S0-ARO-120

MARYBELLE FISHER, PH.D.
MENTAL HEALTH ASSOCIATES
37 DERBY ST., SUITE ONE
HINGHAM, MA 02043

THE IMPACT OF NEW IDEAS

Progress in Self Psychology
Volume 11

Progress in Self Psychology
Editor, Arnold Goldberg, M.D.

EDITORIAL BOARD
Michael F. Basch, M.D.

James L. Fosshage, Ph.D.

Robert Galatzer-Levy, M.D.

Charles Jaffe, M.D.

Robert J. Leider, M.D.

Arthur Malin, M.D.

Anna Ornstein, M.D.

Paul Ornstein, M.D.

Estelle Shane, Ph.D.

Morton Shane, M.D.

Robert D. Stolorow, Ph.D.

Marian Tolpin, M.D.

Paul H. Tolpin, M.D.

Ernest S. Wolf, M.D.

THE IMPACT OF NEW IDEAS

Progress in Self Psychology
Volume 11

Arnold Goldberg
editor

1995   THE ANALYTIC PRESS
Hillsdale, NJ   London

©1995 by The Analytic Press
Hillsdale, NJ 07642

All rights reserved. No part of this book may be reproduced in
any form, by photostat, microfilm, retrieval system, or any other
means, without prior written permission of the publisher.

ISBN 0-88163-213-9
ISSN 0893-5483

Printed in the United States of America
10 9 8 7 6 5 4 3 2 1

Acknowledgment

We would like to thank Ms. Christine Susman, who provided secretarial and editorial assistance.

Contents

III DYING AND MOURNING

IV THEORETICAL AND APPLIED

Contributors

Sharone A. Abramowitz, M.D., Adjunct Professor, Institute for the Psychology of Women, California School of Professional Psychology; Clinical Faculty, Department of Psychiatry, University of California, San Francisco.

Margaret Baker, Ph.D., Consulting Psychologist, Institute of Pennsylvania Hospital, Philadelphia; Clinical Assistant Professor, Institute for Graduate Clinical Psychology, Widener University, Chester, PA.

Donald L. Carveth, Ph.D., Associate Professor of Sociology and Social and Political Thought, York University; Faculty, Toronto Institute of Psychoanalysis and the Toronto Institute for Contemporary Psychoanalysis.

Janet T. Droga, M.S.W., Institute for the Psychoanalytic Study of Subjectivity, New York; Private practice.

Shirley C. Geller, Ph.D., Private practice.

George Hagman, M.S.W., National Psychological Association for Psychoanalysis, New York; Clinical Director, F. S. DuBois Center, Stamford, Connecticut; Private practice in New York City and Connecticut.

Peter J. Kaufmann, Ph.D., Institute for the Psychoanalytic Study of Subjectivity; Instructor, Yeshiva University and the N. I. P.

Sandra Kiersky, Ph.D., Faculty and Supervisor, National Institute for the Psychotherapies; Coordinator of Training, Institute for the Psychoanalytic Study of Subjectivity.

Hans Kilian, M.D., Professor Emeritus of Psychoanalysis and Social Psychology, Department of Human Sciences and Education, University of Kassel, Germany.

Steven H. Knoblauch, Ph.D., Associate, Institute for the Psychoanalytic Study of Subjectivity; Private practice, New York City and Hoboken, NJ.

Frank M. Lachmann, Ph.D., Core Faculty, Institute for the Psychoanalytic Study of Subjectivity; Coauthor (with Joseph Lichtenberg and James Fosshage), *Self and Motivational Systems*.

Ellen J. Lewinberg, B.S.W./Dip. P.S.W./C.S.W./NAAP/MCAPT, Faculty and Supervisor, Toronto Child Psychotherapy Program; Faculty, Training and Research Institute in Self Psychology, New York; Private practice.

Hyman L. Muslin, M.D., Professor of Psychiatry, University of Illinois Medical School, Chicago, IL.

Paul H. Ornstein, M.D., Professor of Psychoanalysis, University of Cincinnati Medical School; Codirector, International Center for the Study of Psychoanalytic Self Psychology; Training and Supervising Analyst, Cincinnati Psychoanalytic Institute.

Sandra R. Palef, Ph.D., Faculty, Toronto Institute of Psychoanalysis; Faculty, Toronto Institute for Contemporary Psychoanalysis; private practice.

Craig Powell, MB BS FRANZCP, Faculty, Australian Psychoanalytical Society, Sydney Branch; Private practice.

Sanford Shapiro, M.D., Training and Supervising Analyst, San Diego Psychoanalytic Society and Institute; Training and Supervising Analyst, Institute of Contemporary Psychoanalysis, Los Angeles; Associate Clinical Professor of Psychiatry, University of California San Diego School of Medicine.

Robert D. Stolorow, Ph.D., Faculty, Training and Supervising Analyst, Institute of Contemporary Psychoanalysis, Los Angeles; Core Faculty, Institute for the Psychoanalytic Study of Subjectivity, New York City.

Jeffrey L. Trop, M.D., Training and Supervising Analyst, Faculty, Institute of Contemporary Psychoanalysis, Los Angeles; Assistant Clinical Professor of Psychiatry, UCLA School of Medicine.

Richard H. Tuch, M.D., Senior Faculty, Los Angeles Psychoanalytic Society and Institute; Assistant Clinical Professor of Psychiatry, UCLA, Neuropsychiatric Institute.

Introduction: Tensions Between Loyalism and Expansionism in Self Psychology

Robert D. Stolorow

What a new system of thought in psychology needs in order to establish the relevance and accuracy of its explanatory approach is not only the concreteness and realism of the innovator and of his close co-workers and friends, but the confirmatory response of workers at a distance from the innovator, of individuals who are not exposed to frequent contact with the teacher figure, and whose views are not influenced by the feelings of loyalty and devotion toward the leader which inevitably arise under these circumstances. The situation that is most favorable in this regard is one in which, not only is there an absence of direct contact, but where we are dealing with individuals who are working in areas that had not been investigated by the primary research.

—H. Kohut (1979, pp. 472–473)

[W]e must turn to a search for something that goes beyond heroes. . . . We gain comfort from our heroes, but they visit a . . . paralysis on us, one that comes from the never-ending test of fidelity. . . . Self psychology has postulated addiction in its many forms as reflecting some sort of psychological deficit, and our need to hang on to the great leaders in our field signifies the same deficit.

—A. Goldberg (1990, pp. 47–48)

In considering some of the controversies that exist within contemporary self psychology, I have found it useful to divide the various current contributors to the self psychology literature into two broad groups. I call them the *loyalists* and the *expansionists*. The loyalists tend to be members of Kohut's original inner circle of former analysands and students who experienced close personal relationships with him. Most of the expansionists, by contrast, know Kohut's work from more of a distance, perhaps primarily from his writings. Correspondingly, whereas most of the first-generation loyalists reside in Chicago or nearby Cincinnati, expansionists are drawn from all over North America—from New York City, New Jersey, Boston, Washington, DC, Los Angeles, Toronto, and Vancouver.

Whereas expansionists, who also tend to be integrationists, wish to bring into self psychology ideas from sources other than Kohut, loyalists, in the words of Lachmann and Beebe (in press), adhere to "the assumption that Kohut's writings constitute the authoritative statement." For loyalists, Kohut's word is the first and the last, and they thus tend to be openly dismissive of the contributions of expansionists. The tensions among loyalists and expansionists are well illustrated in this volume by Paul Ornstein's searing commentary on Trop's essay contrasting the clinical implications of self psychology and intersubjectivity theory. Ornstein, the quintessential loyalist, decries what he deems to be the "unwarranted claims to originality" made by intersubjectivity theorists. In a similar vein, Paul and Anna Ornstein (in press) write that post-Kohut self psychology has achieved "a few relatively minor corrections . . . but cannot claim significant advances in new conceptualizations." The Ornsteins regard attempts to delineate selfobject transferences other than Kohut's original trilogy as only "marginally justified." Paul Ornstein (1994, personal communication) has even gone so far as to declare that people are interested in the theory of intersubjectivity mostly because they "do not know and do not read and do not fully understand Kohut's writings." Kohutian loyalists seem unaware or unconcerned that they respond to expansionists in much the same manner that the Freudian loyalists responded to Kohut.

Unlike loyalists, expansionists have been attempting to integrate ideas from various other sources with those offered by Kohut. Bacal and Newman (1990), for example, have attempted to include within self psychology the contributions of object relations theorists; Lachmann and Beebe (in press), Lichtenberg, Lachmann, and Fosshage (1992), and Shane and Shane (1994), concepts derived from infant research; and my collaborators and I (Atwood and Stolorow, 1984; Stolorow, Brandchaft, and Atwood, 1987; Stolorow and Atwood, 1992), ideas originating in continental philosophy, systems or field theory, and, especially, studies in the psychology of knowledge and the subjective origins of personality theories (Atwood and Stolorow, 1993).[1]

The loyalist and expansionist perspectives seem to be fundamentally incompatible because of their differing origins and distinctly different visions of the future development of self psychology. The house of self psychology described by Lachmann and Beebe (in press) is currently a house divided, and whether it can contain all the diversity that has emerged within it remains to be seen. Historically, psychoanalysts have not been known for their tolerance of differences, and this lamentable history of divisiveness and parochialism seems to repeat itself *ad nauseam*, largely because of the psychological functions served by adherence to psychoanalytic theories (Goldberg, 1990; Atwood and Stolorow, 1993).

A good example of the disagreements separating expansionists and loyalists concerns the status of the selfobject concept within psychoanalytic theory. From my own, intersubjective viewpoint, the term *selfobject* is best understood as referring to a *dimension* of experiencing another, in which a specific bond is required for maintaining, restoring, consolidating, or enhancing a person's sense of selfhood. Selfobject longings are one of several types of principles that unconsciously organize personal, subjective worlds. From this perspective, human experience and human relationships are viewed as fluid and multidimensional (Stolorow and Lachmann, 1984/85; Stolorow et al., 1987). Analytic listening thereby becomes focused on the complex, oscillating figure-ground relationships among the selfobject and other dimensions of experience that take form within a shifting intersubjective context. The psychological system constituted by the ongoing reciprocal interplay between two (or more) oscillating, multidimensional worlds of experience is what my collaborators and I mean when we refer to an intersubjective field.

Loyalists have not taken kindly to this demotion of the selfobject concept to one among many (albeit a ubiquitous one) of the dimensions of experiencing a relationship. Loyalists tend to inflate and reify the selfobject concept so that, for example, the term *self-selfobject relationship* is used to refer to the entirety of a patient's transference experience (see Ornstein, 1991). Here we have either a view of human relationships and of transference narrowed and reduced to only one of their multiple dimensions, or a selfobject concept that, like the ego of classical analysis, has become so all-encompassing as to lose the specificity of its original meaning.

---

[1] I have not listed Basch (1988) among the expansionists because his work seems to me to embody a complex and highly problematic amalgam of loyalism and expansionism (see Stolorow and Atwood, 1992, pp. 18–20).

It has recently become apparent to me, for example, that loyalists tend to use the term *selfobject transference* when referring to two types of relational experience that have distinctly different origins and meanings. In one, the patient longs for the bond with the analyst to supply missing developmental experiences—what Kohut originally meant by selfobject transferences. In the other, the patient seeks responses from the analyst that would counteract invariant organizing principles that are manifestations of what my collaborators and I (Stolorow et al., 1987) call the repetitive dimension of the transference.[2] In the former, the patient longs for something missing; in the latter, the patient seeks an antidote to something crushingly present. Making this distinction has profound implications for the framing of transference interpretations, whereas merging the two types of relational experience into an inflated selfobject concept obscures Kohut's original contribution.

The clinical and theoretical papers collected in this volume richly illustrate the whole spectrum of thought along the loyalism–expansionism continuum. Droga and Kaufmann's chapter on guilt, Hagman's on mourning, Knoblauch's on religious experience, Lachmann and Kiersky's on cross-gender transferences, Palef's on multiple personality disorder, Powell's on internal object relations, Shapiro's on empathic attunement, Trop's on intersubjectivity theory, and Tuch's on writer's block all draw, in varying degrees, on the writings of expansionists. On the other hand, Abramowitz's chapter on suicidality, Baker's on group therapy, Geller's on memories of child abuse, Kilian's on psychohistory, Lewinberg's on child therapy, and Muslin's on termination refer, in their citations of the self psychology literature, primarily to the work of Kohut and Kohutian loyalists.

I doubt that Carveth, self psychology's appreciative but avid critic, would be particularly interested in the tensions among loyalists and expansionists, because his epistemological angst appears to be evoked by all of us. While chastising Atwood and me (Stolorow and Atwood, 1992) for failing to be empathic toward the theorists we have criticized, Carveth, in his contribution to this volume, embarks upon a blistering attack on the philosophical underpinnings of self psychology and, especially, intersubjectivity theory. He employs the procedure known as deconstruction, invented by Derrida and summarized by Sarup (1993) as follows: "This is a method of reading a text so closely that the author's conceptual distinctions on which the text relies are shown to fail on account of the inconsistent and paradoxical use made of these very concepts within the text as a whole" (p. 34).

---

[2] Bacal (1994) alludes to having arrived independently at a similar distinction.

Derrida's method can be applied to any text, including Carveth's. A basic tenet of Derrida's deconstructionism, which Carveth disregards and with which intersubjectivity theory concurs, is that one cannot separate a text from the human contexts in which it was created or is being read.[3]

The exposure of inconsistencies within a text does not necessarily invalidate its thesis. Such inconsistencies are inevitable expressions of the author's personal subjectivity. Carveth's impassioned defense of his objectivity is no less rooted in personal and subjective influences than is Atwood's and my perspectivalism.

It can readily be observed that therapists tend to invoke the concepts of objective reality and distortion when their patients' perceptions of them threaten their sense of self and well-being. A similar phenomenon can be recognized when Ornstein, who in other contexts has been an outspoken critic of objectivist epistemology in psychoanalysis, in this volume makes claims of objectivity in his defense of self psychology against what he perceives to be the menace posed by intersubjectivity theory. My collaborators and I (Stolorow, Atwood, and Brandchaft, 1994) have attempted to show that many common misunderstandings of intersubjectivity theory derive from an array of fears that our ideas seem to evoke in our critics, including the dread of structureless chaos (what Sucharov [1993] calls "Cartesian anxiety"), the dread of an annihilating ad hominem attack, the dread of anarchy in the analytic relationship, and the dread of surrendering one's personal reality. It is this last threat, I believe, that motivates vehement critical reactions to the epistemological stance of self psychology and intersubjectivity theory like the one launched here by Carveth. We have addressed this problem as follows:

> The misreading we are discussing here is the interpretation of our refraining from granting absolute validity to the analyst's reality and not to the patient's as somehow containing an injunction to analysts not to have a theoretical framework to order clinical data. It appears that our critics on this point cannot envision holding to their theoretical ideas without conferring upon those ideas an absolute validity, or at least a greater measure of truth than is ascribed to the patient's ideas. The specter here is of losing a grip on any assumptions at all, of the dissolution of the analyst's personal reality, leaving him adrift in a sea of uncertainty, perhaps in danger of being swept into the vortex of the patient's psychological world. A key distinction lost in this misunderstanding is that between holding an assumption or belief and elevating that assumption to the status of an ultimate, objective truth. Once such an elevation has taken place, the belief necessarily escapes the perimeter of what can be analytically reflected upon [pp. 206–207].

---

[3] I am grateful to Dr. Gary Hayes for calling this point to my attention.

What Carveth and other critics fail to recognize is that neither self psychology nor intersubjectivity theory claims to offer a general epistemology. Instead what they propose is an epistemological stance specifically appropriate for the psychoanalytic method of investigation, as this was eloquently described by Kohut (1959, 1982, 1984) and further refined by intersubjectivity theorists (Stolorow, 1993; Stolorow et al., 1987), including Trop in this volume. None of us claims that objective reality does not exist. What we are arguing is that objective reality is inaccessible and unknowable by the psychoanalytic method, and therefore the concepts of objectivity and distortion have no place within the theoretical lexicon of psychoanalysis. Sucharov (1994), elaborating on the "indivisibility of observer and observed" in psychoanalysis, has suggested "that Kohut's essential lesson was an epistemological one" (pp. 188–189). This is a statement that can be embraced by loyalists and expansionists alike.

REFERENCES

Atwood, G. & Stolorow, R. (1984), *Structures of Subjectivity: Explorations in Psychoanalytic Phenomenology.* Hillsdale, NJ: The Analytic Press.

—— & —— (1993), *Faces in a Cloud*, 2nd ed. Northvale, NJ: Aronson.

Bacal, H. (1994), The analyst's reaction to the analysand's unresponsiveness. Presented at meeting of the Institute of Contemporary Psychoanalysis, Los Angeles, September 12.

—— & Newman, K. (1990), *Theories of Object Relations.* New York: Columbia University Press.

Basch, M. (1988), *Understanding Psychotherapy.* New York: Basic Books.

Goldberg, A. (1990), *The Prisonhouse of Psychoanalysis.* Hillsdale, NJ: The Analytic Press.

Kohut, H. (1959), Introspection, empathy, and psychoanalysis. In: *The Search for the Self, Vol. 1,* ed. P. Ornstein. Madison, CT: International Universities Press, 1978, pp. 205–232.

—— (1979), Remarks on receiving the William A. Schonfeld Distinguished Service Award. In: *The Search for the Self, Vol. 4,* ed. P. Ornstein. Madison, CT: International Universities Press, 1991, pp. 471–474.

—— (1982), Introspection, empathy, and the semicircle of mental health. *Internat. J. Psycho-Anal.,* 63:395–407.

—— (1984), *How Does Analysis Cure?* ed. A. Goldberg & P. Stepansky. Chicago: University of Chicago Press.

Lachmann, F. & Beebe, B. (1995), Self psychology, today. *Psychoanal. Dial.,* 5:375–384.

Lichtenberg, J., Lachmann, F. & Fosshage, J. (1992), *Self and Motivational Systems.* Hillsdale, NJ: The Analytic Press.

Ornstein, P. (1991), Why self psychology is not an object relations theory. In: *The Evolution of Self Psychology, Progress in Self Psychology, Vol. 7,* ed. A. Goldberg. Hillsdale, NJ: The Analytic Press, pp. 17–29.

—— & Ornstein, A. (in press), Untitled contribution to symposium on self psychology. *Psychoanal. Dial.*, 5.

Sarup, M. (1993), *An Introductory Guide to Post-Structuralism and Postmodernism*, 2nd ed. Athens: University of Georgia Press.

Shane, M. & Shane, E. (1994), Self psychology in search of the optimal. Presented at the Seventeenth Annual Conference on the Psychology of the Self, Chicago, October 21–23.

Stolorow, R. (1993), The nature and therapeutic action of psychoanalytic interpretation. In: *The Intersubjective Perspective*, ed. R. Stolorow, G. Atwood & B. Brandchaft. Northvale, NJ: Aronson, 1994, pp. 43–55.

—— & Atwood, G. (1992), *Contexts of Being: The Intersubjective Foundations of Psychological* Life. Hillsdale, NJ: The Analytic Press.

—— —— & Brandchaft, B. (1994), Epilogue. In: *The Intersubjective Perspective*, ed. R. Stolorow, G. Atwood & B. Brandchaft. Northvale, NJ: Aronson, pp. 203–209.

—— Brandchaft, B. & Atwood, G. (1987), *Psychoanalytic Treatment: An Intersubjective Approach.* Hillsdale, NJ: The Analytic Press.

—— & Lachmann, F. (1984/85), Transference: The future of an illusion. *The Annual of Psychoanalysis*, 12/13:19–37. Madison, CT: International Universities Press.

Sucharov, M. (1993), The wise man, the sadist, and Cartesian anxiety. Presented at the Sixteenth Annual Conference on the Psychology of the Self, Toronto, October 29–31.

—— (1994), Psychoanalysis, self psychology, and intersubjectivity. In: *The Intersubjective Perspective*, ed. R. Stolorow, G. Atwood & B. Brandchaft. Northvale, NJ: Aronson, pp. 187–202.

I

Self Psychology and Intersubjectivity

Chapter 1

Self Psychology and the Intersubjective Perspective: A Dialectical Critique

Donald L. Carveth

Because I consider them clinically valuable, especially in the under-standing and resolution of therapeutic impasses in work with more diffi-cult patients, I have for some time been troubled by what I see as signifi-cant epistemological and other theoretical problems in both self psychology (Kohut, 1959, 1971, 1977, 1979, 1984) and the intersubjec-tive approach (Atwood and Stolorow, 1984a, 1984b; Stolorow, Brand-chaft, and Atwood, 1987; Stolorow and Atwood, 1992). In the spirit of the depressive position, I will endeavor in the following "mixed review" to sustain ambivalence without splitting by indicating something of what I value as well as what I reject in these psychoanalytic perpectives. [1]

Although Kohut's method of argument, like Freud's, may be regarded as "dialectical" in the sense in which, deriving from the Greek *dialektos* meaning "discourse" and *dialektike* meaning "debate" (*Concise Oxford Dictionary*, p. 264), dialectic refers to reasoned argument as such, beyond this very general usage the concept is commonly associated with the dialectical logic of Hegel (1807; Singer, 1983). Here thought is held to evolve through the clash of opposites: a thesis gives rise to an

---

[1] Throughout I maintain a distinction between self psychology (or selfobject theory) and the intersubjective approach in light of claims by the authors of the latter that, although widely regarded as an offshoot of the former, their perspective has indepen-dent roots in phenomenology and personology and that it subsumes and transcends self psychology.

antithesis that contradicts it and, out of this opposition, a synthesis emerges that, in its turn, becomes the thesis evoking another antithesis, giving rise to yet another synthesis, and so on. With Marx, Hegel's dialectical *idealism* is brought down to earth, as it were, taking the form of a dialectical *materialism* in which the clashing elements are not ideas but socioeconomic classes, the thesis being the bourgeoisie, the antithesis the proletariat, and the synthesis the socialist state destined to "wither away" with the emergence, at the end of history, of the final communist utopia (Singer, 1980).

Leaving such philosophical origins to one side, the essence of a dialectical approach is its contrast with both monistic and dualistic frameworks. In monism no fundamental conflict is recognized; there is a single force, principle, or process of development, as for example in Freud's libido theory during that brief period between the breakdown (Freud, 1914) of his initial instinctual dualism (sexual versus self-preservative drives) when only the sexual drive was recognized, before dualism was reaffirmed with the introduction (Freud, 1920) of the final dual-drive theory (Eros versus Thanatos). In dualism, the clash of opposites is fundamental and although the form of the conflict may be modified, as from less adaptive to more adaptive compromise-formations (Brenner, 1982), conflict itself is built in to the very nature of reality or the psyche and no fundamental transcendence is possible.

In dialectical thinking, by contrast, conflict is recognized as a necessary but intermediate stage in a three-step developmental process in which an initial monism gives way to a dualistic clash of opposites which is then transcended, however momentarily, in a higher-order synthesis of some type. Whereas the figures one and two are central to monism and dualism respectively, the figure three is fundamental in dialectical thought, whether the three be mother, child, and father or object, self, and the boundary separating these from one another. In this perspective, both monism and dualism reflect flight from and resistance to triangulation or oedipalization (Lacan, 1977).

An argument can be made that whereas Freud's thought entails a mixture of dialectical and dualistic elements—the former being reflected in, for example, his epigenetic model of development and the latter in his instinctual dualisms of sexual vs. self-preservative drives and Eros vs. Thanatos—Kohut's thinking displays both monistic and dualistic trends. In his monistic theory of motivation, for example, Kohut (1977) seeks to abandon a view of human nature based on the conflict model in favor of a perspective emphasizing the centrality of ambition, aspiration, and hope in human subjectivity—a view of "Tragic Man," who, unlike the conflict-driven "Guilty Man" of Freudian theory, is a goal-directed being seeking the "realization . . . of the blueprint for his life that had been laid down in his nuclear self" (p. 133) through relations with his self-object milieu. Beyond this, however, self psychology has presented a range of dualisms: development of narcissism vs. object love; narcissistic vs. object-instinctual transferences; deficit vs. conflict; self-disorder vs. structural neurosis; mirroring selfobject vs. idealizing selfobject; pole of ambitions vs. pole of ideals; and so on.

The differences between monistic, dualistic and dialectical thinking may account for the fact that the proponent of the latter is likely to be misunderstood by both Freudian and Kohutian colleagues. Whereas the former will regard him as a Kohutian fellow traveler, the latter will suspect him of unresolved Freudian or Kleinian tendencies. Although there is something in both these views, the deeper truth is that the dialectical thinker rejects both dualism and monism in whatever form or tradition they happen to appear. He is always looking for the third term, the synthesis, not as any utopian final end to conflict, for allowing that conflict is inevitable, he nevertheless insists that conflict is not all.[2] In dialectical thinking *development through differentiation and integration* is also a reality; evolution is a reality.

For the dialectician, the enduringly valuable aspect of Freud's thinking is not the dualism at the root of his pessimism, but rather his epigenetic model (Freud, 1905; Erikson, 1950, 1959), in which conflicts at one level give rise to a synthesis permitting advance to a higher stage where conflicts emerge once again and so on as development proceeds. Naturally, devolution as well as evolution, regression as well as progression, occurs. The point is only that, against the monists, conflict is a reality; but against the dualists (including the dualistic elements of Freud's own thinking), conflict is neither the only nor the ultimate reality. Refusing views of reality in which conflict is either denied or reified, the dialectician insists that just as it is possible to regress to a primitive monism below conflict, so one can progress to a state beyond it, at least until conflict emerges once again on this higher level. The dialectician's favored image of living systems is the spiral, which in health ascends, but which in illness yields to fixation, stasis, or premature decline.

Dialectical thinking is opposed to either/or thinking. Being essentially allied to the depressive position, it is opposed to schizoparanoid splitting. In a sense it "holds a candle" for both Saint George (Kohut?) and the Dragon (Freud?). Hence, when Freudians attack self psychology, the dialectician defends it. When Kohutians attack Freudianism, he upholds

---

[2] Whereas Hegel, justifiably or not, has frequently been seen as positing an attainable final synthesis, more recent dialecticians, such as Adorno (1966), envisage a progressive but essentially interminable development toward an ultimately incompletely knowable whole (Carveth, 1984, 1987).

it. He sees virtue in both perspectives and yet, because he also sees both as one-sided, he says "a pox on both your camps." He wants both of them to move on toward the ultimately incompletely attainable synthesis. For the dialectician, advancing toward the synthesis (i.e., the depressive position) is our job.[3]

Freudian reductionists will say of the dialectician, here is someone determined to get mother and father together again; while Kohutian reductionists may regard him as a fence-sitter with an inordinate need to be accepted by everyone. But I submit, on the one hand, that recognizing that mother and father rightfully belong together reflects the very oedipal resolution Freudians espouse; and, on the other, that only a peculiarly masochistic fence-sitter would risk alienating both camps by openly disagreeing with each. One is more likely to find the dialectician impaled on the fence (or the Cross), rather than sitting on it.

Both monistic and dualistic perspectives give rise to either/or thinking, that is, to the splitting that characterizes Klein's paranoid-schizoid position and Lacan's Imaginary. For, on the one hand, if there is a unitary principle of right then everything else must be wrong and, on the other hand, if all that exists are the two poles of a binary opposition then one must choose either Scylla or Charybdis. By at least acknowledging both horns of such binary dilemmas, dualistic thinking occasionally gives rise to a dialectical recognition of possible ways of passing between them.

As I have argued elsewhere (Carveth, 1984; 1987), a defining feature of regressive mental functioning is the privileging of one or the other pole of such binary oppositions, affirming thesis over antithesis or vice versa. Correspondingly, the psychoanalytic method may be conceptualized as, in part, a process of dialectical deconstruction (Barratt, 1984) in which the repressed complementarity and mutual dependence of the opposing terms is exposed.

If, as I believe, the foundational opposition constructing psychic reality is *Similarity/Difference* (*Connection/Separation*), some people (the linkers) will tend to privilege the former term over the latter, while others (the separators) will tend to reverse this hierarchy. In contrast, the mark of mature mental functioning is the capacity to achieve and hold the synthesis in which neither pole is concretized or absolutized. Here, instead of the sense of connection or similarity regressing to the level of absolute oneness or identity, and the sense of separation or difference

---

[3] Representing the whole (and, hence, for some, the holy), the final synthesis is (contrary to all idolatry) incompletely achievable or representable. Although it is our responsibility to seek it, we must never delude ourselves that we have found it—although "it" (He? She?) may well find us.

regressing to the level of absolute opposition or antithesis, the recognition of connection within separation and of difference within similarity is retained. Translated into clinical terminology descriptive of the "borderline dilemma" (Carveth, 1993), this refers to a person's capacity to experience separation without abandonment and connection without fusion or engulfment.

Because both analysts and analysands have to struggle with the existential dilemma of oneness vs. separateness, one fruitful way to think of the differing theoretical and technical stances that divide the psychoanalytic community is in terms of their respective biases toward one or the other pole of this fundamental opposition. If the Freudian, Kleinian, and Lacanian traditions can be said to manifest a bias toward separation or dis-integration (Thanatos) in their emphases upon abstinence, frustration, boundary-maintenance, and confrontation with the facts of separateness and "lack" through interpretation leading to insight, mourning, and ultimate accommodation to the reality principle, then various relational and self-psychological perspectives may be said to reflect a bias toward integration (Eros) in their stress upon the importance of affective attunement, empathic linkage or connectedness, holding, and containing as the prerequisites for transmuting internalization of the analyst as a good object or selfobject.

Whereas analysts of the Freudian and related schools tend to define pathology as excessive symbiosis (Langs, 1978) or "forbidden mixture" (Chasseguet-Smirgel, 1984) and, consequently, regard the cure as one or another form of renunciation, resignation, or "acceptance of castration" (Lacan, 1977), those who lean toward the relational and self-psychological schools, regarding states of disconnection and fragmentation as the essence of pathology, prescribe "therapeutic symbiosis" (Searles, 1965), empathic attunement, and the self-selfobject merger entailed in "transmuting internalization" as the very basis for "the restoration of the self" (Kohut, 1977).

By way of contrast, from a dialectical point of view our task is to deconstruct the privileging of either the Thanatic or the Erotic orientation and instead to work toward a synthesis in which the former is tempered by the latter and the latter fortified by the former. In terms of the analyst's concrete struggles with countertransference (broadly defined) in the heat of the analytic situation, the dialectically deconstructive method is one wherein the analyst intentionally "shifts gears" at crucial moments, decentering from the perspective he has been employing and surveying the situation as it appears from the opposing but complementary point of view.

A by-product of Kohut's unitary theory of motivation as the search on the part of the self for attuned selfobject responsiveness is the either/or thinking in which a view of the subject as conflict-driven is opposed to a view of it as pursuing its ambitions, aspirations, and hopes. But why cannot the human subject be seen as both conflict-driven and goal-oriented? Why do we have to choose between "Guilty Man" and "Tragic Man"? Why can't we have both at the same time?[4]

Now permit me to be clear about this. On one level I agree we cannot have our cake and eat it too. If by the conflict model we mean the drive model, the idea that the subject is fundamentally driven by somatically based instinctual drives of sex and aggression as opposed to being fundamentally motivated by attachment or selfobject needs, then the conflict model would have to be abandoned. But why is the conflict model necessarily associated with the drive model? Historically, of course, this was the case, but this association is not a necessary one. We can reject the drive model and yet preserve the conflict model. But here, conflict is not between defenses on the one hand and somatically based drives on the other, but between defenses and the narcissistic rage, archaic longings, and "disintegration products" emerging from frustrated selfobject needs—and also, I would insist, from the inevitable frustration arising from our existential predicament as self-conscious *being-toward-death* (Heidegger, 1927).

It is not only possible for attachment theorists and self psychologists to retain the conflict model while rejecting the drive model, it is necessary for them to do so. For the fact is that people who have had their fundamental attachment and selfobject needs frustrated—by "basic" frustration (the unavoidable existential minimum), "surplus" frustration (due to environmental failure), or both—suffer from varying degrees of conflict.

This distinction between the "surplus" frustration arising from environmental or selfobject failure and the "basic" or existential frustration arising from the human condition as such is necessary in order to combat yet another instance of either/or thinking characteristic of psychoanalytic theory in general. For although virtually everyone pays lip service to the idea that the nature/nurture controversy rests on an essentially false dichotomy and that both hereditary and environmental factors interact in the causation of human behavior, what remains largely missing from psychoanalytic discourse is any adequate recognition of the reality of *Dasein*, or human *being-in-the-world* (Heidegger, 1927), as a uniquely human, existential condition of symbolic self-awareness and

---

[4] If its claim to transcend self psychology through openness to principles organizing subjective experience other than "Tragic Man's" search for selfobject support is valid, then the intersubjective perspective should be able to include the intrapsychic conflicts of "Guilty Man" within its purview.

time-consciousness that is emergent from but irreducible to the interaction of biological and environmental factors.

It remains the case that most schools of psychoanalytic thought (with the exception of the existentialists and the Lacanians)—in their general theory if not in their clinical attitude and praxis—lean heavily toward either a biologism that privileges the somatically rooted drives or an environmentalism that privileges a range of relational factors in the understanding of personality development and psychopathology. There is no need to underestimate the role of biological and environmental factors and their interaction in the determination of human behavior in order to recognize "the uniqueness of man" (Huxley, 1927) and the distinctively human passions (Carveth, 1996) arising from our predicament as symboling animals living not only in the inorganic (prebiological) and organic (biological) worlds, but also in the superorganic (postbiological) world of self-consciousness, signification, and culture.[5]

I will now turn to two additional, interrelated manifestations of either/or thinking in self psychology. Drawing on the philosophical ideas of Dilthey (1961), Weber (1953), and other members of the so-called *verstehende* school of historical and sociological thought, Kohut (1959) alludes to the distinction between the *Naturwissenschaften* (the natural sciences) and the *Geisteswissenschaften* (the human or cultural sciences) and argues that, as a member of the latter group, psychoanalysis necessarily approaches its subject matter—which he defines as the subjectivity of human beings—not from an external, objective, or positivistic point of view, but rather from an internal, subjective, or introspective-empathic perspective. The advocates of the intersubjective approach have simply carried these Kohutian tenets to their logical (from a dialectical standpoint I would say illogical) extreme, while claiming that their work represents an advance over self psychology in that it is open to the discovery of organizing principles structuring the patient's subjective experience other than those of the self-selfobject unit.

Once again the question is, why either/or and not both/and?[6] Although it is true that much of our work as analysts focuses on the patient's and our own subjective *experience* and therefore relies on the

---

[5] Once again, we are in the presence of a trinity: the so-called "three worlds" hypothesis—lithosphere, biosphere, and noösphere (Huxley, 1947)—and the idea that in addition to nature and nurture there exists the tertiary reality of *Dasein*.

[6] This is not the place to develop but only to mention the point that while the Hegelian *both/and* (thesis) is inevitably complemented by the Kierkegaardian *either/or* (antithesis), the very refusal to privilege either of these orientations over the other entails an affirmation of both/and thinking on the higher level (synthesis) on which the necessity and validity of each in different contexts is acknowledged.

empathic/introspective method, surely we are interested in the patient's and our own *behavior* as well, and hence we also resort to objective observation. Attachment theory was greatly influenced both by observation of primate behavior the "strange situation" laboratory of Ainsworth, Blehar, Waters, and Wall (1978) set up for the observation of children and their mothers. Both self psychology and intersubjective studies have themselves been influenced by and draw support from observation of preverbal infant–mother interactions recorded by elaborate video technology (Beebe and Lachmann, 1988).

Even in strictly therapeutic work, analysts observe their patients—and are observed by them—as a central element of the act of empathizing with them. In a real sense, observation and empathy are inseparable, for the latter entails and depends on the former. Beyond this, however, it is a mistake to seek to confine the psychoanalytic method to the empathic study of the patient's subjective world. In optimal psychoanalytic work we need to move back and forth between viewing our patients as subjects and as objects.

The intersubjectivists (Atwood and Stolorow, 1984a) acknowledge the influence of the existential phenomenology of Sartre (1943). But, for Sartre, the peculiar nature of the human being lies in its partaking of both *being-for-itself* and *being-in-itself* (i.e., of being both a subject and an object), denial of either aspect entailing "bad faith." Certainly any psychoanalysis carried on in a Sartrean spirit would in no way confine itself to the exploration of the subject's subjectivity, but would seek to expand that subjectivity through confrontation of the subject with its reality as a historically and socially situated object whose *being-for-others* (including the analyst) and rootedness in *being-in-itself* are as much a part of its reality as its *being-for-itself*.

It is true that whereas we can only view inanimate things from the outside as objects, by employing the empathic-introspective method we are able to view persons (and perhaps, to a degree, animals) as subjects. But it remains the case that we can and need to view people as objects as well. In addition to attuning to and empathizing with the subjectivity of both experiencing patients and experiencing analysts (i.e., their own prereflective experience), I believe it is necessary for analysts to attempt to maintain (or recover if it has been lost) the necessary triangulation of the analytic situation entailed in viewing each of these from a tertiary perspective: that of the observing, including the self-observing (self-reflective), analyst. In so endeavoring to maintain or recover their own "observing ego," analysts simultaneously encourage the development or reestablishment of patients'. Hence, in addition to exploration of patients' subjectivity, I believe it is necessary for analysts to keep in mind in very broad, tentative, and shifting terms such things as their character structure, the quality of their reality-testing, the level of their object-relations, the degree of their regression and capacity to internalize, the state of the therapeutic alliance, the nature of the transference and the countertransference and their interpenetration, and other such considerations.[7]

I believe that analysis helps people not only by assisting them to become more attuned to their subjective, especially their affective, experience but also by enabling them to, in a sense, step outside their subjectivity and view themselves as objects from the standpoint of another (Mead, 1934). It is not at all necessary to assume that this other has privileged access to objective reality in order to recognize the truth in the adage that—phenomena such as folie à deux aside—two heads are generally better than one. I cannot see the back of my own head—without a mirror, that is. The analyst is a mirror (albeit inevitably a flawed one to a greater or lesser extent) in which patients can view themselves in otherwise unavailable ways. Just as a fish living entirely surrounded by water is in no position to know it is all wet, so with the help of our analysts we are enabled to escape subjective self-enclosure to some degree and acquire some approximate knowledge of the sort of objects we may be. Being enabled in this way to see ourselves more objectively for better and for worse is an essential element (but by no means the whole story) of how analysis works.

To someone whose training before becoming an analyst was in the sociology of Max Weber (1953) and the symbolic interactionist social psychology of George Herbert Mead (1934), the psychology of the self with its emphasis on empathic immersion in the perspective of the other (Weber's *verstehen* and Mead's *role-taking*) represents a welcome contribution to the development of a more fully interactional perspective in psychoanalysis. Contributors to selfobject theory and the intersubjective approach add their voices to the critique, developed over many decades by diverse writers in several disciplines, of what Stolorow and Atwood (1992) call "the myth of the isolated mind."

In seeking to transcend the unacceptable individualism of traditional psychoanalysis in favor of a more thorough understanding of the inextricable interconnectedness among *Mind, Self and Society* (to employ the title of Mead's [1934] best-known work), selfobject theory and the intersubjective perspective join a tradition including a wide range of object-

---

[7] For an elaboration of four perspectives upon the analytic interaction—the patient's; the analyst's; the "worm's-eye" view representing a state of confusion and unknowing; and a hypothetical "bird's-eye" or objective view of the reality of the interaction—see Sloane (1986).

relational (Greenberg and Mitchell, 1983; Mitchell, 1988), interpersonal (Sullivan, 1953), bipersonal (Langs, 1976), attachment (Bowlby, 1969–1980), and developmental systems (Stern, 1985; Beebe and Lachmann, 1988) perspectives each of which advocates in one way or another (and of course their differences in approach are as important as their similarities) a more thoroughly social understanding of human nature and of the self.

But while adding their voices to the continuing critique of "one-body" psychology and contributing significantly to the evolution of a more sophisticated and clinically valuable alternative perspective, the inter-subjectivists neglect to situate their contribution within the tradition of the discipline, thus remaining faithful to the time-honored practice in self psychology, beginning with Kohut himself, of failing to enter into dialogue with or even, often enough, to cite the work of predecessors. What, in a notable exception, Bacal and Newman (1990) did for self psychology is now needed for the theory of intersubjectivity.

A central implication of both self psychology and the intersubjective approach is that analysts must seek continually to "decenter" sufficiently from their own perspective and taken-for-granted organizing principles to be able to empathize with and accurately understand the viewpoint of the other.[8] This point is lucidly illustrated in the discussions of the cases of Peter, Robyn, Alice, and Sarah in *Contexts of Being* (Stolorow and Atwood, 1992, ch. 7). Each of these cases illustrates how unconscious organizing principles governing the experience of the analyst sometimes link up with similar unconscious principles shaping the experience of the patient (intersubjective conjunction)—or clash with very different principles at work in the patient (intersubjective disjunction)—resulting in empathic failures and therapeutic impasses of varying types.

The authors argue that the way out of such difficulties is for analysts to become reflectively self-aware of how their hitherto prereflective organizing principles (deep assumptions, attitudes, metaphors, concretized theoretical convictions, and so on) have impaired or distorted—I will defend my use of this term later—their capacity for accurate empathic understanding of the patient's experience and, in this way, to overcome such areas of blindness and the impasses to which they lead. While I would say that, in becoming more reflectively self-aware in this way, analysts are becoming more objective about themselves and insist

---

[8] It is the capacity of the human being existing on the superorganic level of *mind* (noösphere), which depends upon but is irreducible to the organic level of *brain* (biosphere), to "take the role of the other" (Mead, 1934) that constitutes the socio-psychological foundation for the biblical doctrine of charity and its corollary, the Kantian categorical imperative, as well as for the *verstehen* or empathic-introspective method in the human sciences.

that if analysts can become more objective in these ways then so can patients, the authors themselves would never employ this manner of speaking owing to their total excommunication of any reference to objectivity and objective reality from psychoanalytic discourse (see later sections of the chapter).

Unfortunately, while emphasizing the therapeutic importance of accurate empathic understanding of the *patient's* experience, Stolorow and Atwood fail to extend this attitude toward psychoanalytic *colleagues* of other theoretical persuasions. Even if we exempt them from the task of situating their work within the ongoing dialogue that constitutes the collective psychoanalytic self, we cannot absolve them of their responsibility to adopt a respectful and empathic stance toward those psychoanalytic writers to whom they do refer—such as Edith Jacobson, Heinz Kohut, Roy Schafer, and Otto Kernberg—whose work they quote out of context, caricature, and exploit as a foil against which to claim the superiority of the intersubjective approach. Ironically, in their mode of offering "interpretations" to their fellow psychoanalysts, the intersubjectivists resemble the standard self-psychological caricature of the classical analyst—and the cause of intersubjectivity is ill-served in the process.

Schafer (1976), for example, is accused of substantializing and universalizing the experience of personal agency and elevating this to "the ontological core of psychological life" (p. 15). Although there is some truth in this, it is unfair to leave the impression that Schafer is that crude and simplistic a thinker; an examination of *A New Language for Psychoanalysis* reveals that in addition to his major focus upon excessive *disclaiming* of personal agency, Schafer recognizes the existence of excessive *claiming* of responsibility as well, thus refuting the charge that he is blind to the limits of personal freedom.

The "straw man" strategy is again evident in the course of the authors' argument that the "idolatry [sic] of the autonomous mind finds vivid expression in Jacobson's (1964) description of the experiential consequences of superego formation" (p. 13). They state that "prior to this developmental achievement, according to her view, the child's self-esteem is highly vulnerable to the impact of experiences with others. As a result of the consolidation of the superego, by contrast, self-esteem is said to become stabilized and *relatively* [their term, my emphasis] independent of relations with others, so that [and here they quote Jacobson herself] it 'cannot be as easily affected as before by experiences of rejection, frustration, failure and the like' and is 'apt to withstand . . . psychic or even physical injuries to the self' . . ." (p. 13). But having themselves said that she saw self-esteem becoming only *relatively* independent of relations with others after superego consolidation, and having quoted Jacobson herself saying that it "cannot be *as easily affected as before* [my emphasis]," the authors proceed to summarize her view as follows: "The autonomous ego of the healthy older child or adult . . . is presumed to have achieved immunity from the 'slings and arrows' encountered in experiences of the surround" (p. 13). In other words, where Jacobson speaks of *relative* independence and of varying *degrees* of being affected by others, the authors radicalize her position and attribute to her a view of the immunity of the self from influences from the surround that it was never her intention to suggest.

Against Kohut's theory of self-structure formation through "optimal frustration" and "transmuting internalization," which they regard as a variant of the myth of the isolated mind, Stolorow and Atwood (1992) describe improved psychological functioning in terms of "increased affect integration and tolerance" (p. 13); but these attainments would, no doubt, enable the healthier individual, not to be entirely self-reliant, but certainly to rely in less archaic and urgent ways on the selfobject milieu for assistance in affect regulation—which is, after all, what both Jacobson and Kohut had in mind.

The problem is not that Stolorow and Atwood fail to present detailed accounts of the alternative perspectives of these colleagues; that is not the sort of book they set out to write. Rather, the problem is that in choosing to refer to the writings of colleagues to illustrate their adherence to "the myth of the isolated mind," their work is read in a one-sided and polarizing way so that they can be fitted to the authors' stereotype. It is because I share Stolorow and Atwood's view of the importance of sustained empathic inquiry into the subjective world of the other that I believe the method ought to be applied not only in our dealings with *patients* but with *colleagues* as well.

Turning to Stolorow and Atwood's (1992) reconsideration (chapter two), in terms of intersubjectivity, of the concept of unconscious mental processes: instead of viewing the repression barrier as a relatively fixed characteristic of the individual mind, they view it in "two-body" terms as fluid and variable from one intersubjective context to another. This is because, in their view, the motive for repression involves maintaining a tie to a needed object, a tie that would be threatened by self-experiences unacceptable to the object and that therefore come to be dissociated, repressed, or defensively withheld from symbolization (as in Dorpat's [1987] theory of cognitive arrest). Given a different intersubjective situation—say, that of the relationship with the analyst in which the needed tie is ideally less threatened by such self-experiences—the repression barrier may be lifted to a greater or lesser degree.

This it seems to me is a useful reconceptualization of the nature of repression, as are Stolorow and Atwood's (1992) distinctions among the "three realms of the unconscious": the prereflective unconscious, containing "the organizing principles that unconsciously shape and thematize a person's experiences"; the dynamic unconscious, containing "experiences that were denied articulation because they were perceived to threaten needed ties"; and the unvalidated unconscious containing "experiences that could not be articulated because they never evoked the requisite validating responsiveness from the surround" (p. 33).

Although I believe the positing of these three realms, together with the theory of the intersubjective context of repression, goes a long way toward refuting the charge that the intersubjective approach, like self psychology in general, denies the unconscious, for me there is still something significant missing from this account. Specifically, there is as yet in both selfobject and intersubjective theory no adequate account of primary process mentation and the peculiar laws that structure it, which Freud (1900) discovered, namely, condensation (which Lacan, following Roman Jakobson, recognized as metaphor); displacement (metonymy); plastic representation; symbolism; and secondary revision.

No listening stance can be truly intersubjective unless the analyst is able to decode the primary process encodings of the patient's raw perceptions, affects, and phantasies concerning the analytic interaction. As Langs (1978), following Searles (1975), pointed out long ago, if, "listening with the third ear" (Reik, 1948), we know how to *hear* what patients are saying about us and about what they think is going on in us and between us and them on the unconscious level—messages that they frequently expect to be so threatening to their needed tie to us that they must be deeply encoded in a primary-process disguise—then the patient's unconscious can serve as the supervisor of the analysis by pointing out to us, often in almost unbearably blunt terms, what may really be going on, or at least what the patient imagines is going on, in the interaction on the deeper levels.

Although Freud originally linked the idea of the primary process to notions of psychic energy, drive theory, the economic point of view, and so on—concepts now regarded as problematic if not rejected altogether by many contemporary theorists—the important point is that, despite theorizing his insight in terms that many now find unacceptable, he at the same time discovered the existence of another language, another semiotic register, in the mind, to which he gave the name the primary process. Any psychology worthy of being called psychoanalytic must recognize that we are all (at the very least) double in this sense, split between a self that communicates in secondary-process categories and one that communicates in primary-process categories. We all "speak with a forked tongue" and psychoanalysts *do* possess some special insight into the laws and mechanisms of this second language permitting us, not to *know* with any authoritative certainty how to decode its messages, but at least to hazard a range of intelligent and plausible interpretive guesses that will be either supported or disqualified in light of the patient's own associations.

Although, speaking of defensively sequestered affective states, Stolorow and Atwood (1992) refer to "the necessity for disguise when such states are represented in dreams" (p. 31), they fail to explain the mechanisms of such disguise. In speaking of experience that remains unsymbolized or that is defensively withheld from symbolization because it is perceived to threaten a needed tie (p. 33), the authors fail to explore the possibility that such experience may sometimes be symbolized after all—only not in the everyday, secondary process form, but in the archaic language Freud described as the primary process. In discussing a dream as reflecting "a child's expression in metaphorical symbols of the increasing threat to her psychological survival" (pp. 37–38) in the context of sexual abuse by her father, and of psychotic delusions and hallucinations as encoding previously unconscious features of the patient's traumatic history, the authors have insufficient to say regarding the operation of such metaphorical symbols and their decoding. Perhaps the intersubjectivists simply accept and take for granted Freud's theory of the primary process, minus its outmoded energetic accoutrements; if so, it would be nice to hear them say so. If not, there is a deficit in their theory.

The discussion of fantasy formation in chapter five does little to remedy this lacuna. Just as Brandchaft (1993), in his 1991 Kohut Memorial Lecture to the 14th Conference of the Psychology of the Self began to speak of "ghosts" in the psyche at the root of repetitive self-negating processes (p. 12)—thus rediscovering what in other psychoanalytic frameworks is the role of the archaic superego, internal bad objects, the antilibidinal ego or internal saboteur, and so on, in the compulsion to repeat—so in *Contexts of Being* (chapter five), Stolorow and Atwood reaffirm the concepts of internalization and an internal world and revive the concept of the "introject." Here we are witness to the continuing process whereby self psychology comes to reinvent the wheel. But although this chapter does have the virtue of edging toward a rapprochement with object-relations theory by recognizing the existence of the introject, the discussion does not really address the issue of the primary process per se.

Parenthetically, unlike the case vignettes in chapter seven, which so well illustrate the usefulness of the self-psychological principle that analysts must "decenter" from their own perspective and open themselves to that of the other—a principle that the intersubjectivists seem to wish to appropriate and claim as their own—the discussion of the case of

Jessica in chapter five seems quite traditional. The material could equally well have been formulated in the language of object-relations theory, separation-individuation theory, or even the language of superego analysis. One wonders where is the distinctiveness of the intersubjective framework here, because the contribution of the analyst's experience and organizing principles to the therapeutic process is left entirely in the dark.

Perhaps Stolorow and Atwood are reluctant to confront the issue of the primary process precisely because its existence and the analyst's special knowledge of its laws are seen to constitute a basis for the very type of analytic interpretive authoritarianism that the intersubjectivists most deplore. But the fact that knowledge can be abused is no reason to pretend that it does not exist. Besides, his knowledge of the primary process does no more than suggest interpretive possibilities.

Except for his (fortunately only partial) embrace of the "essentializing" method utilized by dream dictionaries and Jungians and to which, following Stekel, he fell victim in the area of the so-called universal language of symbols, Freud's (1900) method was predominantly a "contextualizing" one (Burke, 1939). In this approach, despite his knowledge of primary process mechanisms, the analyst is entirely dependent on the patient's associations to provide the psychic context outside of which interpretation is merely "wild." This is not to deny, however, that many traditional analysts have in practice fallen victim to essentialism and the authoritarianism that follows from it—as, for that matter, have many revisionists; it is merely to insist that this is a departure from rather than an instance of legitimate analytic technique.

Contrary to the idea that any application of knowledge of the primary process must lead to interpretive authoritarianism on the part of the analyst, I think few practitioners have not enjoyed the experience of their patients employing *their* knowledge of the primary process in the conscious interpretation of their therapist's parapraxes, symptomatic actions, nonverbal behavior, and so on. In my experience, this is not a rare event at all and it indicates that the interpretive sword can—and on the unconscious level always does—cut both ways.

Although I have major reservations about other aspects of his work, I think Langs (1980), following Searles (1975), simply hit the nail on the head when some fifteen years ago, he spoke of the fact that sometimes the designated analyst is the functional patient and the designated patient is the functional analyst. But whereas Langs was speaking of a situation he regarded as undesirable, I tend to agree with Searles that, to a degree (and here matters of degree are everything), this is a normal and necessary aspect of every analysis. In a sense, to "listen with the third ear" to what the patient as unconscious supervisor of the analysis is saying is to place oneself in the position of patient to the analysand's unconscious as analyst.

This tendency on the part of intersubjectivists to throw out a valid concept because it may lend itself to authoritarian misuse while remaining blind to its possible employment in a democratic way that undermines authoritarianism is most evident in regard to their rejection of the idea of objective reality. Although Stolorow and Atwood have stated that they are only denying the relevance of this concept insofar as psychoanalytic therapy is concerned and have ridiculed as a misunderstanding reflecting *The Fear of Loss of Reality* the idea that they are doing more than this, I think their work is more ambiguous on this score than they wish to acknowledge.

On reading chapter one of *Contexts of Being* I was momentarily reassured that its authors had pulled back from what I viewed as their earlier epistemological subjectivism (Stolorow, Brandchaft, and Atwood, 1987) in view of their critique (pp. 18–20) of Basch's "radical constructivism verging on solipsism" (p. 19) in which, according to the authors, "even one's mother and father are seen as not possessing any literal existence in a world apart from the self but are regarded instead as examples of 'imaginary entities that exist only in the brain' " (p. 19). Stolorow and Atwood (1992) cogently argue that Basch's position involves a self-contradiction:

> [I]t contains on one level a claim that at another level it denies. On one hand, Basch denies the literal truth of the individual's experience of the independent existence of objects outside the boundaries of the self; he argues that such objects are only "constructions" localized inside the human brain. On the other hand, Basch does accord independent existence to one class of such external objects; the brains themselves [p. 19].

Unfortunately, two pages later, in the context of their critique of Sullivan's concepts of "parataxic distortion" and "consensual validation," Stolorow and Atwood (1992) return to their earlier critique of the idea of "a mind separated from an 'objective' reality that it either accurately apprehends or distorts" (p. 21). In offering this critique the authors give little indication as to whether they mean to restrict it to knowing within the psychoanalytic situation or apply it to knowing in general. Hope arises that they do not mean to deny objective knowledge when they go on to state that in the intersubjective framework "it is assumed that one's personal reality is *always* codetermined by features of the surround and the unique meanings into which these are assimilated" (p. 21). Here, as in their gestures toward a Nietzschean "perspectivalism" as opposed to "radical relativism" (pp. 123–124), Stolorow and Atwood appear to reject radical constructivism—which they rightly critique in Basch—by acknowledging that there does exist a "surround" and that its features are sufficiently potent to "codetermine" one's personal reality.[9]

In this light it seems legitimate to ask to what degree one's personal reality corresponds or fails to correspond to "features of the surround." In the final section of chapter one, entitled "The Genesis of the Sense of the Real," Stolorow and Atwood (1992) express the view that the child's sense of the real develops "through the validating attunement of the caregiving surround" (p. 27). However, this begs the question of the degree to which the child's *sense* of the real is realistic. One can agree with the view that the sense of the real develops from validation (which I regard as inseparable from invalidation because to validate one thing is necessarily to invalidate something else), but at the same time be moved to ask what happens if hallucinations are validated as real? If classical Freudian theory is validated as true by members of the New York Psychoanalytic Institute, does that make it true? I have no doubt that the nonexistence of the Holocaust is psychologically real to those whose experience is validated by the revisionist historians. Does that mean that the Holocaust did not occur?

That such questions are not frivolous and unnecessary is evident from the fact that in their recent new edition of *Faces in a Cloud*, Atwood and Stolorow (1984b) state as one of three interrelated principles of intersubjectivity the assumption that "no personal reality is more true or valid than any other" (p. 189). To me, this is simply a bizarre and indefensible thing to say, not least because it expresses the very radical relativism the authors claim to eschew in their brief and rather belated gesture toward perpectivalism in the "Epilogue" to *Contexts of Being*. If one truly believed this dictum, therapeutic work would be pointless because a patient's posttherapeutic "reality" would by definition be no more true or valid than his or her pretherapeutic perspective. If the

---

[9] Although the correspondence theory of truth has frequently been associated with a naive objectivism or positivism that ignores the role of the subject in construing reality, I believe the very "perspectivalism" to which Stolorow and Atwood pay lip service itself entails a sophisticated version of the correspondence theory. Once again we have a trinity: rejecting either pole of the binary opposition Naive Subjectivism/Naive Objectivism, we embrace a *Perspectivalism* that acknowledges the reality of the object but also that it can only be known from the standpoint of multiple perspectives. Despite the association of this epistemology with continental phenomenology and existential philosophy, I believe it shares a substantial measure of agreement with Popper's (1972) conception of objective knowledge as an evolutionary process in which our conjectures or approximations are progressively accommodated to an ultimately incompletely knowable reality.

authors actually believed what they claim, it would be hard to understand why they bother to write, because the intersubjective perspective they so energetically advocate—which they acknowledge "symbolically crystal-lizes . . . the interplay between our respective worlds of experience through which our theoretical perspective came into being" (*Faces*, 1994, p. 190)—would, by their own principle, be no more valid or true than the psychoanalytic approaches they reject, which similarly embody the personal realities of their authors.

In chapter six of *Contexts* (written in conjunction with Brandchaft) Stolorow and Atwood (1992) state that "the only reality relevant and accessible to psychoanalytic inquiry (that is, to empathy and introspec-tion) is *subjective reality*" (p. 92; original emphasis). When, therefore, in chapter two they acknowledge the "codetermining impact of the analyst on the organization of the patient's experience" (p. 34) and emphasize the importance of "always taking into account what the patient has perceived of the analyst that has leant itself to the patient's anticipations of retraumatization" (p. 34), one would naturally assume the authors mean to beg the question of the relative accuracy or inaccuracy of such perceptions. For to imply that such perceptions may sometimes be accurate (as I, for one, would acknowledge) would be to move beyond the patient's subjective reality to what they regard (but I do not) as unac-ceptable assertions of correspondence with objective reality. However, in contradiction to their own restriction of psychoanalytic work to the field of subjective reality, the authors nevertheless speak of "the kernel of truth" (p. 101) contained in the patient's perceptions and fantasies. There is simply no way that such a kernel of truth can be recognized in a psychology that has ruled reference to objective reality out of court and restricted itself to the exploration of the patient's subjective experience.

In the clinical illustration offered in chapter two Stolorow and Atwood (1992) state that "commencing at the age of two, her father had used his daughter for primarily oral sexual gratification several times each week" (p. 36). This does not sound to me like a statement regarding the patient's experience; it sounds like a statement of objective fact. If pressed by the patient to say whether or not they believed her about this, would the authors hedge and say only that they believed this was her experience? And, if so, what would they reply if she pressed and said, "I know you believe it was my experience, but do you believe my experience corresponds to objective fact or not? Do you believe my father sexually abused me?"

Faced with this question, an intersubjectivist might reply, "Yes, I believe your father abused you," while inwardly maintaining the reserva-tion that in so answering he was doing no more than offering a report on the content of his own subjective reality. However, if in so "validating" his patient's experience he were to make this inner reservation explicit, the patient might well ask, "I believe you believe that I was abused, but is your belief valid or not?" To this the intersubjectivist might well reply, "I believe so," thus leading the discussion into an infinite regress.

Alternatively, an intersubjectivist might feel forced in this situation to reply, "I don't know." Although not exactly "validating," this would nevertheless be an honest answer. The analyst is frequently not in a position to independently verify or falsify various beliefs of the patient. However, against the authors' denial of the very possibility of objective knowledge in psychoanalysis, I would argue that sometimes in clinical as in applied psychoanalysis corroboration of claims about events both within and outside the therapy can be achieved (Hanly, 1991). For example, if the patient's conviction of having been abused were to be supported by, say, her father's admission of having done so and, perhaps, by her mother or sister coming forward and confirming her memories of key events, then the analyst would be justified in going beyond acknowledging his subjective belief in her account to acknowledging that, in want of evidence to the contrary, the account may plausibly be regarded as objectively true.[10]

In chapter six, Stolorow and Atwood (1992) state that "the belief that one's personal reality is objective is an instance of the psychological process of concretization, the symbolic transformation of *configurations of subjective experience* into events and entities that are believed to be *objectively* perceived and known" (p. 92; original emphasis).[11] Regarding the patient discussed previously, they state (chapter two) that two decades of analytic work validating the experience of having been abused resulted in the patient's acquisition of a "felt reality" (p. 39) of

---

[10] In speaking of attainable objective knowledge I refer, like Popper (1972), not to anything resembling absolute truth, but rather to conjectures or approximations that, for the moment at least, resist falsification or, *contra* Popper, enjoy some degree of verification. I find it interesting that here I am the defender of the possibility of validation of the patient's experience through objective verification whereas Stolorow and Atwood are required by their restriction of psychoanalytic inquiry to the field of subjective reality to join the (caricatured) classical analyst in begging the question. But just as the *patient's* experience can sometimes be validated in this way, so can the *analyst's*, even when the validation of the latter's experience entails the invalidation of the former's. Naturally, the validation of the patient's experience may at times invalidate the analyst's.

[11] To me, this statement indicates that, although claiming adherence to a perspectivalism transcending both subjectivism and objectivism, in combating the latter the authors have succumbed to the former, thus regressing from a tertiary or dialectical position into dualism.

having been sexually abused. We now learn, however, that such convictions regarding objective reality amount to concretizations of subjective experience. Is this the sort of progress the therapist intended? Is the aim of therapy to promote the concretizations that allegedly underlie the sense of the real, or is it to undermine such concretizations and, hence, the sense of the real? Or could such theoretical difficulties stem from a defective epistemology which holds that the sense of the real necessarily rests on concretization, rather than on *correspondence* between the subject's experience and the real nature of the object, because the latter position has in practice, if not in rhetorical gestures toward perspectivalism, been rejected in both the intersubjective and self-psychological frameworks?

When Stolorow and Atwood (1992) go on to rail against the concept of distortion that accompanies the appeal to the idea of an objective reality, I am moved to ask with regard to the patient's father—who "pressured her to enjoy the sexual episodes, which he said were akin to the practices of royal families during other historical eras" and who "told her that what was taking place between them heralded the future of parent–child relations" (pp. 36–37)—was he engaged in distortion or was he not? I'm sure what he described reflected his subjective experience, his "felt reality," but was that experience a distortion of the reality of abuse that was taking place or was it not?

Stolorow and Atwood assume that if the notion of an objective reality is allowed into the therapeutic discourse, the analyst will necessarily claim to enjoy a privileged access to it and will dismiss the patient's differing views as distortion. For some reason, the authors appear to believe that the only way to combat this is to rule out of court in psychoanalysis the idea of an objective reality by the standard of which anything might be judged to be a distortion.

But this entirely ignores the democratic possibility that analyst and patient share a belief in the existence of an objective reality, but one that is extremely difficult to perceive and about which the best we ever have are approximations (Popper, 1972) and that even to arrive at our best approximations we have to perpetually seek to purge our conceptions of reality of purely subjective distortions—which are as likely to be present in the analyst's views as in the patient's. In this alternative viewpoint (which differs little from the perspectivalist epistemology that the authors claim but actually fail to sustain), analyst and patient engage in a mutually corrective dialogue in an attempt to approximate the reality of their ongoing encounters; of the patient's psychological, interpersonal, and existential situation; and of his or her past.

In this perspective the concept of distortion carries no authoritarian connotation, for it is recognized that in certain cases of disjunction the analyst may be distorting more than the patient. In this view, every analysis constitutes for the analyst a continuation of the training analysis, for in being open to the patient's messages regarding the analyst's distortions of reality—especially when such messages come from the patient's unconscious—the analyst receives ongoing assistance in reality-testing and ongoing help in recognizing the subjective sources of tendencies to distort in his or her insufficiently analyzed unconscious organizing principles. I think the foregoing account is in the spirit of true intersubjectivity, and I recommend it as a way out of the authors' self-contradictory epistemological cul de sac.

From this alternative epistemological perspective, Stolorow and Atwood's (1992) claim that "when analysts invoke the concept of objective reality along with its corollary concept of distortion, this forecloses and diverts the investigation of the subjective reality encoded in the patient's communications" (p. 93) is seen to have no necessary validity. For I can deny the objective reality of aspects of my patients' perceptions and suggest that they are distorting reality and, at the same time, explore with them the meaning of their experience, of the subjective reality encoded within it, and so on. Similarly, I can seriously consider their claim that I am distorting reality and, if I come to feel this is the case, I can explore, either privately or openly with the patients, the subjective reality encoded in such distortions. In other words, there is no need to assume that disbelief in the objective reality of the patients' or the analysts' perceptions must result in an authoritarianism that closes off inquiry.

If patients and I can agree about reality, and even if we cannot, we can nevertheless explore the possible symbolic meanings encoded in the patients' experience. It is not necessary for me to subscribe to their experience or even to beg the question as to its validity in order for us to analyze it, any more than I have to mistake a dream for a reality, or at least remain open to the possibility that it is more than just a dream, in order to proceed to its analysis.

According to Stolorow and Atwood (1992), "the analyst's acceptance of the validity of the patient's perceptual reality . . . is of inestimable importance in establishing the therapeutic alliance" (p. 94). They write:

> Any threat to the validity of perceptual reality constitutes a deadly threat to the self and to the organization of experience itself. When the analyst insists that the patient's perception is a secondary phenomenon distorted by primary forces, this, more than any other single factor, ushers in the

conflictual transference-countertransference spirals that are so commonly described as resistances to analysis or negative transferences [p. 94].

Although I would agree that total invalidation of the patient's experience would constitute such a threat, as would authoritarian statements about what it *really* means, my point is that one can disconfirm the patient's experience on the literal level as distortion without invalidating it altogether, provided one accompanies the disconfirmation with an expression of one's conviction that it must mean something on another level and of one's genuine interest in working together to learn what that might be.

In my own experience, and that of many other analysts, certain patients feel "held" and "contained" by early interpretations that disconfirm their (sometimes but not always) paranoid fears of the therapist and of therapy and that clarify reality—interpretations that, often enough, permit a therapeutic alliance and a positive selfobject transference to emerge. Again, in my experience, patients sometimes feel reassured and protected when therapists communicate their recognition of the patients' disordered reality-testing and offer to assist them to become more objective—provided this is done with humility, kindness, and in a truly democratic spirit in which therapists remain open to being helped by patients with their own problems in reality-testing.

As part of their critique of the practice of pointing out distortions of reality to patients, Stolorow and Atwood speak of the threat this constitutes for people who are already uncertain about the reality of their experience because it was never validated or had to be disavowed out of a sense that it threatened a needed tie. But, for some reason, the authors seem not to realize that pointing out distortions is a necessary element in the process of helping patients to become more certain of the reality of their experience by validating what is true in that experience and invalidating what is illusory or false.

Ironically, in connection with their criticism of the practice of pointing out distortions, Stolorow and Atwood refer to the "gaslight" genre (p. 95). *But to "gaslight" someone is to distort reality for them, not to help them clarify what is real.* In fact, in the "gaslight" genre in addition to the villain who distorts and mystifies reality for the victim there is usually a hero who works with the victim to dispel the distortions and to clarify the reality, that is, to validate what is real and invalidate what is false or illusory. This surely is the role of the analyst, just as in regard to humanity's collective self it is the role of science.

But Stolorow and Atwood fail to see that validation (which they regard as good) and invalidation (which they view as bad) necessarily go together. For to arrive at the truth it is necessary, on the one hand, to validate what is real and, on the other, to invalidate what is false. Aside from this failure to recognize that validation and invalidation imply one another, the devaluation (not to say demonization) of the latter reflects a failure to appreciate the relief experienced by both children and adults when a trusted other invalidates one's distorted persecutory perceptions or nightmare fears.

Surely it is of little help to patients suffering from uncertainty regarding the validity of their experience to withhold from them our assistance in reality-testing. The authors seem to assume that the analysts are themselves deluded, perhaps by rigid adherence to ideological Freudianism or Kleinianism, and that their attempts to dispel distortions and to clarify reality will necessarily amount to attempts to invalidate patients' valid experience and indoctrinate them with the analyst's ideology. I do not doubt that this occurs, but I hardly think we need to subscribe to the authors' one-sided and self-contradictory denial of the legitimacy of appeals to objective reality in psychoanalytic work in order to critique such ideological abuses of the therapeutic relationship.

It seems to me that if parents sometimes have distorted views of what their children are experiencing, and if analysts sometimes have distorted views of what their patients are experiencing, then it is fair to assume that patients sometimes have distorted views of what their parents and analysts, among others, were or are experiencing. The attempt to clear up some of these distortions is an aspect of the therapeutic process. The authors write that "a milieu in which the patient's perceptual reality is not threatened encourages the patient to develop and expand his own capacity for self-reflection" (p. 96). But I submit that what threatens patients is not the questioning of the validity of their perceptions and beliefs per se, but rather the *spirit* in which such an investigation is carried out—whether it is conducted respectfully, democratically, with an openness to the possibility of one's own views being faulty and a willingness to have one's own distortions corrected with the patient's help, or whether it is conducted in an authoritarian manner.

Writing of Freud's conclusion that fantasies of sexual abuse amounted to mental representations of instincts rather than real events, Stolorow and Atwood (1992) point out that "Freud's dilemma was a false one," for "such fantasies often encode experiences of traumatic developmental derailment," and that "it is common for experiences of abuse and seduction of a non-sexual or covertly sexual nature to be concretized and preserved in sexual symbolism" (p. 101). They go on to state that "this insight into the kernel of truth encoded in a patient's fantasies opens up a whole new pathway for exploration, one that remains foreclosed when a patient's perceptions are dismissed as distortion" (p. 101).

As indicated previously, it is, to say the least, inconsistent to speak of "the kernel of truth" contained in a patient's perceptions while at the same time arguing that the idea of objective reality has no place in psychoanalytic discourse. But for Stolorow and Atwood the notion of objective reality appears acceptable if what is being talked about is the element of truth in a patient's perceptions, but unacceptable when the element of distortion in those perceptions is being discussed. Naturally, the possible kernel of truth in analysts' views—especially in their conviction that patients are distorting—is entirely ignored. Not only is this impossibly one-sided, but it fails to appreciate that in order to even recognize the kernel of truth embedded in distortions, it is necessary to separate this kernel from the distortions in which it is embedded.

Atwood and Stolorow (1984b) support and themselves engage in the practice of tracing psychoanalytic theories to their subjective origins in the personal psychology of their authors. They contribute to the psychoanalysis of their own perspective by noting in the new edition of *Faces in a Cloud* that their postulate that "no personal reality is more true or valid than any other" serves as a "solution to a relentless early experience of invalidation and psychological usurpation" (p. 189).[12]

In this light, it seems legitimate to wonder whether the theoretical problems outlined previously, especially the unquestioning association of objectivist epistemology with authoritarianism, may reflect both the compulsion and the dread of repeating (Ornstein, 1974) the struggle with an authoritarian parent. If so, such a failure to work through, mourn, and in this way move beyond such transference of the early experience of invalidation would have the effect of partially removing the authors' work from the "conflict-free" ego sphere and keeping it embroiled in conflicts of personal origin.[13]

There is an ironic sense in which refusal to work with the idea of objectivity because of its association with authoritarianism (while remaining blind to its democratic uses) itself leads to authoritarianism. For whenever rational and collaborative inquiry into the objective truth is

---

[12] Although, in a certain sense, ad hominem, this strategy is unavoidable in the psychoanalysis of knowledge, including psychoanalytic knowledge. It is perfectly legitimate, however, provided it is clearly understood that psychoanalytic explanation of the subjective foundations of theoretical claims tells us nothing about their scientific validity or invalidity.

[13] It is important to note here that I am not claiming that intersubjective theory is flawed because it may be subjectively motivated by unresolved conflicts with an authoritarian parent. Rather, I have sought to demonstrate its flaws on rational theoretical and clinical grounds alone. Only then have I offered a conjecture regarding the possible basis of these flaws in its authors' taken-for-granted subjective organizing principles.

closed off, unquestioned assumptions and arbitrary actions tend to replace it. Having ruled the concept of objective reality out of court in psychoanalysis, instead of engaging with the patient in a joint search for the objective facts of the case, intersubjectivists may succumb to the assumption that they know what these are and proceed to act accordingly. In this situation, it is as if it is legitimate to *act* as if objective reality exists and one knows what it is, but not to *speak* of this reality, even if to do so opens up the possibility of a genuinely collaborative search for the truth.[14]

As usual, at the root of the theoretical difficulties that bedevil both selfobject and intersubjective theory lies the either/or thinking that entails privileging one or the other term of a false dichotomy. In the present case such binary oppositions as Subjective/Objective, Empathy/Observation, and Validation/Invalidation, among others, are in operation. In each case, the former term seems to be privileged over the latter, when in reality they require and complement one another. However much the intersubjectivists may believe they have transcended self psychology, insofar as both orientations fall victim to these types of either/or thinking they suffer from a common affliction.

SUMMARY

Three patterns of psychoanalytic reasoning are outlined: monism, dualism, and dialectics. Whereas Freud's thought is a mixture of dualistic and dialectical trends, Kohut's thinking manifests both monistic and dualistic elements and displays a marked tendency toward either/or thinking. Various examples of the latter in self psychology are discussed, such as the view that one must be either conflict-driven (Guilty Man) or motivated by the goal of self-fulfillment (Tragic Man). But why not both? Similarly, against the view that psychoanalysis must study human beings purely as subjects via the introspective/empathic method, it is argued that they must be approached—even in psychoanalysis—as what they in fact are: both objects and subjects; in any case, empathy is inseparable from observation. Again, in relation to the intersubjectivist celebration of validation over the invalidation of experience, the two imply one

---

[14] Just as it is a basic principle of Freudian theory that in any conflict it is easier to swing from one pole to the other—as, for example, from saint to sinner and back again —than to genuinely master the conflict, so in the case of epistemological dualism, naive subjectivism, and naive objectivism, although manifestly opposed, frequently enjoy a secret symbiosis, a kind of unholy alliance. Epistemological subjectivism on the level of theory may frequently coexist with an unquestioning and authoritarian objectivism on the level of practice.

another, for to validate one thing is by implication to invalidate something else and vice versa.

It is argued that Stolorow and Atwood's belief (1992) that "analysts embracing an objectivist epistemology presume to have privileged access to the essence of the patient's psychic reality and to the objective truths that the patient's psychic reality obscures" (p. 123) is false. One can embrace a sophisticated objectivist epistemology or perspectivalism without assuming the analyst has privileged access to reality, assuming instead that patient and analyst engage in a mutually corrective and democratic dialogue in search of closer and closer approximations to an ultimately incompletely knowable reality (Carveth, 1984, 1987).

Despite these and other serious theoretical deficiencies, both self psychology and the intersubjective approach contribute, together with a range of other psychoanalytic perspectives, to the evolution of a more thoroughly social conception of the self and the therapeutic encounter and to the enhancement of our understanding of the nature of therapeutic impasses and the ways in which they may be overcome.

REFERENCES

Adorno, T. W. (1966), *Negative Dialectics*, trans. E. B. Ashton. New York: Continuum.

Ainsworth, M., Blehar, M., Waters, E. & Wall, S. (1978), *Patterns of Attachment*. Hilldale, NJ: Lawrence Erlbaum Associates.

Atwood, G. E. & Stolorow, R. D. (1984a), *Structures of Subjectivity: Explorations in Psychoanalytic Phenomenology*. Hillsdale, NJ: The Analytic Press.

—— & —— (1984b), *Faces in a Cloud,* 2nd ed. Northvale, NJ: Aronson, 1994.

✓ Bacal, H. A. & Newman, K. M. (1990), *Theories of Object Relations*. New York: Columbia University Press.

Barratt, B. (1984), *Psychic Reality and Psychoanalytic Knowing. Advances in Psychoanalysis: Theory, Research, and Practice, Vol. 3*. Hillsdale, NJ: The Analytic Press.

Beebe, B. & Lachmann, F. (1988), Mother–infant mutual influence and precursors of psychic structure. In: *Frontiers in Self Psychology: Progress in Self Psychology, Vol. 3*, ed. A. Goldberg. Hillsdale, NJ: The Analytic Press, pp. 3–25.

Bowlby, J. (1969–1980), *Attachment and Loss*, 3 vols. Harmondsworth, Middlesex: Penguin.

Brandchaft, B. (1993), To free the spirit from its cell. The 1991 Kohut Memorial Lecture delivered to the 14th Annual Conference on the Psychology of the Self. In: *The Widening Scope of Self Psychology: Progress in Self Psychology, Vol. 9*, ed. A. Goldberg. Hillsdale, NJ: The Analytic Press, pp. 209–230.

Brenner, C. (1982), *The Mind in Conflict*. New York: International University Press.

Burke, K. (1939), Freud and the analysis of poetry. In: *Freud*, ed. P. Meisel. Englewood Cliffs, NJ: Prentice-Hall, 1981, pp. 73–94.

Carveth, D. L. (1984), The analyst's metaphors: A deconstructionist perspective. *Psychoanal. Contemp. Thought*, 7:491–560.

—— (1987), The epistemological foundations of psychoanalysis: A deconstructionist view of the controversy. *Philos. Social Sci.*, 17:97–115.

—— (1993), The borderline dilemma in *Paris, Texas*: Psychoanalytic approaches to Sam Shepard. *Can. J. Psychoanal./Revue Canad. Psychanalyse*, 1:19–46.

—— (1996), Psychoanalytic conceptions of the passions. In: *Freud and the Passions*, ed. J. O'Neill. University Park: Penn State Press.

Chasseguet-Smirgel, J. (1984), *Creativity and Perversion*. New York: Norton.

Concise Oxford Dictionary of Current English, ed. J. B. Sykes. Oxford: Clarendon Press, 1982.

Dilthey, W. (1961), *Meaning in History*, ed. H. P. Rickman. London: Allen & Unwin.

Dorpat, T. L. (1987), A new look at denial and defense. In: *The Annual of Psychoanalysis*, 15:23–47. Madison, CT: International Universities Press.

Erikson, E. (1950). *Childhood and Society*. New York: Norton.

—— (1959), *Identity and the Life Cycle: Selected Papers*. Psychological Issues Monogr. 1. New York: International Universities Press.

Freud, S. (1900), The interpretation of dreams. *Standard Edition*, 4 & 5. London: Hogarth Press, 1953.

—— (1905), Three essays on the theory of sexuality. *Standard Edition*, 7:135–243. London: Hogarth Press, 1953.

—— (1914), On narcissism: An introduction. *Standard Edition*, 14:73–102. London: Hogarth Press, 1957.

—— (1920), Beyond the Pleasure Principle. *Standard Edition*, 18:7–64. London: Hogarth Press, 1955.

Greenberg, J. R. & Mitchell, S. A. (1983), *Object Relations in Psychoanalytic Theory*. Cambridge, MA: Harvard University Press.

Hanly, C. (1991), *The Problem of Truth in Applied Psychoanalysis*. New York: Guilford.

Hegel, G. W. F. (1807), *The Phenomenology of Mind*, 2 vols., trans. J. Baillie. New York: Macmillan, 1910.

Heidegger, M. (1927), *Being and Time*, trans. J. Macquarrie & E. S. Robinson. New York: Harper, 1962.

Huxley, J. (1927), The uniqueness of man. In: *Man in the Modern World*. New York: Mentor, 1948, pp. 7–28.

—— (1947), Introduction to *The Phenomenon of Man* by Pierre Teilhard de Chardin. London: Fontana, 1965.

Jacobson, E. (1964), *The Self and the Object World*. New York: International Universities Press.

Kohut, H. (1959), Introspection, empathy and psychoanalysis: An examination of the relationship between mode of observation and theory. In: *The Search for the Self*, ed. P. Ornstein. New York: International Universities Press, 1978, pp. 205–232.

—— (1971), *The Analysis of the Self*. New York: International Universities Press.

—— (1977), *The Restoration of the Self*. New York: International Universities Press.

—— (1979), The two analyses of Mr. Z. *Internat. J. Psycho-Anal.*, 60:3–27.

—— (1984), *How Does Analysis Cure?* ed. A. Goldberg & P. Stepansky. Chicago: University of Chicago Press.

Lacan, J. (1977), *Ecrits: A Selection*, trans. A. Sheridan. New York: Norton.

Langs, R. (1976), *The Bipersonal Field*. New York: Aronson.
—— (1978), *Technique in Transition*. New York: Aronson.
—— (1980), Truth therapy/lie therapy. *Internat. J. Psychoanal. Psychother.*, 8:3–34.
Mead, G. H. (1934), *Mind, Self and Society*. Chicago: University of Chicago Press.
Mitchell, S. A. (1988), *Relational Concepts in Psychoanalysis: An Integration*. Cambridge, MA: Harvard University Press.
Ornstein, A. (1974), The dread to repeat and the new beginning. *The Annual of Psychoanalysis*, 2:231–248. New York: International Universities Press.
Popper, K. (1972), *Objective Knowledge: An Evolutionary Approach*. Oxford: Clarendon Press.
Reik, T. (1948), *Listening With the Third Ear*. New York: Arena, 1972.
Sartre, J.-P. (1943), *Being and Nothingness: A Study in Phenomenological Ontology*, trans. H. E. Barnes. New York: Philosophical Library, 1953.
Schafer, R. (1976), *A New Language for Psychoanalysis*. New Haven, CT: Yale University Press.
Searles, H. (1965), *Collected Papers on Schizophrenia and Related Subjects*. New York: International Universities Press.
—— (1975), The patient as therapist to his analyst. In: *Tactics and Techniques in Psychoanalytic Therapy, Vol. 2*, ed. P. L. Giovacchini. New York: Aronson, pp. 95–151. Also in *Countertransference and Related Subjects*. Madison, CT: International Universities Press, 1979, pp. 380–459.
Singer, P. (1980), *Marx*. Oxford: Oxford University Press.
—— (1983), *Hegel*. Oxford: Oxford University Press.
Sloane, J. (1986), Notes on the analytic frame/space. Unpublished paper presented as part of a course on "Intersubjectivity" offered by the Extension Programme of the Toronto Psychoanalytic Society.
Stern, D. (1985), *The Interpersonal World of the Infant: A View From Psychoanalysis and Developmental Psychology*. New York: Basic Books.
—— & Atwood, G. E. (1992), *Contexts of Being: The Intersubjective Foundations of Psychological Life*. Hillsdale, NJ: The Analytic Press.
Stolorow, R. D., Brandchaft, B. & Atwood, G. E. (1987), *Psychoanalytic Treatment: An Intersubjective Approach*. Hillsdale, NJ: The Analytic Press.
Sullivan, H. S. (1953), *The Interpersonal Theory of Psychiatry*. New York: Norton.
Weber, M. (1953), *From Max Weber*, ed. H. H. Gerth & C. Wright Mills. New York: Oxford University Press.

Chapter 2

Self Psychology and Intersubjectivity Theory

Jeffrey L. Trop

The purpose of this chapter is to compare and contrast the clinical theories of self psychology and intersubjectivity. Self psychology and intersubjectivity theory are often seen as synonymous or on a continuum. There are broad and extremely important similarities between the two theories, but there are also important differences between them that have significant clinical implications.

Self psychology and intersubjectivity theory stand together in that both are relational theories and both reject the concept of drive as a primary motivational source. Also, both theories use the stance of empathy and introspection as a central guiding principle. However, the motivational theories of self psychology and intersubjectivity theory differ significantly. The motivational theory of self psychology is centered in the concept of the selfobject. In two significant review papers, entitled "The Selfobject Theory of Motivation and the History of Psychoanalysis" and "Selfobjects and Selfobject Transference: Theoretical Implications," Basch (1984a, b) summarizes the centrality of the selfobject concept for self psychology. In the second paper, describing Kohut's discovery of selfobject transferences, he states:

> Together he called them selfobject transferences, differentiating them from object-instinctual transferences, and indicating that they represented aspects of the development of the self. . . . Indeed, he found that the interpretation and resolution of the selfobject transferences did not lead to formation and resolution of an oedipal transference and then to object love, but to a maturation in the area of ambition and ideals that left the patient free . . . to lead a life that was satisfying and meaningful to him or her [p. 25].

Originally published in *The Intersubjective Perspective*, edited by R. Stolorow, G. Atwood, and B. Brandschaft. Northvale, NJ; Aronson, 1994; reprinted with permission of the editors and publishers.

Kohut (1984), in describing psychoanalytic cure, states that "the essence of the psychoanalytic cure resides in a patient's newly acquired ability to identify and seek out appropriate selfobjects—both mirroring and idealizable—as they present themselves in his realistic surroundings and to be sustained by them" (p. 77). Kohut further goes on to describe his feelings about the unique contribution of self psychology and states, "The only really forward move provided by self psychology is its expansion of psychoanalytic theory, specifically its theoretical elucidation of the whole area of the reactivation of thwarted developmental needs in the transference via the discovery of the selfobject transferences" (p. 104). Self psychological theory thus has as its central tenet that patients will be motivated to mobilize and seek out selfobject experiences to transform developmental deficits.

The motivational principle of intersubjectivity theory is not centered in the concept of the selfobject but in a more broad-based striving to organize and order experience. Atwood and Stolorow (1984) describe their conception of motivation in intersubjectivity theory as follows: "The evolution of our framework has led us to propose an additional, more general supraordinate motivational principle that the need to maintain the organization of experience is a central motive in the patterning of human action" (p. 35).

The intersubjective framework thus proposes that each person establishes unique organizing principles that automatically and unconsciously shape his or her experience. For example, a person, invited to an event where there are unfamiliar people, may enter a room and someone in the room may immediately turn his back. One person may organize this to mean that he is undesirable and repugnant. Another person may conclude that he is better than anyone at the event and assume a haughty indifference. A third person might interpret the other's turning away as a random occurrence, and it would not be assimilated as having a personal meaning regarding his or her entrance into the room. Thus, each person will automatically organize experience according to the unique psychological principles that unconsciously shape his or her subjective world. Atwood and Stolorow (1984) further elaborate their concept of organizing principles as follows:

> The organizing principles of a person's subjective world are themselves unconscious. A person's experiences are shaped by his psychological structures without this shaping becoming the focus of awareness and reflection. . . . In the absence of reflection, a person is unaware of his role as a constitutive subject in elaborating his personal reality. The world in which he lives and moves presents itself as though it were something independently and objectively real. The patterning and thematizing of events that uniquely characterize his personal reality are thus seen

as if they were properties of these events rather than products of his own subjective interpretations and constructions [p. 36].

Intersubjectivity theory does recognize the importance of selfobject longings. Selfobject transferences represent one of a multiplicity of unconscious, automatic, and repetitive ways that patients organize their experience of the analyst. Selfobject transferences, in other words, are a class of invariant organizing principles.

Transference, from an intersubjective vantage point, can thus be conceptualized as unconscious organizing activity. Unconscious organizing principles that have emerged in the interactional system of child and caregiver form the essence of personality development. Intersubjectivity theory thus adds a unique dimension to the concept of empathy. Empathic inquiry can be redefined "as a method of investigating and illuminating the principles that unconsciously organize a patient's experience" (Stolorow, 1993). This definition of empathy emphasizes the elucidation of unconscious organizing principles as a primary focus and differs significantly from Kohut's (1984) characterization of empathy as "the capacity to think and feel oneself into the inner life of another person" (p. 82).

The different definitions of empathy offered by intersubjectivity theory and self psychology are derivative of the significant differences between their motivational theories. These distinctions also lead to very different views of the curative process.

The clinical theory of self psychology emphasizes the strengthening of the weak self through what Wolf (1988) describes as "the disruption-restoration process" (p. 110). Wolf describes the curative process in self psychology as follows:

> The emerging selfobject needs will spontaneously focus on the therapist; that is, a selfobject transference develops. This transference will be disrupted, often very painfully, when inevitably the therapist somehow fails to respond in precisely the manner required by the patient. The therapist then explains and interprets this disruption in all its dimensions but particularly with reference to analogous early and presumably etiological situations with significant persons in the past. These explanations and interpretations restore the previous harmonious selfobject transference, but the mutual understanding achieved and experienced thereby serves to replace the previously frustrated archaic selfobject need with a reciprocal empathic resonance with the therapist, which strengthens the self. The selfobject experience with the therapist strengthens the self and it becomes better able to integrate into a social selfobject matrix, that is, to successfully find responsive selfobject experiences in the social surround unhampered by defenses [p. 97].

Self psychology thus emphasizes a process of cure in which archaic selfobject needs are replaced with an empathic resonance with the therapist. Cure in self psychology is evidenced by the patient's new capacity to seek out appropriate selfobjects. The danger of this formulation is that it underemphasizes the acquisition of reflective self-awareness regarding the patient's constitutive role in shaping his or her own reality. The theory of intersubjectivity pictures the curative process differently. The curative process is conceptualized as resulting from the elucidation and understanding of the unique unconscious organizing principles of the patient that *shape* disruptions of the bond with the therapist. The emphasis, thus, is not only on the restoration of the tie to the analyst but, most centrally, on *understanding the principles that organize the disruption* of the tie.

Intersubjectivity theory therefore has a concept of therapeutic change that differs from that of self psychology. Stolorow et al. (1987) described the oscillation in treatment between the selfobject dimension and the repetitive dimension of the transference. In the selfobject dimension, the patient longs for the analyst to provide selfobject experiences that were missing or insufficient during the formative years. In the repetitive dimension, the patient fears the analyst will repeat previous traumatic experiences from childhood. Each of these two dimensions has unique and specific meanings for the analysand and provides opportunities for the illumination of the unconscious organizing principles that structure the transference.

The presence of a background selfobject transference tie with the analyst provides a trusting relationship for the investigation and illumination of the old repetitive organizing principles both within and outside the transference. The new selfobject experience with the analyst facilitates the development of new, alternative organizing principles and a capacity for self-reflection. Thus the essence of cure within intersubjectivity theory lies in the acquisition of new principles of organizing experience (Stolorow and Atwood, 1992). The capacity for self-reflection enables the patient to recognize the patterns inherent in the mobilization of old, constricting organizing principles and their relational foundation. Stolorow, Atwood, and Brandchaft (1992) summarize their view of the curative process as follows:

> Psychoanalysis, above all else, is a method for illuminating the prereflective unconscious, and it achieves this aim by investigating the ways in which the patient's experience of the analyst and his or her activities is unconsciously and recurrently patterned by the patient according to developmentally preformed meanings and in variant themes. Such analysis, from a position within the patient's subjective frame of reference, always keeping in view the codetermining impact of the analyst on the organization of the patient's experience, both facilitates the engagement and expansion of the patient's capacity for self-reflection and gradually establishes the analyst as an understanding presence to whom the

patient's formerly invariant ordering principles must accommodate, inviting syntheses of alternative modes of experiencing self and other [pp. 28–29].

I now describe two vignettes that illustrate the intersubjective approach. The first situation occurred briefly in the elevator of my building, and I was a peripheral participant. The second vignette is a description of an ongoing case in psychoanalytic treatment.

Joan was a toddler who entered the elevator on the eighth floor with her mother. Joan was sitting in her stroller as her mother walked into the elevator, and she looked at me shyly and started to smile, and then looked away. She then immediately glanced up at the numbers above the doors in the elevator. They were lit up in different shades of colors, and she seemed transfixed and excited by the changing numbers as the elevator descended. Her face was alive and happy with excitement. At this point, her mother looked apprehensive and said to Joan, "Don't worry. The elevator ride will be over in a minute." The elevator stopped at another floor; Joan looked back at her mother quizzically and then resumed looking up at the lights above her. She remained excited and was leaning forward in her chair as she looked at the lights. At this point, her mother bent down with a look of agitation and pushed Joan's chest vigorously, so she was forced backward in her seat. Her mother looked intensely at Joan and repeated angrily her previous admonition and said, "Don't worry. The elevator ride will be over shortly." At this point, Joan stared at her mother's face, became subdued, and leaned back in her chair with a blank look on her face. The mother now faced the front of the elevator and appeared considerably less agitated and more peaceful. The elevator door opened, and her mother pushed Joan into the lobby. I stopped and said to the mother that her daughter had actually seemed excited with the lights and did not seem worried. The mother looked away from me and continued to push Joan's stroller.

This event can be understood in the language of self psychology as a massive deficiency of mirroring and lack of responsiveness to Joan. However, the language of intersubjectivity theory, in particular the concept of unconscious organizing activities and principles, is uniquely suited to describe a situation such as this. Joan's initial feeling of enthusiasm was not only not supported but was reorganized for her as an experience of danger and concern. Joan was told not to worry, even though she did not appear to be worrying at all. Her mother appeared to need Joan to share the mother's feeling about elevators and persisted in presenting her own experience to Joan until there was some evidence that Joan had surrendered her own experience. This helped Joan's mother reestablish her own equilibrium. Here we see an unconscious organizing principle in the making. If her mother is afraid of elevators and requires Joan to share this experience, then Joan will probably grow up frightened of elevators. She in all likelihood will experience her fear of elevators as if it is a property of the machine itself. She will not recognize that her fear has arisen in a conveyed message from her mother, who required her, as a condition of their relationship, to incorporate this anxiety and make it her own. It is also possible that Joan's relationship with her mother could have a more pervasive effect. Her mother's reaction might be a more generalized response to Joan's experiences of aliveness and vitality. In this case, affects related to vitality and aliveness would have to be disavowed more ubiquitously by Joan in order to maintain the tie with her mother. Joan would then unconsciously organize her experience according to a conviction that states of expansiveness were dangerous. While my hypothesis regarding Joan's future is speculative, it seems clear that the concept of unconscious organizing principles has great value in forecasting the legacy and outcome of relational patterns.

David was referred by his family physician at age 28 for symptoms of intense anxiety and panic precipitated by his having inhaled a small amount of a drug while celebrating his graduation from law school. At our first meeting, David, a strikingly handsome man of Scandinavian descent, appeared apprehensive, agitated, and fearful that he had done some permanent damage from which he would never recover. As I inquired about the incident, it became clear that David had become fearful and worried before smoking the drug and that his symptoms had developed immediately after attempting to inhale his first and only puff.

As I listened to him describe the events, I began to inquire about the details, and he became less pressured while talking about the incident. At the end of the first session, he asked me what I thought. I told him that I was very confident that no permanent damage would result from this episode and that his fears did not seem grounded in anything that was inherent in the event. I assured him that he had not harmed himself in any irrevocable way, but I told him that I thought it would be valuable to understand how this event had unfolded in terms of its psychological meanings for him. David became visibly relaxed and said that he would very much like to come in and talk some more.

In the ensuing sessions, he gradually began to tell me his history, and the initial episode began to recede as a source of concern to him. It was my belief at that time that my reassurance had supplied a calming and soothing function and that this had contributed to an underlying idealizing transference that unfolded in subsequent weeks.

David described an extremely tumultuous background. He was an only child, and his mother had abruptly left the family when he was two years old. His father continued to raise David by himself. David remembered his father's intermittent bouts of alcoholism, which were accompanied by rage and even beatings. These were infrequent but terrorizing. He also remembered his father as a man who was kind and loving when not drinking, and who took him all over the city, pointing out beautiful landscapes and sunsets. His father died suddenly when David was six years old. He was told about his father's death in school, and he remembered feeling devastated. He was adopted by a brother of his father who was married and had three other children. David's new parents attempted to integrate him into their family as an equal sibling. They were dedicated to giving him every economic and educational opportunity and were delighted at his graduation from law school.

In the first several months of our work, David and I tried to understand what had precipitated his initial feeling of panic. We discovered that his relationship to his adoptive parents was dominated by their reactions to issues concerning his expansiveness and health. His father was preoccupied with drug abuse and used any opportunity to drum into David how dangerous drugs were and how one could "go crazy or become brain damaged with drugs." This "ammunition" was presented to David incessantly, long after it would have been useful to him from any educational perspective. There was also a more general feature of the relationship to his father that involved his father's reactions to David's states of expansiveness. David described how he would run exuberantly at the beach when he was growing up. His father would invariably be concerned and tell him repeatedly to settle down.

Thus it became clear that one of David's organizing principles was that states of intense excitement and aliveness were dangerous and that his tie with his father repeatedly conveyed this meaning to him. I interpreted that the act of smoking a drug had taken on enormous symbolic meaning for him. He was at a party feeling excited and expansive and was unconsciously attempting to free himself of the relationship with his father and its constricting impact. He wanted to have his own experience of being alive and excited. He had, however, become reactively panicked. I told him that he had not recognized his act of taking the drug as an attempt to free himself from his father's view of him as fragile and vulnerable. He felt that my interpretation was correct, and he felt very relieved.

As we talked together in the ensuing months, David began to describe a recurrent and painful experience in relationships. He had difficulty dating women and feeling at ease with himself. He felt wary of losing himself and being taken over in a relationship and had a pervasive feeling that he would not measure up. In particular, if he went out with a woman who was dating someone else, he would inevitably have a feeling that she would choose the other man, and he would act on this feeling by withdrawing morosely. He would be similarly threatened if he was talking to a woman and another male friend merely walked up to them. He would feel anxious, exposed, and unacceptable. Any situation involving a triangle with another man was organized by David as a certain threat and a confirmation that he would never be special. He described a relationship with a high school sweetheart that had ended with her dating someone else on the side. He was thrown into turmoil and a sense of devastating betrayal, and he remembered his pledge to himself never to get hurt again. His emotional devastation was compounded by his adopted mother's reaction to the event. She became extremely solicitous and concerned about his reaction. Her solicitousness and concern were voiced daily, with inquiries about his state of mind and about whether he was still feeling depressed. This had a paradoxical effect on David. Her intense concern actually reinforced his anguish. He felt that she must know that something was really wrong with him, because her concern communicated a fear that he would not be able to manage his feelings.

About four months into our work together, an episode unfolded that stimulated these intense feelings of vulnerability in David's relationship with me. One day he was in the waiting room and came in looking subdued and glum. He began to talk about his work at his law firm but seemed to have none of his customary enthusiasm or energy. I commented on this, and at first David said that he was feeling good earlier in the day and that he could not account for his feeling of glumness. I asked if anything had taken place between us. David was silent and then confided shamefully that he had heard a woman leaving my consulting room and she had been laughing and joking with me. He said that he knew that it did not make any sense to be depressed, but he did feel down. As we explored the specific meaning of this experience, David said that he had always felt I was fond of him, but that he had had a sudden feeling of competitiveness with this woman, and he began to feel that he would not interest me as much as she did. After all, he said, how could he compete with a beautiful and funny woman? He felt now that he had misconstrued our relationship and that he must be boring and vacuous. I commented that the conversation between me and the woman patient had left him feeling excluded and destitute of any concept of his value in my eyes. I clarified for David how he had automatically organized the meaning of my interchange with her as a confirmation that he was not interesting or compelling in his own right. He agreed, and we both noted how quickly this could occur for him.

As we continued to explore his family background, David and I identified one aspect of his relationship with his original father that had set the stage for this way of organizing his experience of himself. His father, when he was drinking, would take David with him when he went to see women. This occurred repeatedly until the time the father died. The setting was usually a dingy, one-room apartment where David would be confined to a bathroom or balcony. His father would have sexual relations with the woman while David was sequestered in the hallway or behind the door. David remembered hearing noises and that he would try to block his awareness of the sounds and smells. As we reconstructed his feelings about these episodes, I hypothesized that one of the origins of his feeling of not measuring up was the sudden loss of his father and the repeated experience of abandonment in isolated hallways. It made sense to both of us that this experience had repeatedly established the central theme that he would not be the one who was chosen. At various times I attempted to understand the impact on him of his mother's leaving him, but David said that he had very few memories of her and did not feel much about her leaving the family.

As we discussed these issues, David gradually grew more confident and more enthusiastic about his life. This began to manifest itself in several ways. He began doing more painting, a passion that he had given up at the age of 9 or 10. He and I established that his artistic nature and interest in painting had been displeasing to his adopted parents, because they wanted him to have a professional career. He had thus renounced his interest in art and ended up going to law school. At this point in the treatment, he also began feeling more confident with women and began dating. Over the next year, he dated several women. Although none of the relationships worked out, the two of us were able to observe the recurring pattern of his feeling threatened by the women's interest in other men, and the feeling of threat began to lessen.

Soon David met a woman he truly liked. He described Ruth as funny, lively, and attractive. He had met her at a party where she was joking and being very playful. He confided that she was the type of woman that in the past he would have avoided and would have admired from a distance. He said she was just too desirable, and he knew that other men would find her attractive. The relationship proceeded, and David found himself falling in love with her. She was supportive, kind, and very interested in him. David responded to her vivacious and outgoing nature. She was very friendly and would start up conversations with many people. David would become intensely anxious and apprehensive and would feel as if he were losing her. On several occasions, when she was engaged in talking to a man at a party or at a restaurant, David became agitated and angry with her. She became hurt and confused and withdrew from him. David and I explored these episodes and understood his reactions as a manifestation of his old way of unconsciously organizing his experience. I noted David's difficulty maintaining a feeling of well-being when her interests were directed at other people. I interpreted this reaction as an automatic and unconscious revival of the meaning of the experience of being suddenly abandoned by his father.

Soon after this discussion, David came to a session in an acute state of agitation and rage. He told me that he thought his relationship with Ruth was over. Ruth had told him the night before that she was taking a walk and would be back in 10 minutes, but she actually returned in an hour. When she came home he felt enraged with her and told her that she was totally irresponsible. It was about 11 o'clock at night, and he had told her that he had almost called the police. He also told her that he was afraid that something dangerous had befallen her or that she had been kidnapped. She had never seen him so angry and she broke down in tears. They did not talk about this episode in the morning, and he still felt enraged with her. He looked at me incredulously and asked, "Do you want to hear her explanation of what had happened to her?" He said that she had told him that she had been transfixed by the moon and the stars and had lost all concept of time, because the air and the stars were so beautiful. He looked at me intensely and said, "Can you believe that?!"

At this point, for the first time in my relationship with David, I felt in the grip of a dilemma within myself. Clearly he was turning vigorously to me for support. He felt extremely upset with Ruth and wanted me to validate the correctness of his experience. I felt conflicted, because there was a bitterness in his tone that seemed to mask some underlying painful feelings about himself. I also began to reflect on the tie that had developed between David and me. I had always felt that David and I had developed a good rapport since our initial meeting when I reassured him. David had developed an idealizing transference: he looked up to me and admired me. I wondered if our tie would be damaged if I conveyed my perception of his vulnerability. Could David tolerate my communicating to him my understanding of the episode, which was distinctively different from his?

I decided to articulate my dilemma. I told David that I could certainly agree that what Ruth had done was an act of unreliability. I also said that it seemed clear that he wanted my support, not only as a confirmation that what she had done was unreliable, but for his perception that this meant there was something centrally flawed about Ruth. I told him that I was reluctant to support this perception because I felt there were feelings underlying his rage that would be valuable to explore. David brushed aside my concerns about our relationship and said, "I trust you and I want to know what you think."

I said that there was a tone in his reaction to Ruth that I wanted to understand further, that it felt to me that he was reacting as if she had chosen to be with the stars and had not chosen him. I told him that her action seemed to have reexposed him to a familiar feeling that he was not special and valuable. I asked him what he had been thinking when she was away, if there were any other thoughts that had occurred to him. He was silent for a while and said that his other thoughts were difficult for him to disclose because they made him feel embarrassed and humiliated. While she was gone, he had imagined that she had gone to someone's house. He admitted further that the worst fantasy was that she had gone to see an old boyfriend. That thought, however, had soon become buried beneath a torrent of rage at Ruth. I said that his rage seemed to be an attempt to recover his equilibrium and that his anger had been codetermined by her thoughtlessness and his automatically and unconsciously organizing her lateness to mean that he was not compelling and special to her. The sky and the stars were equivalent to the other man in the triangle, and anything that engaged Ruth and took her away from him was experienced as a confirmation of some defect in himself. He smiled ruefully and asked plaintively, "Will this always sneak up on me? Will I ever be free of this?" I replied that I was confident that he would come to recognize this pattern, but that I also thought there were aspects of his reactions that awaited further understanding.

Several sessions after this, David came in feeling anxious and agitated. He had repaired the relationship with Ruth and had been feeling better, but had a dream that left him feeling shaken. He had dreamed that he was in an automobile or a machine that was going back in time. The vehicle was shaking as images flashed before his eyes and eventually stopped at some time in his past. A very young baby boy had been thrown out of the car, and he felt frantic as he looked for him. Finally he found him at the side of the road, alive but wrapped up in bandages.

He was clearly shaken by this dream, and I asked him what he thought. He said that the dream was about an infant and he felt scared and confused, but he knew the dream was important. He said that maybe the dream had to do with his mother. I said that I also wondered if the dream might pertain to feelings or memories that he had about his original mother and her abandonment of him when he was two years old. He became tearful, and over the next several sessions many memories and feelings that had been repressed began to emerge.

David did not recall his mother's leaving, but he did begin to remember other reactions and feelings that he had had subsequently. His mother lived several blocks away from his original father's apartment. He remembered that when he was four or five years old he would wander over to her house and play in front of her yard. He longed for her to see him, recognize him, and come out and be with him. He thought that she could easily see him, but that she just refused to look at him or turn toward him. He played in front of her house many times, but she never came out. He remembered feeling subdued and crestfallen and more and more depressed. He also recalled an early incident that happened with a five- or six-year-old girl at about that time. They were playing together in a playground, and she ran away from him to play with another friend. He felt that she had left him because he was repulsive and disgusting. Thus, his central organizing principle was established—that he could never be centrally important to a woman.

David then recalled that he had gone back to see his mother when he was 16 years old. He knocked on her door, and she opened it. He told her that he was her son and tried to talk to her, and she refused to speak to him and closed the door. David then went and talked to the neighbors about his mother. They described her as reclusive and paranoid. He recalled these events tearfully, and we both recognized the powerful role these experiences had played in shaping his core feelings about himself.

These memories supplied the foundation for our understanding that he had unconsciously organized her repetitive abandonment of him as a confirmation of a central and loathsome defect in himself, leaving him feeling that he could never be central to a woman. No one, including his natural father, had ever talked to him about his experience of her abandoning him.

The new understanding of his mother's impact on him proved to be pivotal to David. He was increasingly able to recognize how he automatically assimilated Ruth's enthusiastic interest in other things as a confirmation of his defectiveness. It was Ruth's capacity for aliveness, vitality, and engagement that stimulated his own archaic organizing principles. The very qualities about her that he valued most when they were directed at him were the source of the most profound pain when exhibited outside the relationship. David now understood his reactions to Ruth as replicating the way he unconsciously organized his experiences of abandonment by both his mother and his father. The earlier experience with his mother had been reinforced by his having been repeatedly left isolated and alone while his father had sexual relations. This new awareness helped David to understand his reactive rage and withdrawal as attempts to protect himself from these painful meanings. He has continued to develop a greater capacity for affect tolerance and self-reflection through our work together.

I have presented two vignettes to illustrate the clinical unfolding of an intersubjective vantage point. An unwavering focus on the unconscious principles that prereflectively organize experience creates a significant shift in emphasis from that of self psychology. The emphasis in self psychology on the disruption-restoration sequence lends itself to a particular therapeutic stance. The task of the analyst, from such a perspective, is to restore the analytic bond, thereby providing the patient with an empathic attunement that promotes a gradual internalization of the analyst's selfobject functions. The central therapeutic outcome of the self psychological curative process is the patient's enhanced capacity to choose more mature selfobjects in future relationships. This theory of cure directs the analyst's attention to the impact on the patient of disruptions of the therapeutic tie and leads to a preoccupation with the selfobject dimension of the patient's experience. In self psychology, the patient's attainment of self-reflective awareness of his own constitutive role in structuring his reality is not emphasized.

In the case of Joan, her mother required Joan to alter her own unique experience of the elevator ride as a condition of maintaining her tie to her mother. Joan's initial experience of excitement had to be surrendered, and she became subdued and crestfallen. The theory of self psychology, with its emphasis on selfobject longings, does not illuminate adequately the interactional dynamics of this situation. Describing this event as entailing an absence of selfobject responsiveness does not provide a full understanding of the meaning of this experience for Joan. The outcome of repeated experiences of usurpation is an unconscious organizing principle. Joan will probably repetitively organize affects related to vitality and excitement as a source of apprehension and danger. The theory of intersubjectivity, with its central focus on how experience becomes unconsciously organized, is uniquely suited to facilitate a clinical understanding of the patterning and thematizing of experience when selfobject functions are missing.

In the case of David, at a critical juncture in our work he had an intense experience of Ruth as unreliable and flawed. The underlying impasse that David experienced with Ruth did not primarily involve Ruth's inability to provide selfobject responses to him. The impasse was a consequence of David's unconsciously and automatically assimilating her interest in outside activities as a confirmation of a central defect in him. He defended himself against this painful awareness by a reactive rage and devaluation of Ruth. David's wish for me to support his devaluation of Ruth was also a wish for me to support a defensive avoidance of the painful affective experience of not feeling special to her.

Self psychology, because of its emphasis on the selfobject dimension of experience, lends itself to seeing all transference wishes as selfobject longings. There is thus a significant danger of reinforcing the patient's defenses by misinterpreting defensive transference wishes as selfobject longings. This has the effect of covering over painful affective experiences that derive from repetitive organizing principles. My interpretations to David touched on his selfobject longing to feel special. However, I primarily emphasized the repetitive organizing principle underlying his rage—his belief that he would never be centrally important to any woman. In this situation, an exclusive emphasis on the selfobject dimension would have focused on the absence of mirroring and its impact on David. However, such a focus would have neglected what was centrally present—his repetitive experience that he did not even exist in her mind.

Intersubjectivity theory conceptualizes the disruption of selfobject transference ties as an inevitable by-product of the interaction of the unique and different organizing principles of patient and therapist. Intersubjectivity theory recognizes the importance of selfobject transferences as a very important class of organizing principles. The emergence of selfobject transferences and the elucidation of unconscious repetitive organizations are two indivisible aspects of a unitary process. The illumination of old organizing principles occurs in the context of a new selfobject experience with the analyst. The process of cure in the case of David required an awareness of his organizing principles in the selfobject dimension *and* the repetitive dimension. David's initial experience with me was that I provided a calming and soothing selfobject function. There was also a disjunctive episode involving his overhearing a woman patient, and it was crucial that I did not reject his reactive feelings of injury. I gradually became established as a longed-for parental figure. The stability of his experience of a selfobject bond allowed David to make use of my analysis of the repetitive dimension of his experience with me and with Ruth. The analysis of this repetitive dimension opened up the possibility of an alternative organizing principle—that he could be special to a woman.

The curative process as seen from the perspective of intersubjectivity theory is thus distinctively different from what is pictured from the perspective of self psychology. Intersubjectivity theory emphasizes the opportunity for the patient to become aware that the legacy of absent selfobject responses during childhood is the constricting and limiting way of unconsciously organizing experiences. I contend that it is primarily by acquiring self-reflective awareness of their own unique organizing principles, in concert with the new selfobject experience with the analyst, that patients can develop alternative ways of organizing their experience so that they can be free of this pathogenic legacy.

REFERENCES

Atwood, G. & Stolorow, R. (1984), *Structures of Subjectivity: Explorations in Psychoanalytic Phenomenology*. Hillsdale, NJ: The Analytic Press.

Basch, M. (1984a), The selfobject theory of motivation and the history of psychoanalysis. In: *Kohut's Legacy*, ed. P. Stepansky & A. Goldberg. Hillsdale, NJ: The Analytic Press, pp. 3–17.

—— (1984b), Selfobjects and selfobject transference: Theoretical implications. In: *Kohut's Legacy*, ed. P. Stepansky & A. Goldberg. Hillsdale, NJ: The Analytic Press, pp. 21–41.

Kohut, H. (1984), *How Does Analysis Cure?* ed. A. Goldberg & P. Stepansky. Chicago: University of Chicago Press.

Stolorow, R. (1993), Thoughts on the nature and therapeutic action of psychoanalytic interpretation. In: *The Widening Scope of Self Psychology, Progress in Self Psychology, Vol. 9*, ed. A. Goldberg. Hillsdale, NJ: The Analytic Press, pp. 31–43.

—— & Atwood, G. (1992), *Contexts of Being: The Intersubjective Foundations of Psychological Life*. Hillsdale, NJ: The Analytic Press.

—— —— & Brandchaft, B. (1992), Three realms of the unconscious and their therapeutic transformation. *Psychoanal. Rev.*, 79:25–30.

—— Brandchaft, B. & Atwood, G. (1987), *Psychoanalytic Treatment: An Intersubjective Approach*. Hillsdale, NJ: The Analytic Press.

Wolf, E. (1988), *Treating the Self*. New York: Guilford.

Chapter 3

Critical Reflections on a Comparative Analysis of "Self Psychology and Intersubjectivity Theory"

Paul H. Ornstein

Intersubjectivity theory, as elaborated by Stolorow, Atwood, and Brand-chaft in their numerous publications (1984, 1987, 1992, 1994), began as a special emphasis and direction in self psychology. It highlighted and clearly articulated what was often only implicit in self psychology or somewhat obscured for many (but not for all) since Kohut's language originated in classical analysis, especially ego psychology. Because Stolorow et al. at first seemed to push the method of empathy to its possible limits—more than some of those who followed Kohut—I was enthusiastic about their contributions to self psychology. These efforts of Stolorow et al. only became controversial within self psychology when the proponents of intersubjectivity theory claimed originality and funda-mental difference from the theoretical system out of which intersubjec-tivity theory (largely[1]) arose, and began to disregard the original sources

---

[1] I say "largely" because Stolorow et al. do refer to the German phenomenologist philoso-phers, Heidegger and Husserl, as their other sources. Husserl's intersubjectivity theory includes such ideas as "pre-reflective and reflective consciousness" and "invariant organizing principles," to name only a few. F. von Broembsen (1993, personal communication) called many other overlapping basic concepts in Husserl's philosophy to my attention. These additional concepts would have to be examined for a more comprehensive study of Stolorow's intersubjectivity theory, which is not the purpose of this chapter.

of many of their ideas. Perhaps even some of these unwarranted claims to originality would not have elicited the sharp criticisms that have ultimately emerged, if the theories proposed would have led to clearly demonstrable differences in the clinical process beyond those already advocated by Kohut and some other self psychologists. There might have been some resistance to their acceptance initially, but truly innovative changes in theory that lead to significant demonstrable results in the clinical approach will ultimately triumph. Theoretical claims and formulations that do not visibly alter the interpretive process are of little consequence in our everyday clinical work and therefore, by themselves, seldom provoke intense discussions among clinicians.

Criticisms of intersubjectivity theory have become more intense and more sharply focused because some of the recent clinical presentations (e.g., Thompson, 1994; Trop, 1994) guided by intersubjectivity theory have violated the central feature of the treatment approach guided by self psychology: listening and interpreting from the perspective of the patient's subjective experience; the search for understanding before explanations. These and other recent presentations and discussions raise the question anew: Just what *is* intersubjectivity theory and the clinical process it guides as either a part of or as distinct from self psychology?

A recently published book edited by Stolorow, Atwood, and Brandchaft (1994) contains a chapter by Trop entitled "Self Psychology and Intersubjectivity Theory," which is an example of this drastic shift in the treatment approach just mentioned, along with claims that self psychology and intersubjectivity theory are two separate albeit interrelated and clearly distinguishable psychologies and treatment approaches. I shall put these claims and the treatment approach to which they have guided Trop under my own clinical-theoretical microscope for a detailed assessment. The particular value in examining Trop's chapter in this fashion lies in the fact that in his clinical vignette he is quite explicit about what he had done and why he had done so. The "devil is in the details," as they say, and Trop supplies the bare minimum of these details; a few more illustrative interchanges would have allowed us an independent study of the relationship between his theory and his clinical approach.

Trop's chapter consists of three parts. In the first part (pp. 77–81) he introduces what he considers to be the core concepts of self psychology and intersubjectivity theory; in the second part (pp. 81–89) he presents a chance observation and a clinical report—a most useful segment for us to study; and in the third part (pp. 89–91) he draws far-reaching conclusions, some of which are not warranted on the basis of the data presented.

It will take time before a dispassionate account of the areas of sameness, similarities, and differences in the two approaches can be expected. Passions notwithstanding, I believe there is a way to discuss these matters with some objectivity, if we can establish a method for such discussions and thereby elevate the debate (to the degree possible) above partisanship. None of us can be expected to feel equidistant from the various existing psychoanalytic theories and simply treat our own as just one of them. Equidistance is not possible because each of us had chosen a particular theory for complex, idiosyncratic, personal reasons as well as elaborately justifiable (or unjustifiable, as the case may be) scientific (i.e., logically and clinically as well as theoretically based) reasons—and these have a strong hold on us all. Meanwhile, comparative psychoanalysis, to which Trop's chapter is a highly problematic contribution, is still in its infancy, without explicit rules or a suitable language for the exercise. Detailed process notes (or long samples of them) would be necessary to make the comparison and contrast more meaningful and the far-reaching claims more plausible. I have long been concerned with the difficulties inherent in comparative psychoanalysis (see, for example, P. H. Ornstein, 1983, 1990a, b, 1991a, b, 1992) and therefore sought the challenge of discussing Trop's chapter.

One of the central problems of a comparative psychoanalysis resides in the fact that from any one of the psychoanalytic perspectives the theories and data of any other framework are viewed as inevitably flawed. Thus, remaining within our own theoretical and clinical perspective unavoidably leads us to judge the approach and data of the other as incomplete or even inadequate. However, this may not be intrinsically so, but only because we view them from our own perspective. It is imperative that we step out of our own framework and enter the framework under consideration. Only from within the perspective of that other theoretical system can we discover its essence, its explanatory range and limitations. In other words, only by entering the respective frameworks of self psychology and intersubjectivity theory can we be led to their reasonably fair assessment. There are no reliable, external, scientific—hence generally compelling—criteria for such a comparative study of the various psychoanalytic approaches and their therapeutic outcome. Claims to the contrary are hard to adjudicate. There are strong convictions; plenty of anecdotal clinical evidence; striking improvements that are not fully explicable; and equally striking failures with each approach that often weigh heavily in the minds of individual practitioners in favor of or against one or another theory.

In the following I shall (1) examine Trop's juxtaposition of the core concepts of self psychology and intersubjectivity theory; (2) look at his chance encounter with a mother and her toddler in the elevator, and then examine the case of David at greater length; and finally (3) sum up.

My task requires a two-pronged approach. First, in relation to Trop's comparison and contrast of the two theories I shall examine the validity of his claims in the light of my own knowledge of self psychology, mindful of Trop's view of intersubjectivity theory as a broader and more encompassing one, and therefore an advance beyond self psychology. Second, in relation to his observational and clinical examples, I shall try to enter his observational field (the interaction of Joan and her mother) and his clinical experience (with David) and assess Trop's approach in relation to his implicit and explicit claims from within his own perspective. In other words, I shall be interested in determining whether Trop's conduct of the analysis of David is truly more encompassing and whether his findings do indeed go beyond what would be found in a self psychology–based analysis. If his findings do not turn up anything more or different, I shall consider his claims invalid.

THE CORE CONCEPTS OF SELF PSYCHOLOGY AND INTER-SUBJECTIVITY THEORY: SIMILARITIES AND DIFFERENCES

I wish to state at the outset that I am not offering a comparative assessment of self psychology and intersubjectivity theory as a whole in this discussion. I am only examining Trop's views of them as expressed in his chapter, and my critique is directed explicitly at his formulations and clinical approach. My data are in his text, and I shall endeavor to produce a textual analysis. It will not come as a surprise, I am sure, that my assessment of the comparison and contrast of the two systems will be significantly different from Trop's.

Trop sees "extremely important similarities" between the two theories as well as "important differences" with "significant clinical implications." He sees the similarities "in that both are relational theories and both reject the concept of drive as a primary motivational source." In addition, he notes that both theories use "empathy and introspection as a central guiding principle." However, as I shall discuss later, the two theories do *not* use the same method of observation. (I prefer to use the term *method* rather than *guiding principle* in this connection and consider the respective *theories* as the guiding principles in using the method.) The significant task for us is to examine whether the clinical vignettes do in fact reveal the same usage of empathy and introspection as treatment processes guided by self psychology do.

The Motivational Theories

Trop sees the sharpest difference in the respective motivational theories of self psychology and intersubjectivity theory. I believe he is on very slippery ground here. Trop recognizes the selfobject concept as central to the motivational theory of self psychology and contrasts this with "a more broad-based striving for connection in order to organize and order experience" in intersubjectivity theory. Trop calls this general statement about motivation "more broad-based," perhaps because he fails to recognize that an equally broad-based, general theory of motivation in self psychology is formulated as the striving to achieve cohesiveness (wholeness, unity) and vitality of the nuclear self—clearly, an effort to organize and order experience. The need to organize and order experience is a well-recognized and accepted basic motivation in modern developmental theory, and as such it does not, by itself, characterize the difference between self psychology and intersubjectivity theory.

But if we leave the concept at this level of generality, we have only made a widely accepted, nondifferentiating, statement about motivation. We then have to make this general statement operationally (i.e., clinically) useful by filling in the details. Self psychology fills in the details by postulating that once the cohesiveness of the nuclear self is achieved to a reasonable degree, it is the striving to live out the "inner program or design" laid down in the nuclear self that becomes the specific way in which organizing and ordering of experience takes place. It is then the unimpeded, further unfolding and actualization of this inner program that is at the root of self psychology's motivational theory. The selfobject concept addresses how the cohesiveness of the self and the capacity for the expression of one's inner design occur under favorable circumstances and what happens to these same developmental processes under unfavorable (traumatic) circumstances. We might put it this way: The fundamental human motive is the establishment and maintenance of a cohesive self. Once cohesion has been achieved, living out one's inner design in keeping with one's ambitions and ideals, while maintaining connection to others, are lifelong, basic motives. When these efforts at living out our inner program and maintaining connection to mature selfobjects are successful, this success is the mark of mental health in self psychology. Kohut described "disorganization" (fragmentation, enfeeblement) of the self and showed us how we achieve organization and ordering of experience with the aid of archaic selfobjects (i.e., through selfobject experiences) and how as adults we maintain the capacity for organizing and ordering experience through connectedness to mature selfobjects. Such organizing and ordering is inconceivable in self psychology without selfobject-experiences and cannot be separated from them, except in abstract theory. We organize and order specific experiences from the very beginning. What is being organized and ordered for structure building (i.e., for the laying down of "invariant ordering principles") and what is simply organized and ordered ad hoc (without laying down "invariant ordering principles") is thus immediately part of this fundamental motivational system.

The claim that the motivation for organizing and ordering experience is "more broad-based" than the selfobject theory of motivation, even if accurate in the abstract, without the selfobject theory of motivation (or some equivalent) such a broadly based abstraction cannot deal explicitly with *what* is being organized and ordered—which alone can give it clinical meaning.[2]

Once we add the specifics that bring the general theory to life in the clinical situation, we may have many different theories with the same broad, nondifferentiating base. Trop's (1994) example of the many possible reactions to the same event is instructive: ". . . a person, invited to an event where there are unfamiliar people, may enter a room and someone in the room may immediately turn his back. One person may organize this to mean that he is undesirable and repugnant. Another person may conclude that he is better than anyone at the event and assume a haughty indifference. A third person might interpret the other's turning away as a random occurrence, and it would not be assimilated as having a personal meaning" (p. 78). These examples demonstrate clearly the nonspecificity of the proposition "that each person establishes unique organizing principles that automatically and unconsciously shape his experiences." Of course. In what psychoanalytic theory would such different reactions *not* be viewed in terms of the impact of early experiences (the invariant, repetitive aspects of the transference)? How else could "personal meaning" affect current perception? I cannot see Trop's claim as a differentiating feature of intersubjectivity theory, when it is every modem psychoanalyst's daily bread—by whatever name the general motivational theory is known in the developmental and psychoanalytic literature. The explanations as to the exact origin and pathogenesis of these differing "invariant" reactions do diverge, but not the fact that such reactions are ascribed to the influence of early experiences and are seen as "invariant" in each of us. However, in the clinical situation we have to ask just how "invariant" these transference reactions are when we observe great variations in them in differ-

---

[2] See the analysis of David, where Trop repeatedly formulates his intervention in this abstract theoretical language.

ent patient–analyst pairs. In other words, even these so-called invariant organizing principles are not entirely the property of the patient alone, but emerge differently in different analytic contexts; the particular self-object experience within the analytic process will codetermine what will appear as "invariant" and how invariant will be whatever appears.

What comparative psychoanalysis has to recognize here is that sometimes the use of a different language expresses a fundamental difference, but other times, more or less felicitously, different languages express the same well-known assumptions or facts. Basch (1988) would say in this connection that the selfobject theory of motivation is just one clinically significant example of the general theory, which describes a basic function of the brain and he would not see any incompatibility between the two formulations. "Affect management," for example, is an aspect of this fundamental striving to organize and order experience; it is affect management that is always at the center of our interest as clinicians, and not the organizing and ordering principles per se. Lichtenberg (1989) would say that leaving motivational theory at that general level, although absolutely correct, leads to a reductionistic approach. The general theory does need to be filled in with the details, which he had elaborated on in his broad-based motivational theory. I would only add here that the brain's tendency (capacity or function) for organizing and ordering experience—a biological given—becomes a psychologically significant process through the selfobject experiences of the infant, child, and later on the adult. There is thus no antithesis between the two motivational theories Trop sees as so sharply divergent. In fact, underplaying or neglecting the pivotal role of the selfobject transferences in their function as organizing and ordering experiences deprives Trop's version of intersubjectivity theory—and his treatment approach based on it—of a much-needed clinical focus, as I shall later discuss regarding the treatment of David.

Still under the heading of similarities and differences, Trop focuses on the concepts of transference, empathy, and cure and derives their changed conception for intersubjectivity theory and their decisive difference from self psychology from the differing motivational theories of the two systems. It is in relation to the changed definition and use of empathy (tied up, as he says, with the proposed definitions of transference and cure) that I have my greatest reservations about Trop's notion of intersubjectivity theory as broader than, and by implication superior to, self psychology. Superiority or inferiority, as I already indicated earlier, cannot yet be *scientifically* adjudicated. But we can study the premises and deeper implications of the various concepts and the way they are actually used in the clinical situation by comparing and contrasting them on the basis of the clinical data they yield and not simply on the basis of abstract claims. This is how we can, to a degree, objectify our method for comparative psychoanalysis.

Transference, Cure, and Empathy

My reservations about Trop's definition of transference and cure (as fundamentally different in self psychology and intersubjectivity theory) are exactly the same as those in relation to his claim about the antithetical relation between the motivational theories. Trop (1994) says: "Transference, from an intersubjective vantage point, can thus be conceptualized as *unconscious organizing activity*. Unconscious organizing principles that have emerged in the interactional system of child and caregiver form the essence of personality development" (p. 79, italics added). This again is merely the generally acceptable conceptual shell that has to be filled out with the specifics. The conceptual shell does not contradict the formulation of the nature of the selfobject transferences, which focus on the wished-for experiences with the analyst while clearly acknowledging the old, repetitive, invariant aspects of the transference and thus bring nothing new to self psychology (see, for example, A. Ornstein, 1974, 1991). In fact, by not dividing the two aspects of transference into the "selfobject dimension" and the "repetitive dimension" so sharply, self psychology succeeds in focusing on the significant question of what interaction with the analyst changes the one into the other at any particular moment in the analysis. The shift from one dimension to the other does not occur in a vacuum and is not an event in the mind as a closed system. I have always thought that the intersubjective approach stressed the analyst's inevitable contributions to the configuration of the transference (as did self psychology from its inception) including the various shifts in the transference. There is no reference to the analyst's contribution to these shifts in the theoretical section of Trop's presentation, nor is there any in the clinical report.

Without further explanation Trop (1994) adds the following to his definition of the transference: "Intersubjectivity theory thus [?] adds a unique dimension to the concept of empathy. Empathic inquiry can be *redefined* 'as a method of investigating and illuminating the principles that unconsciously organize the patient's experience' (Stolorow, 1993). This definition of empathy emphasizes the elucidation of unconscious organizing principles as a *primary focus*. Indeed, this definition differs significantly from Kohut's (1984) characterization of empathy as 'the capacity to think and feel oneself into the inner life of another person' (p. 82)" (p. 79, italics added). Because of the change in the primary focus, which is no longer on the subjective experience, this view of empathy changes the nature of the interpretive process significantly. We can see this most clearly in David's treatment.

Because I now consider this alteration of the basic method as the most significant distinction between self psychology and intersubjectivity theory as presented by Trop,[3] I need to elaborate on my misgivings in some detail. I shall do so by first recounting an event I witnessed many years ago. Anna Ornstein presented a clinical-theoretical paper at the San Francisco Psychoanalytic Institute and Society in the late 1970s. At the end of her presentation, in the course of the discussion that followed, Victor Calef remarked that he now understood more clearly what the difference was between the approach of self psychologists and traditional analysts. He said: "We [traditional analysts] listen for drive-derivatives and you [self psychologists] listen for the patient's subjective experiences and that is a big difference!" When it was my turn to comment, I said that Dr. Calef was absolutely right: we had a very different listening perspective indeed by not narrowing it to drive-derivatives only. In our listening perspective we cannot decide a priori what to listen for and what not to listen for, but have to choose the broadest perspective given to us in the patient's subjective experiences. Our theory then, as every other theory, calls attention to what are the centrally significant data in the patient's presentation: drive-derivatives in traditional analysis and subjective experiences reflecting the state of the self and its selfobjects in self psychology–based analysis.

Thus, Trop's claim (1994) that the revised definition of empathy, which emphasizes that the elucidation of "unconscious organizing principles as a primary focus *adds a unique dimension to the concept of empathy*" (p. 79, italics added), is a return to the narrow way of listening. In fact, this redefinition detracts from the unique dimension of the concept of empathy as it is generally understood and as self psychology understands it. This revised definition is now at the core of what is different in the two systems. Trop's definition deprives the concept of empathy (and of empathic inquiry) of its unique dimension in capturing the broadest range of subjective inner experience, whatever its earliest origin. His narrow focus on the unconscious organizing principles leads

---

[3] Until the study of Trop's chapter I could not think of any sharply distinguishing and compellingly different features in intersubjectivity theory. I have, however, always appreciated the approach it dictated as an effort to push the empathic observational mode to its limits and formulate a pure psychology as Kohut endeavored to do—and possibly carrying it further, because Kohut still had one leg (linguistically, and to a much lesser degree, conceptually) in the old tradition. I have therefore also appreciated some of the more felicitous new terms introduced by Stolorow et al. over the years, without discerning in them a departure from self psychology. In relation to Trop's presentation I have been repeatedly confronted with the question: Where is the subjectivity in his theory of intersubjectivity?

Trop almost exclusively to the invariant aspects of the transference. This is reminiscent of viewing transference as repetition and displacement only. By treating the selfobject dimension as peripheral, the focus on the repetitive aspects cannot address the "thwarted need to grow"—the essence of a transference based on developmental arrests. A further problem here is that the assumption of "unconscious, automatic, organizing principles" is a theoretical construct and we cannot empathize with theory. We can only empathize with subjective experience. No wonder then that the decision to focus primarily on "organizing principles" necessitated a redefinition of empathy for that purpose, because the exploration of the invariant organizing principles in Trop's case example does *not* seem to take place from within the patient's own perspective.[4]

If empathy is a method of observation (vicarious introspection), as Kohut defined it, linking the method a priori and inextricably with what is to be observed leads to a highly undesirable circular reasoning and greatly limits new observations. To my knowledge, no one has yet proposed a better and more widely accepted definition of empathy than "feeling oneself and thinking oneself into the inner life of another," a process that greatly facilitates the recognition of the specific features of a selfobject transference. Disagreements regarding the definition of empathy as feeling and thinking oneself into the inner life of another are only related to what such a process of empathy consists of; whether it requires a channel separate from our five senses to achieve its goal; and whether it is central to the psychoanalytic method or not.[5] It should be noted that many biographers and historians also claim the necessity for prolonged empathic immersion in their subjects to grasp their inner lives, and what they say about their modus operandi verifies Kohut's conceptualization of the empathic process. Empathy does lead psychoanalysts, biographers, and historians to the formulation of "organizing and ordering principles" in their subjects' lives (be these adaptive or mal-

---

[4] It should be added here that empathy cannot directly reach the unconscious invariant organizing principles. Empathy can only reach subjective experience. If properly responded to, patients will feel increasing safety with their analysts; empathic understanding will then significantly contribute to the restoration of the cohesiveness and vitality of the self, so that more of what had been unavailable to consciousness before will then emerge. Empathy can only indirectly enlarge the sphere of consciousness. What becomes known in this fashion will then give rise to the analyst's conceptualization of the patient's hitherto unconscious, invariant organizing principles. I can well imagine "empathic inquiry" achieving that—with the accent falling equally on empathy and inquiry. It is then the ongoing inquiry, led from the empathic vantage point, that allows the conceptualization of the patient's invariant organizing principles. But "empathic inquiry" is then simply a felicitous term for how the analysis is supposed to be conducted.

[5] For some additional discussions on empathy see Basch (1983), Goldberg (1988), and Ornstein, P. H. (1979).

adaptive) but these principles derive secondarily from the empathically discerned subjective experiences under study. It is only in relation to Trop's observations of Joan, and more particularly in relation to David in the treatment process, that we may be able to determine the nature of Trop's conduct of his inquiry: empathic or nonempathic (i.e., conducted from the perspective of the external observer), as the case may be.

Trop's comparison and contrast of cure in self psychology and intersubjectivity theory suffers from a serious misconception of the curative process as envisioned by self psychology. He states (1994): "Self psychology . . . emphasizes a process of cure in which archaic selfobject needs are replaced with an empathic resonance with the therapist. Cure in self psychology is evidenced by the patient's new capacity to seek out appropriate selfobjects. The *danger* of this formulation is . . . that *it underemphasizes the acquisition of reflective self-awareness regarding the patient's constitutive role in shaping his own reality*" (p. 80, italics added). The problem is that Trop takes a particular view of the outcome or the result of analysis (namely, the replacement of archaic selfobject needs with an empathic resonance with the therapist) without considering how that is achieved. It is only this neglect of the treatment method itself that could have led Trop to state that self-reflective awareness regarding the patient's constitutive role in shaping his or her own reality is underemphasized in the treatment process in self psychology. Far from it. Here again, Trop elevates a desirable result and an inevitable accompaniment of all forms of analysis into a conception specific to intersubjectivity theory. The fact of the matter is that only feeling understood can bring about a self-reflective attitude. The two steps in the interpretive process, "understanding and explaining" (the "therapeutic unit" as Kohut called them), are part and parcel of the analytic approach guided by the theory of self psychology. However, self psychology does not consider the acquisition of self-reflective awareness per se as necessarily the prime curative factor. Self-reflective awareness, or insight, as it is commonly referred to, may well precede or follow cure or may be concomitant with the curative process, which is based on the belated acquisition of psychic structure—an improved capacity to organize and order experience.[6] A telling example of how self-reflective awareness

---

[6] Here is where designating self psychology simply as a "relational psychology" misses the point. Self psychology is a structural psychology in that by definition, it pays attention to the invariant organizing principles (here called structures)—even though it recognizes that both the original "structure" formation and the subsequent maintenance of the integrity of these structures throughout life occur in a (descriptively) "relational" context. However—and this is the important distinction —the self-selfobject concept brings external reality (the other in the relationship) into the inner world of the self. Psychoanalytic focus, therefore, is *not* on what goes on *between* people, but on what goes on *inside* of them. The focus in the clinical situation is on how patient experiences analyst

emerges in a well-conducted analysis guided by self psychology is the following: A patient responded to the analyst at one point by saying: "It is not what *you* may say, but what *I* may hear in your voice that scares me" (A. Ornstein, 1991).

A glance at Trop's view of cure according to intersubjectivity theory is quite instructive. This is what he says (1994): "The theory of intersubjectivity pictures the curative process differently [than does self psychology]. The curative process is conceptualized as resulting from the elucidation and understanding of the unique unconscious organizing principles of the patient that *shape* disruptions of the bond with the therapist. The emphasis, thus, is not only on the restoration of the tie to the analyst but, most centrally, on *understanding the principles that organize the disruption* of the tie" (p. 80, italics in the original). The emphasis here is on "insight" as the main curative process rather than on the inevitable combination of the properties of the relationship (which strengthen the self) along with the equally inevitable gain from the explanations that are jointly arrived at. Trop's emphasis is a return to a long-discredited supremacy of "insight" in the psychoanalytic curative process. His formulation bypasses the countless references by Kohut and the subsequent self psychology literature to the singular opportunities disruptions present both for recognizing the analyst's impact on the patient and for elucidating the invariant organizing principles (the repetitive aspects of the transference), in having created the "soft spots" at which disruptions inevitably occur.

In an analysis conducted from within a self-psychological perspective the curative process results from the systematic application of understanding *and* explaining, leading to a strengthening of the cohesiveness and vitality of the self—a self that may then pursue its ambitions in keeping with its values and actualize its innate program. The restoration of the disrupted tie to the analyst occurs through the understanding and elucidation of what has led to the disruption—the current precipitant of the disruption in the analyst–patient interaction and the antecedent spe-

---

and how analyst experiences patient (the two subjectivities affect each other!). The impact of each on the other is clearly recognized in self psychology and is central in this analytic focus on the inner world. Kohut's psychoanalytic "intrapsychic focus" is thereby more felicitous and fully in keeping with modern trends in many other fields. To put it differently, the analytic focus in self psychology is on the "state of the self" in its selfobject matrix. Clearly and unambiguously, this self-selfobject matrix embraces both subjectivities and their inevitable influence on each other in the analytic situation. To call this "intersubjective" adds nothing useful *theoretically*. In fact, it muddies the psychoanalytic waters with the external observer's "one-person," "two-person," and "three-person" constructs and by focusing on what is intersubjective (i.e., between the two subjectivities) and often misses what is *within* each of them. Perhaps the redefinition of empathy also contributes to this fact. (See the case of David in this respect.)

cific vulnerabilities of the self that give special meaning to the disruption of the tie, thereby offering both a cross-sectional and a longitudinal view of the personality and psychopathology.

To conclude the discussion of the theoretical part of Trop's comparison and contrast, I should like to add the following: The concept-by-concept juxtaposition of the two theories—although necessary and an important preliminary step—does not reveal the true nature of either system because "the whole is more than the sum of its parts," and particular emphases or overemphases alter the inner design of the theories and their impact on the treatment process. It is the whole ensemble, the specific relation of the parts of the theory to each other and the fact that they cannot be taken out of this total context, that makes comparative psychoanalysis such a difficult enterprise. I therefore trust the exploration of the clinical data, which reflect more accurately the *actual* usage of theory and technique, to give us a more reliable picture of similarities and differences. I shall now turn to Trop's observation of Joan and her mother and his clinical experience with David, where I shall discuss the impact that intersubjectivity theory had on the organization of his data and his manner of response.

THE OBSERVATIONAL AND CLINICAL EXAMPLES

Joan and Her Mother

Trop described his observations of Joan's excitement in the elevator and her mother's visible anxiety (which she insistently attributed to Joan) vividly and with sensitivity. I accept his observations as the basis for my own discussion. It is Trop's comment to the mother at the end of the ride that I shall use as my entry into his interpretation of the experience. At the end of the elevator ride Trop turned to the mother and said "that her daughter had actually seemed excited with the lights and did not seem worried. The mother looked away from [Trop] and continued to push Joan's stroller." I believe that Trop's offer to the mother of a correction of her "distorted" perception of Joan's experience led her to turn away, indicating (to me) with her behavior, that she found this "interpretation" of her "distorted perception" an unwelcome intrusion, not capturing her subjective experience. In the treatment situation this might have continued as a nonempathic inquiry.

A self-psychological understanding might have induced the observer to make an empathically based comment, such as "You tried to calm your daughter's worries, but it wasn't easy—you both made it down the elevator successfully at the end." I imagine that the mother might not have turned away then, because she would have felt at least partially understood and affirmed in her subjective experience. She might have smiled in response and might even have said, "I don't know which of us was more anxious, Joan or I?"—a beginning reflection on her own anxiety, in response to having felt understood. In a treatment situation this would have initiated an empathic inquiry.[7]

Let us look at Trop's view of the experience; admittedly, it is highly speculative, but because this is a demonstration of his clinical application of intersubjectivity theory, I consider it to be a demonstration of his clinical thinking and response, just as my interpretations will be a demonstration of my clinical thinking and response.

Trop underestimates the explanatory power of self psychology when he says that "this event [in the elevator] can be understood . . . [only] as a massive deficiency in mirroring and lack of responsiveness to Joan" (p. 82). Does Trop seriously believe that that is *all* self psychology can say about his observations? He goes on to say that "the language of intersubjectivity theory, in particular the concept of unconscious organizing activities and principles, is *uniquely suited* to describe the situation such as this" (p. 82, italics added). He then elaborates with different "keywords" what any good self psychologist would instantly consider, namely, that the mother was not simply withholding her mirroring responses, but inflicted on the daughter her own anxiety, and was not only unable to participate in her daughter's excitement and curiosity, but actively squelched them.[8] This might indeed be "an unconscious organizing principle in the making," if the mother's response to Joan was chronic and not just occasional, which occurs in elevators of which the mother might be phobic. Be that as it may, Trop's claim that "the concept of unconscious organizing principles has great value in forecasting the legacy and outcome of relational pattens" is in no way different from similar speculative forecasts on the basis of recognizing the nature of the self-selfobject experiences. We psychoanalysts are not so reliable in our forecasting—we are better at explaining retrospectively what might have happened in the process of pathogenesis.

Assuming that this mother was in treatment with Trop and told him the story just as vividly and with the same details as he told it to us, my question regarding Joan and her mother would be this: Would Trop

---

[7] James L. Fosshage (in a personal communication) suggested an alternative interpretation, which I liked better than my own, hence I wish to quote it: "You felt your daughter was worried and upset and you did your best at trying to calm her—it wasn't easy, but both of you made it down the elevator successfully at the end." This interpretation may well have captured the mother's subjective experience more accurately.

[8] See Ornstein and Ornstein (1985) for details about the child's being used as a selfobject by the caretaker, originally proposed by Kohut.

focus in his inquiry on the treatment setting with the mother's *distortion* of her daughter's experience and thereby directly deny the validity of her own (albeit, from the perspective of the external observer, "distorted") perceptions? How does that differ from the traditional pursuit of the distortions in the transference? How could such an approach be called an "empathic inquiry"—a study of subjective experience from within the patient's own perspective? It is just the opposite: it is the external observer's insistence on the validity of his own observations. The clinically relevant question is, Could a denial of the mother's experience change her attitude toward the child? What is the nature of the curative process that such confrontations promote? The answer comes not from me, but from Joan's mother herself. She turned away from Trop. Her response to such a confrontation might not be very different in the treatment setting and might well lead to a stalemate.

The Analysis of David

Because this is the clinical centerpiece of Trop's claims regarding the relations between self psychology and intersubjectivity theory, Trop's analysis of David should be thoroughly scrutinized from the "outside" and the "inside."

A quick overview and first impression

My first reading left me with a number of disquieting impressions. Although David undoubtedly benefited from his experience with Trop, whose interest and concern must have made an impression on him very early, I shall forgo the pursuit of the intriguing question of how David's improvement might have occurred.

Although the formulations of David's formative experiences are frequently too general and macroscopic, hence often quite imprecise, for this discussion I shall accept them as given. They are, on the whole, broadly compatible with what self psychologists might reconstruct through the analysis of the selfobject transferences and then describe more microscopically (i.e., with more details of the patient's inner experiences). Such microscopic descriptions would make the clinical findings not only more plausible but also emotionally more compelling to both patient and analyst, and anyone else studying the transcript. The formulations offered in the text in a summary form are not placed adequately into the context of the evolving analytic process (i.e., they are not correlated with what went on between Trop and David at that time, which would have provided the necessary "intersubjective" context) and are therefore not really suitable for a comparative analysis.[9] The formulations given in the report appear to have been arrived at mainly on the basis of the patient's recollections and the content of his communications, and were then applied directly to the elucidation of the meaning of previous events, while disregarding their possible meaning in the here-and-now of the analytic relationship. Thus, the intersubjective elements (the experiences within the self-selfobject matrix of the analysis), which would more firmly anchor the meaning and validity of Trop's formulations, are largely missing in these reconstructions from the patient's narrative. These intersubjective elements are always crucial, but here even more so, because Trop has set out to use these examples to demonstrate the validity of his claims. It is the context of the relationship in which the patient's "history" is narrated in the analytic process that provides and anchors the meaning of this history. This meaning cannot be reliably reached if we skip the communicative aspects in the here-and-now of the patient's narrative, and if we do not use these immediate experiences as a basis for the reconstruction of the meaning of the earlier ones. It is the leap from the patient's developmental history to psychogenetics, as it was practiced primarily by psychoanalytically oriented psychotherapists, that psychoanalytic self psychology has been successful in correcting (see, for example, Ornstein and Ornstein, 1977, 1990).

A detailed look from the inside

I shall restrict myself to the examination of the three episodes with direct interchanges, where the contributions of both the patient and the analyst are immediately visible and therefore do not necessitate that we speculatively reach beyond the given clinical material. It is at these interchanges (I call these "encounters"[10]) that I shall try to enter the analytic process. Entry into the analytic process is difficult elsewhere in the text, because Trop's main focus there is on the narrative account of the patient, the "content" David brings to the sessions, and on his own formulations of

---

[9] What would make these summary statements suitable for comparative analysis would be the demonstration of the emergence of the data from the interpretation and working through of the selfobject transferences, which Trop claims are important but which are essentially shunted aside in this analysis.

[10] What I call encounters consist of three steps: (1) the patient says or does something that warrants a response; (2) the analyst either does or does not respond; and (3) the patient reacts to the response or its absence. Such encounters reveal what patient and analyst *actually* contribute to the emerging analytic process and permit us an independent discovery of whether they talk to each other on the same wavelength or talk past each other. And this judgment can be made without the use of our respective theoretical systems.

their meaning. In this format, naturally, we cannot be privy to how meaning was negotiated between David and his analyst. What we see instead is that Trop assigns meanings to events that he gained mainly from David's *history*. It is this history, interspersed with some poignant recollections and one dream, that serves as the focal point for Trop's interpretations and reconstructions.

The three reported actual interchanges however, do permit us an entry into the analysis and I shall now turn to these.

Encounter #1

David came to Trop with a recent history of "intense anxiety and panic" and during the first interview "appeared apprehensive, agitated and fearful that he had done some permanent damage [to himself, by inhaling a small amount of a drug] from which he would never recover." Although he was at once convinced that David's inhaling "his first and only puff" seemed an unlikely cause of his current, acute symptoms, and David also "became less pressured while talking about the incident"—indicating in my view that perhaps contact-making already helped—Trop, nevertheless, took David's question at the end of the session *literally* and responded to it with a lengthy, detailed, reassuring comment. The exact wording of the comment is of interest. This is what Trop said (1994): "I told him that I was *very confident* that no permanent damage would result from this episode and that his fears did not seem grounded in anything that was inherent in the event. I assured him that he had not harmed himself in any irrevocable way, but told him that I thought it would be valuable to try to understand how this event had unfolded in terms of its psychological meanings for him. David became visibly relaxed and said that he would very much like to come in and talk some more" (p. 83, italics added).

Two additional significant statements follow, both of which I shall also quote verbatim: (1) "In the ensuing sessions [David] gradually began to tell me his *history*, and the initial episode began to recede as a source of concern to him" (italics added); (2) "It was my belief at that time that my reassurance had supplied a calming and soothing function and that this had contributed to an underlying idealizing transference that unfolded in subsequent weeks."

It is helpful for us to see how David is initiated into the analytic process. Recognizing and grasping the meaning of this first step is necessary to understand the subsequent course of the analysis, because contributions of both participants forge the emerging data: understanding, as it unfolds in the course of analysis, is highly context-bound. Although an initial reassurance might not do any harm and on occasion might even be useful, the very confidence and certainty, the authoritativeness, with which it was pronounced by Trop—if continued—would interfere with the unfolding of a truly analytic climate and an analytically workable selfobject transference. The reason this issue concerns me here is because of Trop's remark (1994) that "in the ensuing sessions [the patient] gradually began to tell me his *history*" (p. 83, italics added). Trop's focus does not appear to be on what David communicates about his experiences of him, but on the information David's story contains about his past, without the filter of the transference experience in the analysis. Only through the meaning of David's communication within the transference could we discern the impact of his "history" on his early life, and thus on his personality development and psychopathology. Otherwise, our understanding and explanations of the developmental history—no matter how plausible—remain mere conjectures.

Trop's assumption that his reassurance "supplied a calming and soothing function," though reasonable, neglects other possibilities. For instance, it could also be that David responded by becoming "visibly relaxed" once he was invited to explore his anxieties further—because of the contact he made with Trop, as I said earlier. After all, he reached out to Trop with these anxieties, which appear to have considerably lessened as soon as his plea for help was accepted. We might say that David's communication achieved its immediate goal the moment he succeeded in enlisting Trop's interest and concern. But the claim that the reassurance per se "had contributed to an underlying idealizing transference" has to be questioned on both clinical and theoretical grounds. An idealizing transference generally arises out of a previously traumatically thwarted developmental need to idealize; patients often come to us with a readiness for an idealizing transference, which will unfold in a proper climate or which we can inadvertently nip in the bud. Other times there is a great deal of inner resistance to its mobilization, for fear of renewed traumatization. Reassurance usually cannot allay those fears of retraumatization, only an analytic response to those fears can, which then permits the emergence of a hitherto thwarted developmental need to idealize. Premature and especially authoritative reassurance interferes with the emergence of any kind of transference, including and especially a selfobject transference. By not rushing in with such a reassurance we leave the door open for the remobilization of a selfobject transference. Trop could have gotten hold of the "invariant organizing principles" in David's life more meaningfully from David's own perspective, had he chosen such a path. What Trop calls an idealizing transference here is not a repetition of a "thwarted developmental need to grow" (hence not a genuine idealizing transference) but a reaction to his actual behavior (his kind, reassuring, authoritative presence). Because

Trop's focus in his presentation is almost exclusively on the invariant organizing principles (the repetitive aspects of the transference), however, we cannot independently determine whether an idealizing transference ever developed in David's case or not. (Encounter #3 will further clarify this issue.)

This initial encounter had a follow-up to it several months later, when Trop (1994) offered the following reconstructive interpretation:

> [T]he act of smoking the drug had taken on an enormous symbolic meaning for [David]. He was at a party feeling excited and expansive and was unconsciously attempting to free himself of the relationship with his father and its constricting impact. He wanted to have his own experience of being alive and excited. He had, however, become reactively panicked. I told him that the panic, which became attached to the drug, had not been understood by him as an attempt to free himself from his father's view of him as fragile and vulnerable. He felt that my interpretation was correct and he felt relieved [p. 84].

I do not see any substantive divergence or novelty here as a self psychologist; this reconstructive interpretation is quite to the point and describes David's experience essentially from within his own subjective view. What I cannot judge without more detailed process notes is the timeliness of this intervention. I would have changed the phrase *enormous symbolic meaning* to spelling out what that meaning was, so as not to sound so abstract, and I would also have changed the word *unconsciously*, because David could neither verify nor deny this internal process, if it was put to him that way and not experientially. What David did or felt *unconsciously* is *our* theory of *his* experience, but such a theoretical statement does not address what he felt when it is worded so abstractly. Furthermore, and this is where I would place the emphasis, talking about the various details of his history, we cannot tell what it was that David was communicating to Trop about his day-to-day experiences in the analysis, because this remained outside of Trop's focus. (See, for instance, David's dream in Encounter #3.)

Let me try, then, to characterize how David and Trop met, and thereby invite the reader to capture what each participant contributed to the beginning of their encounter. David reached out for help in acute distress, signaling that something in his life was amiss and he feared that he inflicted (in a somewhat peculiar fashion, by inhaling "his first and only puff" of a drug) the damage on himself. Trop responded to this distress directly, in spite of recognizing that the story on the manifest level did not quite make sense to him. He rushed in with his reassurance, rather than initiating an analytic inquiry (hence ultimately an analytic process) by simply recognizing David's intense anxiety and concern and staying with David's agony and fear, to explore what David himself made of his experience and simultaneously listen for what David wanted and expected from him. Had he done so, Trop might have discovered that his own calm presence and sincere engagement of David in the exploration of what his manifest symptoms represented might have served at that moment as an adequate reassurance, without the risk of blocking analytic inquiry. Trop responded instead with an authoritative, definitive reassurance that David's fears were unwarranted and that he could not have damaged himself permanently. David did in fact calm down and expressed interest in returning for further talks after he was invited to do so. Thus, at this point, there seems to be no *visible* draw-back to the reassurance, or more importantly to Trop's direct response to David's manifest complaint. (But see p. 33 for another key question taken literally.)

I shall now trace what happened in the analysis subsequently by focusing on the two additional interchanges and look at what patient and analyst said to each other, and how each experienced the other (in the manifest and the latent content of their communications) in order to identify the nature of their interactions from their subjective perspectives and thereby determine the respective contributions of self psychology and intersubjectivity theory to this analysis. (This is how I shall try to minimize, as much as possible, the intrusion of my own bias in assessing the clinical process.)

Encounter #2

Following the reconstructive interpretation of the meaning of David's inhalation of a drug, quoted previously (which was on the whole in keeping with self psychology, without any noticeable additions from intersubjectivity theory), "David began to describe a recurrent and painful experience in relationships. He had difficulty dating women and feeling at ease with himself. He felt wary of losing himself and being taken over in a relationship and had a pervasive feeling that he would not measure up" (p. 84). About four months into the treatment some of these issues entered briefly into the analytic relationship: "One day . . . [David] came in[to the office] looking subdued and glum." On exploring this at one point, Trop asked whether anything had taken place between them that could account for the way David felt. David, after a brief silence, finally "confided shamefully" that he overheard a woman patient leaving the office and "she had been laughing and joking," which stimu-lated his competitiveness and "he began to feel that he would not inter-est [Trop] as much as she did." David went even further: this episode also made him feel that he misconstrued the positive aspects of his earlier relationship to Trop and now felt that he must be "boring and vacu-ous" (compared to Trop's woman patient). Trop captured some aspects of David's self-experience when he stated in response "that the conver-sation between me and the woman patient had left him feeling excluded and destitute of any concept of his value in my eyes."

He continued: "I *clarified* with David how he had *automatically organized* the meaning of my interchange with [the woman] as a con-firmation that he was not interesting or compelling in his own right" (p. 85, italics added). This addition, although it might in principle be correct, again focuses on David's flawed "automatic organizing principles," as if he could consciously decide to organize his experiences differently, by simply being told about it. Such abstract and cognitive comments are reminiscent of the traditional approach to interpretations. A self-psy-chologically sophisticated analyst might have said something like this (to acknowledge the validity of David's subjective feelings): "No wonder you drew those conclusions from what you heard. Based on your past expe-riences [giving some of the details to make it concrete] your feeling unwanted and valueless was only confirmed again. Now we can under-stand better why you felt depressed and glum when you entered the office this morning." This would underscore the legitimacy of David's feelings in the light of his past experiences and validate his self-experi-ence of the moment (without having to take sides); it would also make a defensive withdrawal on his part less necessary. David could then, as a consequence of the strengthening of his self, raise the questions himself about the current validity of his conclusions and be thus progressively freed up from his chronic "automatic, unconscious organizing principles" (without the need for confrontations). Without such a previous accretion of structure (i.e., strengthening of his self) even friendly and well-meant confrontations accomplish very little—in fact, they might injure him fur-ther or drive his "selfobject longings" underground.[11]

When such interventions appear to be successful—as in this instance when David agreed with Trop's intervention (although it is not entirely clear what exactly he agreed with)—it is probably more on account of what he could extract from the relationship than on the basis of the spe-cific intervention itself. But we shall never know. There is no question that David's progress here, as presented, was quite significant: he recap-tured an earlier, long-thwarted passion for painting, became more confi-dent, began dating, and began to feel less threatened by the interest in

___

[11] Historically, it was the relentless search for the repetitive aspects of the transference that blocked analytic vision from the discovery of the structure-building selfobject needs, which self psy-chology has unambiguously placed at the center of analytic concerns, both developmentally and clinically. Trop seems to have returned, in the one remark he made to Joan's mother and in David's analysis, to this earlier interpretive stance.

other men of the women he dated. The question for us here is only, What discernible element of intersubjectivity theory contributed to the success of this interchange? I see absolutely none. It is the way Trop captured David's self-experience in the first part of his intervention that seems to have contributed to its success.

Encounter #3

David soon fell in love with Ruth, who was "a funny, lively and attractive" woman. In the past, David would only have admired her from afar because she was "too desirable" and "other men would find her attractive." In response to her contacts with other men, even casual contacts at a party or a restaurant, David would become agitated and angry with Ruth; whereupon she would become hurt and confused and would withdraw from him.

Trop's interpretation of these episodes (1994) is of interest as we embark on examining the third and most illuminating encounter. "David and I explored these episodes," Trop says, "and understood his reactions as a manifestation of his old way of unconsciously organizing his experience" (p. 86). Trop noted "David's difficulty maintaining a feeling of well-being when her interests were directed at other people," and he "interpreted this reaction as an automatic and unconscious revival of the meaning of the experience of being suddenly abandoned by his father" (p. 86). Does the phrase "[we] understood his reactions as a manifestation of his old way of unconsciously organizing his experience" reflect a meaningful understanding? Hardly. It is an attempt at an explanation, but in reality it does not explain anything—it simply restates the abstract theory. In the next sentence Trop came closer to a potentially more meaningful intervention, when he recognized (at least implicitly) that Ruth served David as a mirroring selfobject whose diverted attention deprived him of his feeling of well-being. But instead of translating this into a communicable empathic understanding of David's state of mind and exploring its nature and origin, Trop again resorted to his by now almost sloganlike repetitive statements that David's reaction was "an automatic and unconscious revival of the meaning of the experience of being suddenly abandoned by his father." How do we know that? Why not the abrupt and cruel abandonment by his mother, with whom he tried later to resume contact with a further traumatic rejection? Maybe the origin of this kind of reaction is in both of those experiences (as Trop himself recognized later on). It may be the expression of the structural "defect" and its defensive overlay left behind in the wake of those experiences.

Understanding first what *function* David unconsciously assigned to Ruth and what his falling in love with her meant to him would have served as a safer, less abstract, less speculative bridge to the past. Here is where David's selfobject needs and their painful disappointment in his relations to Ruth could have been meaningfully engaged analytically. (See A. Ornstein, 1991, regarding "extra-analytic" transference interpretations.) Both Trop and David would then have understood what he was searching for, what he needed for his well-being, how he needed Ruth to strengthen his fragile self, and why he reacted with such intense disappointment to Ruth's behavior with other men. Competitiveness, feeling left out, and problems in triangular relationships are merely descriptive and not explanatory—they do not capture clearly enough David's selfobject needs and the manner in which he is trying to fill them. The approach I am suggesting here might have led Trop to explore David's profound self-pathology and would also have provided both of them with an opportunity to learn about David's "invariant, unconscious organizing principles" in such a way that their findings and explanations, when jointly arrived at, could make immediate sense to him. No wonder Trop underplays the importance of the selfobject transferences in his actual clinical work as presented (in contrast to his claim of its importance in the theoretical section)—he repeatedly *interfered* with their emergence through his relentless search for the "distorting" organizing principles, the invariant, repetitive aspects of transference—as if Kohut never existed. This is most regrettable, because it was the selfobject concept and the recognition of selfobject transferences that had drastically revised the classical view of transference and the curative process.

It is with Ruth that David appears to have lived out his mirroring and idealizing needs (his extra-analytic transferences), and perhaps he also signaled through the expression of his longings for Ruth and his disappointments in her what he needed from his analyst. But Trop's "empathy" was directed at the invariant unconscious organizing principles, so he could not, or preferred not to, recognize his transference significance for David. Trop spoke of David's archaic longings vis à vis Ruth, but never vis à vis himself. Had he allowed these longings to emerge toward himself, he would inevitably have witnessed the disruptions, which would have meaningfully brought to his attention the repetitive aspects of the transference. We learn that one day David came to his session "in an acute state of agitation and rage" and "thought [that] his relationship with Ruth was over" (p. 86). The night before Ruth ostensibly went for a 10-minute walk, but returned a whole hour later. In his rage David told her "that she was totally irresponsible." He already thought of the many possible dangers that could have befallen her and even thought of calling the police. She burst into tears and offered the explanation that "she had been transfixed by the moon and the stars and had lost all concept of time, because the air and the stars were so beautiful" (p. 86). Trop remarked that "[David] looked at me intensely and asked: 'Can you believe that?!'"

This is the juncture at which Trop's "dilemma" and response to David is most revealing of the analytic climate and the nature of the interpretive process in this analysis. Trop again, just as in the initial encounter, takes David's question literally—as if he were asked to believe in something that he feels he cannot possibly believe in and give a direct answer to. He says (1994): "for the first time in my relationship with David, I felt in the grip of a dilemma within myself. [David] was clearly turning vigorously to me for support . . . and wanted my validation for the correctness of his experience" (p. 86). Trop's conflict related to his perception of "a bitterness in [David's] tone that [he] felt masked some underlying painful feelings about himself." Why not acknowledge those feelings then, by saying something to the effect that "Ruth's explanation must have sounded unbelievable and outrageously contrived to you; this seems to have added to your agony. I sense a bitterness in your tone, you sound deeply disappointed."

Yes, David did seem to have turned "vigorously" to Trop for support and did indeed wish for a validation of his subjective experience—but not for the "correctness" of it; he did not need a "reality check." "Can you believe it?!" sounds to me like David's expression of his consternation and request for the validation of his experience, not for a direct answer of whether Ruth is objectively trustworthy or not. Even if that were David's request, how could his analyst ever answer that? How could he assume the role of being the arbiter of David's reality? What follows is a peculiar explanation: Trop was reluctant to answer the question because he was afraid that he would damage the tie that developed between him and David, should he convey his perception of David's vulnerability (p. 86). Having to consider David as too vulnerable to his communication of "the truth," Trop faced two problems: (1) he misconceived his own function as an analyst by taking on the role of arbiter of David's reality; and (2) having discarded the empathic observational perspective of self psychology, he could not reflect on David's subjective experience as an element of the interpretive process. Eventually he settled on being a reluctant arbiter of part of David's subjective reality and said, ". . . I could certainly agree that what Ruth had done was an act of unreliability" (p. 87). How does Trop know about Ruth's unreliability? Such an intervention seriously interferes with the analytic process. "[He] also said that it seemed clear [!] that [David] wanted my support, not only as a confirmation that what she had done was unreliable, but for his perception that this meant there was something centrally flawed with Ruth" (p. 87). Trop assumed that he knew what David wanted from him without searching for David's meaning of "support." What follows is meant as an explanation, but it lacks cogency: "I told him that I was reluctant to *support* this perception because I felt there were feelings of underlying rage that would be valuable to explore" (p. 87). I do not believe that a simultaneous exploration of rage and analytic support is contradictory. David's "vulnerability" and his rage are both legitimate analytic concerns. A statement acknowledging that Ruth's behavior played into David's vulnerability would have accomplished that. This could have naturally led to an exploration of David's vulnerability and his effort to remedy it. Such an interpretive comment is part of the process of working through as it inevitably encompasses (especially at points of disruption) the repetitive aspects of the selfobject transference as well.

There is no stronger support in an analysis than the nonjudgmental, noncondemning acceptance of what the patient presents, and the effort to grasp and validate the patient's self-experience by conveying our understanding. Instead, Trop condemned Ruth's action as "unreliable" but refused to see this action as reflecting "something centrally flawed in Ruth." Once more, the notion of support is taken literally and not analytically, and Trop decided which part of David's claim was true and which part was not! David was essentially asking Trop, "Tell me, am I crazy to feel the way I do?" The analytic answer should pose no dilemma: "Of course not, your reaction makes sense in the light of Ruth's turning away from you. Ruth's other interests and activities deprive you of her unfailingly ever-present emotional support you feel you need and expect from her." Such an interpretive statement (however formulated) would acknowledge how Ruth's behavior played into David's vulnerability. A comment like this enhances self-reflection as it refers to the patient's, and not someone else's, subjectivity. But Trop went on to state that "[David's] anger had been codetermined by [Ruth's] thoughtlessness [!] and by his automatically and unconsciously organizing her lateness to mean that he was not compelling and special to her." In ordinary English, in the interpretive mode, this would sound something like: "You experienced Ruth as thoughtless and became angry at her because her lateness meant to you that she didn't give a damn about you." This unambiguous statement about David's subjective experience could naturally lead into an exploration of how Ruth's lateness came to mean for David that he did not matter to her.

Had Trop not challenged the validity of David's communication, David's core psychopathology (his mirror-hungry personality?) might have been analytically engaged in this treatment process. Trop does not seem to give David room to bring the full weight of his self-disorder into their relationship through one of the selfobject transferences. He short-circuits these by reaching directly and repeatedly for the invariant unconscious organizing principles.

A dream at this point strikingly reveals what is missing in this analysis. "David came in feeling anxious and agitated. He had repaired the relationship with Ruth and had been feeling better, but had a dream that left him feeling shaken.

He had dreamed that he was in an automobile or a machine that was going back in time. The vehicle was shaking as images flashed before his eyes and eventually stopped at some time in his past. A very young baby boy had been thrown out of the car, and he felt frantic as he looked for him. Finally he found him at the side of the road, alive, but wrapped up in bandages" (p. 87).

A gripping dream that says much and I shall not try to reinterpret it, because where it led David and Trop in their reconstruction of David's past is essentially compatible with self psychology, again without any discernible special contribution from intersubjectivity theory. The only point I wish to make is that both patient and analyst rushed to interpret the dream in light of the patient's past history. But what would have served here as a bridge to the past would have been the exploration of the phrase of "an automobile or machine going back in time" as a possible reference to the analysis, and the shaking vehicle as a possible reference to what might have been going on in the analytic situation that was disturbing and frightening to David. This focus might have brought the past more meaningfully into the present; it would have brought the "intersubjective" (self-selfobject) elements into the foreground they deserve. In spite of that distancing from the present by both patient and analyst, the analytic conversation (as reported) was deepened, and significant, affect-laden memories have emerged following the dream and its interpretation.

But memories alone are hardly trustworthy. Their embeddedness in the transference had become a sine qua non for the interpretation of their meaning in the here-and-now. And yet Trop says: "These memories supplied the *foundation* for our understanding that [David] had unconsciously organized [his mother's] repetitive abandonment of him as a confirmation of a central and loathsome defect in him, leaving him feeling that he could never be central to a woman" (p. 88, italics added).

Focusing on the content of his memories and how the recall of significant events might have affected David's unconscious organizing principles leads to some very imprecise formulations. "David was [now] increasingly able to recognize how he automatically assimilated Ruth's enthusiastic interest in other things as a confirmation of his *defectiveness*. It was Ruth's capacity for aliveness, vitality, and engagement that stimulated his own 'archaic organizing principles.' The very qualities about her that he valued most when they were directed at him were the source of the most profound pain when exhibited outside the relationship" (p. 88, italics added). This quote once more highlights the price Trop paid for deciding to avoid the insights of self psychology in order to claim the superiority of his intersubjectivity theory. The problem is this: Trop recognized that David's self-experience was one of "defectiveness." It is then plausible that his attachment to Ruth may well have been "stimulated" precisely on account of her "aliveness, vitality, and engagement," which served to enliven, vitalize, and engage him in the activities around him, to compensate for his "defectiveness." We are dealing with David's archaic longings here—even more strongly, with his archaic *needs*. And the pain is the direct result of his feeling that those qualities in Ruth are (even if only temporarily) not available to him to make him feel alive and whole. The statement that "David now understood his reactions to Ruth as replicating the way he unconsciously organized his experience of abandonment by both his mother and father" (p. 88, italics added) restates Trop's theory in a language that does not illuminate for David just exactly what he is seeking in Ruth and why. Is this "replication" without purpose? Is David not attempting to accomplish something essential, such as experiencing himself as vital and alive in her presence? Self psychology assumes that such a replication indeed has a purpose; it is a search for a response that would heal his defectiveness, both within and outside of the therapeutic setting. This is a key discovery of self psychology. Without such an assumption (or some equivalent) Trop does not have a meaningful explanation as to why people are compelled to repeat. He only has an abstract metapsychology, which he cannot operationalize.

The relentless repetitive interpretation of unconscious, automatic, invariant organizing principles as explanations for David's varied behavior and difficulties (I counted ten such interventions) bypasses David's subjective experience in the treatment situation and does not bring to awareness or explain the fundamental nature of his psychopathology, nor does it touch on how he strives to remedy his "defectiveness" inside or outside of the therapeutic setting.

SUMMING UP

The purpose of this study, the detailed textual analysis of the clinical report of David's analysis, was to examine the validity of Trop's claims of intersubjectivity theory as superior to self psychology—that it is broader and more encompassing because intersubjectivity theory incorporated the concept of selfobject longings into its theoretical and clinical approach. In this view the relation between the two separate systems is reduced to the fact that both are "relational theories," reject "drive as a primary source of motivation," and use "the empathic-introspective method of observation and inquiry."

A detailed inspection of Trop's observation and interpretation of Joan and her mother and his report of the analysis of David points to a wide gap between his claims and what he actually demonstrated to us clinically. Based on my reading of his clinical report, Trop does not use the empathic-introspective observational method systematically (he stumbles into it on two occasions) but uses the notion of an "invariant, unconscious organizing principle" as his motivational theory in a highly stereotyped fashion. The formulations of his interventions do not seem to convey to David what he would need to understand about the way he conducts his life. Instead, Trop's interventions repetitively confront him with his outdated invariant organizing principles and invite him to drop these in favor of some other, more appropriate ones. Trop is certainly willing to lend David his own view of reality—he arbitrarily decides which claims of David's to accept and which ones to reject.

Although Trop sees these organizing principles as the fundamental motivational factors, his formulations do not contain references to how, why, and for what purpose these principles "motivate" David's maladaptive behavior and, especially, how he is struggling to remedy his "defectiveness" both inside and outside of the analysis. He does not explain satisfactorily how self-reflective awareness can change the unconscious, automatic, invariant organizing principles and implies that simply making them conscious will alter them. It seems to be a puzzling paradox that in attempting to present the superiority of intersubjectivity theory, instead of focusing on intersubjective processes, Trop focuses his entire interpretive process on the *invariant* aspects of David's psychopathology and presents these as if self psychology disregarded them.

In my view Trop succeeded only in one respect. He succeeded in demonstrating a sharp dichotomy between the observational methods of self psychology and intersubjectivity theory by accepting Stolorow's redefinition of empathy. This redefinition of empathy does indeed sharply separate self psychology and intersubjectivity theory. As a result there is a one-sided emphasis in the case report on the repetitive aspects of the transference. Trop has thereby relinquished the advances made by self psychology and lost a significant *psychoanalytic* therapeutic leverage.

There is a profound contradiction in presenting intersubjectivity theory in sharp contrast to self psychology as an interpersonal versus an intrapsychic psychology. Self psychology in its core concept of the selfobject encompasses self-experience in a selfobject matrix and thereby pays due attention to the mutual influence of self and other. Analytic focus is on the self-experience of both partners as they affect each other in the psychoanalytic dialogue. Central to this dialogue is that what transpires in the present has a past, which weighs heavily (in the form of the repetitive aspects of the transference) on the present. This past is inevitably enacted and becomes especially visible in the disruptions of the selfobject transferences that express the striving for the resumption of the thwarted developmental need to grow—its powerful motivational foundation.

Intersubjectivity theory is viewed by Trop as superior because self psychology supposedly disregards the "invariant organizing principles." This, as I have already indicated, is not a correct reading of self psychology. Rather, the opposite is true: attending to the selfobject transferences results in the increase in self-cohesion that makes self-reflection possible and lessens the need for the repetitive deployment of the maladaptive "invariant organizing principles" in new situations (see A. Ornstein, 1991). When changes in habitual ways of responding are achieved by the consolidation of the self, they are the consequence of *analytic change*, related to the belated acquisition of psychic structures. Psychoanalysis is supposed to address the kind of vulnerability that David suffered from by facilitating an increase in self-cohesion; only a well-consolidated self is able to relinquish habitual patterns that had become established in the past in relation to childhood traumatic experiences.

If Trop (1994) had started his presentation with his concluding remark that "[t]he emergence of selfobject transferences and the elucidation of unconscious repetitive organizations are *two indivisible aspects of a unitary process* [and that] the illumination of old organizing principles occurs in the context of a new selfobject experience with the analyst" (p. 23) and his clinical material had actually illustrated this, I would have applauded his chapter wholeheartedly and would not have written such a long and arduous discussion. In Trop's general statement (quoted previously) I see no contradiction between the two psychologies, nor do I see any substantive differences between them. But I no longer believe in the validity of general statements without their being demonstrated in the clinical process.

REFERENCES

Atwood, G. E. & Stolorow, R. D. (1984), *Structures of Subjectivity: Explorations in Psychoanalytic Phenomenology*. Hillsdale, NJ: The Analytic Press.

Basch, M. F. (1983), Empathic understanding: A review of the concept and some theoretical considerations. *J. Amer. Psychoanal. Assn.*, 31:101–126.

—— (1988), *Understanding Psychotherapy: The Science Behind the Art.* New York: Basic Books.

Goldberg, A. (1988), *A Fresh Look at Psychoanalysis: A View from Self Psychology.* Hillsdale, NJ: The Analytic Press.

Kohut, H. (1984), *How Does Analysis Cure?* ed. A. Goldberg & P. Stepansky. Chicago: Chicago University Press.

Lichtenberg, J. D. (1989), *Psychoanalysis and Motivation.* Hillsdale, NJ: The Analytic Press.

Ornstein, A. (1974). The dread to repeat and the new beginning: Contribution to the psychoanalytic treatment of narcissistic personality disorders. *The Annual of Psychoanalysis,* 2:231–248. New York: International Universities Press.

 —— (1991a), Selfobject transferences, intersubjectivity and countertransference in the analytic process. In: *The Evolution of Self Psychology, Progress in Self Psychology, Vol. 7,* ed. A. Goldberg. Hillsdale, NJ: The Analytic Press, pp. 93–99.

—— (1991b), The dread to repeat: Comments on the working through process in psychoanalysis. *J. Amer. Psychoanal. Assn.,* 39:377–398.

—— & Ornstein, P. H. (1985), Parenting as a function of the adult self. A psychoanalytic developmental perspective. In: *Parental Influences in Health and Disease,* ed. J. Anthony & G. Pollock. Boston: Little Brown, pp. 181–231.

—— & —— (1990), The process of psychoanalytic psychotherapy: A self psychological perspective. In: *Review of Psychiatry, Vol. 9,* ed. A. Tasman, S. M. Goldinger & C. A. Kaufman. Washington, DC: American Psychiatric Press, pp. 323–340.

Ornstein, P. H. (1979), Remarks on the central position of empathy in psychoanalysis. *Bull. Assn. Psychoanal. Med.,* 18:95–109.

—— (1983), Discussion of papers by Drs. Goldberg, Stolorow, and Wallerstein. In: *Reflections on Self Psychology,* ed. J. D. Lichtenberg & S. Kaplan. Hillsdale, NJ: The Analytic Press, pp. 339–384.

—— (1990a), How to enter a psychoanalytic process conducted by another analyst? *Psychoanal. Inq.,* 10:478–497.

—— (1990b), A case discussion. The self psychological perspective. In: *New Perspectives on Narcissism,* ed. E. M. Plakun. Washington, DC: American Psychiatric Press, pp. 205–252.

—— (1991a), From narcissism to ego psychology to self psychology. In: *Freud's On Narcissism: An Introduction,* ed. J. Sandler, E. S. Person & P. Fonagy. International Psychoanalytic Association. New Haven, CT: Yale University Press, pp. 175–194.

—— (1991b), A self-psychological perspective on conflict and compromise. In: *Conflict and Compromise: Therapeutic Implications.* Monogr. 7, ed. S. Dowling. Workshop Series of the American Psychoanalytic Association. Madison, CT: International Universities Press, pp. 133–171.

—— (1992), How to read *The Basic Fault?* An introduction to Michael Balint's seminal ideas on the psychoanalytic treatment process. In: *The Basic Fault,* M. Balint. Evanston, IL: Northwestern University Press, pp. vii–xxv.

—— & Ornstein, A. (1977), On the continuing evolution of psychoanalytic psychotherapy: Reflections and predictions. In: *The Annual of Psychoanalysis,* 5:329–355. New York: International Universities Press.

Stolorow, R. D. (1993), Thoughts on the nature and therapeutic action of psychoanalytic interpretation. In: *The Widening Scope of Self Psychology, Progress in Self Psychology, Vol. 9,* ed. A. Goldberg, pp. 31–43. Hillsdale, NJ: The Analytic Press.

—— & Atwood, G. E. (1992), *Contexts of Being: The Intersubjective Foundations of Psychological Life*. Hillsdale, NJ: The Analytic Press.

—— —— & Brandchaft, B., eds. (1994), *The Intersubjective Perspective*. Northvale, NJ: Aronson.

—— Brandchaft, B. & Atwood, G. E. (1987), *Psychoanalytic Treatment: An Intersubjective Approach*. Hillsdale, NJ: The Analytic Press.

Thompson, P. G. (1994), Countertransference. In: *The Intersubjective Perspective,* ed. R. D. Stolorow, G. E. Atwood & B. Brandchaft. Northvale, NJ: Aronson.

Trop, J. L. (1994), Self psychology and intersubjectivity theory. In: *The Intersubjective Perspective,* ed. R. D. Stolorow, G. E. Atwood & B. Brandchaft. Northvale, NJ: Aronson.

Chapter 4

Reply to Ornstein

Jeffrey L. Trop

Paul Ornstein's discussion of my article, "Self Psychology and Inter-subjectivity Theory: A Clinical Comparison" (1994; also in this volume), highlights the differing perspectives of and similarities between self psychology and intersubjectivity theory. It will not be possible for me to consider all of Ornstein's criticisms, so I intend to address certain key issues.

As someone who has profound respect for the contributions of self psychology, I welcome the opportunity to continue this dialogue. Stephen Mitchell (1992) has commented on the importance of comparing the nuances of modern theories of psychoanalysis in his discussion of a paper by Trop and Stolorow (1992). He states:

> In my view, the battle against orthodoxy has been largely won; the real vitality and creativity in this field have shifted to efforts, like the present one, to develop postclassical, broadly relational approaches to mind, development, and the analytic situation. Because the battle has been won, it is now less interesting to recount the deficiencies of the classical model than to explore the subtle but quite important differences among postclassical perspectives [p. 443].

My original article and Ornstein's response to it represent two attempts to explore these types of differences among postclassical perspectives in

The author would like to thank Dr. Robert Stolorow for his assistance.

an attempt to compare and contrast self psychology and intersubjectivity theory.

Kohut's first article (1959a) on introspection and empathy, presented at the Chicago Institute for Psychoanalysis, was a nodal point in the history of psychoanalysis. In this article, Kohut boldly stated: "We designate phenomena as mental, psychic, or psychological if our mode of observation includes introspection and empathy as an essential constituent" (p. 209). In his last article (1982), entitled "Introspection, Empathy, and the Semicircle of Mental Health," Kohut again returned to an examination of empathy. In this poignant essay, Kohut summarizes his basic position on empathy. He states:

> I will, in other words, be talking about empathy in an epistemological context. In this context, it should go without saying, empathy is a value-neutral mode of observation; a mode of observation attuned to the inner life of man, just as extrospection is a mode of observation attuned to the external world [p. 396].

Kohut's noteworthy comments on empathy illuminate a significant problem with the tenor and tone of Ornstein's discussion. In his response to me, Ornstein invokes the concept of *objectivity*. He states: "I believe there is a way to discuss these matters with some objectivity" (p. 3). As Kohut clarifies again and again in his writing, it is not possible for *anyone* to discuss these matters with any objectivity whatsoever, without the discussion being intensely colored by the principles that organize one's own experience. The entire tenor of Ornstein's discussion derives from his resurrecting the concept of true objectivity, which violates all that Kohut has discussed regarding the concept of objectivity. As Kohut (1982) states: "I had never seriously considered the fact that I would have to define or defend my operationalism, my clearly established knowledge that reality per se, whether extrospective or introspective, is unknowable and that we can only describe what we see within the framework of what we have done to see it" (p. 400). In striking violation of Kohut's epistemological stance, Ornstein here elevates his own intense subjective reaction to my comparison of self psychology and intersubjectivity theory to the status of "objectivity."

I will now address myself to some of Ornstein's specific statements regarding intersubjectivity theory. Ornstein's claim that "intersubjectivity theory . . . began as a special emphasis and direction in self psychology" and that self psychology was "the theoretical system from which intersubjectivity theory arose" is simply factually incorrect. As has been chronicled now in a number of contexts (e.g., Stolorow, 1992; Stolorow and Atwood, 1992; Atwood and Stolorow, 1993), the "original sources" of the theory of intersubjectivity can be found in a series of psychobiographical studies conducted in the early 1970s in which Stolorow and Atwood explored the personal, subjective origins of the theoretical systems of Freud, Jung, Reich, and Rank. From these studies, which formed the basis of Stolorow and Atwood's first book, *Faces in a Cloud* (1979), they concluded that, because psychological theories derive to a significant degree from the subjective concerns of their creators, what psychoanalysis needs is a theory of subjectivity itself—a unifying framework that can account not only for the phenomena that other theories address but also for these theories themselves.

Although the concept of *inter*subjectivity was not yet a formal component of the skeletal framework introduced in *Faces in a Cloud*, it was clearly implicit in the demonstrations of how the subjective world of a psychological theorist influences his understanding of other persons' experiences. The therapeutic implications of intersubjectivity were explored in an early clinical paper (Stolorow, Atwood, and Ross, 1978), and soon thereafter, in the late 1970s and early 1980s, the intersubjective perspective and self psychology came together in a mutually enriching dialogue when Stolorow and Brandchaft became deeply involved in the self psychology movement (see Stolorow, 1992).

One of Ornstein's central criticisms concerns my revised definition of empathy, which includes the illumination of unconscious organizing principles. As I state (Trop, 1994), this "adds a unique dimension to the concept of empathy" (p. 79). Ornstein claims that my "narrow focus on the unconscious organizing principles leads Trop almost exclusively to the invariant aspects of the transference." Ornstein repeatedly misunderstands the use of the word *invariant* to mean only the repetitive aspect of the transference. The concept of invariant, automatic organizing principles encompasses *both* the repetitive and the selfobject dimensions of experience.

Ornstein (1995) states emphatically several times that I thus engage in "treating the selfobject dimension as peripheral." There are several problems with Ornstein's understanding of my comments. In the discussion of the case of David, I emphasized the repetitive unconscious organizing principles that occurred primarily with Ruth and also in an episode with me when I was saying good-bye to another patient. At those moments, David experienced himself as deprived of the selfobject functions he needed to maintain cohesion and unconsciously organized his experience as a confirmation of a central defect in himself. The unconscious and automatic meaning he assigned to her absence and my engagement with the other patient were revivals of the recurrent meanings that he experienced when playing outside his mother's house. At this time, he frantically longed for his mother's mirroring responsiveness and in its absence felt increasingly repulsive, repugnant, and deserving of the abandonment he received. It is in this episode that one can see the pervasive impact on David of the absence of selfobject responsiveness.

Although my presentation of this particular case thus focused more on the repetitive dimension of experience, I make it clear that the understanding of the selfobject dimension of experience is also critical in understanding all patients. Certain aspects of David's treatment were highlighted to emphasize specific areas of significant difference from self psychology, perhaps leading to an artifactually one-sided focus in the clinical discussion. However, as I stated in my article, the concept of unconscious organizing principles does *not* imply an exclusive focus on the repetitive aspects of the transference or relegation of the selfobject dimension to the periphery. Atwood and Stolorow (1993) have described the selfobject and repetitive dimensions of transference as "two broad classes of unconscious organizing principles" (p. 184). Thus the concept of unconscious organizing principles clearly encompasses *both* dimensions.

To return to my expansion of the definition of empathy, Ornstein (1995) states: "To my knowledge, no one has yet proposed a better and more widely accepted definition of empathy than 'feeling oneself and thinking oneself into the inner life of another,' a process that greatly facilitates the recognition of the specific features of a selfobject transference." My emphasis on unconscious organizing principles, which encompasses multiple dimensions of transference, does not narrow the way of listening but rather extends the range of possibilities. The emphasis on a broad range of unconscious organization in addition to selfobject longings sharpens the concept of empathy as a mode of investigation. I am attempting to define specifically the constellations that the therapist is striving to illuminate through analytic inquiry. Contrary to Ornstein's claim, the redefinition of analytic empathy offered by intersubjectivity theory does *not* diminish the analyst's primary focus on subjective experience. On the contrary, it sharpens this focus by highlighting how subjective experience is recurrently and unconsciously organized.

I will now take up briefly certain of Ornstein's other statements regarding intersubjectivity before I then address some of his specific clinical comments.

Focusing on what is intersubjective does *not* lead to a neglect of inner experience. Stolorow and Atwood (1992) write: "The concept of an intersubjective system brings to focus *both* the individual's world of inner experience *and* its embeddedness with other such worlds in a continual flow of reciprocal mutual influence" (p. 18).

Intersubjectivity theory does *not* emphasize insight, as opposed to relationship, as the main curative agent in psychoanalysis. Responding to this false dichotomy, Stolorow, Brandchaft, and Atwood (1987) write: "Insight through interpretation, affective bonding through empathic attunement, and the facilitation of psychological integration are indissoluble facets of a unitary therapeutic process" (p. 105).

Intersubjectivity theory does *not* claim that self-reflective awareness can change invariant organizing principles. Stolorow and Atwood (1992) write:

> Successful psychoanalytic treatment, in our view, does not produce therapeutic change by altering or eliminating the patient's invariant organizing principles. Rather, through new relational experiences with the analyst in concert with enhancements of the patient's capacity for reflective self-awareness, it facilitates the establishment and consolidation of alternative principles and thereby enlarges the patient's experiential repertoire [p. 25].

Ornstein's comments about my communication to Joan's mother highlight a significant difference in approach. Ornstein (1995) stated that he would have said the following to Joan's mother: "You tried to calm your daughter's worries, but it wasn't easy—you both made it down the elevator successfully at the end." This represents to me an example of squeezing an interaction into the selfobject dimension of experience. My subjective experience was the opposite of what Ornstein recommends be articulated. I did not experience the mother as trying to calm her daughter's worries but rather as trying to calm herself by using her daughter to provide a twinship experience. My subjective experience was that she was using her daughter, but Ornstein recommends that I *not* use my subjective experience but rather ignore it. In my opinion, presenting his comments to the mother would serve to reinforce an archaic and embedded meaning pertaining to the mother's own sense of subjective danger.

Thus, one can see here that intersubjectivity theory, focused on the interplay between our two differing subjectivities, would promote a dialogue whereby subjective experiences that are at variance can be discussed and used to illuminate the patient's (and analyst's) own unique organizing principles. I do certainly agree with Ornstein's implication that if I were seeing her in an office setting, I would explore her feelings about the elevator ride and the evidence she deduced to conclude that her child was anxious. Ornstein's description of his comment to her, however, asks the analyst to surrender his own subjectivity to enact a selfobject responsiveness, with the consequence of reinforcing archaic meanings. It is this kind of intervention that evokes the criticism that self psychology sanitizes the underlying painful affective meanings of disruptive states and covers over central repetitive configurations of experience.

In turning to the case of David, Ornstein (1995) states that my discussion of David's reactions ignores the fundamental nature of his psychopathology. He feels that my comments to David do

> not illuminate for David just exactly what he is seeking in Ruth and why. Is this "replication" without purpose? Is David not attempting something essential, such as experiencing himself as vital and alive in her presence? Self psychology assumes that such a replication has a purpose: it is a search for a response that would heal his defectiveness—both within and outside of the therapeutic setting [p. 73].

Ornstein's comments here deserve careful reflection. Clearly, Ruth served important selfobject functions for David. She helped him feel a sense of his own specialness, and indeed Ornstein is correct in his comments about David "experiencing himself as vital and alive in her presence." I also recognized this in the therapy with David, as I stated (Trop, 1994): "My interpretations to David touched on his selfobject longing to feel special" (p. 90). It is thus difficult to understand Ornstein's criticism of my ignoring David's selfobject needs when I specifically mentioned his mirroring needs in relation to Ruth and his idealizing needs in relation to me. In essence, I have no disagreement with his comments about Ruth's selfobject functions, and in fact repeatedly communicated them to David. I think our differences lie in our understanding of what was centrally salient for David at this time in his therapy. I saw as centrally salient David's disruptive affective reactions to the *loss* of Ruth's selfobject responsiveness and the unconscious meanings that structured these reactions. The illumination of the repetitive meanings of his reactions to his perceptions of abandonment was my central focus. The understanding of the meanings of his reactions to abandonment occurred in the context of his therapeutic selfobject tie. This facilitated the acquisition of a new organizing principle, namely, that he could experience himself as centrally important to a woman.

It is clear that Ornstein and I continue to see both the clinical material and some theoretical constructs differently. In a pivotal article, Shane and Shane (1993) describe the different approaches within self psychology stemming from a variety of divergent theoretical stances within the field. They catalogue the similarities and differences among several theoreticians—Basch, Gedo, Wolf, Goldberg, Lichtenberg, Stolorow, and Bacal and Newman. The title of their article is "Self Psychology After Kohut: One Theory or Many?" They summarize their answer as follows:

As for the question we raise—one self psychology or many?—it is clear that the authors we have discussed are original contributors, dedicated to their own unique perspectives, less interested in sounding like one another, or Kohut, than in clearly defining and putting forth their own views. As the situation stands today, we would have to conclude that there are many self psychologies, not just one, reflecting not only the state of psychoanalysis in general, but also the vigor and ferment that constitutes health in any growing and changing science [pp. 795–796].

Shane and Shane thus delineate the important divergences among different frameworks. They also describe the similarities in approach and find useful ways to attempt to integrate various vantage points. Despite Ornstein's and my differences in regard to self psychology and intersubjectivity theory, I commend Ornstein for his detailed examination of my chapter. Efforts to identify the similarities and differences among various postclassical theories provide important clarifications of the theoretical assumptions underlying our clinical work.

REFERENCES

Atwood, G. & Stolorow, R. (1993), *Faces in a Cloud*, 2nd ed. Northvale, NJ: Aronson.

Kohut, H. (1959), Introspection, empathy, and psychoanalysis: An examination of the relationship between mode of observation and theory. In: *The Search for the Self*, ed. P. Ornstein. New York: International Universities Press, 1978, pp. 205–232.

—— (1982), Introspection, empathy, and the semicircle of mental health. *Internat. J. Psycho-Anal.*, 63:395–407.

Mitchell, S. (1992), Commentary on Trop and Stolorow's "Defense analysis in self psychology." *Psychoanal. Dial.*, 2: 443–453.

Ornstein, P. (1995), Critical reflections on a comparison and contrast of self psychology and intersubjectivity theory. In: *The Impact of New Ideas, Progress in Self Psychology, Vol. 11*, ed. A. Goldberg. Hillsdale, NJ: The Analytic Press, pp. 47–77.

Shane, M. & Shane, E. (1993), Self psychology after Kohut: One theory or many? *J. Amer. Psychoanal. Assn.*, 41:777–797.

Stolorow, R. (1992), Subjectivity and self psychology. In: *The Intersubjective Perspective*, ed. R. Stolorow, G. Atwood & B. Brandchaft. Northvale, NJ: Aronson, 1994, pp. 31–39.

—— & Atwood, G. (1979), *Faces in a Cloud*. Northvale, NJ: Aronson.

—— & —— (1992), *Contexts of Being*. Hillsdale, NJ: The Analytic Press.

—— —— & Ross, J. (1978), The representational world in psychoanalytic therapy. *Internat. Rev. Psycho-Anal.*, 5:247–256.

—— Brandchaft, B. & Atwood, G. (1987), *Psychoanalytic Treatment: An Intersubjective Approach*. Hillsdale, NJ: The Analytic Press.

—— (1994), Self psychology and intersubjectivity theory. In: *The Intersubjective Perspective*, ed. R. Stolorow, G. Atwood & B. Brandchaft. Northvale, NJ: Aronson, pp. 77–91.

—— & Stolorow, R. (1992), Defense analysis in self psychology: A developmental view. *Psychoanal. Dial.*, 2:427–442.

Chapter 5

Internal Object Relations as Intersubjective Phenomena

Craig Powell

Although Kohut held the view that "transmuting internalization" (Kohut, 1971, p. 49) was the means by which both healthy development and analytic cure proceeded, he did not—in contrast to theorists like Fairbairn and Melanie Klein in Britain, and Kernberg in the United States—develop a theory of internal object relations.

In one sense this need not surprise us. Klein and Kernberg, in differing ways, remain committed to drive theory, whereas self psychology may be seen (Bacal, 1990) as "a systematically elaborated 'object relations' theory where the significance of the link with the object that is experienced as providing a selfobject function is central" (p. 13). Drives are relegated to the periphery, or viewed as fragmentation products.

Furthermore, schemata of internal object relations such as Klein and Kernberg have proposed have an *extrospective* quality. We could think of them as hypothetical maps of psychic development in which "the development of 'rewarding' (libidinally gratifying) and 'punishing' (painful, frustrating, frightening experiences triggering aggression) experiences in the early mother–child interaction [develop] into early intrapsychic structures culminating in a set of structures representing 'internal object relations'" (Kernberg, 1972, p. 233). Such internalized object relations are considered "primitive" when "cathectic processes that involve object and self-representations are reflected in introjective-projective relatedness; primitive splitting supported by denial is the dominant mechanism of defense: and the presence of primitive splitting indicates failure to achieve a tolerance of ambivalence" (Volkan, 1976, pp. 29–30).

The wariness that self psychologically informed analysts have shown toward such schemata has arisen in part from this extrospective quality, that of an observational stance outside the patient's experiential field. Although such schemata may acknowledge the part played by early self-objects in the formation of these structures, one finds less frequently an acknowledgment of the influence of the analytic observer, as though any number of different assessments of the same patient would result in the same intrapsychic map.

Nevertheless we are faced with the fact that patients frequently experience themselves as internally divided and look for ways to articulate this. Grotstein (1983) has observed, "We are normally more dissociated than we have imagined. This multiplicity or dissociation of selves is not apparent thanks to the normal cohesion of the self but, when this cohesion fails and we become fragmented, our separate subselves begin to emerge" (p. 172). For an example of this I will turn initially not to a first-hand clinical vignette but to a passage from a narrative poem, "The Floor of Heaven," by the Australian poet John Tranter (1992). The scene is a therapy group. The therapist is addressing one of the group members who has handed him a bundle of notes:

> "I think I see what you want.
> You'd like one of us to read it out,
> is that your plan, Gloria?" He turned
> and swung his smile on her like a spotlight.
> Was she going to faint? She wavered;
> weed under running water. "Unhhh . . ."
> was all Gloria could manage, blushing.
> One of the pale animals in her lap
> seemed to be on the verge of triumph,
> grasping and choking the other, which had
> reddened under the sudden attack. A ring—
> I hadn't noticed the glittering engagement ring
> before—was being twisted violently [pp. 4–5].

In this scene the therapist responds to the patient's tentative offer of her personal notes by shaming her in front of the group. One possible interpretation is that, deprived of the needed selfobject response, the patient suffers fragmentation. She is unable to form words. But her hands enact her internal division. One hand becomes triumphant and attacking, as she might experience the therapist; the other is the strangled victim. The engagement ring is also "twisted violently." Something might be symbolically expressed here about Gloria's relation with her fiancé and other people in her past and present selfobject milieu, and perhaps also about the hope she might have held for an engagement with the group and the group leader.

We could imagine an internal drama with a cast of metaphorical characters such as Fairbairn might have provided. Among the British object relations theorists Fairbairn's work is remarkably congruent with self psychology because, as Ernest Jones remarked in his introduction to *Psychoanalytic Studies of the Personality* (1952), "Instead of starting, as Freud did, from stimulation of the nervous system proceeding from various erotogenic zones and internal tension arising from gonadal activity, Dr. Fairbairn starts at the centre of the personality, the ego, and depicts its strivings and difficulties in its endeavour to reach an object where it might find support." In addition, Fairbairn hypothesized that intrapsychic splitting is not present at birth but arises in response to frustrations of attachment needs and that the splitting follows a particular pattern, like the cleavage lines of a diamond. The conscious experience of self and other Fairbairn referred to as the Central Ego, linked to the Acceptable Object. Within the unconscious are the imagos of early self-with-object experiences, split into all good and all bad—in Fairbairn's terminology, the Exciting Object and the Rejecting Object. A portion of the self is attached to and identified with each—the Libidinal Ego and the Antilibidinal Ego, respectively. Fairbairn regarded the combined structure of Exciting Object–Libidinal Ego as having many of the functions of the id, as described by Freud, while the Rejecting Object–Antilibidinal Ego, which he also called the Internal Saboteur, formed the equivalent of the archaic superego. The Central Ego attempts to keep both structures in repression while, within the unconscious, the Rejecting Object–Antilibidinal Ego also directs aggression against the Exciting Object–Libidinal Ego (Fairbairn, 1944). Here, as I suggested, might be the metaphorical characters beneath the surface of the drama depicted in the poem. Gloria is crushed and inarticulate under the shaming gaze of the therapist. But one part of her is not crushed at all, but rather "on the verge of triumph." One hand, presumably the right, which would not be wearing the engagement ring, proceeds to strenuously attack the other. Included in the attack is the engagement ring, the symbol of libidinal attachment.

However, caution must be applied to any system of metaphors. Reification is an ever-present snare, whether one is talking about "internalization," "id, ego, and superego," or, for that matter, "the bipolar self." Schafer (1976) has drawn attention to the spatial and physicalistic reifications that can be brought about by the use of the term *internalization*. When Kohut wrote of "transmuting internalization" he was referring to the acquisition of self-regulating *functions* when such regulation had previously come from the environment—the parental self-objects, the analyst, or both.

Although Kohut did not attempt a theory of internal object relations, the nearest he came was in his metaphor of the vertical and horizontal splits within the self, first described in his essay "Narcissism as a Resistance and as a Driving Force in Psychoanalysis" (Kohut, 1970) and later in *The Analysis of the Self* (Kohut, 1971). Although there are some areas of commonality with Fairbairn's "map" in the splitting between grandiose and depleted, vulnerable aspects of the self, there are also important differences in that Kohut does not conceptualize a splitting of the *selfobject* experience. Implicitly, in this schema, the maternal selfobject is present to make "narcissistic use of the child's performance" or is not felt to be present at all. Indeed, self psychological writers seem to have said little about the acquisition of functions that are not self-regulatory but self-sabotaging and indeed self-destructive. Fairbairn believed that "bad objects" were internalized as a means of controlling them. From a more self psychological stance we might say that the need for selfobjects is so compelling that they will be attached to and taken in even when experienced as destructive. All internal representations, according to Beebe and Lachmann (1988) constitute "interiorized *interaction*: not simply the infant's action, nor simply the environment's response, but the dynamic mutual influence between the two. Interiorized patterns include actions, perception, cognition, affect and proprioceptive experience" (p. 8). Moreover, such "interiorized interaction," when brought to us by our patients, whether in action (Gloria's hand movements in the group), in conscious verbalizations, or in dreams, should be received within the intersubjective context of patient and therapist in which they arise (Stolorow, Brandchaft, and Atwood, 1987). Not only is the patient's communication profoundly influenced by the state of the selfobject transference, but the therapist's observation is shaped by his or her theoretical stance, and "every . . . act of understanding resets the field, i.e., it changes what we study as well as ourselves" (Goldberg, 1994).

CLINICAL EXAMPLE

Mrs. R is a professional woman in her mid-40s, married with no children. She came to analysis complaining of a pervasive depression, saying that she felt "full of other people." She had left her native Argentina in her early 20s and migrated to Australia, where nobody spoke Spanish. She polished her rudimentary English and gained a university degree, eventually establishing a career in health administration. She had married relatively late, and explained to her analyst that she could never *plan* a pregnancy. "I don't believe in life. How could I give it to someone who might have to endure it for 90 years?"

She is the older of two children. She has a younger brother who still lives with their parents and shows signs of a chronic mental illness. The mother emerges from Mrs. R's account as a pious, masochistic lady, absorbed in her Catholicism and the suffering of her son. She describes her father as an explosive, paranoid man who was nonetheless not physically violent. As a child and adolescent she was clearly her father's favorite, and the only person whose mere presence could soothe his rages, yet there was always a rigid blocking out of any oedipal sensuality in the relationship. She remarked sardonically, "He despises women. I think it troubles him that his favorite person is one of them." She described occasions when she and her mother would attempt to establish an intimate conversation and her father would exclaim, "That smells of shit!" During her adolescence she had longed for the day when she could move half the world away from the pain and chaos of her family. Then, she believed, her real life would begin. But when she was eventually able to make the geographic separation she was mortified to discover how anxious and unhappy she was, still haunted by the humiliation and guilt of her early life, where the most scathing accusation was that she was taking notice of her own words. This was often conveyed through a vernacular Argentinian insult, "¡Mira que hablas al pedo!" This roughly translates as "Look how you're talking nothing but farts!"

The following passages describe a Friday session after she had been in analysis four times per week for a little more than a year. In the previous session she had spoken in distress of a phone call from her brother in Buenos Aires, who seemed in a severely regressed state, making angry and impossible demands of the patient. Shortly afterward her mother also phoned to lament how difficult it was to cope with her brother. The patient spoke of her mother as the child she had always had to care for, but that her mother had also helped the patient by sacrificing herself. She also said that through the generations of her family the men had ruthlessly "fed off" the women and could not cope without them. If her mother had not been sacrificed for her father and her brother, the patient herself would have had to do it and could never have managed any kind of escape.

She began this session by remarking, "You weren't really on my wavelength yesterday, and I was trying to push through my own barrier of 'Who do you think you are?' I couldn't really get across how it affected me." She recalled a story—"not really *my* story." During her research in a Community Health Project some years earlier she had reviewed a large number of files. One was that of an immigrant woman from a Middle Eastern country. This woman had migrated to Australia at the age of 16 for an arranged marriage to a man she had never met and had had five children in five years. Her husband brought her to the psychiatric service because she was depressed and was not a "good wife." She had been given antidepressants and E.C.T. At one point she had begged the staff not to send her home because she could not cope and feared she would be sent back to her family, who would kill her for bringing dishonor upon them. Nonetheless she was repeatedly sent home. "In the next to last note there is a record of someone suggesting to the husband that maybe he should treat his wife better. Then there's a later footnote, saying it's been heard she went back to her native country and three weeks later met with an accidental death." The patient wept with bitter outrage, exclaiming, "It was so cruel and unfair! No one cared. And he could just get another mail-order bride, someone to look after the children." The analyst responded that it was indeed an appalling story, and perhaps it somehow *was* her own story.

She answered, "I guess I'd better tell you the dream I had last night. I was in a room with a man . . . a doctor . . . and this young girl. She was like a sexual object . . . and he was playing with her . . . without any real feeling. Then he seemed to go into the next room and then I was touching her. . . . I reached into her sex. . . . I pulled out her womb and showed it to her. It seemed sadistic, but she made no protest. Then I put it back in, but back to front, so I reached in and twisted it back the right way. Then I said, 'Next time I'll do it to your anus!'"

She added that the cruelty in the dream was very distressing, but she herself had been doing it. "A womb or an arse-hole, it makes no difference. . . . Yesterday I was trying to tell you about myself and my mother. I had a dream about her last Saturday night." Mrs. R had often remarked that her Saturday night dreams were particularly desolate and lonely and this, it will be remembered, was a Friday session. "My mother was telling me how empty she felt inside. And I told her I felt empty also. Then we touched our abdomens against each other. I wanted to feel close to her, to understand her pain. I wanted her to know all about mine. When I was talking to you yesterday I felt so terribly constricted . . . this feeling of 'Who do you think you are? . . . ¡Mira que hablas al pedo!' I'm both people . . . the cruel person and the young girl who's the victim. I do it to myself. I wrench out my own insides."

The analyst replied, "You felt I didn't know yesterday how much it affected you, how powerful the cruelty was. I left you alone with it. The doctor went into another room." She answered, "Yes, and I couldn't really show you what I felt. I talked without feeling." The analyst suggested, "Without the womb, without the guts." She said, "Yes. Exactly."

DISCUSSION

Perhaps there is enough in that session, and those two dreams, for an infinite number of essays. But for the purposes of this one I wish to narrow my focus onto the internal object relations as expressed in the dreams and in the context of this particular analyst–analysand relationship. The patient presents herself as two subselves in relation to each other, the patient-victim and the woman who cruelly abuses her as the doctor leaves the room. The abusive self takes on the callous attitude of the abandoning male. In Fairbairn's metaphors, we could say that the Antilibidinal Ego, linked with the Rejecting Object, directs aggression toward the Exciting Object–Libidinal Ego. What is attacked is her vulnerable feminine selfhood, her sexuality. To say "A womb or an arsehole, it makes no difference," is to affirm that feminine intimacy "smells of shit." She is thus hollowed out, like her mother, impotent as the woman sent back to the Middle East to be killed, and painfully aware that somehow she herself has played a part in this.

This is part of an intrapsychic map viewed in terms of her relationship with childhood selfobjects. Yet the dream also expresses her frustration within the intersubjective matrix with her (male) analyst, and indeed becomes a way of telling him what otherwise could not be spoken. In the previous session, in some crucial sense she had not felt understood. From the viewpoint of the analyst's subjectivity, he had indeed been stirred by the patient's saying that whatever freedom she enjoyed seemed purchased with her mother's sacrifice, but he had missed the transference nuance and had not enabled her to explore this meaning in greater depth. In that sense he *became* the destructive father with whom she identified, the doctor who "played" with her with no feeling and callously went into another room. There were, after all, any number of "mail order" (male order) patients coming after her.

Guntrip (1968) has written of how the Antilibidinal Ego makes "natural maturing" impossible, yet it "must be respected as the patient's desperate struggle to keep himself functioning in the absence of genuine help" (p. 190). That is, it is a partially failed attempt at self-regulation. A perverse (i.e., sadomasochistic) self-selfobject relationship is internally maintained and provides a measure of cohesion. But to the external observer, and often indeed to the patient, what is more compelling is the quality of sabotage. In a later session in which this dream again came into focus, the analyst suggested, "Perhaps in the dream you're saying you can maintain a bond with me even when I fail you, but to do that you have to betray your own deepest self." Mrs. R replied thoughtfully, "It doesn't quite feel like that. It's more that, when you're not with me, I'm left alone with my own self-destructiveness."

In Fosshage's view (1983), "the supraordinate function of dreams is the development, maintenance (regulation), and, when necessary, restoration of psychic processes, structure and organization" (p. 657). The structures we are concerned with are both intrapsychic (or "endopsychic," to use Fairbairn's term) and intersubjective. Elsewhere Fosshage says (1988), "Dreaming mentation not only serves to maintain organization, but contributes to the development of new organizations" (p. 164). By experiencing the dream and then relating it in the session the patient both records her own internal organization and the self-selfobject relationship with her analyst, and also restructures them. She is listening to her own words.

THE PLACE FOR A THEORY OF INTERNAL OBJECT RELATIONS

As I stated at the beginning, Kohut's original formulations were object relational, in that he spoke (1971) of psychic structure formation through "transmuting internalization" in the context of a self-selfobject relationship (p. 49). What is taken in from the selfobject, under conditions of "optimal frustration," to become part of the self is not "the total human context of the personality" but "certain of its specific functions."

Just as Fairbairn had to revise his original hypothesis that only "bad" experiences with the object led to internalization, so self psychological authors have questioned Kohut's assumption that structure formation occurs only in a context of "optimal frustration." Bacal (1985) has indeed proposed the concept of "optimal responsiveness."

Furthermore, Kohut's formulation concentrates on the development of a "cohesive self," with derailment of the process predisposing to a poorly structured, fragmentation-prone self. It is a "deficit" rather than a "conflict" model. Stechler (1983) acknowledged the need for a more inclusive approach when he wrote, "Deficits can be seen as part of the process whereby early failures in the dialectic process become structuralized and through that structural failure exert lasting influence on the later dialectic defined as conflict" (p. 48).

Our model needs to take cognizance of the functions of a *far less than optimally* frustrating selfobject becoming structuralized within the self, to become simultaneously a locus of painful conflict and a soothing bond with a familiar selfobject relation, the sadomasochistic attachment referred to earlier. Such an internal image may be described in Atwood and Stolorow's (1984) terms as "concretization," with the function of maintaining "the organization of experience" (p. 85).

Such concretization products "cannot be fully comprehended psychoanalytically apart from the intersubjective contexts in which they arise and recede" (Atwood and Stolorow, 1984, p. 117). In the vignette of Mrs. R the imagery in her dream was profoundly influenced by the rupture in the self-selfobject bond with her analyst, and her need to tell him about this, to transform psychic pain into more organized discourse. But equally, the metaphors employed in the writing of the vignette could only come from an analyst for whom the ideas of Kohut and Fairbairn have the function of internal idealized selfobjects, helping to organize the experience of being with this patient. The metaphors are thus provisional, more or less useful in furthering an analytic dialogue and in assisting the self-cohesion of the analyst.

Perhaps, then, this is the place for a *theory* of internal object relations—as a portion of the analyst's experiential world that becomes part of his or her contribution to the intersubjective encounter with the patient. Theories of internal object relations in the analytic literature are legion and, often enough, mutually contradictory. We can only ask of any system of metaphors that it be useful, not that it be authoritative. Indeed, with the first clamor for authority its usefulness ends.

REFERENCES

Atwood, G. & Stolorow, R. (1984), *Structures of Subjectivity.* Hillsdale, NJ: The Analytic Press.

Bacal, H. (1985), Optimal responsiveness and the therapeutic process. In: *Progress in Self Psychology, Vol. 1,* ed. A. Goldberg. New York: Guilford, pp. 202–227.

—— & Newman, K. (1990), *Theories of Object Relations: Bridges to Self Psychology.* New York: Columbia University Press.

Beebe, B. & Lachmann, F. (1988), Mother–infant mutual influence and precursors of psychic structure. In: *Frontiers in Self Psychology: Progress in Self Psychology, Vol. 3,* ed. A. Goldberg. Hillsdale, NJ: The Analytic Press, pp. 3–25.

Fairbairn, W. R. D. (1944), Endopsychic structure considered in terms of object relationships. Reprinted in *Psychoanalytic Studies of the Personality.* London: Tavistock, 1952.

Fosshage, J. (1983), The psychological function of dreams: A revised psychoanalytic perspective. *Psychoanal. Contemp. Thought,* 6:641–669.

—— (1988), Dream interpretation revisited. In: *Progress in Self Psychology, Vol. 3,* ed. A. Goldberg. Hillsdale, NJ: The Analytic Press, pp. 161–175.

Goldberg, A. (1994), Farewell to the objective analyst. *Internat. J. Psycho-Anal.,* 75:21–30.

Grotstein, J. (1983), Some perspectives on self psychology. In: *The Future of Psychoanalysis,* ed. A. Goldberg. New York: International Universities Press, p. 172.

Guntrip, H. (1968), *Schizoid Phenomena, Object Relations, and the Self.* London: Hogarth Press.

Jones, E. (1952), Preface to *Psychoanalytic Studies of the Personality,* by W. R. D. Fairbairn. London: Tavistock.

Kernberg, O. (1972), Early ego integration and object relations. *Annals NY Acad. Sci.,* 193:233–247.

Kohut, H. (1970), Narcissism as a resistance and as a driving force in psychoanalysis. Reprinted in *The Search for the Self: Selected Writings of Heinz Kohut 1950–1978*, ed. P. Ornstein. New York: International Universities Press, 1978.

—— (1971), *The Analysis of the Self*. New York: International Universities Press.

Schafer, R. (1976), *A New Language for Psychoanalysis*. New Haven, CT: Yale University Press.

Stechler, G. (1983), Infancy research: A contribution to self psychology. In: *Reflections on Self Psychology*, ed. J. Lichtenberg & S. Kaplan. Hillsdale, NJ: The Analytic Press, pp. 43–48.

Stolorow, R. Brandchaft, B. & Atwood, G. (1987), *Psychoanalytic Treatment: An Intersubjective Approach*. Hillsdale, NJ: The Analytic Press.

Tranter, J. (1992), *The Floor of Heaven*. Sydney, Australia: Collins Angus & Robertson.

Volkan, V. (1976), *Primitive Internalized Object Relations*. New York: International Universities Press.

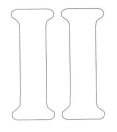

Treatment: Clinical Studies

Chapter 6

Why Can't a Woman Be a Man . . . in the Transference?

Frank M. Lachmann
Sandra Kiersky

Interest in the impact of the analyst's gender in psychoanalytic treatment has revived an interest in distinguishing transference from the "real" factors in the analytic relationship. To some extent this harks back to Greenson's (1967) distinction between transference and the "real" relationship between patient and analyst. Implicit in that distinction was the belief that some aspects of the analytic relationship were distorted by the patient whereas others were free from interference because the patient was healthy enough to retain a "real" relationship with the analyst. However, what may appear to be a "real" relationship to the analyst—and may even be desired by the analyst as a "real connection" —may be far from "realistically perceived" by the patient (Stolorow and Lachmann, 1980). Though "objective" or "realistic" aspects of the analytic encounter, such as the analyst's gender, appearance, or age and the prevailing cultural climate and stereotypes help shape the therapeutic situation, it is their *meaning* to the patient that is assimilated into the imagery and metaphors that organize a patient's subjective life. These meanings are the focus of our chapter.

Transference has been defined as the organization of the totality of the patient's experience in the treatment situation. This refers to all the ways in which the patient's experience of the analytic relationship is shaped by archaically rooted configurations of self and object that unconsciously organize subjective experience (Stolorow and Lachmann, 1984/1985; Stolorow, Atwood and Ross, 1978). At the most general level, transference is an instance of organizing activity through which the patient assimilates (Piaget, 1954) the experience of the treatment into the distinctive, thematic structures of a personal universe. This framework, rather than reducing transference to a regression, distortion, or projection from the past, recognizes the contribution of *both* the ongoing analyst-patient interaction and the patient's repetitive themes or representational configurations (Lachmann and Beebe, 1992; Stolorow, Brandchaft, and Atwood, 1987; Stolorow and Lachmann, 1984/1985). It can, therefore, encompass various dimensions of the transference and the multiple, psychological functions it can serve.

For example, the contributions of the analyst–patient interaction includes similarities and differences in gender between analyst and patient. The subjective, individualized *meanings* of these similarities or differences in gender are then assimilated into the repetitive themes or representational configurations of the patient. No part of the patient–analyst interaction is immune to transferential influence or to the impact of immediate situational factors. All aspects of the analyst–patient encounter are, to some extent, transferentially shaped.

Though patients may respond to us as the men and women we are, this level of the analytic relationship stirs up a variety of social conventions, stereotypes, and characterological ways of relating to same or different-gendered people. For example, a same-sex patient–analyst dyad may stimulate homosexual imagery and associations. In the case to be described, a female patient expressed sensual/sexual longings for her female analyst and thereby used her analyst's gender as an experimental field in which to test out shame-ridden, conflicted aspects of herself.

Alongside these consciously expressed longings, analytic inquiry addresses the patient's repetitive configurations of self and other that shape the transference in accordance with the unconscious meanings that the patient brings to her experience. It is on this level that the patient to be described construed her female analyst as a "phallic" presence, a father with a large, potentially dangerous penis. Her construction was consistent with a need to work through a traumatic experience of early exposure to her father's penis and a later sexual molestation by an unknown man. Thus, it is at this level of the transference that the actual gender of the analyst is relatively uninfluential and a woman can indeed be a man. It is at this level that working through occurs, in that the patient both repeats and attempts to transform unconsciously organized, past traumatic experience. It is also at this level that the analyst's technique and theory have the greatest impact on treatment.

Self psychology, in particular, stresses the necessity for understanding the patient from within his or her subjective experience. This perspective minimizes the risk of disruptions based on the analyst's expectations that the patient relate to him or her as a separate, distinct man or woman. A selfobject tie is engaged that permits attention to be directed to the patient's unconsciously organized themes and rigid, repetitive patterns of organization as they shape the transference and become available for analytic work.

In the present chapter we focus on the patient's construction of a specific representational configuration of herself as frightened and withdrawn with her awesome, rejecting, and potentially sexually dangerous father. The analyst's real "quality," her femaleness, proved to be an obstacle neither to the emergence of this father transference configuration nor to its analysis. Moreover, the analyst neither confronted the patient nor required her to recognize the unconsciously determined "distortions" of the analyst's gender and to relinquish or correct them. Rather, by permitting the patient's repetitive, organizing themes to crystallize in the transference as metaphors, these configurations could be explored with respect to their origins and current functions. and thus, they could be transformed. In this particular case, it became possible to distinguish between the patient's surface transference as an activation of unfulfilled sensual longings toward her mother and an underlying, imperative need to rework, through the transference, traumatic, elaborated oedipal configurations of her idealized father.

The patient, Lisa, was 23 when she began her analysis with Sandra Kiersky. She suffered from a variety of vague symptoms, felt "spacy," as though she was "losing her body," and described difficulties in her work and social life. The early phase of the analysis, which lasted about three years, focused on her fragmented sense of self. It was characterized by severe difficulties in communicating and trusting the analyst and by long stretches of silence. These initial difficulties in communicating decreased as she addressed her fears of abandonment, which were associated with her mother and her maternal grandmother. The decrease of this symptomatology was a consequence of the analyst's persistent efforts to maintain an ambience of acceptance. Maintaining this focus on the patient from within her subjective experience gradually permitted a stable, selfobject tie to be engaged. Disappointments and other ruptures in this tie were addressed from the standpoint of their effect on the patient. During this period, the patient developed the expectation that she would be valued, understood, and accepted. Through the establishment and maintenance of this selfobject tie, some sense of self-cohesion was restored.

During the second phase of the analysis, about four years, Lisa's relationship with her analyst was essentially organized around her experience of her mother and grandmother. Fears of abandonment, the wish to be loved and nurtured as a unique individual, and the dread of overwhelming and depressing her analyst took center stage.

Conspicuously absent from Lisa's associations were references to her relationship with her father, her three older brothers, and her identical twin sister. Early in the analysis, however, she had described her father as the dominant figure of the household, "a brilliant, successful academic more interested in his work and students than in his family," preferring her brothers and contemptuous of the twins since they were "babies . . . and, after all, only girls." She reported that she had been angry with her father for years. They fought a great deal because she would not "obey his orders as everyone else in the family did."

The seventh year of the analysis marked a dramatic shift in Lisa's experience of her analyst. Following the summer vacation, she returned, feeling abandoned and vulnerable, and found it difficult to reconnect with her analyst after the separation. She said, "I felt that you put your needs before mine in going away," and now, "you seem bored and otherwise engaged—probably with your students and more interesting patients." She added, "I feel that you don't want to be pestered by me anymore, especially with how angry and resentful I feel about your absence." She acknowledged that she felt better, but this only made her afraid that when she really got better the analytic relationship would be over and her analyst would "breathe a sigh of relief."

Lisa's reaction after the vacation was promoted by an increasing sense of well-being after the working through of the abandonment fears associated with her mother and grandmother. A series of dreams and fantasies about the analyst then ushered in a third phase of the analysis. She felt that her analyst's life was "busy and full" without her and that she was "extraneous," a description that applied to both her relationship with her father and her twin sister. Therapeutic attention turned more and more to her father's inaccessibility during her growing up years. He was always in his study or out of the house, engaged in some intellectually stimulating activity (probably), she imagined, with women who were exciting and unique.

In the context of describing her feelings about her father, Lisa's maternally directed sensual/sexual longings emerged. She speculated about the analyst, "I imagine what it would be like to be touched by you, by your body." Ostensibly, Lisa referred here to the analyst as a desirable woman. She was conscious of not wanting her analyst to have any other relationships, particularly sexual ones. These fantasies, Lisa lamented, were arousing and upsetting, for they evoked longings that she felt could never be fulfilled.

The comparisons between Lisa's experiences with her father and those with her mother supported the impression that her longings, though manifestly along maternal lines, were organized by her according to unfulfilled needs and conflicted wishes associated with her father. She asked, "How can I stop creating this feeling that you are like my father? That you are not on my side. Talking about it is hard, because it puts me into the position I'm creating and want to escape. When I was describing last time the girl I didn't like at work, I felt you laughed at me . . . I said she was whiny and pompous and I felt that you were thinking, she's just like me . . . I continue to kick you. If I were a baby and you were trying to hold me, I'd just keep kicking. I'm always on the defensive. I don't trust you completely and it seems bad to me. I don't want to be in love with you and yet I have this feeling. It seems so immature. Actually, I don't want to feel anything about you at all. I have images of you in your pink dress and in your chair . . . and distant, just like my father. I just feel insignificant, as though it doesn't matter what I do, and I feel that with you, too."

Sometime after this session, Lisa learned that, because her mother had been severely depressed after the birth of the twins, her father had actually done much of the infant caretaking, and it is likely that the image of the "kicking, whiny baby," though elaborated over time, recalled a sensory/kinesthetic configuration of experience from this early time. As a twin, Lisa felt a constant disruption of contact when attention was paid to the second baby. During this period of the analysis, the analyst underlined how difficult it was for Lisa to feel special and unique, to feel held. Lisa added that she desperately wanted to be the one and only.

As these connections were integrated, Lisa's transference was shaped by an upsurge and intensification of sexual feelings and associated concerns that her body was not desirable. She became preoccupied with an intense wish to "turn the analyst on" and a fear that if she succeeded, the analyst would become very angry. She desperately wanted to be noticed in some way other than as a kicking, whiny baby. She imagined that this baby was her father's enduring characterization of her, one that marked her as eternally undesirable and that she felt helpless to alter.

The kicking, whiny baby metaphor contained the longing to be taken care of by her mother and the humiliating, enduring relationship with her father. In her characterological whining and kicking, she protected herself against the dreaded, anticipated rejection by her father. The exploration and working through of this configuration permitted it to recede and be transformed. Lisa then expressed her desire to woo the "woman with the pencil."

The analyst's possession of a pencil, taking notes during the sessions, distinguished her, for Lisa, as "powerful," "self-confident," "brilliant," "dazzling," and most of all, "well equipped." Lisa felt the analyst was comfortable with her body and she wished she could be, too. She wanted something from the analyst, perhaps the pencil. Lisa wondered if she could ever have a pencil of her own. She felt the analyst remained "indifferent" behind her pencil, creating an unbridgeable gap between them. In the context of describing these fantasies, Lisa suddenly became alarmed. She feared that her longings and sexual feelings would not be acknowledged. She wanted her analyst to find her body desirable and feared she would be looked upon as presumptuous. The analyst commented that Lisa expected her longings and sexual feelings to be neither acknowledged nor understood. As with her father, Lisa could not believe that she could have any effect on her analyst.

These sessions revived memories from Lisa's adolescence and her first attempts to enter the mysterious world of men and women. The metaphor of the "woman with the pencil" combined a number of themes: an upsurge of sexual feelings, longings for someone of her own to be with, and her first serious wish to be a writer. All three themes were rooted in her adolescence. The "pencil" metaphor contained rich, sensual bodily memories and longings and the added element of ambitious and creative strivings.

Lisa recalled her father teasing and mocking her about the shy young men who came to take her out on dates. She felt humiliated in her attempts to be attractive to them and soon withdrew completely. She imagined becoming a famous writer and having safer sexual encounters with women. She stopped dating and turned to fantasizing, which continued until the time her analysis began.

As Lisa recalled her humiliating experiences with her father, she considered withdrawing from treatment. She explained, "I'll always want something from you that I can't get and I understand that it comes from my relationship with my father, but it's still unbearable. What I want is my own life. I have a body, but I don't own it." The analyst interpreted this statement to mean that Lisa again feared being ridiculed about any attempt on her part to make a life of her own and express herself sexually.

Lisa remained in analysis and proceeded to describe sexual feelings toward a girlfriend. The significance of this richly determined theme at this point in the analysis was interpreted as a tentative test to determine whether she was safe to venture into the world of sensuality and sexuality in whatever way she chose. Would the analyst view her current forays as derisively and critically as had her father? She then brought up the following dream:

> I had to go to the bathroom. It was as if I could see that part of my body and there was a certain pleasure in not going. When I did, it came out and I smushed it back between my legs. I guess it was a masturbation dream. I woke up and didn't feel sexual but, for some reason, I decided

to masturbate. I had been to the farmer's market and bought a lot of vegetables and flowers and I also got an eggplant that, when I saw it, I thought it was kind of phallic . . . and I used it as an object. I was aware of feeling like it was something entering me very deep.

The analyst inquired about any accompanying fantasy and Lisa responded:

There was, afterwards. It occurred to me that it seemed like my father's penis because it was a long and big object to go into me. I've always had the notion, because he's very tall and very big, that he's bigger than most men . . . well, this is embarrassing, but bigger than all men actually and it made me think of little boys comparing themselves to their fathers.

The analyst commented that it would be hard for little boys to compete with the biggest pencil in the world. Lisa laughed and agreed. A shift in the material followed. The metaphor of "the woman with the pencil" faded, and the sessions were filled with Lisa's desire to excite the analyst sexually.

After a session, a few weeks later, Lisa stopped in the waiting room on her way out and asked if she might borrow a particular word-processing program from the analyst to copy in her computer. She wondered if the analyst's disk would fit into her disk drive. The analyst suggested to Lisa that she might raise this issue at the next session.

Lisa began the next session by describing how excited she became after the session. She felt "thrilled" that she had been able to "get" the analyst "outside" her office. She felt she had "crossed a line or taboo" and could not stop thinking about it. She wondered, "What if you did give me your diskettes? What would it mean? Would they fit? Do we have the same drive or are they different?"

The analysis had entered the heady world of diskettes and drives, a world in which anatomy and prohibitions, desires and taboos were prominent. Interpretation remained at the level of Lisa's metaphor, Lisa's concern about equipment—hers and the analyst's. Did the analyst have equipment that Lisa did not have but needed? Would the analyst give it to her or lend it to her? What about the size of the analyst's equipment? If Lisa tried to fit some part of the analyst's equipment into her own, would there be any damage? Lisa recognized the metaphors that she and her analyst shared as useful in reconstructing central themes in her development that reappeared as rigid, configurations in the transference. These were formulated as feelings of fright and awe in relation to her large, phallic, potentially hurtful father; her sexual curiosity and fear of being damaged; and the wish to be as exciting to her father as he had been to her.

Exploration of these themes first enabled Lisa to recall seeing her father in their bathroom urinating and her amazement at his size and the sight of him. She then recovered in detail the experience of being molested in the woods near their summer home. One afternoon she had gone, on her own, to have a bicycle tire repaired. She met a boy with a dog who asked her to come into the woods with him. He would show her something interesting. The boy reminded her of her brother and so she felt safe. She also remembered having felt excited and curious about what he wanted to show her. He pushed her up against a tree, took off her pants and his own and jammed his penis against her. When he ejaculated, she recalled thinking it looked like milk and wondered what it was. She thought his penis was gigantic also, like her father's. She was afraid that she would be hurt or damaged in some way but she also felt excited. It was not clear to her how she had been bad, but she felt she was. She was afraid to tell her parents, especially her father, about the molestation. She thought he would blame her for what had happened. In the analysis, she recounted the experience anxiously, clearly worried that her analyst would judge her as well.

Lisa said that she had put the experience away after a few days but recalled that some years later, when she was about nine she became depressed, agitated, and hauntedy memories of the event. It was then that she began to have fights at home, especially with her father, and was labeled the family troublemaker.

Following the recovery of the details of the sexual molestation, Lisa described herself as the "Berlin Wall" coming down. She no longer needed the protective barriers she had built between herself and others. The repressed memory of the molestation had been recovered with its associated affects and had been integrated into broader, more evolved configurations of self and other. More importantly, however, the "father" transference had remained intact, which enabled her to work through the anticipated disgust and shame at her revelation.

The working through of the "father" transference set the stage for a dramatic change in Lisa's relationship with her father. They were beginning to enjoy each other's company. She felt more comfortable with men and with her analyst. Her interests turned to a young man she had met and, with whom, she now became seriously involved. The transference shifted to concerns that the analyst might feel abandoned and angry with her because Lisa now loved someone else. As Lisa's acceptance of her satisfying love relationship became more firm and her prohibiting tie to her father was reworked, her competitive and ambitious strivings were freed. She began to sell some articles she had written and soon was able to shift from occasional, temporary work as a typist to a stimulating, challenging job with a magazine.

As the end of the seventh year of the analysis drew to a close, Lisa recovered her first *positive* memory of an experience with her father. She recalled, in first grade, tearing up her homework while working on it. She became very upset and her father took the time to sit with her and paste it back together so that she would not be embarrassed in school the next day. She called this an occasion in which her father protected her from a trauma.

DISCUSSION AND CONCLUSION

We have described the analysis of a young woman who felt irredeemably damaged and fated to be excluded by and from her father's life and world. She depicted her father as a sexually awesome man who was rejecting and critical of her sexual and intellectual development. These configurations were traumatically amplified by an experience of sexual molestation at about age seven.

The fact that the analyst in this treatment was a woman did not interfere with the emergence or analysis of a sexually complex paternal transference. The patient's erotic feelings toward the analyst, though assimilating her actual gender, were based on her need to rework repressed configurations of awe, fear, and sexual desire toward her father. The patient's reactions to the analyst as a woman became part of her conscious associative network before the emergence of the paternal transference and maternal transference themes appeared. These were initially organized around the patient's fear that her needs and desires would burden and "overwhelm" the analyst, whom she experienced at that time as "vulnerable, soft, self-sacrificing, and warm." Lisa described feeling "stirred" by the analyst's smell and wanted to be "held and cherished" by her as a unique individual without fear of "being dropped" and "left alone." These configurations drew on Lisa's experience as a twin.

Thus, the predominating metaphors of the two transferences were quite distinct. The maternal transference was characterized by sensual longings and fears that her desires for sensual and bodily experiences would be denied her because of a preferred rival. They were indeed associated with her mother, and she used the analyst's gender as an opportunity to disconfirm grim beliefs about her unacceptability (Weiss and Sampson, 1986). These issues were also rooted in aspects of her experience with her father where her unacceptability received continuous confirmation. In relation to the analyst, she tested whether she would again be deemed unacceptable.

Through the analysis of these metaphors, central, representational configurations of self and other could be worked through. Lisa expanded the "kicking baby" into a challenging adult, the idealized "pencil" was transformed into a desire to be a writer, and the "disk drive" metaphor evolved into a sense of herself as a desiring and desirable, sexual woman.

SUMMARY

Interest in the effect of the analyst's "real" qualities on the therapeutic relationship has led to distinguishing transference from the "real" relationship. We define transference as an instance of organizing activity and hold that although "objective" aspects help shape the therapeutic situation, they are assimilated into the imagery and metaphors of the patient's subjective life. When the transference unfolds without interference from the analyst's need to have his or her "real" qualities acknowledged, the patient's invariant organizing principles crystallize as a foreground dimension of the transference as in the case described here. A female patient transformed her female analyst into an idealized "phallic" presence. The analyst's "femaleness" was neither an obstacle to the transference analysis nor used by the analyst as a "reality" the patient had to recognize in order to correct her "distortions." The case also illustrates the therapeutic value in distinguishing between the patient's maternal and oedipal transference love.

REFERENCES

Greenson, R. (1967), *The Technique and Practise of Psychoanalysis*. New York: International Universities Press.

Lachmann, F. & Beebe, B. (1992), Representational and selfobject transferences: A developmental perspective. In: *New Therapeutic Visions: Progress in Self Psychology, Vol. 8*. Hillsdale, NJ: The Analytic Press, pp. 3–15.

Piaget, J. (1954), *The Construction of Reality in the Child*. New York: Basic Books.

Stolorow, R., Atwood, G. & Ross, J. (1978), The representational world in psychoanalytic therapy. *Internat. Rev. Psycho-Anal.*, 5:247–356.

—— Brandchaft, B. & Atwood, G. (1987), *Psychoanalytic Treatment: An Intersubjective Approach*. Hillsdale, NJ: The Analytic Press.

—— & Lachmann, F. (1980), *Psychoanalysis of Developmental Arrests*. New York: International Universities Press.

—— & —— (1984/85), Transference: The future of an illusion. *The Annual of Psychoanalysis*, 12/13:19–38. New York: International Universities Press.

Weiss, E. & Sampson, H. (1986), *The Psychoanalytic Process*. New York: Guilford.

Chapter 7

The Complementary Function of Individual and Group Psychotherapy in the Management and Working Through of Archaic Selfobject Transferences

Margaret Baker

There are people who are unable to risk the development of an archaic selfobject transference, because it will overwhelm a precariously maintained self structure. Kohut (1977) has commented on this and has suggested that when this kind of patient withdraws from therapy in an obviously "premature" fashion, it may be best to respect this wish. For him or her, continued immersion in an archaic selfobject transference may provoke an irreversible regression and loss of essential, basic self-organization. It is as if either a successful and regressed selfobject transference or an empathically failed selfobject transference will overburden the patient's capacity to process what is happening. Perhaps most of these patients will not withdraw from therapy. Instead, they will continue and distance the transference in a way that does not really offer the potential for genuine psychological growth. It will be as if they are in therapy, as if something like a selfobject transference has occurred, but they will, in fact, be presenting a false self (Winnicott, 1965) for analysis.

Even the most astute clinician may be unable to break through this defensive posture. It has, however, been my experience that some of these patients may be able to make surprising gains in combined individual and group psychotherapy. Because of a peculiar combination of more directly gratifying and more indirect vicarious interactions, the group may offer a variety of selfobject experiences that these people can both permit and sustain.

There are frequent interactions among group members that satisfy mirroring, idealizing and twinship needs. As the members provide these needs for each other, some may vicariously grasp what is happening with other members. As this distance provides safety, they may gradually internalize new possibilities for interactions, behaviors, motivations, and affect management.

I understand the treatment process as an effort to reformulate one's existing intrapsychic patterns of organizing experience. For example, if we believe that people are basically out for themselves and will exploit us, that organizing principle will indelibly color what we perecive in life. These sorts of preconscious or unconscious schemas will organize our expectations and behavior. One goal of treatment is to expand our organizational perspectives and come to realize that there are other possibilites than those that we have been ruled by. Any form of treatment that accomplishes this goal seems worthwhile, even if the results are theoretically incomplete.

This chapter will attempt to understand the usefulness of adding group therapy to individual therapy when the resistance to exploration of archaic selfobject transferences is truncated by the habitual defensive posture of the patient. After introducing the patient, Joseph, I will present the definition of three qualitatively different types of selfobject experiences that helped clarify the patient's subjective experience. I will then outline how the complementary process of individual and group therapy worked together to deepen and elucidate the archaic selfobject transferences in individual therapy that had created the initial therapeutic impasse. I will then describe how the patient developed an archaic transference, what therapeutic gains he made, and how he worked through the transference. I have included samples of the patient's own written account of his experience in therapy, in keeping with self psychology's emphasis on subjective experience.

Joseph came to therapy when his wife threatened to break up the relationship if he did not. Their marriage of more than 10 years had produced two children and was the perfect picture of what a family should be. However, Joseph's flirtation with his secretary had become problematic.

When I first saw Joseph I was impressed with his high level of anxiety, his need for intellectualization and control, and his apparent need to comply and be viewed as a cooperative, nice guy. Seemingly eager, he would do very well in treatment, I thought, once his anxiety diminished and he settled into the process. Although he was extremely responsible about coming to sessions, it became clear during the initial phase of treatment that his anxiety was not being ameliorated, nor was he able to use the sessions to help him calm down. He was distracted and unable to focus on what he wanted to say when sitting face to face. He was relieved when I suggested using the couch. At first, this helped him focus better. We worked twice a week for two years this way. My hope was that he would grow to develop an archaic transference to me spontaneously. In fact, this did happen. He became exquisitely sensitive to me and felt he had to comply with what he thought I wanted him to be. At the same time he resented it. My responses to him were experienced as attempts to control him. Efforts to analyze his affects in the transference met with intellectualized rebuffs and emotional distancing. What he said he wanted from me were revelations about my own experiences that were similar to his. It was not enough to interpret his need for twinship responses; he wanted my personal confession. The fact that he wanted something he knew was out of bounds of treatment, just as his secretary was out of bounds in his marriage, did not stop him from feeling that it was only his experiencing my feelings that would create a "big bang" event for him. This would function to change or sooth his internal struggle. He was locked in to his habitual defensive posture with me. My attempts to be optimally responsive were not breaking through his defensive shield. His immediate needs for reassurance and twinship seemed so intense, just as a drowning man needs air, he could not do anything but try to breathe.

He feared being retraumatized in his "dread to repeat" developmental disappointments. Traumas and disappointments had heightened in therapy, particularly in the mirroring sector of his transference. His fanatically religious, scrupulous, and depressed mother had never been attuned to her bright and energetic son. (Although his father was a more benign force and offered him a basically kind, masculine personality to idealize, he was afraid of his wife, was given to sudden outbursts of rage, and worked long hours.) My approach to Joseph's seemingly intractable fear was to empathize with him and understand, clarify, and communicate that understanding to him. My countertransference included the belief that in order for him to reorganize his internal experience, he needed to spontaneously develop and reinstate his unmet archaic needs with me for understanding and interpretation. Although he had developed an idealizing and mirroring transference merger with me, he remained unable to use it for effective exploration of his structural deficits. He may well have sensed my commitment to therapeutic beliefs as he experienced his mother's fanatical religious beliefs, with the anticipation that once again he would not be heard.

Joseph exhibited several traits that seemed to interfere with his benefiting from his archaic transferences: his automatic distancing of affects through intellectualization, his constant anxiety, his extreme sensitivity to feeling controlled and diminished, and his demand that I share my personal feelings with him. I felt that I was trying very hard to understand him and that what I did understand was accurate. It was frustrating that what should have led to progress in fact resulted in an impasse.

At this point I thought that adding concurrent group therapy might be useful. There he might find actual reassurance and twinship experiences that he seemed to crave so intensely. What was available in individual therapy was principally an opportunity to elucidate and analyze these needs. Gratification was limited to the experience of being understood. He seemed to need some level of gratification beyond what was available in individual therapy. It was as if he simply could not operate without *actual* twinship experiences.

I considered whether I was acting out in the countertransference to ameliorate my frustration and helplessness. I suggested the group experience when I was reasonably convinced I was doing it for him, not me. He readily and enthusiastically agreed to be in the group.

THEORETICAL CONSIDERATIONS

Although Kohut introduced the concept of the selfobject, other more contemporary self psychological thinkers such as Lichtenberg, Lachmann, and Fosshage (1992) and Lichtenberg (personal communication) prefer the term *selfobject experience*. Many interactions with others have essentially no impact on self organization. They neither enhance or solidify self-experience nor do they complicate or weaken it. By contrast, other interactions are *self-defining experiences*. Because of them the sense of self may be enhanced, calmed, envigorated, consolidated, or usefully reorganized. These self-defining experiences are *selfobject experiences*. Other experiences may disorganize, deplete, agitate, confuse, or perniciously reorganize the self. The term *self-disruptive experiences* has been reserved for them. An example is when a person experiences narcissistic injury or misattunement from a person who has salience for them.

I would like to propose the following distinctions amongst selfobject experiences.[1] First are *transforming selfobject experiences*. They are generated in authentic interactions with parents and close friends or through creative activities and effective psychotherapy. They lead to intrapsychic consolidation, reorganization, and meaningful and lasting transformations. Transforming selfobject experiences need not be rare, but they are not routine. An example would be when patients realize emotionally that efforts at trying to help them were geared toward supporting their efforts for self-development rather than attempts to control them or force them to conform to therapists' expectations. Second are *restorative selfobject experiences*. These are interactions that restore a sense of self-cohesion in a way that is regularly necessary, but they neither lead to growth nor have destructive elements. An example is the normal encouragement from a spouse after a difficult day. Third are *maintaining selfobject experiences*. These interactions maintain a self-cohesion in an ongoing way. They neither restore nor dismantle the self, and they are usually not obvious until they are missing. An example is a particular daily routine. Fourth, *chimerical selfobject experiences* are interactions that offer temporary relief from painful experiences of self-fragmentation and self-depletion, but hold within them inevitable deleterious consequences. An example would be the temporary relief provided by alcohol, drugs, or compulsive sex.

Group therapy creates opportunities for a wide variety of selfobject experiences. There are possibilities for the patient to obtain overt, direct, and often needed selfobject experiences from group members. Less obviously, when group members are able to watch others interact, they may be able to vicariously observe others offering and receiving selfobject experiences. They are able to participate one step removed. These interactions may feel safer because the patient is not directly involved. From this more protected distance, there is less chance that interactions will risk alteration of self organization or the need to control beyond the patient's ability to tolerate. They can thus gradually move into more direct selfobject experiences.

Adding group to individual therapy may help elucidate a person's archaic self needs in a variety of ways, and this may clarify the selfobject transferences as they become manifest in individual sessions. This may be true particularly for patients who are afraid of merger and archaic rage, because the group gives them the opportunity to feel these affects less claustrophobically. Seeing the therapist interact in the group can build trust in her authenticity. Because the group itself offers the oppor-

---

[1]These distinctions among selfobject experiences were formulated in conjunction with Howard S. Baker, M.D.

tunity for the direct generation of a variety of selfobject experiences, considerable self-consolidation can result. Because of added resilience, and because future group interactions can be counted on for self-restoration, it will be possible for some patients to risk the deeper levels of self examination in which more archaic transferences can be elucidated.

The group provides opportunities to observe the patient in entirely new ways. For example, what became heightened for me in the group was the intensity, pervasiveness, and seeming inability for Joseph to find even a moment's relief from his anxiety. His hyperarousal was always there, infused in every statement and move he made, much like a baby with colic. The constant intensity of his anxiety was startling in the group. In individual sessions I had become so accustomed to and immersed in it that it had lost its heightened impact.

Joseph's anxiety, his scattered patterns of communication, and his illegible half-printing, half-writing style placed his early erratic school history in a new light, leading me to suspect he might have Attention Deficit Disorder. (When he was evaluated for ADD, the examining psychiatrist agreed he had it, and this also opened up new treatment possibilities.)

The therapist may have new eyes in the group for reasons more subtle than the opportunity for different observations. Just as the group can distance the patient from intolerable transferences, it also distances the therapist. Interactions that develop between group members can contain transferences that are initially experienced as unbearable in a one-to-one situation. The lessened affective charge is then more manageable. It is, of course, also true that this can so diminish the intensity as to alter its essence, but I think that a thoughtful combination of the two modalities can afford a particularly helpful dialectic of transference and counter-transference intensities.

Doing group therapy from a self psychological perspective focuses on the generation of self-relevant experiences within the object relational matrix of the group. Aspects of the interactions, whether between members or between a member and the leader, will interact with the intrapsychic structuring of the members (including the leader); this will determine whether and in what way the relationship can be used to generate selfobject experiences. Real growth can occur quite independently of the therapist. But she is afforded good opportunities to observe resistances and the consequences of both self-defining and self-dismantling experiences. These can be worked through in the group and during individual therapy. Making reference to group process during individual sessions can be useful in itself and as a means to soften resistances and defenses.

EXTENDED CLINICAL ILLUSTRATION

Extensive clinical material about Joseph follows and is intended to illustrate the theoretical points just made.

Joseph's experience in the group opened selfobject opportunities for him immediately. The members responded to him readily. He was elated by their acceptance and literally thrilled to hear that the issues the other group members were struggling with were similar to his. At the same time he had difficulty taking in the group's positive feedback directly. Joseph writes about what happened to him in the group:

> Peter said to me and another person, "You are a good man, You're a good man, You're a good man." I couldn't quite let that in . . . I came closer to feeling this for myself when the same person that said this to me said it to another group member. The monitoring in me could almost see the person it was said to as me and the reassurance in "You're a good man" rang true for both him and me. When it was said to me, I was too anxious to be able to let it in in the same way. I would like to think that perhaps by "knowing" myself better through individual and group "processes" that are in so many ways difficult and frustrating for me, I can come to "know the good" in me and, then, through that "knowing," to love the good. I suppose I'll know when that happens because the monitor will let me feel the, "You're a good man" when it is said to me again.

Joseph communicates in his own words the trouble he has letting any emotionally laden feedback affect him. Despite his longing for it, his habitual resistance through the rational monitor filters communications directed at him.

To reiterate, Joseph's inadequate early mirroring experiences, his lack of other adequate adults to turn to in childhood, and his constitutional vulnerability as manifested in his Attention Deficit Disorder made it difficult for him to experience compliments as real. A secondhand experiencing of similar interactions could be observed without excessive stimulation. A new concept began to emerge: people can compliment and enjoy one another and honestly mean what they say!

Joseph was unable to open himself to an archaic selfobject transference, fearing he would be overwhelmed both by the intensity of his longing and by the excitement of being enjoyed. He could not trust in his intrapsychic capacities to contain these affects, and he was convinced that I would eventually disappoint him. On the other hand, not establishing such a transference was failure. This Scylla and Charybdis left an impossibly narrow passage of safety, and Joseph would periodically wish to withdraw from therapy for fear that further involvement would risk his destruction, or in our terms, precipitate an irreversible, regressive loss of self-cohesion. When, however, he could safely observe others generating selfobject experiences, he was able to grasp new potentials at a safe distance. Paradoxically, the danger of regression was contained both through a more distant stance in the individual transference and through direct participation in actual "here and now" group interactions.

The act of coming to the group on a weekly basis would be considered a maintaining selfobject experience. In the group, Joseph most often experienced self-restorative selfobject experiences by having his need for twinship responded to and gratified. He began to see how bothered he was if another person did not feel exactly the way he felt. The temporary relief he got from the group's understanding and intermittent gratification of his twinship needs maintained his self cohesion but did not expand it. When I commented about how disappointed he must feel when others did not share his feelings, he reacted by telling me I was distant, superior, and critical of him. Similar empathic ruptures in individual sessions still could throw him back into his habitual defensive posture, but this happened with less intensity and for less time. When he was just in individual therapy, his frustration would become so overwhelming we would get locked in an impasse.

A particular event became a transforming selfobject experience. A woman member talked about one of her struggles, and Joseph related that he also struggled with the same issue. When she was understanding to him, he let down his guard enough to say that he worked hard to intellectualize and distance the support she and others gave him. To feel anything directly was too terrifying. When he got groupwide empathy about his terror, he began to recognize what he lost when he held himself at an emotional distance. His resistance to participating emotionally in the therapeutic process or making his needs known started to diminish. The event potentiated a genuine internal reorganization and thus acted as a transforming selfobject experience.

An example of a self-disruptive experience occurred during a group session when one of the men, Peter, who likes and identifies with Joseph, confronted him. Peter told Joseph that he talked just to fill up time, adding that Joseph wasn't "really there." Joseph was deflated by Peter's criticism. In the following individual session, Joseph then praised my masterfulness in the group as a way of maintaining selfobject relatedness with me in the absence of Peter's support. He talked about Becky (his secretary, with whom he almost had an affair) and sex and how he felt loved when he thought of how much she enjoyed and initiated sexual expression. Their relatively raw sexual encounter was intense and yet safely distant. Although ultimately dangerous and potentially destructive, it was the best he could do; he attempted to use the memory to maintain his self-cohesion. This was not enough to prevent his decline into a fragmented state, a self-disruptive experience.

The group and I tried to reach out to him. He could not take in our empathic concern. He stayed isolated and withdrawn for several days. Other members' attempts at understanding his feelings during the next week's group session helped restore his relatedness to Peter and the group as a whole.

Joseph could, in the moment, feel safer when he held himself separate and apart and when he was so anxious he couldn't focus on what he felt internally. He also tended to develop eczema and back pain when he was unusually stressed. These manuevers kept him in homeostatic balance, but at a high cost. These are examples of chimerical selfobject experiences.

As Joseph became increasingly involved in the group process over the ensuing months, the quality of his selfobject transferences in individual sessions became more negative. His fear and distrust surfaced more directly. He told me how menacing I was. I did not greet him warmly. I was a smug, distant "know-it-all" who diminished him. When I said I held the ultimate threat for him in his fear that I would be critical and judgmental about his feelings, he agreed and sighed with relief. In contrast, during the group sessions he had much more of a sense of my warmth and empathy. He saw concern in my face, not menace. He felt both calmed and stimulated by the group members' presence, although his anxiety and obsessive concern about the group were never far from consciousness. As he said in his own words:

Until the morning of the group thoughts about the group are never very far away. I think in terms of "I'll say this and get into this" or I would like to say X but I don't think I can. "I guess I'll hide out this week and hope that X just comes out spontaneously in some group session." In this thought process I think of the individual members of the group and what their reactions to me will be. I actually practice little speeches in my mind and picture myself saying it and the reactions. As group time approaches I can't seem to help thinking about what I want to say or bring up. I try not to do this because I enjoy the spontaneity of doing it in the group. I try to just tuck the thoughts away—even though they come to mind as little essays—with the idea that they are "there" and they will come out in one way or another at some point, if not in the group session . . . I drive the hour back to work and think, usually what happened in the group. Sometimes I think about something that happened and see something that happened and see something I didn't see before. Mostly I'm trying to figure out why I had the reaction I had. I will often be pretty hard on myself and feel like an "idiot" for something I said in the group or a reaction I had. If I catch myself getting too analytical about it, though, I will turn on the radio or a tape (I'm not sure why I resist getting too analytical about it). It is often at this point that I go through the "I'm quitting therapy," thought process, which is never very far out of my mind. Interestingly, it's always the individual therapy I am most "sure" I want to quit and it has to become extreme for me to include group with the "process" that I want to give up on. When I do my rational mind seizes on the artificiality of the group process—coming together with people you don't know and paying money to pour out your feelings, emotions, problems, etc. "IT DOESN'T MAKE SENSE."

Joseph shows us how intellectualized, anxious, ambivalent, and self-critical he is. He is afraid of turning on himself for not "doing it right" and he resents the pressure to have to "get it right." He does and he doesn't want to think about the group. He is frightened his thoughts may evoke feelings, particularly negative ones, that will get out of control. The "holding" function of the group allows Joseph to make meaningful connections to group members, even though, as illustrated by what he wrote previously, it is hard for him to readily take in what the group has to offer.

Inevitable disruptions of selfobject relatedness happened in group sessions as they had in individual sessions. When this occurred, Joseph experienced varying degrees of fragmentation. At these junctures he could then use his relationship with me in individual sessions to restore him as he worked to bridge a rupture with someone in the group. The complementary shifting from group to individual selfobject transferences can help patients maintain some type of selfobject connection.

The group has functioned to soften the impasse Joseph and I were in. It has provided the opportunity for varieties of selfobject relatedness that are not as conflictual as experiencing the archaic transferences and his resistances to them in individual therapy. To reiterate, one goal in combined treatment is to provide enough selfobject experiences in the group to fortify a person's ability to tolerate a more threatening, archaic transference in individual sessions. Another goal is to provide a safe place for the working through process if it is not possible to sustain all the working through in individual therapy.

With the group's added support, Joseph continued to surface his experience of me in individual sessions as menacing, imperious, and detached. At the same time, he allowed himself to be somewhat touched by my interpretations about his unmet childhood needs for mirroring from his rigid and unattuned mother. He has self-protectively developed an aversion to his own neediness, as he writes:

There is a ME, ME, ME, phenomenon that operates for me in the group and in individual therapy. It is some sort of fear of selfishness. In the group it manifests itself as a reluctance to take up the group's time with my musings. . . . pushing me in the other direction is to speak up and say whatever is on my mind is, I think, what I call the "rules." It is what you are supposed to say in group—"say, feel, emote." So what I say is, of course, partly a function of how strongly I feel something (or how sure I am that I "really" feel it) but partly a function of maintaining a balance between the "ME, ME, ME" pull and the "rules" telling me to speak up. . . . I don't trust that "experiencing my feelings" will lead anywhere useful. This probably keeps me from being able to experience them fully.

I just sit there monitoring my thoughts and emotions. I no sooner "feel" or "think" something than the monitor (the "me" above "me" that watches "me") starts asking, "What does this feeling mean?"; "Am I really feeling it?"; "Am I making this up?" Then when a feeling "takes over," the monitor panics, "You are really scared, what does this mean?" "Such a strong emotion." "This is dangerous!" "This is stupid, why do I come here?" "I can tell from X's look he thinks I'm an idiot. No. Calm down, you're projecting (or something similar)."

I suppose I'm describing anxiety or fear. When I become the center of attention this feeling of needing to control myself becomes pretty intense even as the monitor is telling me "Just relax, you can do this, it shouldn't be threatening," some other voice is sending the "This is really danger-ous" message. The net effect of all this is exhausting and "claustropho-bic," in the sense that all of these conflicting thoughts seem to close in on me and sort of make me paralyzed in a numb sort of way.

By maintaining a chronic level of high anxiety, Joseph removes him-self from the substantive content of his internal war. He focuses his attention on putting out the fires his anxiety lights up, on arguing with himself and being self-effacing and nice. As much as his archaic needs for mirroring push to the fore, he defends against them. Even though Joseph regards his desires as selfish and immature, he is beginning to experience these old, deep longings.

During an individual session, Joseph reported the following dream: He was back in school, unprepared and neglecting his studies because he was pursuing other activities. Then he was looking at two regal women with white hair walking their dogs. One of them was having a heart attack. The other woman pulled back on the leash and began attacking her dog, killing it. His associations included that he just lies there and blabbers away and it wouldn't matter who sat in my chair, he just rambles on. I say, "You mean I'm just sitting here detached?" And he says how he wishes that I would jump in and organize him the way the group members do. They keep him from getting so lost (he fails to mention that when, on occasion, I have done that he feels controlled). I suggested the issue was the power he felt I had over him as he experi-enced me as detached while he, at the other extreme, was hot wired to me. He agreed. I think he was also talking about his detachment from me and his fear that my power to hurt him was so great he could not risk experiencing his archaic dependence on me.

In the following session he talked about his own desires and how hopeless he was. He dreamed of an old man deteriorating, never having any time for anything but his family. I said I thought it was hard for him to consider his own needs in the face of others' demands, especially when he wasn't sure what he wanted. I added that he wished I could prevent his decline and lead him out into the light. He started to cry.

In his idealizing selfobject transference to me, Joseph wanted me to define what he wants empathically and accurately, so that he experiences through me what he feels, thus making it legitimate and at the same time not losing the protection of his merged relationship to me. This contrasts to his mother, who would consider his needs self-indulgent enough to lead him to hell.

In a subsequent individual session he talked about his mother and her rigid, distancing, religious attitudes. I kept saying how difficult she must have been for him. With no response to what I said, I asked him if he had any reactions to my comments. He said he felt very detached. He then remembered how in awe of his children his father was and that his mother never conveyed that delight. (Perhaps he felt that I also didn't praise him enough.) In any event, he cried deeply as he talked of his father. In the following session he was able to talk about how angry and frustrated he is that his mother is and was so anxious and inaccessible. She leaves him anxious and abandoned. His declaration of negative feelings was expressed with little confounding anxiety and distance. As a result of his deepening selfobject transference Joseph seemed to respond more positively to his wife's caring. He became less critical of her shortcomings. Increasingly, he saw his own needs as legitimate. Other gains he had sustained and consolidated were a deeper involvement with his children, a more aggressive and self directed attitude at work, and an increasing desire and ability to develop male friendships.

After eight months of being in the group and at the time he was allowing himself to feel his archaic mirroring transference to me in individual therapy more freely, he said he wanted to terminate individual therapy in June rather than the following January. He had fixed the January date in his mind a year before. I asked why he changed to June. He replied that he was pleased with his progress. However, if he continued to feel so dependent on me he would be with me forever. He'd better go sooner than later to avoid being overwhelmed by this consuming dependency. He then reported a dream where a closet was about to explode open with its contents. Panicked, he worked feverishly to put the key in the lock. Against the formidable weight of the closet's contents, he managed to get the door locked and was once again safe.

Despite the fact that he understood what the dream meant to him (part of himself had to be blocked off, it was probably sexual and even though he knew he "should" deal with it, he did not want to break up his family or lose what he already had) he had made up his mind to finish in June, not January. From my perspective, he had finally trusted me enough to allow the interpretations of his archaic longings to evoke a meaningful emotional response in him. As he experienced this newly evolved archaic attachment to me, though, something in him signaled flight over continued involvement.

In *The Restoration of the Self,* Kohut (1977) talks about what may result when the mirroring selfobject, in this case Joseph's mother, is not able to respond adequately. He writes:

> Not only must he (Mr. M.) have been traumatized by the repeated failure of his mother to respond appropriately to his needs during the preverbal period, but behind these layers of frustration there hovered always a nameless preverbal depression, apathy, sense of deadness, and diffuse rage that related to the primordial trauma of his life. [My patient, Joseph, reported that he had had colic, was hyperactive, and had then undiagnosed Attention Deficit Disorder. As an adult, one of his presenting complaints was preoccupation with and catastrophizing of hypochondriacal symptoms.] Such primal states, however, can neither be recalled through verbalized memories, as can traumata occurring after speech has developed, nor expressed through psychosomatic symptoms, as can the more organized rages of later preverbal experience. The effect of the primordial trauma on the patient's psychological organization is attested to only by his fear that further analysis would be "addictive"—by the vague dread, in other words, of a regressive voyage from which there is no return. . . . Translating this question into practical clinical terms, we would have to ask ourselves whether the patient's fear of an irreversible regression is the fear of the total loss of the self in the form of a permanent profound apathy, or the fear of the reactivation of the experience of oscillations between intense greed, diffuse rage, and contentless depression [p. 25].

I suspect that Joseph feared both a profound irreversible regression and the intensification of his archaic greed, rage, and depression. In these ways he is similar to Kohut's patient, Mr. M. Kohut (1977) believed that Mr. M "dimly recognized that the activation of certain aspects of the mirror transference would expose him to the danger of permanent psychological disruption through the re-experience of primordial rage and greed, and that he indirectly expressed his awareness of these potential dangers in two ways: by developing a psychosomatic symptom, a rash on his elbow, . . . and by saying that remaining in analysis much longer could become 'addictive'" (p. 24).

Joseph made it clear at the beginning of therapy that he wanted treatment that would help him understand and know himself. He didn't trust emotions. Throughout treatment it was hard for him to experience his feelings or allow primary process material to emerge. He would exclaim at times that for brief seconds he could really feel something other than his "rational monitor." Perhaps he was saying all along that there was a point beyond which he could not allow himself to go.

It is also important to consider the effect his ADD may have had on his ability to let go enough to experience a full therapeutic regression. A characteristic of ADD is to be more than usually reactive to both internal and external stimuli. A compensatory mechanism is to build up rigid internal structures to diminish a constitutionally based tendency to disorganize in the face of overstimulation. A therapeutic regression demands that control be given up. For a person who has had to work hard to build in control to regulate a constitutional vulnerability, letting go of it can feel like certain death. Thus in Joseph's case, his lack of early mirroring and his constitutional vulnerability may have combined to necessitate flight from a sustained regressed transference. As Kohut said, the patient's experience of his limitation should be respected, especially in cases where there has already been marked improvement.

I met with Joseph in individual sessions through the end of June. During his sessions he minimized the abruptness of his decision. He told me how much better his life was going. He definitely wanted to stay in the group. He also again expressed his fear, as mentioned previously, that he was afraid he would stay forever in individual therapy unless he stopped now. His archaic mirror transference had been reactivated. Consequently, his vulnerability to my responsiveness was heightened. His archaic transference and his need to be in control (a result of his ADD) had two results. It precipitated his need to distance himself from any possibility that I would fail him and it relieved his own sense of impotent dependency on me. He was driven to take control of the individual sessions and end them. He was going to do therapy his way. I complied with this need and encouraged his work in the group.

Through the summer and fall Joseph participated in the group sessions, with only a brief mention that he had terminated individual therapy. He was not very interested in the group's feedback. Although they didn't push him about individual therapy, they continued to give him honest feedback about his behavior in the group. He continued to use the group for self-restorative selfobject experiences. Group members often commented that they thought he was being defensive. When he reported his life was great, he communicated with an air of boredom and resentment. When he got angry that one member was always listened to and he was accused of "filling up air time," one group member said to him, "You just want to be accepted and loved for who you are, don't you?" To this he sighed with relief and said yes. This interaction acted as a transforming selfobject experience.

One and a half years later, Joseph's group therapy continues to play a critical role in his continued development. He can use the group to work through the deficiencies in the mirroring sectors of his personality. It is important that I am in the group to watch. He has the added benefit of the group member's experience and responses to buffer disappointment he may feel from me. His controlling the distance-closeness variable between us frees him from the more constricting effects of his terror in the individual transference. It is my hope that the group will both stabilize him and facilitate enough selfobject experiences to reorganize and transform his intrapsychic experience.

In summary, there are intricacies involved when group and individual therapeutic transferences operate simultaneously. Combined therapy provides several advantages. When one modality is disrupted, the other may be usefully available. This can facilitate the development of archaic transferences. Indeed, this happened in the earlier phases of Joseph's treatment. The group transferences often provide direct gratification of selfobject needs as well as understanding. Finally, by observing the interactions of others, selfobject experiences may occur at a distance, or one step removed. Particularly when archaic transferences threaten to overwhelm self-cohesion, these more distanced transference experiences may be more valuable and facilitate continuing growth and development.

REFERENCES

Kohut, H. (1977), *The Restoration of the Self*. New York: International Universities Press, pp. 15–54.

Lichtenberg, J. D., Lachmann, F. M. & Fosshage, J. L. (1992), *Self and Motivational Systems*. Hillsdale, NJ: The Analytic Press.

Winnicott, D. W. (1965), *Maturational Processes and the Facilitating Environment*. New York: International Universities Press.

Chapter 8

Jacquie: The Working Through of Selfobject Transferences with a Latency-Aged Girl

Ellen J. Lewinberg

The unfolding and working through of selfobject transferences in our work with adults is familiar. What I will demonstrate in this chapter is that, despite the fact that a child's self experience is in the process of developing, many of the technical and theoretical aspects of self psychology and intersubjectivity are equally helpful in work with children. Transference and countertransference issues play a central role in therapy. The evidence for this appears, not merely in the content of the play, but in the process and interactions between child and therapist. To illustrate my contention, I present the case of Jacquie.

Jacquie was referred when she was eight years old. Reasons for referral included a nervous blink and, according to her mother, a very poor self-image. She was unable to get along with people at home or at school. If she did not understand or could not do something right away, she panicked and felt that she could not do it at all. She was described as being very sensitive, emotional, and perpetually convinced that she was being unfairly treated. In response to the anger of others, she would become self-denigrating, call herself a stupid, rotten person, and threaten suicide. She could not bear to be teased. Jacquie was in conflict with her sisters, who were close to each other. Jacquie and her mother often entered into power struggles in which both became irrational and could not stop harping at one another.

Jacquie was a beautiful, tall, slim girl with medium blond hair, blue eyes, and a lovely but rare smile. She dressed stylishly, did well in school, was very musical, and was good at ballet. She had a best friend and felt she was popular at school, but always worried about her place in friendships. Jacquie was possessive about her things and tidy to an obsessional degree.

Jacquie is the middle child in a family of three girls. She was described as always having been difficult, a whiny baby who cried a lot. Jacquie was breast-fed and weaned gradually. Her milestones were described as "normal." However, her parents felt that they got nothing positive from her. Her mother complained that she had no fun with Jacquie because she was always so cranky. Jacquie had recurrent ear infections that resulted in two attempts to put tubes in her ears before she was two years old.

When Jacquie was two, the family went on a vacation to an isolated place far from any medical facilities. Jacquie's mother was pregnant at the time, and began to hemorrhage. She was flown to a hospital and was carried off on a stretcher. Jacquie became very upset and could not be comforted. She was left with her four-year-old sister, her grandmother, and a new maid. Her father accompanied her mother, and they did not return for four or five days.

At two-and-a-half, Jacquie tore off her big toenail while bike-riding. Soon after this, her older sister slammed Jacquie's finger in a door, severing the tip. Both parents were at work and her mother could not be reached. Her father came home and took her to a hospital, where she was placed in restraint in order to suture the severed tip in place. Between the ages of two and three years, Jacquie would throw rocks and bite other children. When she was upset, she would cry for hours and could not be comforted. As Jacquie grew up, she disliked being away from home, did not like sleepovers at friends' houses, and returned early from sleepover camp.

Jacquie's mother was the youngest daughter in a wealthy family with three children. She worked part-time in one of the helping professions. Her father came from a middle-class background. He had three siblings, worked hard in a profession, and was not home much.

I saw Jacquie three times a week in intensive psychotherapy, and her parents once a month. Jacquie engaged quickly in therapy. She spent her time describing how unfairly she was treated in school, at home, and in her ballet class but was very concerned with being good in my office, always asking permission to use equipment and so on. My interpretations, which used her play as a metaphor, were from a self-psychological perspective. I surmised that she wished to experience me as a mirroring selfobject and she felt that this would be contingent on good behavior, undoubtedly a reflection of her feeling at home that she had to excel.

She would also bring in schoolwork and drawings for me to admire in an apparent effort to elicit mirroring responses.

The unfolding of the transference reflected the family situation and the traumas she had experienced early on. Because of her early history, there were serious difficulties in the development of her self experience. She could not experience herself as special or valuable. How special could she be if her parents could not enjoy her or could abandon her? She felt therefore that the only way to be special was to be perfect. She was also perfectionist in her demands, even at times insinuating that I was not a good enough therapist. This created a transference\counter-transference configuration that resulted in a number of selfobject failures, which I will discuss later.

The more Jacquie experienced me as providing the needed selfobject experiences, the more she was able to reveal her experience of herself as special. She decided to apply to the National Ballet School (a private, very selective institution for which she had to audition) and also tried out for a part in a school play. Other indications of the reactivation of her archaic grandiosity were demonstrated in her detailed descriptions of her relatives' wealth, possessions, homes, and so on.

About the third month into the therapy, Jacquie became upset when she saw another child leave my office. I surmised that this disrupted the beginnings of a mirror transference and probably created tremendous anxiety and rage. Although she knew I was Jewish, she illustrated her anger at me by talking about her German aunt and about Hitler and her feelings that he was right in what he did. She began to wonder how special she could be for me and accused me of wanting to help her only for the fee. She worried that I would prefer other patients, as her mother preferred her sisters. When the connection was restored she expressed the wish that I could be her mother and began a theme of play in the dollhouse: a baby is hidden in the cupboard; all the members of the family are killed in a war; the people who move into the house are wealthy and distinguished, find the baby, and raise it as their own. She was content for me to sit and watch her play and ask questions about it, and she basked in my acceptance and appreciation of her.

Jacquie's drawings at this time were very stereotypical and devoid of people. She drew houses, grass, trees, or patterns that she colored very carefully. She would show me techniques she had learned in art class at school and suggested I might be able to teach others who came to see me. She was relying on what she already knew in order to elicit mirroring responses and be appreciated by the therapist, and was attempting to deny her competitive feelings.

At the time that Jacquie was about to have her first separation from therapy (after five months) to go on a family vacation, an intensification occurred in her symptoms, which had subsided for a time. Jacquie wrote a poem describing how she felt. She wanted to commit suicide because everyone was being so mean to her.

> The Way I Feel
> An evil goblin or a witch's pet,
> A horrid lonely swamp that's slimy and wet.
> The Way I Don't Feel
> Beautiful silk dresses and fairies magical dust,
> Brave strong hearted warriors that say
> "Fighting we must."

> To: Paper;
> You might be plain but I'll write on you anyway.
> I wanted to say I feel terrible.
> Horribly truly,

> Jacquie.

After talking about her poem for a while, it emerged that she was angry about the forthcoming long weekend, the family vacation, and the fact that she would have to wait four days before she saw me again; she did not know if I cared about her. She could not imagine that I could keep her in mind all that time and felt that separations meant that I was being mean to her. It appeared that she experienced weekends and the family vacation as selfobject failures on my part; the selfobject functions I performed for her could not be sustained when a break in the therapy was imminent. Stern (1985) suggests that from 15 months onward the consolidation of verbal language marks the first point at which one can infer the initial consolidation of internalized representation of self and object. I suggest that Jacquie's traumatic experience of abandonment represented the crystallization of her early experiences of the relative unavailability of empathic parental responsiveness before and after the trauma. When she faced a separation from me, she feared the loss of the selfobject responses that I provided, and her symptomatology increased. What she feared in the transference was a retraumatization—I would abandon her as she had been abandoned when she was two years old. This would prove that she was not special.

Jacquie's play in the dollhouse continued. She wished it were *her* dollhouse and behaved as though it were. She would leave it set up in a particular way and would check it each session to see that nothing had been rearranged. She would rearrange the whole house if she saw that even one thing had been moved. A girl lived alone in the dollhouse; her parents were allowed to visit only occasionally. I surmised that Jacquie was expressing her feelings of isolation and her longing to be unique and special to me. She would set up elaborate games with dolls. For example, the dolls were put into teams, the girls in one and the boys in another. One girl was always excluded. But she would perform incredible feats and win the others' friendship, a clear representation of Jacquie's self-experience.

With the approach of the summer holidays (eleven months into the therapy) and, consequently, the next break in the therapy, a shift in the transference occurred again. Jacquie began to feel that she had nothing to talk about. She felt that I was sitting and waiting for her to talk, but she could not think. She worried that I would be displeased if she didn't talk and that I would get bored and lose interest. She began to complain that I did not give her enough advice. She wanted advice about what to say to her teacher when she cried and was told to "grow up." I later discovered that the wish for advice signaled her experience of my selfobject failure. My sense is that one does not wish to be mirrored by someone whom one cannot idealize. When Jacquie experienced a selfobject failure on my part, she no longer felt mirrored and therefore could no longer idealize me. Her requests for advice were perhaps attempts to reinstate me as idealizable, so that I could provide the mirroring selfobject functions she so desperately needed.

Because of the impending break, Jacquie was concerned that I would not be able to respond to her mirroring needs. When her attempt to reinstate me failed, she became critical of me to counter her fear that I saw her as inadequate and would fail to provide mirroring selfobject responses. At times, when she did not feel understood by me, she would tidy her drawer repeatedly. (Each child I see is given a drawer in which to keep anything that they draw or make in the therapy.)

With impending separations, Jacquie's obsessional features increased both within and outside of the therapy. She would spend sessions lining up toy animals or rearranging the dollhouse, ending up with the identical arrangement each time. She would have enormous difficulty at home and threaten not to go on family trips. (I will discuss the role of the obsessional behavior in following passages.)

Each of the family trips heralded an increase in Jacquie's symptomatology and, preceding each, her bid for mirroring would become more desperate. She would spend most of her sessions describing how well she was doing in the different areas of her life other than personal relationships: in school, sport, music, and ballet. She felt very envious of Angie, who was favored by the ballet teacher; she kept wondering whether to discontinue ballet class. She knew Angie's parents could not afford ballet tuition and that Angie had been given a scholarship.

Jacquie felt that Angie did not deserve one and that if her parents could not afford it she ought not to come. Her efforts to be regarded as special increased and indicated the intensification of her selfobject needs that result when the normal processes of self development are disrupted.

The third trip, seventeen months into the therapy, was to a destination halfway around the world, which in some ways would replicate her experience at age two, in that the family was traveling with relatives, was staying with other relatives whom Jacquie did not know very well, and involved a three-day side trip by her parents. Before the trip, I talked to Jacquie about her previous traumatic vacation. She listened, but said nothing.

On the eve of her departure, she brought me a Christmas present. I wondered aloud what she felt about bringing me a present, and also whether she perhaps wished we might exchange gifts. She immediately stated that I thought she was greedy. It emerged that the gift had not been her idea, but her mother's. She became very upset and left the session in tears. She telephoned that evening, just before the family was to leave, saying she could not leave that way. After talking for a while on the phone and stating over and over again that she did not want a present from me, I said that I thought that we had had a terrible "misunderstanding." This calmed her. She fixed on the word, repeating a number of times: "It was just a misunderstanding." If she thought that I felt she was a greedy child, I could no longer fill a mirroring role.

On her return a month later, Jacquie said she did not have a good time. She complained mostly of being unable to sleep. This had started when her parents took their side trip and left the children with relatives. Her sleep disruption continued after their return. She described how she experienced a terrible feeling in the pit of her stomach as soon as it grew dark. She felt helpless and very alone when everyone else in the family was asleep and she was awake. She would wake up her mother, who would become enraged and impatient with her. Jacquie's difficulty sleeping subsided a few weeks after her return home.

The transference seemed to deepen after this and, feeling more sure of me, Jacquie risked acknowledging that she was a bit annoyed with me for something I had said about her wanting to feel special at ballet. She referred to the earlier conversation during which she had felt indignant about special treatment Angie was getting at ballet, and I suggested that perhaps she also wanted special treatment. She thought I was wrong; she just did not think it was fair that someone got a scholarship or that the ballet teacher paid for her ballet shoes, or took her to the ballet. She did want to feel special with me and wanted to go over the "misunderstanding" from before the break in therapy. She said that if it had been her idea to buy me a present, then maybe I would have been right about her wanting to exchange presents. She always gave her teachers presents and did not expect any from them; that is why she did not expect one from me. I said I understood why she had felt so upset at the thought I might feel she was greedy.

Her play changed after her return. She spent a lot of time using blocks to build long bridges that would span the room. I talked about them as connections she was building to reestablish her connection with me. She did not comment. Terman (1988) writes that structure is built through "participation and response in the formation of a pattern" and Bacal (1985, 1988) writes that "optimal responsiveness is necessary for growth and change to occur." I feel that, overall, Jacquie was able to accept the selfobject functions I was providing for her; as a result, we entered a period of relative calm. Jacquie was functioning well at school and at home; there were fewer descriptions of her fragmentation.

Separations continued to be difficult for Jacquie. When her mother went away for a long weekend, Jacquie made a lot of plans to fill the time, and told me she might have to call me. She did not phone, and was able to sleep while her mother was away. I think this was owed to the mirroring transference's having been stabilized, allowing Jacquie to feel that she could rely on me to keep her in mind even when she did not see me.

One particular day Jacquie arrived quite upset about a grade she had received in math. Katy, her friend, had done much better. She was busy drawing a rabbit and telling me she was in a bad mood because of the grade. She wanted me to help her draw the rabbit, saying she couldn't do it by herself. She told me that Katy's mark was out of 50 and hers was out of 30. I was unable to tell if Jacquie did in fact have a lower mark. Also, I wanted to make her feel better. I worked out the percentages and it turned out that Katy had about 8 percent more than Jacquie did. Jacquie became furious with me and burst into tears: she had not asked me to work out the percentages; it was worse than she thought; she was really dumb; Katy never got anything wrong and she did all the time.

Jacquie felt I had worked out the percentages because I had wanted to show her how badly she had done and that I was just the same as everyone else. She never wanted to see me again; if her parents made her continue therapy, she would not talk to me; I liked Katy better than I liked her, in fact, I didn't care about her at all; I didn't think she was in the least bit special; she was not getting any better; I did not give her advice, so there was no point in her coming to see me anyway. Jacquie tore up the rabbit she was drawing and put it and a painting she had brought from school to show me into the garbage. She began to tidy her drawer. She then said that she always regretted things she did and went to look at the pictures in the garbage. She said she was stupid.

I wondered aloud if she felt that I thought she was stupid. This upset her even more because she felt that I *was* saying that she was stupid. After I told her I had made a mistake and should never have worked out the percentages when she did not ask me to, she calmed down. She took the painting out of the garbage and told me that she regretted tearing up the rabbit. The response that she had needed was for me to stay with her distress. Therefore, my trying to make her feel better represented a selfobject failure in the mirroring transference.

At this point, I became aware that, in addition to needing mirroring selfobject responses, Jacquie appears to have been using me as an alter ego selfobject (Brothers, 1993) who embodied the disavowed aspects of herself. For example, Jacquie described just how terrible the fights with her sisters were. They bugged her and she hit, bit, and scratched them. She described how she did not want to behave that way but did not seem to be able to stop herself. I asked Jacquie how she felt when she bugged her sisters. She told me that she wanted her younger sister to get really upset. Jacquie experienced my question as a criticism and she again felt that I was useless and of no value to her. She became very angry with me: I was not helping her; I was not telling her what to do or say; I was not giving her advice; I did not help her in her fighting with her sisters; in fact, I thought she was bad. She again remembered how I had hurt her when I had worked out the percentages. Maybe I wanted to hurt her. Did I think she was "psycho"? Is that why she was coming to see me? If I am a psychotherapist, she must be "psycho." Why is she the only person in the world to come and see me?

Her criticism of me demonstrated her wish to disavow the negative aspects of herself that tended to overwhelm her in the face of my failing her in the mirror transference. She was then filled with her own badness, which she wished to disavow. To repair the ruptured selfobject tie, I said that I thought I had hurt her again when I asked what happened when she bugged her sisters. I wondered if she felt that I was criticizing her. She said then that she felt confused. She felt she behaved badly when she got angry with me. I told her that I thought that had happened because she was so hurt that she wanted to hurt me and that I knew she felt badly afterward. She told me she did not want to forget these grievances. I replied that I understood it was important that she not forget them until she could really trust me.

At this point in the therapy, Jacquie decided to make a puppet similar to one in my office. She began by painting a cone and then decided to do two paintings. They were very messy, using all the colors, one on top of the other. She seemed quite depressed and made no attempt to conceal this from me. There had been a failure in the mirroring transference that she did not want to forget.

Jacquie continued to criticize me, this time for not having the "stuff" she needed to make an identical puppet, while at the same time asking me continuously how to make it. Toward the end of one session, I felt that I was unable to give Jacquie what she needed. I answered in an abrupt manner that she could make it whichever way she chose. She became upset and told me she would bring something for the hair from home.

On the following day, Jacquie made a nose for her puppet that she did not like and got angry. She said that I had made her do the puppet my way, not hers; the "stuff" I had was no good. She could not make it look like the original. She dumped it all in the garbage and then worried that I thought badly of her. What was she coming here for, anyway? Maybe she should stop. I said that I understood that she felt that I did not have the right stuff for her, and added that I could see that she was really upset. I also said that I knew—because she had told me—that when she was upset, she did things she really regretted later. She decided to take the puppet out of the garbage and put it in her drawer. She asked me whether I could bring some cotton wool for the hair next time.

At that time (two and a half years into therapy) during one of the monthly meetings I had with her parents, they said they felt Jacquie was doing better at home. There was less fighting and crying. She was now developing a sense of humor. We agreed that she was making progress.

In the following session Jacquie was quite subdued. It appeared that she was reacting to my having told her parents that she was making progress. If she was perfect, how could she be making progress? And if she were making progress, it would mean that she might lose me by ending the therapy. I would be sending her back to her unempathic mother. She claimed the dollhouse as hers even more by painting one of the rooms pink, and then continued with her puppet. She asked me about my childhood in South Africa. Was I part of the aristocracy, and did I have servants? She was wishing to reestablish an idealizing tie with me so that I could once again serve as a mirroring selfobject for her. She also told me that she did not think she was getting any better. She then asked me whether I could get one round wooden bead to put at the bottom of the stick for the puppet.

At this point, Jacquie was using me as an alter ego selfobject (Brothers, 1993), and my countertransference got in the way. I had been feeling criticized, accused of not giving Jacquie the "right stuff" for her puppet. This made me feel that I was a bad therapist. I went to a craft store to buy the wooden bead and saw there all the "stuff" she had originally needed for the puppet; I bought it for her. I was going to be the perfect therapist who provided for all of Jacquie's needs.

When Jacquie saw the new materials at the following session, she seemed a bit put out. She tried to use the hair I had bought; it would not work. She then tried to use the original puppet head, and became very frustrated. I was feeling unappreciated, and said that whatever I got for her was not good enough. With that she took the whole lot of "stuff" and threw it into the garbage, saying that I had only bought all this because I had thought *her* puppet was so awful. She became enraged and would not listen to anything I had to say. However, just before the end of the session, she took the "stuff" out of the garbage and wanted to take it home. I said that it would have to stay in her drawer. She slammed it shut and stormed out.

The following session, she was still very angry. She did not wish to talk. She went to the dollhouse but could not engage in playing there. She decided to draw instead. She said she was angry that I told her mother that we were making progress. She didn't feel we were. She did not want to come and see me anymore. She drew a picture of a woman (me?) with a bomb going through her heart. She wrote that she wanted to die, and wrote her name and the word *nobody* over and over. She said that she felt like a nobody with her father and mother, and with me.

I told Jacquie that I thought that she felt that I wanted to get rid of her when I told her parents that she was making progress, and that, in fact, I did not mean that therapy would end before she was ready. She kept saying that, because of the last session, she was sure that I was angry with her and did not like her. I replied that she felt I was criticizing her puppet when I brought the new "stuff" and I could understand why she became so upset. I said that I had felt badly early on when I did not have the "stuff" she needed, so that when I saw it, I bought it without realizing that she no longer needed it.

At the end of the session, she was very thoughtful and wondered how I could stay so calm. She told me that the day before her mother had gotten so mad at her on the way to a concert, she had kicked her out of the car. Her mother had driven away and told Jacquie to walk home. However, she had relented, driven around the block, and had then come to pick her up. Jacquie had not wanted to get back in the car, but was too scared to return home alone.

The next session began with Jacquie sitting silently staring at me. She looked upset and then burst out that she was upset about always having to start everything. Why didn't *I* start the sessions? I said that I had seen that she was upset, and I should have asked her what was happening. She was upset at her teacher.

As a consequence of my countertransference reaction, which led me to buy the materials for the puppet, Jacquie's anger intensified. Jacquie now felt that everyone was angry with her: her mother, who kicked her out of the car; her teacher; and me, for what happened during the previous session. She wanted to kill herself. This was a reaction to a disruption in the alter ego transference (Brothers, 1993). It was impossible for her to see me as embodying her hurtfulness, and she responded with self-directed rage. She went round the room looking for sharp objects with which to hurt herself. I followed behind her and took them away, saying that I was sorry that she was feeling so badly, but I could not let her hurt herself. She told me we might as well say good-bye, because she would not be back on Monday. She would be dead and in hell where she belonged. I told her I did not think she belonged there, and that I took her threat very seriously. I told her I felt that she was in danger, and that I would have to let her parents know. She said that they would not care. I then said that in that case I would have to make sure that she was in a place where people did care for her and would not let her hurt herself. She asked what I meant, and I replied, perhaps a hospital. She became very upset and accused me of thinking she was "psycho." I told her that I did not think so, but if she was so upset that she wanted to kill herself I had to protect her.

Jacquie then accused me of acting to protect my reputation. She suddenly stopped and asked me if my feelings were hurt. I said yes, but that I thought hers were, too. She agreed. I said another thing we could do was for me to see her for an extra session, so that we could continue to talk about what was happening. She agreed; then I agreed not to tell her parents about her suicidal feelings. Jacquie was demonstrating for the first time a capacity for empathy when she wondered whether my feelings were hurt. This was a major change. She was concerned about my feelings but was also gratified that she had had an impact on me. The issue of my selfobject failure was worked through because I did not become defensive, and she was able to calm down.

The following session Jacquie seemed calmer, but my selfobject failure was not yet repaired. She continued to make her puppet, and at the end was pleased with it. Throughout, however, she would ask why I told her parents that she was making progress. She did feel that I was saying that I did not want to see her anymore. She could not understand how behaving badly with me was progress. (An aspect that I should perhaps have explored with her had to do with the reactivation of her expansive sense of herself. If she was perfect, how could she be "making progress"? I must think that there was something wrong with her.)

A few days later Jacquie told me she was feeling better with me. She was not sure why. We were able to work things out. It was not like at her home, where nothing ever got resolved.

The issue of my telling her parents she was making progress remained prominent and was raised on a number of subsequent occasions when I did not understand her. For example, in one session she commented on my haircut, saying she liked my hair better long. She talked about difficulties she had with her sister and began to build a jail with blocks, into which she put a girl doll. I wondered if she wished her sister would go to jail. She laughed and said she wished sometimes her parents would police things better. She then started talking about her own hair and how she was going to grow it really long. I said that if I had not cut mine, we would both have long hair, and perhaps she wished we could both be the same. She became very angry and insulted at this comment, and accused me of wanting her to like me better than her mother. She refused to talk about it or to listen to me. She also refused to let me help her tidy up. She worried about liking me more, as if that might further endanger her connection to her mother. The transference was that making progress would cause her to lose me, and she would feel abandoned again.

During the following session Jacquie again felt that she did not wish to continue. I had told her mother that we were making progress, which meant that the therapy could end. Anyway, she felt worse here than before she came. Everything outside was awful. She and her best friend were not getting along; she was fighting with everyone; therapy was not helping, so why should she come? She could not stop thinking about all the awful things I had done to her. She wanted to feel in control of the ending to avert the catastrophe of an abandonment and therefore decided she would leave me. I said that I did not think now was a good time to stop. She said she worried that if she got better, she would lose me, so she might as well leave now. I disagreed and said we still had work to do, and that she should not leave until she felt ready to.

It took a number of sessions for the selfobject bond to be restored—sessions in which Jacquie went over all the things that had gone wrong between us. She was eventually able to say, however, that she could see it was very important to sort things out, because when things were wrong here, they were wrong everywhere, and she blamed me for that.

The approach of the next break (the summer holidays, three years into the therapy) proved a difficult time for Jacquie. I will describe the working through of some of the disruptions at that time, because these events, and some events outside the therapy, heralded a shift in Jacquie's self-experience that led to our talking about and setting a termination date. She mentioned being worried about the long summer break, and wondered if she could phone me once a week. I agreed. The selfobject tie being secure calmed her and she talked in a cheerful way about her friends and all sorts of things she had done. At our next session Jacquie told me that she was nervous about an athletics competition. She had told her mother she had wanted to call me again during the break, and her mother had said that this was fine, but that it would be up to her to keep track of the day and the time. She felt that this was a tremendous burden and that she could not do it. She never knew what day it was while she was at the cottage. Her ability to keep track of dates would indicate her lessened need of me. She was not yet ready to end the sessions.

Jacquie then related the following dream. She is with her family at the cottage. There is no food there. They have to go to the hotel across the lake. Her parents and older sister get into the motorboat and leave. She and her younger sister are in the canoe. She decides to go along the shore because it is too scary in the middle of the lake in a canoe. She sees dolphins, but when she gets closer, she sees that they are killer whales. She tries to scramble onto a neighbor's dock. Her sister falls in. She saves her in the nick of time; the whale's mouth is already over her sister. Suddenly she is in a concentration camp. Then she is sent to a far away country to live with a poor family.

Jacquie said that she thought the dolphins were there because she was doing a dolphin project. I said I thought it was a very interesting dream and asked if she had any thoughts about it. She shrugged. I said her parents were leaving her to fend for herself, by her having to row herself and her sister across the lake, and related this to her having to be responsible for remembering to call me. She said she did not want to talk about it. She thought she was the heroine and saved her sister. In retrospect I feel when I noted the inadequacy of Jacquie's parenting, she experienced me as critical and not mirroring.

She returned from the summer vacation feeling that she had done very well at camp and at home. She felt happier, there was less fighting with her sisters, and she felt that she and her mother were getting along much better. She was attending a new school and felt that she would be making a new start there.

After a few months in the new school, Jacquie frequently felt that she was too busy with friends and her new school to continue the therapy. We decided to set a termination date. In the new school she was admired for her competence, both academically and socially, and the mirroring selfobject functions I had been providing for her were therefore provided by the school.

DISCUSSION

It is hard to know whether Jacquie was a constitutionally difficult baby, whether there was a temperamental mismatch between Jacquie and her mother (Chess and Thomas, 1974) or whether Jacquie's frequent ear infections caused her to be so difficult. Whatever the reason, her mother was not able to enjoy her development and be affectively attuned or empathic with Jacquie, feeling that she was a burden, always sick, and always cranky. Daniel Stern (1985) has described the difficulties encountered when affect attunement and empathy are missing from birth until the verbal self develops, about 15 months to two years. Basch (1985) draws on the work of Stern and states that through

> affective attunement the mother is serving as the quintessential selfobject for her baby, sharing the infant's experience, confirming it in its activity, building a sensorimotor model for what shall become the self concept. Affect attunement leads to a shared world of emotional meanings. . . . If affective attunement is not present or is ineffective during those early years, the lack of shared experience may well create a sense of isolation and a belief that one's affective needs generally are somehow unacceptable and shameful [p. 35].

This was true for Jacquie.

Jacquie's mother, although at times attuned, was unable to modulate her own affect and was therefore unable to perform this selfobject function for Jacquie. Her empathic capacity was invested in herself and she experienced Jacquie as a threat to her own self-cohesion, as when she forced an anxious and panicking Jacquie out of the car. In Jacquie's case there were problems on two fronts. Her mother was, at times, tuned in emotionally and experienced Jacquie's intense affects as overwhelming her own feelings. Hence, her mother felt compelled to distance herself from Jacquie and reject her feelings. She was unable to enjoy Jacquie so that Jacquie was unable to experience her as a mirroring selfobject. Tolpin (1986) suggests that "the child whose mirroring, idealizing or alterego needs are not adequately met by one parent, . . . may emerge from his disappointment with new resources with which to turn to the other parent" (p. 116). However, this path was not available to Jacquie because her father, although more able to calm her, was for the most part not available to either Jacquie or to her mother, because of his long work day and his absorption in his work.

Jacquie's early crankiness, and her later behavior of throwing rocks and fighting with other children, made her parents angry and interfered with their ability to provide mirroring, idealizing, or alter ego selfobject functions for her. Consequently, Jacquie could not admire or have an idealizing experience with parents who could not soothe or admire her. Without this, Jacquie could not develop a stable self structure. Added to this was Jacquie's traumatic experience when she was two years old and in the process of acquiring verbal language, but not yet able to express or perhaps even define her feelings. Jacquie's traumatic experience of being abandoned under very dramatic circumstances served to crystallize her earlier experience of the relative unavailability of empathic parental responsiveness. The development of her self-experience was arrested. Without a stable self structure, being apart from her mother at camp or at home left Jacquie without an evocable representation of her mother as a soothing selfobject and resulted in her fragmentation. At other times, Jacquie was able to elicit the mirroring selfobject functions she needed from me and, as a result, spoke of me in an idealizing way at home.

Jacquie's perfectionism was the result of the untransformed nature of her grandiose fantasies (Ulman and Brothers, 1988). She relegated all her difficulties to the outside. Her externalizations reflected her disavowal of all aspects of herself that she felt would interfere with the possibility of receiving mirroring selfobject responses. She sought others as alter ego selfobjects who might embody the disavowed aspects of herself. In the treatment, when she felt that I hated her or was deliberately being mean to her, she evidenced aspects of an alter ego transference (Brothers, 1993) in which she was trying to reconnect to the disavowed aspects of herself.

Jacquie's obsessional behavior can be understood as an attempt to master feelings of helplessness and anger. She was trying to institute self-calming and self-soothing selfobject functions that were not experienced in the transference because of selfobject failures or anticipated disruptions in the therapy. I suggest that obsessionality isolates and denies affect and is an effort to ward off fragmentation resulting from selfobject failure.

On the eve of her departure for the vacation after she had given me the gift, and as a result of the repair of the empathic failure, Jacquie was able to use my word "misunderstanding" as a transitional phenomenon (Winnicott, 1951) to soothe herself. When she returned, she needed to make sure that I understood her position before she could trust me again.

The impediments to the development of her cohesive selfhood colored the treatment process. Treatment provided an opportunity for the resumption of her arrested development, in the form of transferences in which the therapist provided mirroring, idealizing, and alter ego experiences. Aspects of her early development were revived in the treatment as a result of the therapist's empathic failures. Through the play and the repair of the selfobject failures, the selfobject needs that had been traumatically aborted early in Jacquie's development reemerged and were worked through. This enabled her to continue the development of her self.

ACKNOWLEDGMENT

I wish to thank Dr. Doris Brothers for all her support and encouragement in the writing of this chapter.

REFERENCES

Bacal, H. A. (1985), Optimal responsiveness and the therapeutic process. In: *Progress in Self Psychology, Vol. 1*, ed. A. Goldberg. New York: Guilford, pp. 202–228.
—— (1988), Reflections on "optimum frustration." In: *Learning from Kohut: Progress in Self Psychology, Vol. 4*, ed. A. Goldberg. Hillsdale, NJ: The Analytic Press, pp. 127–133.
Basch, M. F. (1985), Interpretation: Toward a developmental model. In: *Progress in Self Psychology, Vol. 1*, ed. A. Goldberg. New York: Guilford, pp. 33–43.
Brothers, D. (1993), The search for the hidden self: A fresh look at alter ego transferences. In: *The Widening Scope of Self Psychology: Progress in Self Psychology, Vol. 9*, ed. A. Goldberg. Hillsdale, NJ: The Analytic Press, pp. 191–207.
Chess, S. & Thomas, A. (1974), Temperament in the normal infant. In: *Individual Differences in Children*, ed. J. Westman. New York: Wiley, pp. 83–103.
Stern, D. N. (1985), *The Interpersonal World of the Infant*. New York: Basic Books.
Terman, D. M. (1988), Optimum frustration: Structuralization and the therapeutic process. In: *Learning from Kohut: Progress in Self Psychology, Vol. 4*, ed. A. Goldberg. Hillsdale, NJ: The Analytic Press, pp. 113–126.
Tolpin, M. (1986), The self and its selfobjects: A different baby. In: *Progress in Self Psychology, Vol. 2*, ed. A. Goldberg. New York: Guilford, pp. 115–128.
Ulman, R. & Brothers, D. (1988), *The Shattered Self: A Psychoanalytic Study of Trauma*. Hillsdale, NJ: The Analytic Press.
Winnicott, D. W. (1951), Transitional objects and transitional phenomena. In: *Through Pediatrics to Psychoanalysis*. New York: Basic Books, 1975, pp. 229–242.

Chapter 9

The Termination Phase in Psychoanalysis: A Self Psychology Study

Hyman L. Muslin

The self psychology view of the termination of analysis, as Kohut articulated (1977), stresses that a recovery of the self, a "functional rehabilitation" in Kohut's terms, comprises that stage when the analyzed self has "become firm, when it has ceased to react to the loss of self objects with fragmentation, serious enfeeblement, or uncontrollable rage" (p. 138). Kohut later added that the endpoint of an analysis was reached when the patient is enabled to seek out and invest in appropriate selfobjects for the sustenance—from mature selfobjects —required from time to time of the now-cohesive self (1984).

From the classical psychoanalytic view, there is consensus that although symptom removal is an important criterion of termination-readiness, it is an unreliable criterion as an indicator of genuine intrapsychic change (Firestein, 1973). Most analytic observers agree that for the patient to be considered ready for termination of the analysis, the patient's symptoms of psychic distress be traced to genetic conflicts in which the oedipal neurosis has been identified and the infantile amnesia uncovered. Further changes would indicate that object relations have proceeded to more mature levels along with psychosexual functioning, the latter attaining full genitality. In this same connection, penis envy and castration anxiety are expected to be mastered. The ego changes would include the attainment of maximum secondary autonomy but also the ability to tolerate delay, experience pleasure without guilt, lessen acting out, have an increase in the strength of sublimations, and accomplish the shift from autoplastic to alloplastic conflict solutions. Although transference resolution continues in the postanalytic period, most authors who have written on termination express the conviction that termination and transference resolution are intertwined, in effect that termination *is* the resolution of the transference (Ferenczi, 1927; Freud, 1937; Buxbaum, 1950; Macalpine, 1950; Rangell, 1966; Kubie 1968).

It is a commonplace occurrence that patients respond to the onset of the termination phase with an exacerbation of their symptom picture or from another view, with a return of their preanalysis self-state (Dewald, 1972). In the classical literature, there are many instances of these episodes of recrudescence of symptoms in the termination, and many explanations are offered. Thus, Fenichel (1945) spoke of symptomatic worsening to spite the analyst who is not fulfilling transference wishes. Anne Reich (1950) similarly wrote of exacerbations as "weapons of revenge." Ekstein (1960) spoke of "the final captive act of mastery." Kubie (1968) spoke of the end of analysis as a "desperate intensification" of the analytic process.

Kohut (1977) wrote similarly of the termination process in self psychology analyses. He stated:

In the analysis of those narcissistic personality disorders where working through had on the whole concerned a primary defect in the structure of the patient's self resulting in a gradual healing of the defect via the acquisition of new structures through transmuting internalization, the terminal phase can be seen to parallel that of the usual transference neuroses. The analysand is exposed to the impact of the realization that he has to face the ultimate separation from the analyst as a selfobject. As a result of the pressure of this difficult emotional task, a temporary regression takes place in the analysand, creating a situation in which the healing of the structural defect seems to be again undone. A condition supervenes, in other words, in which it appears that the healing was only sham, that the patient's improved functioning was not a consequence of newly acquired psychic structure, but depended on the actual presence of the selfobject. Or, to describe the situation in still different terms, it suddenly seems as if the processes of working-through had not brought about those optimal frustrations which, through minute internalizations, lay down psychic structure and make the patient independent of the analyst, but that the patient had improved by leaning on the external selfobject or, at best, by having borrowed the selfobject's (the analyst's) functions through gross, unstable identifications with him. Among the manifestations of the terminal phase in the analysis of these cases, signs indicating the temporary reconcretization of the relation to the selfobject are therefore often in evidence. Once more the patient feels that the analyst is substituting for his psychic structure—once more he sees him as the supplier of self-esteem, as the integrator of his ambitions, as the concretely present idealized power that dispenses approval and other forms of narcissistic sustenance [pp. 15–16].

These comments on the terminal phase of analysis indicate that a spectrum of reactions in termination may be expected and studied in any sample of cases surveyed. The following questions are germane to the student of termination: What did the announcement of termination evoke in the patient? What in the patient's background explains the nature of the termination response? What in the analyst is therapeutic or distressing to the patient in termination? What in the patient's self may still be needy of working through as revealed by the termination response?

Termination of an analysis unleashes archaic wishes to consummate the unfulfilled yearnings of one's earliest self intertwined with the remembrances of one's disappointments and consequent despair, rage, and anxieties. Regardless of what has been worked out or developed in the analysis, there is therefore at the moment of separation—ofttimes an elongated moment—a gamut of experiences which is unleashed that reflect the early life of the analysand and its impact on the cohesiveness of the self. These termination experiences, as has been amply described in many contributions in our literature, range from massive despair and a "long drawn out leave taking" (Loewald, 1962) to manifestations of fragmentation and, as has been reported in some instances (Freud, 1937), terminations without any manifestations of disarray. Apart from the considerations raised about the background explanations for these varied termination reactions, one must add that in some analysands the capacity of the self to remove itself from fixed self positions is limited (Muslin, 1989). Another variation of this motif is the unique constitutional or functional capacity of a particular self to internalize new structure, one of the essential ingredients in an analytic cure from the viewpoint of self psychology (Kohut, 1977). Thus, in some analysands, there can be no terminable analysis in the sense of cure, the injuries to their selves have permanently interfered with their capacities to internalize over time the structures needed for maintenance of their cohesiveness. These patients may require continued visits after "termination"—therapeutic interviews from time to time—to maintain their cohesive self-state because their self-structures require the support of the selfobject analyst. In other instances after termination, there is, as Freud said, a permanent farewell, a *rebus bene gestis* in those cases in which internalization was effective over time (Freud, 1937).

Perhaps this variety of resolutions of an analysis reflects the wisdom of Kohut's final communication on the postanalytic self and the essence of cure in psychoanalysis. Kohut pointed out that for man the self/selfobject dyad is like oxygen to cerebral tissue—without it the tissue, like the self, will expire. He asserted that the germane issue in analysis was to be able to establish a channel between the self and its required selfobject supports. In this manner, he explicated the central issue in man's despair—the fear of being exposed to repeated traumata of disappointment from one's fellow man. Analysis is the quintessentially best method of diminishing the impact of the past on the present. Once the entire array of interferences with selfobject gratifications is "known" to patient and analyst, and its impact diminished (i.e., the defense transference has abated), the patient can now, due to the new experience of her- or himself, look to a life of continuing support from empathically resonating, mature selfobjects (Kohut, 1984). Thus Kohut's views make clear that the endpoint of an analysis, the so-called cure, is in essence the removal of impediments to the necessary ingredients for self-survival. In the end, it seems to me self psychology has given an answer to Freud's query directed to the terminability of analysis (Freud, 1937). The answer from Kohut is that analysis is the process by which our patients who had been stifled can now reveal their longings for sustenance of their selves, and that this continuing process of obtaining self-nurturance is, of course, interminable. The analysis, the preparation for a life of mature selfobject involvement when needed, is a terminable process in many if not most instances, but it is only a preparation for life after analysis in which the patient can now in safety form the human bonds that maintain the cohesive self (Kohut, 1984).

A CASE STUDY

Pertinent History

The patient, Ms. H.D., came to analysis years ago after experiencing what she called a depression that had persisted for more than six months. She was at that time in mourning for her father, then dead for one year. She had given birth to her last child (her second) four months prior to the time she came to see me. At the time of her first visit, she was a slightly built and fragile-appearing 32-year-old. She related that she had been both in analysis and psychotherapy since she was 18. Her mother, who had been ill since the patient's high school days with a depression, had become even further depressed since she entered college. Our patient, reacting to her mother's distress, became depressed and agitated and arranged for psychotherapy. After her mother's death from breast cancer when the patient was 18, she arranged for her first analysis, which continued until her marriage and was terminated with "good results." One of the good results was that she had become able to socialize more easily and overcome her fear of an intimate relationship with a man. The analysis was as she put it, "all about my Oedipus complex, my wish to dethrone my mother."

The major data that she came to reveal in this analysis—after a long interval—was that she had had a depressing life from the earliest of her remembrances, a life without the uplifting of an adequate mirroring presence throughout her entire development. Her mother, she recalled, was unable to calm her at any time. She became in fact so distressed over her mother's ministrations, which were apparently inconsistent and rejecting, that she cried and became agitated whenever her mother attempted to hold her. The patient was told innumerable times that her first years were marked by her being a "colicky" infant and that she had been considered as a candidate for surgery in her first year of life (probably due to a pyloric stenosis) for this condition. Her only memories alluding to this period were that throughout her childhood she was frightened of being picked up and held by her mother; she recalled a vivid scene at her third birthday party when her mother picked her up and she panicked and couldn't be calmed. It was only through the reconstructions in the second year of her analysis that it became clear she associated her mother's presence and touch with the psychic pain of forced isolation—when her mother picked her up, she always carried the threat of ultimately rejecting her by either placing her in the crib or by putting her down without further contact. Undoubtedly, her mother's presence was further associated with the physiologic distress of abdominal pain—a pain that could not be eased. How much our patient's constant agitation had an impact on her mother's functioning we do not know, but clearly, for both the patient and her mother her childhood provided few gratifications.

Thus the major instigator of her lifelong psychic distress was revealed to be her experience of her mother as an imprisoner. Although she could and did clamor for interest throughout her life, including in her analysis, the capacity to receive, and therefore accrete self-structure, was always interfered with by the fear of dismissal, which led to her inability to allow any relationship to be consummated. She was confined to being on the outside in all her relationships, a victim of the unconscious equation of closeness with imprisonment. It is of course no surprise that she never came to her mother for aid, fearing either coldness or criticism, and so she became an isolate in her own home, always lonely, always feeling cold. She was also commonly agitated in school and at home; she could not sit for any length of time and therefore could not comfortably sink into books, movies, or conversations. She was not totally without stimulation, it was just that there was no capacity on her part to completely unfold herself and be lifted up physically or emotionally. It was always too frightening to be receptive to her mother. The stimulation that she did get was that her mother, a former piano teacher, ran the house like a military installation, with rules and fines, until she became ill when the patient was 12. Her siblings, she reported, were somewhat less awed or frightened by her mother and were less nervous than she, but the atmosphere in the house was cold for all, and no one touched, hugged, kissed, or even smiled at one another when Mother was around.

Her father, toward whom she felt more positive, was a warmer person. He did show good humor and he did try to engage her later in her early teens in his sports, fishing, and boating, to which she responded. However, in the first several years of her life, he was not often at home a great deal, away on business and coming home mainly on weekends. In later years, he took the entire family on trips in which she participated with pleasure in the fishing and boating and hiking, but always as one of the family; she did not have an exclusive relationship with him. He remained in her self-experience as an idealized persona from afar who did not utilize his powers to teach, guide, or even influence her destinies in any of her intellectual and social activities.

Her experiences in school paralleled those at home. She became superficially attached to a group of young women and practiced what she had perfected at home, to be the accommodating friend and never display self-needs. Unfortunately for her learning, she experienced an interference with her capacity to "take in" information from her instructors and the books, and she could not enter into a dialogue with teachers or authors. In high school she did not date, nor did she enter into any social activities. One reason was that since early high school days her mother became more and more isolated and was diagnosed as suffering with a depression. Her home situation was so depressing that neither she nor her siblings ever brought friends into their home. When she was 18 and started college in her hometown, her mother's condition worsened, necessitating hospitalization. It was at this time that she started psychotherapy. In her senior year at college, it was discovered that her mother had a breast cancer that had already widely metastasized. The patient reacted to her mother's death, only one year after the discovery of cancer, with a mixture of sadness and relief at the end of her mother's many years of suffering.

The patient's first analysis was, as had been previously noted, helpful to her in many ways. She became able to relate to men at the elementary school where she taught, albeit with anxiety, and began going to group parties and dances. Her first analyst concentrated on her special feeling of competitiveness with her mother for her father's interest and did not focus on her childhood of isolation.

She met her first beau at a dance; two months afterward they married. She had great respect for his serious approach to life and devotion to ideals in his work and family ties. Her relationship to him had been until this analysis marred by her lifelong difficulty in receptivity. Although he had been somewhat reserved in his manner, her barriers to being cherished were the major obstacle to their romantic involvement. In relating to her children, a similar pattern of inhibition was revealed so that she could not enter into the parent–child bond and could only perform in a dutiful manner as wife and mother. Her equilibrium was disrupted again after her first analysis when her father suddenly died of a cerebrovascular accident. She experienced this event as a catastrophe of aloneness although she had seen him infrequently over the years since her mother's death. As she later came to understand, this event symbolized the end of any aspirations to achieve fulfillment of her archaic needs for union with her parental selfobjects.

Review of the Analysis

In a nutshell, as Kohut often said, the entire analysis concerned itself with the vicissitudes of her fixation on a life of restraint and vigilance toward potential invaders of her life space. Her previous work in analysis had not given her the knowledge or experiences necessary to extricate her from her self-in-isolation, a self filled with barriers to intimacy in many forms—toward mirroring, toward calming, toward being led. Her fixations onto this self had led to her experience of life as being empty, but she was unaware that she was functionally unable to partake of the supports that were offered from her milieu. She was filled with "empty complaints," that is, those that she could not pursue to gratification of her needs. Many other methods of maintaining this self-in-isolation became evident through the analysis—dueling with me, withholding information, curtailing the length of her sessions by coming late and leaving early—and, at times the emergence of panic when her intrapsychic walls became permeable and she began attaching herself to me.

The analysis began with the patient's expressions of fear of allowing me to enter into her psychic life in a manner (from her view) similar to her first analysis. Further, she stated that her behaviors and even her voice seemed the same as if she were revisiting her first analysis. From my side, I witnessed a person remarkably responsive to any physical movement on my part, to which she would react with intense anxiety. I can still recall the first years of her analysis when she was frightened of her contact with me and her voice would approach the intensity of shrieking. Several segments from different phases of her analysis will now be presented to give the gist of the analytic work while presenting the entire analytic process in this chapter focused on the termination phase of analysis.

A segment from a session in this phase of her analysis will now be recounted from the original record. After several minutes the patient speaks in a muffled and garbled tone.

Patient: I'm getting more from my husband. I'm close to him because I'm reaching out these days. . . . I have to take it, I always have to be the leader. We had sex last night because I started it, I always have to be the leader, I'm always the one that has to do it all, wherever I go. That gets me so angry. [After several minutes of silence, patient repeated the same comments.]

Analyst: In here too you have to do everything. I don't do enough.

Patient: [interrupts] I'll run the whole show in here too. [voice rises to a shriek]

Analyst: In here too, you have to do everything, I don't do enough.

Patient: [interrupts again almost simultaneously with analyst's comments] I can do it, I can do it [shrieking] . . . What did you say?

Analyst: For some time now each time I speak, you—

Patient: Interrupt . . . I can do it myself, everything . . . [quieter, silent for several minutes]. I always have to do it alone, I'm always alone, I'm always alone. . . . [quiet, several minutes of silence]

Analyst: It's difficult for you to let yourself be with me and open yourself up to me. Each time you begin to open up, you get frightened and push me away.

Patient: [silent for several minutes] I can't do it, I can't let you in. . . . I can't let you in . . . I want to work with somebody [shrieking again] . . . I don't know how to work with somebody. . . . I don't know how to do it. [silent for several minutes, analyst moves slightly in chair] What are you doing back there? [voice quite loud] Are you getting up? That's scary! [silent again for several minutes]

Analyst: Letting yourself enter into a relationship with me stirs up so much danger—before you know it, you're pushing me away, responding to the feelings of danger you're suddenly filled with.

Patient: [quiet, silent for several minutes] That's right.

I quickly learned that my task was to provide a milieu with minimal interventions over a long period of time so that she would begin to experience a safe environment free from any unprecipitated "controlling" on my part. Little by little, the manner in which she structured her life emerged in which she managed to keep everyone, emotionally speaking, at bay. Although she expressed many complaints about her unfulfilled longings, the complaints could not proceed to any fulfillment of these longings since the posture of receptivity required could not be experienced without panic. In this way she maintained herself in equilibrium—empty and lonely but safe. She began now to repeat in the analysis this defensive pattern with complaints of loneliness while at the same time exhibiting defenses against gratification of her needs for contact. Sometimes the resistance came in the form of nonverbal behaviors—late coming, early leaving—other times in her verbal behaviors such as rejections at times of any and all comments of mine. I was able in the early part of the analysis at times very tentatively and infrequently, to explain to her the repetitiousness in her experience of me as yet another source of danger, not a source of succor.

At the end of the second year, she responded to these interventions and the analytic milieu by recounting the history of her early days with her mother. The session in which she responded to the analytic interventions was a dramatic one, occurring 18 months after the beginning of the analysis (condensed from original record).

The patient entered room quickly; she was in an agitated state, and as soon as she lay down, she turned to the wall. Several minutes of silence was interrupted by her coughing, and finally she turned to a supine position.

Patient: Everything's the same [sad tone, slowly expressed] . . . I'm still all alone, I mean inside. . . . [several more minutes]

Analyst: Keeping away from me is safe but *it's so lonely.*

Patient: [several more minutes] You'll just walk away, you'll just put me down. . . . That's the feeling. . . . [several more minutes]

Analyst: As long as you keep away from me—stay behind that wall—I won't pick you up and then put you down and desert you. . . . This must have happened before. . . .

Patient: [long silence] I would never let *her* [mother] touch me—she was trying to touch me with the usual stuff, I never let her. . . . I remember, I must have been three, she tried to pick me up I suppose to kiss me and I went berserk. It was a birthday party, mine I guess. . . . I never let her touch me, well I guess later before she died, I did. I guess I was always antsy around my mother. . . . You know I had that stomach problem when I was a kid, colitis. I guess I was a handful, always bawling. She told me I was supposed to have surgery if I couldn't stop crying. I just never remember wanting to be with her, sit on her lap, get hugs you know, all that stuff. I remember that birthday party of mine clearly now. I remember her, I remember crying. I guess I was always frightened around her. And you know I never did feel comfortable around her. I mean always, as a kid, as a teenager, never could truly relax around her. You know what I mean. I could never simply close both eyes around her not knowing I guess what she'd do.

Over the next long period of time, this archaic pattern of distancing herself, which had been so necessary for her survival as a child, waned and she began to experience, not just complaints of my "indifference," but wishes for more and more expressions of comfort from me.

The following session was from one year later.

Patient: It was a long weekend, I guess I missed you. . . . [long silence] I feel dead today. . . . [long silence] I guess I better leave. . . . [long silence]

Analyst: It's so clear to you that as soon as you unfold your wishes to me to be for you it is dangerous. I'll leave you as soon as you get close to me.

Patient: [long silence] I guess that pattern's going to hound me all my life. She was always walking away from me—you know I told you she was down, she was depressed. She got sicker and sicker. I never could tell her or anyone what was going on in my life. Can you imagine a teenager not telling *anyone* anything about themselves?

The analyst's interventions are directed to the patient's wishes for his continuing and uninterrupted presence in the room with her. The complete intervention has to include the fear of his dangerous dismissal (i.e., the past suddenly emerging in the here-and-now present).

Finally, the actual experiences—not just wishes—of being calmed emerged in the analysis. Her behaviors now revealed that her mothering patterns had changed—she could now touch and hold her children and husband. There were a variety of changes in her life that were now manifest, from getting along well with her children to asking for warmth from her husband to resuming contacts with her siblings, whom she previously had avoided.

Patient: Did I give you a check for last month, I guess so. I used to be so compulsive about money. [silence] I haven't seen you for a couple of days. I guess that relates to me not coming in yesterday. I didn't call you till the morning, my son was sick. Actually I was going to bring him and come in. [silence] My kids and I are getting along, I guess. I'm watching them easier, I know what they're doing. [silence]

Analyst: I wonder if these comments relate to how much care and concern *I* felt about you yesterday.

Patient: I don't think you were worried about me yesterday. [mild laughter]

Analyst: Well, there must be something more to why you waited so long to call me yesterday.

Patient: Funny, I started to call you the night before. I thought, that's too much time. Then all of a sudden I almost didn't call, of course then you *would* have been worried. [silence, several minutes] Went out to dinner last night with my husband and friends, [sad tone, slowed-down speech] he's so unassertive, we waited and waited for a table, he never speaks up for us. [silence] He never takes charge, I made turkey last weekend, he can never carve it up, he always gets me to do it. [silence, few minutes] I considered bringing my son here but he was too sick. You know, I don't feel as frightened as I used to about his illness.

Analyst: What we're looking at here are your wishes that *I* do more for you, that I encourage you so that you get your needs met, like to make sure you get here and get taken care of.

Patient: [silence] I was disappointed yesterday, I did want to see you.

Analyst: Hard to get it out in the open—your needs—in here with me like it was so often in the past to let anyone in on what you wanted. So often in the past it was futile, no one listened, no one was special for you.

Patient: [silent] You know my father's birthday was last week. Last night I was with some people and there was an elderly couple there who talked of their grandchildren. It reminded me of what I didn't get in my life, what could have been. [silence, several minutes]

Analyst: I guess you take it for granted that I'll behave towards you like your father did.

Patient: [silent] Last session I did expect more from you, more of I guess an appreciation of what I was going through—thinking of my father—even though I didn't tell you. [quiet, slowed-down, occasionally crying, then [silent for several minutes]

Analyst: Maybe you've been trying to tell me for some time that you want more comforting from me. Remember that dream about the friend who suddenly was lost . . . ?

Patient: Yeah, right. I was frantic in the dream I couldn't find him. There must be some connection to my son in this, my son's birthday is coming up. I used to have the fantasy that I was going to lose my son to other people like I lost my father. Five years later here I am—only five years later I feel he's gone, he's not mine. [cries] I guess I'm concerned about losing you. I've had such a resistance in taking from you—taking fatherlike care, father protection. I guess it's getting easier.

Here again the analyst's interventions are attempts to help the patient become aware of her wants and longings admixed with fear of the analyst's selfobject care. Comments such as "you want more comforting of me" and "you take it for granted that I'll behave towards you like your father did" were helpful to her, allowing her to see the past in the present so as to detumesce the many painful experiences from her sorrow and lonely past.

In analysis, she could now enter into the work with enthusiasm because as she said, she no longer experienced my comments and other observations as "putdowns" that had blocked her in the past. Now the work centered on the emergence of her assertive strivings quickly followed by the fear that I would be disapproving or abandon her, followed usually by a resumption of the old experiences of empty complaining, and then back again in the here-and-now benevolent milieu of analysis. A typical pattern would be that of telling me of a weekend in which she had a lovemaking experience with her husband that was "good," followed by associations to worries of an impending separation from me, and then to an emerging memory of showing her mother a homework assignment only to have it taken over by her mother.

Following is a segment condensed from the original record.

Patient: It was good over the weekend with my husband and me. I told you we went to the resort just to get away. [silence] I don't know why I'm being quiet again like I used to be in here. . . . We made love, it's funny but he's been starting the sex for some time now. I haven't mentioned that in here. . . . I'm nervous again in here. . . . what's going on again . . . I know it's uneasiness about telling you I set it up with this trip and I really set up the sex, etc., etc. Oh shit, I'm really nervous. . . . [long silence]

Analyst: You're nervous because you're concerned that I'm angry at you for being so assertive without checking it out with me. If you continue in this fashion I'll dismiss you.

Patient: Wait a minute, I know you're not mad when I do things by myself. . . . [silence] Yeah, well, it never was that way at home. I remember bringing home an English assignment once, just once—and asked her for help. We started to work on it and every time I said . . . something about my ideas, she would get angry and dismiss me. I finally got so upset I ran to my room and locked myself in while she stood outside shouting at me. I never asked again, I never showed her my stuff again. . . . That's so sad. It was so sad.

Analyst: Yes, it was as if I too will take anything you do out of your hands unless you check with me.

When she announced that she wished to terminate, it seemed to be a reasonable decision. She had over the past two years been able to engage in her life pursuits with enthusiasm, free from her previous shackles of restraint. As mother, wife, and friend she now seemed to excel consistently. In her analysis, there was little evidence of either the old defense patterns of silence or the exquisite sensitivities to interruptions or empathic errors by retreat into the pattern of withdrawal or panic reactions. However, shortly after she announced her intention to terminate, the analytic sessions revealed that she was uneasy about leaving her treatment and declaring a termination date. The focus now shifted to her wish to have me reassure her that I was not simply dismissing her by allowing her to terminate; I was pleased with her achievements and she matched my ideal for an analyzed person. Five months afterward she decided that she could terminate.

The Termination Phase

The material in the sessions directly after the setting of the termination date found her experiencing great agitation. In her view, she could not leave me or "had to have me to live," expressions that were coupled with the experiences that I was not "sufficiently" involved with her and that I was dismissing her out of disappointment with her performance in analysis. These comments evoked associations to her mother whose interest in her, minimal as it was, only emerged when she was in great need, indeed when she clamored or actually fought for interest. On the other hand, because of her childhood of deprivation, she had been uneasy around her mother, fearing any physical contact with her. The interpretations I made at this point, one month after the date-setting, were that she was structuring her relationship with me so that I would stop the termination and *make* her continue the analysis indefinitely. Her subsequent associations to this interpretation confirmed this interpretation. Thus directly after setting the date of termination, the patient's experience of the analyst heightened considerably and led to a revival of the relationship with me that repeated the earlier phases of her analysis. In this defense transference, the patient experienced me as withdrawn, withholding, and unempathic or dangerously intrusive. This pattern of defending herself was previously reconstructed in her analysis as having two roots; one was traced to her mother, who many times was aloof, distracted, and unavailable to her children. The patient also experienced her mother at times as a frightening presence who might imprison her. In her early life, she had been a colicky infant and could not be calmed. She had never experienced her mother's embraces as calming, only as leading to isolation in her crib without relief of her physiological and psychological pain.

Now, suddenly, so it seemed, after this initial post–date-setting phase of the heightened defense transference, a break in this mode of interaction transpired and she became receptive again to my presence and my words; she experienced calming and enhanced worth without resistance. For the remainder of the months of her termination process, this cyclic pattern—the resumption of her defense transference and the working through of this pattern, followed by the acceptance of my interest and the enhancing of her self-value and cohesiveness—continued to be repeated.

In the next month of her analysis, her defense transference was now reenacted with me and also in relation to her husband and their three children: once again, in her view, she had to be the "cement" of the family, obeying only what she interpreted as their needs and her role in gratifying these needs. "He's not like my partner, I have to take care of everything. It's me taking care of myself again. No one on my side. I never felt anyone on my side—my younger sister, my younger brothers. Now my three children, my husband." And then, on the following day of the analysis, she would say: "I had to tell you how terrible it was, regardless of what you were saying or doing. I still want you to hear how bad it's been." On this same following day, she would experience and articulate the idea that she had been very helped by my presence in sharing and understanding her burdens from the past and present. I told her that I too was experienced as a nongiver and that she was in effect dismissing me and not deriving any support from me. These comments liberated remembrances from her past of her years of caretaking of a cancer-ridden mother, a well-meaning but ineffectual father, and a vivid, previously repressed memory of the death scene of her mother. When I interpreted her transference onto me as one who was also identified as a nongiver, she responded that I too overvalued her capacities as a caretaker and in this way I too was not genuinely appreciating her. At the end of this intense period of reliving the experience of being unappreciated, unrecognized, and only living for others—her "rightful place in the sun"—she quietly expressed the feeling that she would miss her analysis and the help she derived from it in sharing her inner life. In fact, she became uneasy, stating, "How do I do life without you? What am I going to do when I quit seeing you?"

This period ended with a flurry of feelings of being accepted and of experiencing an enhancement of self-value, albeit with the concern ". . . how long that took to make you part of me. Hope it'll last. I hope termination will not take it away. I've never experienced this feeling before. You've always been there, I've always been too scared to acknowledge it, such a struggle to get here! I've always had the feeling—from her—that I've asked for too much. It's like you've always said: 'Here, have me!'" These comments were in relation to a dream that in form and meaning was repeated somewhat later in the termination. The dream was: "You and I were going on a trip where you were to give a series of lectures and I would be your secretary. Your wife became enraged and tried to stop it but you arranged it so that we left while she was away visiting her relative."

The next session also centered on a dream: "I was riding a motorcycle in a strange place. I paused at a gas station to rest. It was hot. I debated for a long time with myself over whether I had enough gas; finally I told the attendant to fill my tank."

The associations all led to the uncovering of an experience still new to her, the overt wish to obtain reassurance of my continuing interest even as she was terminating her formal relationship with me.

The following sessions were predictably filled with material of being "on the outside," in fact, the clearest "acting in" of the self-state of childhood we had ever witnessed. The patient complained of the tension of this phase. She was sad and alone but unable to remove herself from being immersed in despair, the experience of being uncared for, which she now related solely to me and her analysis, complaining that the sadness was only in "here." Her reaction to my clarifying comments relating her past to her present and to me was a torrent of the most intense anger in the entire analysis, ending up with this statement: "You don't care, you don't care, you don't tell me what to do—analysis is all washed up." And now for the first time in six years, she exhibited the behavior she had demonstrated in the early part of her analysis—a massive outpouring of rage in a shrieking and sobbing outburst during which she was unable to control herself for extended periods.

Here was another example of her wish to stay hidden and deprived under the umbrella of the defense transference. She would continue to complain of her malevolent surround but—and this is the crucial point—I would, in her transference distortion, continue to overlook her and "be" the unempathic and therefore ungiving archaic selfobject.

With the termination two weeks away, she now stated: "I should not terminate, I'm not ready." I proposed delaying it; it seemed to me (and I interpreted these considerations to her) that she was pursuing a course in which she would end up her analysis in a manner that mimicked her actual early life experiences—the self-state of the youngster deprived of nourishment of her self by a lack of applause and secondarily by the absence of calming, soothing, direction, and standards.

She was surprised at her own reactions to my suggestion that we delay the termination. She took the suggestion without resistance and said, "It felt good to have you in control. I was obedient to my mother but never truly accepting. This was different, you were responding to me. This was not duty." There were of course reactions to her acceptance. She had an anxiety dream in which she was driving endlessly over dangerous rocky mountains, but not really driving, only steering. Her associations to this dream centered on her uneasiness at giving over control intermingled with her satisfaction in this regard (only steering, not being in charge). Another dream dealt with a violinist who played at her command. In connection with this dream, she reminded herself of all the gifts she had never experienced in her life; she was now going to take it all from me.

The next period—the final month—dealt with her feeling flooded by her wishes to attach herself permanently to me. She felt that coming to analysis was crucial, and she was distressed at the prospect of losing me and not having a replacement for me. This expression of my importance to her was a new experience. The grief that she was now living through was focused on her separation from me, without displacements now, and highlighted in a dream of aloneness:

> I had an appointment to see you in a large foreign city. There was a sudden burst of rain on the city, stopping traffic, I could hardly see through the window from my car. I stopped to ask a policeman for direction, it was two miles in the opposite direction. I decided to walk and suddenly in front of me, I saw an awesome church which made me stop and view it in wonder. The Vatican? St. Paul's. I woke up before I could see you.

The awesome church made her think of her overpowering feeling of loss at the end of analysis and the loss of me without replacements. The main associations dealt with her impending loss, the grief of "feeling you inside of me and now it's going to hurt to lose you."

The last three weeks were a mixture of complaints of not feeling well, feeling incomplete, and questioning why she "had to leave." I repeated my interpretations to her of her wish to leave analysis as a sad, deprived person still living out her life with the experiences of being unvalued, not wanting more mirroring, reinforcing her need to *stay* deprived and therefore be in the ancient self-selfobject dyad. She had a series of confirmatory dreams all relating to the theme of being with a person (a man) who rejected her. She complained at length of her inability to celebrate her achievement in terminating the analysis and related it to her mother, who was never present for her triumphs in school or elsewhere. She said, "I've changed unbelievably, it's hard to remember what I was like. I'm so different in my self-esteem, I just don't have problems anymore, I've just not felt cherished in *here*." The tension of experiencing the intense relived deprivation during one session evoked in her a cry for help that I wasn't providing. She had a dream in which a friend was in need of financial aid. She went to the bank and talked the loan officer into giving her friend a loan. Her associations to this dream culminated in her awareness that she needed me to be her advocate. She said, "Why am I having this dream now? I'm not starting, I'm terminating."

Finally, three sessions before the end, she recounted that the "sad period is over." All the relived pain of deprivation was seemingly at an end and a mixture of pleasurable feelings and sadness now entered the analysis. She had a triumphal dream in which she was singled out by a man and in the process ". . . outshone the other woman who was competing for him." However, as she stated, ". . . the other woman without anger recognized it." She said in her elaboration and interpretation of the dream, "They both felt good about me, I didn't have any ulterior motive. I just didn't have to hold back, I felt recognized for my worth." She associated to the lifelong pattern of her unrewarded and guilt-ridden strivings for outclassing her mother, which were finally resolved in the dream. The next material dealt with her sadness that life would be difficult without me to know of her and recognize her accomplishments, and then came the last session.

The last session began with a gift, a wall hanging that she said would remind me of her. She then recounted her final dream:

Patient: Here is the dream. I'm in Marshall Field's. I'm looking in a mirror and I am trying on mother's fur hat. (I have it at home usually, I only wear it once in a while.) I'm looking to see if I look OK in her hat with my black coat. I like it. (I guess I'm trying to see what part of Mother fits with me.) [short silence]
I really do want to hear from you today. I want to know how you send your children away when they go on a big trip. What advice do you give them? [cries]

Analyst: This must be your association between the mirror in your dream and me. Your reflection in the mirror pleased you, I guess you want to know if I am pleased at the way you look at the end of your analysis.

Patient: Yeah, I do. [quiet, short-lived] You know, Mother was a fine seamstress, I didn't keep enough of her outfits. It's like I didn't take enough from her. [silence]

Analyst: I guess you want to be sure you take enough from me. My stamp of approval.

Patient: Yeah. I've gotten that from you. It does feel good. It's good to look good. I guess I want parting wisdom's words from you.

Analyst: I tell my children when they go off, "You look good to me!" Just like I'm telling you.

Patient: You tell them that. [cries] Do you go visit them? You tell them you're pleased with them.

Analyst: It's pleasure, it's a joy to an analyst when a person you've worked with can go forward by themselves.

Patient: I feel good. Yesterday I realized, when the kids were jumping around, I can calm myself.

She then associated to a time in her college days when her mother paid her a visit and suggested she would like to live with her permanently, which frightened her. She discounted my comment that she was harboring a concern over whether I was genuinely pleased over her new-found confidence by telling me that she knew I was pleased "without strings attached." She said, "I've never been able to feel important and special. I've gotten enough. I have tools to straighten myself out if I get down. I guess I've grown up. We haven't left anything out."

DISCUSSION

The discussion will be centered on the three findings from the termination phase of the analysis: 1) The intensity of the recapitulated defense transference, 2) the seeming dissolution of the gains in the termination phase from previous analytic work, and 3) the telescoped nature of the activity in the termination—from defensiveness to well-being and back again.

The defense transference from the self psychology viewpoint is the unconscious experience of the patient that the analyst's self is akin to the patient's selfobjects of her childhood (Muslin, 1981). The patient then experiences those needs, also from childhood, to posture herself—the defense part of the defense transference—in a manner guaranteed to derive optimum gratification (or at least safety) from this "new" selfobject, the analyst. Thus, a patient will maintain a self-state based on disavowal or repression if the defense transference dictates that one "must" relate in this manner in the recapitulated self-selfobject relationship of the analysis to derive some measure of acceptance. The factors that enable the patient and the analyst to work through the defense transference are well known to every analyst. They include the patient's capacity to be allied with the analyst in the work of observing and ultimately disarming the self posturing itself for "protection" in relation to the selfobject. If the patient's encounters with selfobjects during the formative years of the self-selfobject dyads have been overwhelmingly negative, the defense transference phase of his or her analysis may not be overcome as the patient continues forever to defend *against* the immersion into the basic mirroring, idealizing, or twinship selfobject transference and with it the experience of the gratifications of being understood, valued, or calmed, which ultimately lead to the structure-building of analysis.

Other factors that are instrumental in overcoming the defense transference are also well known, including the maxim that the analyst is to provide an atmosphere of understanding so that the intrapsychic malevolence is sufficiently diminished to allow for the formation of a selfobject transference. The atmosphere of understanding includes in some cases the protracted period of silent acceptance of the patient's experiences; in other instances, the analyst interprets, with tact in relation to dosage and timing, those experiences that are necessary to call attention to in order to give the patient freedom from unconscious repetitive experiences that interfere with growth and, more specifically, with the formation of the basic therapeutic transference (Daniels, 1976; Muslin, 1981; Kohut, 1984).

The termination period in this analysis centered on the working out of a recapitulated defense transference of intense proportions. In the process of working this pattern out, more intense experiences of need and wishes for gratifications of needs emerged along with the experiences of feeling affirmed and calmed in the analysis. The crucial question at termination, however, focuses on whether there is evidence of internalization of structure at the end, not just the experience of being appreciated or calmed in the analysis but the evidence of *self*-calming and *self*-valuing. Further evidence of a successful analysis includes an enhancement of self-cohesiveness with lessened vulnerability to fragmentation. There should also be a diminution in the patient's need to enter into archaic transferences, and above all there should be an increase in the capacity to enter into mature selfobject relationships based on empathic resonance, not merger. All these findings are evidence of a more cohesive self—a self *not* fixed on archaic selfobjects and the limited gratifications available in these mergers. In sum, a successful analysis results in a self that is considerably less frightened to go beyond the limitations of archaic self-selfobject relationships.

In the case material presented, there were no new findings in the termination sessions in the sense of historical material or emergence of patterns of self-states previously undetected. There was, however, an intensity, a desperateness in the termination sessions in which the patient, perhaps for the last time in her life, attempted to eke out from a fantasied, aloof, at times frightening, and distracted *parent-in-fantasy*—the analyst—nurturance and direction. Once again, the mission was a "failure" on two counts: she experienced the analyst in the transference as unresponsive to her archaic needs and herself as being stifled in her ability to be sufficiently demanding. She finally relinquished her ancient self, with its strivings and its fears, and was again receptive to her here-and-now world and her here-and-now self and its mature self-objects, including the analyst.

Can this desperate attempt to reenact the old drama of her archaic strivings for self-structure be conceived of as a ubiquitous finding in the termination period of analyses, or self-psychologically conducted analyses? It is true of course that termination, regardless of the joy at the achievement or crying at the happy-ending aspect, indicates the relationship is at an end, and therefore ushers in the modal associations to separation. Patients who are ending their analyses which, if successful, have only recently removed themselves from the imprisonment of a stunted self (assuming the analyses were successful). The analyst, in terminating with his patient, is thus removing himself as a selfobject support to a fledgling self that has only recently interiorized sufficient in the way of selfobject strengths to have established the features of *self*-calming and *self*-admiration. Thus, the newly analyzed self is a vulnerable self and therefore, under the stress of permanent separation from the selfobject analyst, relives and reenacts the ancient pathways to archaic bonds—this was Kohut's hypothesis. The intensity of the termination-reliving will be determined by the successes and failures of the patient's previous archaic selfobject encounters. The intensity of the termination and the successes or failures of the working through phase of the analysis will be determined in part by the patient's fears of removing herself/himself from these archaic patterns to strive for acknowledgment and support of wishes for greater selfhood.

Perhaps the most important overview of termination as a phase of psychoanalytic treatment is that it is needed, perhaps required, for the patient to attempt to cement the gains of the psychoanalysis by reviving again, this time with more awareness, the mission to achieve ancient selfobject gratifications, albeit stultifying to self-growth, in order to finally relinquish the strivings to repeat the archaic self-selfobject involvements. And perhaps this is all one should say. Looking at the disarray in the termination phase reported here, especially the flurry of the reemerging defense transference, would lead one, it is suggested here, to a distorted version of the gains in a patient's self from psychoanalytic treatment. There was, after all, in the material presented more than an eruption of her archaic patterns of being and seeming. She did continue to come to her analytic sessions and focused much if not most of her strivings onto the analyst. Although there was a great deal of intensity about her old patterns of feeling-and-being, there was little in the way of reenacting these dramas into the outside world, as had previously been her pattern. There was as reported earlier an alternation in the material rather than the fixity that characterized the first phase of her analysis. She did continue to respond with appropriate associations to the interventions of the analyst. She did continue to maintain her introspective functioning and complained of the painful state of affairs—the reemerging defense transference—from which she felt unable to escape. Her final dreams and her self-posture revealed that her direct wishes for acceptance and admiration in the direct manner in which it was revealed were in the end the major self-alterations. These data reminded us that we were not just witnessing a dissolution of the gains of her analysis but rather a *telescoped* or *recapitulated* analysis. Some would surmise that if earlier defensive attitudes and behavior recur at the end of an analysis in a massive form they raise legitimate questions about the extent and success of the working-through, but it is clear that in this case, the massive upheaval was a temporary phenomenon and ultimately helpful in cementing the gains of the analyses.

Thus, the final session revealed the patient's newfound capacity to unfold her needs to the analyst for guidance and warmth, "parting wisdom's words," in a direct, unimpeded, and undisguised manner. This patient, after all, had entered analysis unable to relate any of her strivings in a direct manner and was imprisoned in her resistance to any human encounter throughout her life before her analysis.

In sum, the discussion of the termination of the case described has centered on what emerged in the last five months of the patient's analysis, essentially the intense telescoping of the major movements in the analysis revisited and highlighting what was for her the central issue, the final attempts to remake—through *realized* gratifications from the analyst of her archaic needs—her archaic self-selfobject relationships. Termination viewed as a telescoped phase of analysis in which each patient in greater or lesser quantities relives and reenacts ancient dramas before the final separation, was presented as an explanatory hypothesis. Thus, some patients, reflecting the strength of their early ties, would either pass easily through this phase without much disarray whereas others, as in the case described, experience much anguish reflecting the strength of their archaic selfobject bonds and their fears of separation from these intense and malignant bonds. It remains to be seen whether there is a special quality to the terminations of analyses conducted utilizing the strategies and tactics of self psychology, a reasonable surmise. Perhaps further microscopic evaluations of terminations will uncover characteristic movements, phases, or processes beyond what has been described, granted that one makes room for the uniqueness of each patient (the nature of the psychopathology and its residual impact on what is free in the self and what is frozen) and the uniqueness of therapists—their capacity for empathy, their transferences and countertransferences.

Although some may argue that termination does not, on the whole, bring back any prolonged defense transference (i.e., an intense reliving of the preanalyzed self), one must examine each case of an analysis, as our predecessors taught, as a research project. Some may even assert that termination should not be considered a legitimate phase of analysis. To the contrary, I would assert, as this case teaches, that termination may be helpful and even essential to cementing the gains of an analysis—at least it proved so in this case. To repeat an assertion made earlier, in those cases in which there has been massive trauma, their intense fixations of patients do not easily become disengaged from their original position, which defuses the strength of their resistance to structural changes. During the stress of separation-abandonment in the termination phase, these selves revert back to their original defensive postures.

This patient had a recovery from such a massive fixation, which had culminated in a narcissistically deficient self and a compulsion to reenact her malignant transference with everyone in her life, including her therapists. This report offers a documented validation of the import of a self analysis with a person with massive developmental traumata.

In harmony with the views expressed here pertaining to the need to examine each termination as a research project, it is germane to examine Kohut's views on the differences in the termination phase as reflecting the differences of the analytic task in patients with different lesions of the self. Kohut (1977) mentioned two varieties of the termination syndrome: "the well investigated pathological events that take place in the terminal phase of the analysis of the classical transference neuroses and the so far comparatively uninvestigated psychological events that tend to occur in the terminal phase of the analyses of narcissistic personality disorders" (p. 33). He went on to note the difference in termination of those in which the work had concerned a primary structural defect (Mr. I) and those in whom the work concerned the rehabilitation of compensatory structures (Mr. M). In both instances, during the termination phase (Goldberg, 1978), the material of the sessions revealed that "all the results that had been obtained via the working-through processes had been sham . . ." (p. 34). In the instance of Mr. I, it appeared that "all the progress of transmuting the self-object into psychological structure had been sham" (p. 33). In the case of Mr. M, it appeared that the compensatory structures "had not really become stronger" (p. 34).

A final note may be in order pertaining to the termination process from the side of the analyst and his or her personal reactions. Again, one must be careful to isolate those unique characteristics of the analyst that make for more or less responsivity to certain material or certain needs of the patient. Analysts, like parents, vary, as Kohut said, in their empathic capacity for different developmental experiences: some can identify easily with the self of a mirror-hungry person, others cannot. Certainly analysts form transferences—not just reactions of opposition or dislike to their patient's transferences, the so-called countertransferences—onto their patients and may experience them, albeit in a limited manner, as figures to be admired.

Apart from all these considerations of the idiosyncracies of the patient and the analyst, it is my surmise that an analyst preoccupied with the considerations of empathy—not drive-defense awareness—throughout an analysis experiences more self-reverberations throughout the analysis and therefore experiences more in the way of separation experiences at the end. These experiences may take the form of difficulties in terminating and may be experienced as excess concern over the patient's welfare or doubts over the completeness of the analysis. The analyst has little certitude that a given patient has reached his or her limits of structure-growth in the self. It is always, as Freud would put it, a case of *non liquet*, because in some, the possibility exists that further internalization may yet be forthcoming with the continuation of the analysis; in others this limit has been reached. We must be mindful in the study of self psychology analyses that our notion of cure is not on the resolution of the transference neuroses but on the accretion of self-structure, the transmuting internalizations that eventuate after the basic selfobject transferences are established. It is therefore a judgment made by patient and analyst that sufficient structure has been established in the self.

The transformations in the analysand's self-experience of the analyst after the analysis concern the analyst being experienced as the one to whom the analysand can turn during times of tragedy or other crises. Perhaps one of the major events in an analysis is that the analysand no longer experiences the analyst at the end as an archaic selfobject. The permanent memory traces of the analyst in the analysand's experiences in my view have become that of a mature selfobject. The patient holds the conviction that, if a crisis occurs, hopefully the therapist will continue to "be there"; the analyst's experiences range from reflections of interest in the analysand's current circumstances to concerns over whether the self-changes after analysis perdure.

REFERENCES

Buxbaum, E. (1950), Technique of terminating analysis. *Internat. J. Psycho-Anal.*, 31:14–190.

Daniels, R. (1976), Manifestations of transference: Their implications for the first phase of psychoanalysis. *J. Amer. Psychoanal. Assn.*, 17:991–1014.

Dewald, P. (1972), The clinical assessment of structural change. *J. Amer. Psychoanal. Assn.,* 20:302–324.

Ekstein, R. (1960), Working through and termination of analysis. *J. Amer. Psychoanal. Assn.,* 13:57–78.

Fenichel, O. (1924), From the terminal phase of analysis. In: *Collected Papers, Vol. 1.* New York: Norton, 1953, pp. 27–31.

Ferenczi, S. (1927), The problem of termination of psycho-analysis. In: *Final Contribution to Psycho-Analysis.* New York: Basic Books, 1955, pp. 77–86.

Firestein, S. (1973), *Termination in Psychoanalysis.* New York: International Universities Press.

Freud, S. (1937), Analysis terminable and interminable. *Standard Edition,* 23:209–254. London: Hogarth Press, 1964.

Goldberg, A. (1978), *Psychology of the Self.* New York: International Universities Press.

Kohut, H. (1977), *The Restoration of the Self.* New York: International Universities Press.

—— (1984), *How Does Analysis Cure?* ed. A. Goldberg & P. Stepansky. Chicago: University of Chicago Press.

Kubie, L. (1968), Unsolved problems in the resolution of the transference. *Psychoanal. Quart.,* 37:331–352.

Loewald, H. (1962), Internalization, separation, mourning, and the superego. *Psychoanal. Quart.,* 31:483–504.

Macalpine, I. (1950), The development of the transference. *Psychoanal. Quart.,* 19:501–539.

Muslin, H. (1981), On working through in self psychology. In: *Progress in Self Psychology,* ed. A. Goldberg. Hillsdale, NJ: The Analytic Press.

Muslin, H. (1989), Analysis terminable and interminable revisited. In: *Progress in Self Psychology, Vol. 5,* ed. A. Goldberg. Hillsdale, NJ: The Analytic Press.

Rangell, L. (1966), An overview of the ending of an analysis. In: *Psychoanalysis in the Americas,* ed. R. E. Litman. New York: International Universities Press, pp. 141–165.

Reich, A. (1950), On the termination of analysis. In: *Psychoanalytic Contributions.* New York: International Universities Press, 1973, pp. 121–135.

Chapter 10

A Self-Psychological Perspective on Multiple Personality Disorder

Sandra R. Palef

There is a Janus-faced quality to multiple personality disorder (MPD), consisting on the one hand of a rejection of traumatic early experiences, and on the other of an attempt to maintain and solidify those very experiences. Because the parents of these patients never acknowledged the painful affect states their children were enduring, these states cannot be acknowledged by the patients. But they are an essential part of the child's self-experience and must therefore be maintained at all costs. The child's dilemma is how to preserve some measure of self-organization when her experiences are intolerable handled alone; when they are treated by others with indifference or disbelief; and when their outward expression is extinguished by means of punishment and threats of death. What can happen is that the huge empathic gap between the child's affective experience and the parents' response is replicated in the patient's self-organization by means of dissociations and the subjective experience that the walled-off affects are not real, or not hers. This allows the child to preserve a tie to the caregiver who is still needed but who, for his or her own reasons, cannot acknowledge the child's reactions. However, the more the affects are treated as unreal, the more they have to be reified in order to maintain the self. The MPD patient's creative solution to this dilemma is not only to dissociate the painful affect states but also to concretize them in the form of individual personalities with their own names, ages, voices, looks, memories, and characters.

My understanding of MPD is a self-psychological one[1] because it emphasizes both the need for selfobjects to provide attuned responsiveness to the child's affect states and the need to maintain the organization of subjective experience by concretizing it in various ways. Kohut (1971, 1977) explored and conceptualized these needs, and his ideas were later developed by other analysts. More specifically, in four recent books (Stolorow and Lachmann, 1980; Atwood and Stolorow, 1984; Stolorow, Brandchaft, and Atwood, 1987; Stolorow and Atwood, 1992), it has been argued that affects are the organizers of self-experience. The need for selfobjects is fundamentally the need for caregivers to affirm, accept, differentiate, synthesize, and contain varying affect states. When such affect attunement is absent, the child develops a propensity to dissociate or disavow his affects and they cannot become integrated into the organization of his self-experience. They argue further that painful experiences in and of themselves need not be traumatic. It is only the absence of the caregiver's attuned responsiveness to the child's painful affects that produces states of mind characterized as unbearable, traumatic, overwhelmed, and disintegrated.

At the same time, these authors have proposed that a supraordinate principle of human motivation is the need to maintain the organization of subjective experience. This may be done by concretizing experience in various ways, including neurotic symptoms, symbolic objects, behavioral enactments, and dreams. They argue further that dramatic and even bizarre enactments, as well as delusions and hallucinations, are concretizations used by severely traumatized people to restore or maintain a self-organization they experience as unstable and likely to disintegrate. According to Stolorow, Brandchaft, and Atwood (1987) the psychotic person uses concrete delusional images to "dramatize and reify his endangered psychic reality, casting it in a material and substantial form, thereby restoring his vanishing belief in its validity" (p. 133). It may be true that the more severe the trauma, the more unstable is the self-organization, and in turn the greater is the need for more dramatic concretizations.

In all of their books, these authors continually emphasize the intersubjective contexts in which these concretizations of personal experience arise and recede. They argue that when the therapist understands and validates the patient's subjective truth symbolized in the concretization, whether it be an enactment or a delusion, then the concretization is no longer necessary and disappears. If the patient is tenacious about it, it

---

[1] For reviews of the literature on MPD as well as case studies, see the following: Lasky (1978), Marmer (1980), Berman (1981), Lampl-de Groot (1981), Kluft (1985), Putnam (1989), and Ross and Loewenstein (1992).

points to a continuing disruption in the validating function of the therapeutic tie. Many cases are presented beginning with concretizations that dissolve once a selfobject transference is well established, and appear again only when the empathic bond is disrupted. In MPD, on the other hand, such concretizations survive for years even when a validating therapeutic relationship has been well established. Indeed, it is only when the MPD patient sufficiently trusts in the attuned responsiveness of her therapist that she will be willing to expose her inner world of concretized selves. The MPD case that I will present is both an attempt to apply the principles of self psychology to an understanding of MPD and an attempt to demonstrate that the concretizations demanded by massive selfobject failure in childhood may have to persist for many years before the affects they dramatize may be thoroughly understood, validated, and integrated.

I will illustrate my theme that MPD arises out of a dual need to dissociate and to concretize unacknowledged childhood experiences by organizing my presentation of the case along the following lines. First, I will present examples of the patient's voices, dreams, and use of visual metaphor, hallucination, and perception that come from points in the analysis before diagnosis. Second, I will describe how I directly acknowledged the patient's voices and how this led to the unfolding of 15 separate personalities of which the patient had almost total amnesia. Finally, I will discuss an example postdiagnosis of my failure to acknowledge some of the patient's voices and how the working through of this failure led to some integration.

About the patient I will say only that she is middle-aged, separated with two children, and conducts a successful business. I'll call her Jane. As is typical of MPD patients, she is a survivor of father–daughter incest, which in her case began in her infancy and continued until she was 17. Her adolescence and early adulthood were filled with suicide attempts and hospitalizations, along with numerous diagnoses, numerous therapists, and numerous psychiatric and psychopharmacological treatments, none of which seemed to help her very much.

Let me turn first to Jane's voices, which I understand as an expression of her dual need to rid herself of the affects of her traumatic past and maintain and solidify them by concretizing them. In the period before diagnosis, Jane heard voices only sporadically and most of the time could not differentiate them or hear their words clearly. An exception occurred six months into the analysis when Jane's parents arrived for a two-month visit and Jane panicked. She heard someone say he or she hated her. She thought she heard *me* say I wanted her to leave. She interrupted a session to ask me, "Why did you let me do those things with him?" The affects of self-hatred and guilt these voices dramatize belong, in Jane's experience, not to her but to others, including me. In fact, she reported that she was in a constant battle with the voices because they tell her that I don't care about her and will eventually hate her and abandon her, and that she should stop telling me things and kill herself. She was terrified that the voices were like gangrene and would take over her mind. As I began to realize that Jane's voices were the concretized expression of a dissociated part of her childhood experience, an experience that was probably never heard or never believed but needed to be maintained and validated, I communicated this under-standing to her and began to speak directly to the voices. It was only later that I came to see that the voices did not represent a unitary part of her but rather a whole system of separate selves; furthermore, their full discovery required not only my speaking to them but also their speaking to me. Every time Jane asked me, "Can you hear them?" I realized that my not hearing them repeated for her the experience of not being heard in childhood.

Under the pressure of her parents' visit, Jane reported dreams that also reflected her need to dissociate and concretize. In the first dream, she had a bump on her foot and the doctor said he would cut the foot off, but if the problem appeared on the other foot, it meant "it" had gone right through her body. It had. In the second dream there were a bunch of heads, including hers and mine, decapitated, sitting on ice. Jane's associations to these dreams led to her fear that the gangrenous voices would take her over, and to her wish to cut off or freeze out the parts of herself she feared. A third dream was about two men in compe-tition; the loser had to have a limb cut off, and one man had already lost both hands and feet. To this dream, Jane associated to feeling numb about her parents' visit. One may argue that the dream images of ampu-tations, decapitations, and multiple heads depict in concrete anatomical form Jane's many dissociations, and that the ice symbolizes the dissoci-ated experiences being preserved. Note that I am one of the heads on ice, a needed container perhaps for the experiences Jane still had to dis-sociate because I, like her parents, had not fully acknowledged them.

Later on in the analysis, after I had heard all about the incest but before diagnosis, Jane reported visual metaphors, hallucinations, and perceptions that also expressed her need to dissociate her painful affect states, and her growing desire not only to preserve but to unify them. For example, again under the pressure of an upcoming visit by her father, Jane became very frightened and told me that she wanted to put all her dangerous feelings in safety-deposit boxes, to be safe. She imag-ined a whole wall of them. This image beautifully captured the nature of Jane's self-structure, portraying not only how her affects were dissoci-ated from each other and from herself, but also how they were being maintained and preserved like valuable possessions one might lock away for the future. When her father was about to arrive, Jane had visual hallucinations of blocks that did not fit together. She kept trying desperately to fit them together, but they kept coming apart. We understood that in trying to "block" her memories of the incest lest her father see her fear or anger and become enraged himself, Jane was keeping the various parts of herself from fitting together. She wanted to integrate herself, but her feelings for her father were too disparate. On one hand, she loved him, sent him money to visit her, and craved his love; on the other hand, she wanted to be dead before he arrived because she feared and hated him so much. She was aware of feeling she was in pieces, and associated to how she sees herself in a mirror, that is, only her eyes, or only her mouth, or only her nose, but never her whole face.

It was in this context that I asked Jane's voices to speak to me.[2] More specifically, I said, "Do the voices know who I am?" She said yes. I said, "Can they hear me?" She said yes. I said, "Will they speak to me?" She said no. They hated me because I wanted her to live and they all wanted to die. Nevertheless, Jane spontaneously began to tell me about them, outlining seven different personalities, as follows: 1) a baby, maybe two years old, who whimpers and cries and doesn't talk, who wants me to look after her and speak softly to her as I sometimes do; 2) an older child who cries uncontrollably and who took over recently when Jane was at work; 3) an angry man who wants Jane to kill herself; 4) an authoritarian man with a deep voice who tells Jane to be strong; 5) a man with a normal voice; 6) a woman with a screechy voice who ridicules her and tells her she is a wimp; 7) a competent, confident woman who is independent, doesn't need anyone, has a sense of humor the others think is sick, and is responsible for conducting Jane's business. Jane said she would like to be the competent one. She was afraid to leave at the end of this session, afraid that one of the voices would take over forever but would be unable to cope. She said that she had never really acknowledged the voices the way she had today, and thought that maybe we shouldn't; they should just go away.

In the following session, the voices began to speak to me directly. Jane began the session by telling me that she had stayed in town the previous night because of a bad snowstorm. Then, in a whiny, pleading, babylike voice I had heard before, she asked me to speak to her in soft tones the way I sometimes did. I said softly that I knew that she liked to be spoken to gently, like a baby, and when she smiled contentedly as she usually did when I spoke to her this way, I thought perhaps this was

---

[2] I am indebted to Dr. Douglas W. Detrick for suggesting that I use this approach with Jane.

one of the baby personalities she had identified that I was now speaking to. Jane's voice then changed to one that was quick, mumbled, and pouty, one I had also heard before. I asked whom I was speaking to and was told it was a child who is so alone she withdraws and doesn't want to be with anybody or talk to anybody. I asked if she had a name and an age and was told only that she was about 12. There was also a 17-year-old who remembers the incest, but I do not know who told me that. Then I was speaking to the competent woman who told me that it was she who conducted Jane's business, and that she didn't need me and didn't care about anything. She did say, however, that she enjoyed her work and liked making money. I felt triumphant now because Jane had always insisted that she was incapable of experiencing pleasure. I asked to speak to the angry man, and another voice told me that the angry man refused to speak to me but *he* would speak to him for me. He identified himself simply as another man. He told me that the angry man wanted to murder people by choking them to death with his bare hands. That included me. He wouldn't actually do it though; he was choking on his own anger.

Then Jane began complaining that the session had been wasted. When I asked her if she was aware of our talking about her loneliness or her work or her anger, she said that all she could remember was our discussion of her activities the night before. I explained that I had been talking to the voices, and mentioned talking softly to the baby and talking about anger with a male voice. She said that she had been a skinny child with a runny nose who always sucked her thumb and whose genitals hurt. And she said that she was frightened by the angry man. She was shocked that she couldn't remember any of our conversation; she was frightened and wanted to know if she was a multiple personality. I said yes, hedging in case she couldn't handle it. Again she said that this was the first time we had acknowledged the voices, and she wasn't sure we should do it because they might gain control. And she complained that there wasn't enough time for her today. She said it felt as if there were a hundred people behind bars clamoring to touch me, for me to rescue them.

In subsequent sessions, 15 personalities competed with Jane for full control of her behavior, most of whom had names and ages and all of whom spoke differently, related to me differently, had unique memories, and were organized around a particular affect or characteristic. Jane was usually so completely amnesic when the voices were out that she lost time in the sessions and was convinced that I was making the clock go faster. She complained vociferously that by listening to the voices I was depriving her of needed time with me, and only relented again when I concentrated on her and she felt strong enough to let another voice be heard. Whenever Jane heard some of what the voices said, or when I reported it to her, she would insist that it was all "just imaginings," not real, and definitely not her. A year later, after I had acknowledged Jane's voices, listed to their memories and feelings, witnessed their flashback experiences, and understood and validated them, Jane still needed to keep her voices separate from herself.

My final example concerns a failure to acknowledge aspects of my patient and how the understanding and working through of the disruption led to the beginnings of integration. One Christmas, about a year after diagnosis, Jane informed me in angry and defiant tones that if I could take a two-week holiday so could she, and she decided to take a two-week trip with her daughter immediately following mine. At the same time she insisted that I continue to be available to her by telephone during my break but not during hers. Now it was my turn to feel angry that she could have a holiday but I could not. The night before she was to depart, she telephoned me to say that she was in pieces and couldn't decide what to do. Robin, the lonely one, wanted to cancel the trip and stay with me; the angry man wanted to stay away from me; and a mother personality felt obligated to accompany her daughter. Her solution was to cancel the trip, kick her daughter out of the house, and terminate her work with me. Shocked, and with no time for analysis, I told Jane that I didn't think her solution would work and advised her to think again. She did go on her trip, and on her return reported that she enjoyed herself and didn't hear her voices at all.

But over the next few months I heard repeatedly how much I had failed her by not sufficiently acknowledging the lonely and frightened parts of her that didn't want to go. In particular, Robin complained that I had forgotten about her, that she hid on the trip, came out only once, got scared, and went back in. The sessions were filled with Jane, Robin, the angry man, Janet the hopeless one, and Jenny the bad, guilty one all complaining that I had denied the validity of Jane's needs, had failed to acknowledge the little ones and Robin, and only wanted to acknowledge the competent part of her. They presumed I did so for my own selfish reasons, namely, that I wanted a holiday and resented having to be available to look after her. I was like her father, who denied her existence so that he could have what he wanted. As a result, she denies the existence of the needy ones, too. Jane said that I must continue to acknowledge the needy ones in order for her to do the same.

As I began to explore with Jane what I came to see as my failure to acknowledge simultaneously both the needy and competent parts of her, she became increasingly able to do so for herself. In particular, I explained to Jane that given the contradiction between her need for me during my holiday and the competent, angry, and even defiant attitude she maintained about hers, and given my desire for a holiday free of her needs, I believed in the moment that the competent and angry parts of her were the only real parts, and that the needy parts were not real. I believe I experienced at that moment what Jane experienced on a regular basis, namely, that what is out is real and what is more hidden (and unwanted) is not real. And I began to interpret at every opportunity that the part of her that was being expressed at the moment was a valid part but only a part, and all her disparate parts were real and belonged to her. She especially needed me to remind her, when the angry and hopeless parts of her threatened to walk out and never return, that there were parts of her that still wanted and needed to stay. Jane expressed appreciation to me for helping her deal with the frightening angry man in this manner.

Jane was now beginning to integrate different versions of herself, versions of me, and versions of others. The degree of her self-integration seemed to vary with her willingness to acknowledge all of her feelings. She was aware, for example, that the more she fought and blocked the angry man, the more loudly she experienced him shouting at her. One day, after I had become accustomed to speaking about aspects of her as voices, she was able to say, "Don't talk to me as if the hopelessness and anger are not part of me, 'cause they are." At the same time, she struggled to integrate different versions of me. In the past when I would fail her she would insist that her version of me as a caring person was just an illusion and the uncaring me was the only reality, but now she was able to hold two very different experiences of me almost simultaneously. On one occasion she reported that as she was talking happily to me, she heard someone say, "Don't talk to her anymore," and thought it must be the angry man; or she heard someone say, "It doesn't matter, nothing matters," and thought that must be the hopeless one. She was aware that at one moment she wanted to put her head in my lap and at the very next wanted to leave; she wanted to listen to me speaking and immediately afterward wanted to tell me to get lost. Jane said this gave her "a splitting headache." At times she was more integrated still, saying that the limitations in my caring for her were "so disappointing." I allowed her to make me the most important person in her life, and then I disappointed her by not being everything she needed me to be. Jane began to integrate the positive and negative qualities of her friends, and for the first time in her memory experienced impatience and irritability with her mother.

In summary, the case of Jane illustrates in a number of ways my theme that MPD arises out of a dual need to dissociate and concretize unacknowledged childhood experiences. What began, in Jane's analysis, as a tension between her need to reject the memories and affects of her traumatic past on one hand, and her need to preserve and concretize them on the other hand has given way, through acknowledgment, containment, and synthesis in the transference, to the beginnings of integration.

REFERENCES

Atwood, G. E. & Stolorow, R. D. (1984), *Structures of Subjectivity: Explorations in Psychoanalytic Phenomenology*. Hillsdale, NJ: The Analytic Press.

Berman, E. (1981), Multiple personality: Psychoanalytic perspectives. *Internat. J. Psycho-Anal.*, 62:283–300.

Kluft, R. P., ed. (1985), *Childhood Antecedents of Multiple Personality*. Washington, DC: American Psychiatric Press.

Kohut, H. (1971), *The Analysis of the Self*. New York: International Universities Press.

—— (1977), *The Restoration of the Self*. New York: International Universities Press.

Lampl-de Groot, J. (1981), Notes on "multiple personality." *Psychoanal. Quart.*, 50:614–624.

Lasky, R. (1978), The psychoanalytic treatment of a case of multiple personality. *Psychoanal. Rev.*, 65:355–380.

Marmer, S. S. (1980), Psychoanalysis of multiple personality. *Internat. J. Psycho-Anal.*, 61:439–459.

Putnam, F. W. (1989), *Diagnosis and Treatment of Multiple Personality Disorder*. New York: Guilford.

Ross, D. R. & Loewenstein, R. J., eds. (1992), Perspectives on multiple personality disorder. *Psychoanal. Inq.*, 12:1–173.

Stolorow, R. D. & Atwood, G. E. (1992), *Contexts of Being: The Intersubjective Foundations of Psychological Life*. Hillsdale, NJ: The Analytic Press.

—— Brandchaft, B. & Atwood, G. E. (1987), *Psychoanalytic Treatment: An Intersubjective Approach*. Hillsdale, NJ: The Analytic Press.

—— & Lachmann, F. M. (1980), *Psychoanalysis of Developmental Arrests: Theory and Treatment*. New York: International Universities Press.

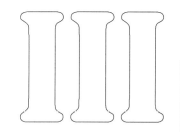

Dying
and
Mourning

Killing the Needy Self: Women Professionals and Suicide (A Critique of Winnicott's False Self Theory)

Sharone A. Abramowitz

Women professionals, including physicians (Steppacher, 1974; Pitts, 1979; Sakinofsky, 1980), medical students (Pepitone-Areola-Rockwell, 1981), psychologists (Steppacher, 1973), chemists (Li, 1969), pharmacists (Steppacher, 1973), and the intellectually gifted (Shneidman, 1971) have suicide rates from two to four times the rate of the general female population. Although women professionals suicide at about the same frequency as their male colleagues, male professionals have suicide rates that are similar to the general male population (Shneidman, 1971; Council on Scientific Affairs, 1987; Rich and Pitts 1979). In one community survey, 47% of women physicians reported experiencing suicidal feelings, as did 58% of female psychologists (Clayton, 1992).

The paradox of why a successful professional wants to end her life perplexes not only her acquaintances but often the people who feel closest to her. The confusion grows out of mistaking a facade for the deeper psychological structure it hides. For these women a vast chasm separates the outer persona from the inner psyche. The wide disparity between that which shows and that which is hidden shapes these women's psychologies. This disparity also imprisons them.

I wrote this chapter in response to two female physicians' suicidal crises. They never knew one another, but these physicians were close in

The author would like to thank Dr. Anna Ornstein, Dr. Lynn Schroeder, Dr. Michelle Dhanak, Rachel Wahba, L.C.S.W., and Susan Frankel, M.F.C.C. for their thoughtful comments.

age, at the same stage in their successful careers, and in committed relationships with other physicians. They each projected capable and friendly images while hiding their inner despair. Even their suicide acts matched one another. They both resorted to types of bloodletting —gestures as disheartening and desperate as they were meaningful in their symbolism. One woman, a colleague, died before receiving treatment. The other woman, whom I will call Dr. Serrano, my patient, survived. Those who die, as did my colleague, tragically live and end their lives hidden behind façades. Only the survivors, like Dr. Serrano, can be known.

People who appear socially adept and "good" on the outside, while internally feeling so insecure and unseen, are often described as having divided selves. Since Winnicott (1960) first published his compelling essay on the False Self/True Self split, many psychotherapists have used his theory to understand these psychodynamics. Winnicott's essay is evocative and illustrates his fine clinical acumen, but I believe that his core thesis is flawed. I contend that falsity versus truth does not define this dangerously dichotomized self. Drawing on Kohut's (1977) description of compensatory self-structures, I will argue that each sector of this divided self carries authenticity; it is the lack of self-integration that is problematic.

Following a presentation of Dr. Serrano's case and a self-psychological critique of Winnicott's False Self/True Self thesis, I will review some of the gender issues that contribute to suicidal crises in these women. First, how does the professional setting, with its bias in favor of men, impact these narcissistically vulnerable women? Second, how does the gendered socialized pull to mirror men, who in turn provide idealized functions, contribute to these women's suicidal dynamics?

CASE DISCUSSION

Dr. Serrano was completing her radiology training when she began psychotherapy. She sought help after she lost a coveted fellowship to her husband. The loss caught her by surprise and humiliated her. She felt depleted and depressed, and this frightened her. She believed that losing the fellowship "shouldn't have bothered [her] so much."

Dr. Serrano shrank at the thought that she might be like her mother, whom she viewed as "over emotional, needy and self-centered." Whenever her mother felt uncared for, she erupted into rages or dissolved into needy tears. At times she threatened suicide. Dr. Serrano's father typically responded to his wife's outbursts with a resigned shrug. Instead of protecting his daughter, he warned her to not upset her mother. Dr. Serrano withdrew from her mother's outbursts with cold disgust.

Control preoccupied Dr. Serrano. In adolescence she trained in gymnastics, and reported feeling "narcissistic gratification" when she held precise postures. When her husband tried to comfort her during the rare times that she cried at work, she found his sympathy jarring. She believed that work, like her family, left "no space for tears." In *control* she felt strong and competent; she wished to be seen. In *need* she felt self-loathing and shame; she wished to hide. She named these two states her "independent self" and her "needy self." [1]

A couple of months after beginning treatment, Dr. Serrano found herself resorting to a dramatic maneuver to stay in control. She called for an additional session. This was a highly unusual request, because she initially insisted on only once-a-week sessions despite my strong recommendation that I see her more frequently. Exhausted, pale, and sounding detached, she confessed that after the previous session she went home to insert an intravenous line and watch her blood pour into a sink. During the previous hour I had commented on how distressed she looked, but she felt disappointed that, as she put it, I did not "magically know" of her suicidal intentions. Her intense shame prevented her from directly telling me that she had the intravenous equipment ready to go in her car. She told me that as she bled she felt "detached, relieved and in control." Only later did she feel isolation, panic, and a yearning to be comforted. She feared looking melodramatic and manipulative like her mother.

Dr. Serrano told me of bloodletting several more times, mostly at work. She kept hoping that her colleagues and husband (as she had hoped I could) would see her suffering without her having to explicitly tell them. She seemed to wish for what Kohut has described as an archaic merger selfobject experience (Kohut, 1971, 1984). [2] Only after she nearly passed out from anemia did Dr. Serrano confess her terrible secret to her husband. As he panicked she took pleasure in telling him "not to overreact." She privately savored his concern while minimizing to him her need for attention. The sector of herself that felt needy enjoyed the caretaking, and her independent side felt relief at appearing in control and not looking like her volatile mother.

Dr. Serrano feared that I would act like her mother and "overreact and humiliate" her by sending her to a hospital. Turning the physician

---

[1] Despite the reifying terms of *independent self* and *needy self*, the patient was referring to two sectors of the self. They were not the seemingly separate subjectivities that highly dissociated individuals possess. They were conflictual dimensions of self-experience (Lee and Martin, 1991).

[2] Kohut (1971) defined a merger selfobject experience as "an experience of the grandiose self which first regressively diffuses its borders to include the analyst" (p. 114). He goes on to say: "the analyst is experienced as a part of the self, the analysand—within the sector of the specific, therapeutically mobilized regression—expects unquestioned dominance over him" (p. 115).

(the independent self state) into the patient (the needy self state) would rip from her the identity on which her self-esteem most depended and thrust a tenuous, frightening, and humiliating bridge between these two parts of herself. Her methodical bloodletting condensed the competent physician and the needy bleeding patient into one symbolic whole, and allowed her to remain the doctor to her patient-self.[3]

As she feared, I did insist on hospitalization. Although Dr. Serrano's shame at being hospitalized never disappeared, she quickly grew happy to meet for our daily sessions. Being forced into an overtly dependent relationship with me allowed Dr. Serrano the safety to work through her defenses against exposing her selfobject longings. For example, at the start of one session she angrily said, "I don't know how to relate to you—as a friend or as a professional?" She continued, "I don't like feeling dependent!" The later hour of our meeting bothered her, because she assumed that like her I resented seeing all but "special" patients then. "Physicians are not close to their patients," she declared. Just as she distanced herself from "needy" patients, her "needy" mother, and her own neediness, she imagined that I too wanted to remain distant from her needs. After we discussed this dynamic, she ended the hour with a pleasant memory of the time a psychiatrist friend told her that a dream she once had meant that she did not want a career in gymnastics (i.e., a life committed to keeping her dependency needs under strict control).

As we came to understand the interrelationship between her shame-ridden needy-self state and her proud independent state, Dr. Serrano eased her defenses. Her selfobject longings to have her vulnerabilities attuned to, soothed, and understood surfaced. She began to establish both a quiet, idealized selfobject transference and a mirroring transference.[4] Even when a blood transfusion was recommended, she refused. She "wanted to feel how bad it was and not pretend that it was all better." Over the following months, she came to feel that if others were "to know" her they would have to understand what happened to her. She grew to be a strong proponent of psychotherapy's helpfulness.

Dr. Serrano eventually found an apt analogy for her suicidal crisis. She viewed her needy-self state as a primitive, ugly, and shameful worm. This worm emerged from its hiding place underground and tried

---

[3] The author would like to thank Dr. Patricia White for this insight.

[4] "Silent idealization" is a concept of Gedo's (1975), which Lee and Martin (1971) discuss. They point out its difference from "defensive idealization": "The silent idealizing transference repeats a more archaic experience where the selfobject's availability and perfection are taken for granted . . ." (p. 143). They add: "This kind of idealization is frequently expressed in a patient's referring friends to the therapist" (p. 143)—while otherwise saying little about the idealization feelings directly. This was true in this case.

to show itself, but a cold steel manhole cover above ground (her independent-self state) pushed it back down. We came to understand her
bloodletting as a concretization of these two images. Her worm-like
veins were what her independent self sector, with cold calculation, pene-
trated with the steel intravenous needle, and her bloodletting was a literal attempt to drain away her unmet needs.[5]

A SELF PSYCHOLOGICAL CRITIQUE OF WINNICOTT'S FALSE SELF THEORY

In shame-based suicidal crises such as Dr. Serrano's, or what Reiser
(1986) terms "narcissistic suicides," hidden suffering, duplicity of presentation, and precipitation by a narcissistically compromising event are
characteristic. The organization of the self, instead of traditional risk factors such as depression or substance abuse, becomes critical. We can
see Dr. Serrano in Reiser's description of a mirror-hungry individual
who, like a "psychological chameleon," quickly attunes to the narcissistic
needs of important others. Mercilessly and perfectionistically she tries to
accommodate them while ridiculing her own emotions.

Winnicott's evocative discussion of the False Self/True Self split
(1960) is often used to explain this type of self-organization. Miller
(1981), Bacal and Newman (1990), and others argue that this split is
caused by false compliance with the parents and suppression of an
authentic self in order to maintain vital relational ties. Bacal and Newman explain that these dynamics result from "the conflict [that] arises
when the declaration of needs is felt to threaten the links that would
ensure the provision of whatever selfobject responsiveness may be
available" (p. 240). Certainly Dr. Serrano suffered from this "fundamental psychic conflict" (Stolorow, Brandchaft, and Atwood, 1987, pp.
52, 90; quoted in Bacal and Newman, 1990, p. 240).

Winnicott's ideas are compelling because they accurately describe
how a self-organization splits into two parts if the child is pressured to
comply with parental narcissistic needs in the service of attachment.
They are also evocative, because the term *false self* resonates for people who suffer from the experience of forcing themselves into a lifetime
of contrived accommodation.[6] Nevertheless, it is critical to evaluate
Winnicott's fundamental assumption that this type of divided psychology

---

[5] One could argue that this act of bloodletting was not a suicide attempt. It could be viewed as
carrying the same dynamics that "cutting" or other cases of self-mutilation do. In this case I believe
that would be a wrong understanding. The patient subjectively felt this act to be an attempt to kill
herself, or at least a sector of herself. Although it served a self-cohesive function, as do most acts of
self-mutilation, the suicide act can also serve this function (as I discuss later).

[6] The author would like to thank Dr. Kenneth Newman for this observation.

organizes itself around falsity versus truth. Mitchell (1991) criticizes Winnicott for reifying "authentic experience into a 'true self,'" but is Winnicott's paradigm "a very useful starting point in distinguishing between authentic and inauthentic experience," as Mitchell suggests (p. 133)?

My critique of Winnicott begins with an analysis of Dr. Serrano's own metaphor for her suicidal crisis: the independent self tried to place a "manhole cover" over the emerging "worm," the needy self. Like a manhole cover lying on top of a road, Dr. Serrano consciously maintained a rigid identification with a stereotypical masculine ideal. This ideal, valued by her profession and her father, respects emotional control, ambition, and competency. Dr. Serrano utilized her independent side to achieve this ideal and distance herself from her emotionally messy mother. Although an extrospective view of this self sector might see it as compliant, ungenuine, and "false," Dr. Serrano internally experienced it as highly authentic. She built this side of herself out of the genuine and reliable talents and skills that she could use relationally to recruit vital efficacy, idealizing, twinship, and mirroring selfobject needs (Wolf, 1988), whether as a child trying to imitate and gain the attention of an emotionally muted father, as a gymnast maintaining control and precision for a respected coach, or as a physician receiving admiration for skillfully completing a complex medical procedure.

The other half of Dr. Serrano's metaphor, the worm, depicts a primitive creature hidden underground protected by a manhole cover, the masculine ideal. This side carries the shame-ridden, unmirrored dimension of self-experience. This dimension was stuck in a more archaic form, because it was the sector that her father most ignored and her mother most humiliated. It was the sector of herself that Dr. Serrano sacrificed an expectation of responsiveness to. This needy-self state is no more authentic or "true" than the independent-self state. Both sectors derive from a split of a whole self-organization. It is the imbalance caused by the split, with the person's intense identification with one side (and its subsequent hypertrophy), and disavowal and repression of the other side (and its subsequent atrophy) that feels ungenuine and "false." I believe that this is the source of the inauthenticity that makes Winnicott's (inaccurate) term *false self* so evocative and popular.

Kohut's concept of *compensatory self structure* (1977) offers a better explanation of this self-organization. When a child must sacrifice mirroring of her whole self, she feels defective. And when she is left alone to face the angry demands of a selfobject-hungry parent, she will rigidly defend against her own unmet idealizing needs for protection and soothing. The result will be a self-organization that develops a "compensatory structure" that, according to Kohut (1977), "rather than merely covering a defect in the self, it compensates for this defect" (p.

3). Kohut goes on to explain in *Restoration of the Self* (1977), "the child's acquisition of compensatory structures are best explained in the context of his having been able to shift from a frustrating self-object to a nonfrustrating or less frustrating one. The decisive issue, in other words, is . . . that a self that had been threatened in its cohesion and functioning in *one* sector has managed to survive by shifting its psychological point of gravity toward *another* one" (p. 83). When the child disavows the authentic dimensions of self-experience that the parents devalued and develops other authentic sectors of the self that best recruit vital relational ties, a divided-self system is created based on a "compensatory structure." The sector that received the most responsiveness is consciously identified with as "me." It seems to protect and hide the shame-ridden and under-responded-to dimensions of the self, the sector that is related to as "not me."

This divided-self system works well as long as the fragile legs it stands on do not collapse. When the legs collapse, a suicidal crisis can develop. Kay (1989) links suicidal behaviors in these individuals to an incomplete "compensatory process" of seeking out "restorative experiences that promote self-cohesion." He goes on to say that they remain with "a specific vulnerability that is likely to be reactivated when future selfobject failures occur" (p. 176). In other words, when the primary vehicle for meeting selfobject needs is assaulted, suicide can result, as when Dr. Serrano faced the humiliating loss of the fellowship to her husband.

Reiser (1986) suggests that the narcissistic suicidal crisis is due to "self fragmentation." Yet when one looks closer a different picture emerges. Dr. Serrano described feeling "perfection" as she bled. She carried out this act with the meticulous skill that characterized her work style. Rather than resulting from "self fragmentation," the suicide behavior seemed to be a defensive attempt to *maintain* self-cohesion. Ironically, although suicide assaults the body, it can be an attempt to achieve psychological stabilization.

A critical issue to explore is how an analytic psychotherapy allowed Dr. Serrano to survive. Winnicott describes how analysands with a "false self" system must pass through a phase of regressed dependency on the analyst for the "true self" to safely emerge. He explains (1960) that often the patient will have an illness to allow the analyst to take over the caretaker function of the False Self (p. 151). Although this could describe what happened for Dr. Serrano through the period of the suicidal crisis and the subsequent hospitalization, the shift in dependence was not, in my view, from the "false self" onto the therapist. It was a shift from extreme dependence on one way of recruiting selfobject responsiveness to include others.

The shift occurred by simultaneously analyzing the ongoing selfobject needs of both the independent-self state and the needy-self state. If I had followed Winnicott's theory and positioned a dimension of self-experience as inauthentic against a dimension that was considered authentic, a countertransferential pull to overvalue the newly exposed needy sector and devalue the independent sector would have occurred. I would have then been placed outside the patient's subjective experience of herself, and in an unempathic position. If this type of bias occurs, the patient will (at best) fight to have both sides of herself validated, (at worst) leave treatment because she feels unempathized with, or (most often) overtly comply (as she is used to doing since childhood) with the therapist's view and hide her differences. If instead the therapist responds to and analyzes the authentic selfobject needs of *both self sectors*, the divided system can then begin to integrate, and the tragic consequences of a completed suicide can be averted.

THE GENDER ISSUES

One could ignore the gender issues in these shame-based suicides. Both men and women fall victim to "narcissistic suicides." Nevertheless, the significantly higher suicide rates of women professionals compared to women in the general population imply that the professional work setting faces career women with unique gender issues. These issues fall into two general categories. The first involves the issues that arise when women work in a "man's world." Pressures from the ongoing strain of workplace sexism and changing role expectations can overburden vulnerable professional women. The second category arises out of the clash between female and male gender roles with the differing relational styles that these roles encourage.

The culture of a professional setting, whether it be a corporation, a law firm, or a training hospital, rewards achievement and competency and devalues anything that obstructs productivity and performance (e.g., fatigue, crying, and maternity leave). To illustrate this, an intern once explained to me why his colleague refused his offer to relieve his large work load during a busy clinic day. The other intern did not want to seem "weak."

The modern work setting's high valuation of a *heroic ideal*, which places the demands of career first and denies limitations, complements the dynamics of the divided self. Brightman's (1984) description of the "grandiose professional self" nicely illustrates the attributes of this ideal. His description was of psychotherapy trainees, but it applies to most professional settings. He states that "omniscience," "benevolence," and "omnipotence" "appear to serve as powerful determinants of professional self esteem" (p. 297). The consequence of living up to this institutionally valued heroic ideal selectively mirrors the ambitiousness and intellectual exhibitionism of the divided-self organization while colluding with the shame-ridden hiding of suffering and vulnerability.

For women like Dr. Serrano, being attracted to a profession that highly encourages external achievement and discourages exposure of inner emotions is at first glance a comfortable road to follow. The problem is that these work settings were originally designed only for men. To thrive and survive in an environment that promotes such a deep psychic division, the male professional historically depended on a woman at home to consciously attend to his disavowed and repressed sectors. As long as a woman was in the wings ready to nurture him, the work setting could neglect large domains of need and only focus on the cultivation of intellect and ambition.

If the ambitious woman, dependent on a compensatory structure like the independent-self state, enters the professional world and has a partner who can sensitively attune to her, she too can manage the split at work. She is also more equipped to handle the narcissistic injuries caused by the sexist setbacks of receiving less affirmation or being assumed to be less competent than her male colleagues. If instead she finds herself in a more traditional male–female dynamic, where her partner offers idealized functions and she provides him with mirroring, her psychic split and the crises it can generate will demand something he cannot give.

During her crisis, Dr. Serrano, like many of her contemporaries, was involved with a man as professionally ambitious as she was. She greatly admired him and saw him as a role model. Her husband offered the idealized selfobject functions of guidance and protection that her passive father and volatile mother failed to provide. Unfortunately, this type of idealized relationship can also set up the women who participate in them for a huge sense of personal failure. When male professionals actively assert themselves, often they easily receive admiration for their achievements. Their expressions of competitiveness and exhibitionism are not viewed as "castrating" or "too masculine." Yet in the equal-opportunity mores of today's professional settings both men and women are overtly expected to achieve comparably. The sexism that still exists is rarely acknowledged (Notman and Nadelson, 1973; Nadelson, Notman, and Bennet, 1978; Charney and Russel, 1994). This leaves women like Dr. Serrano feeling pressured and not quite able to live up to the high standards of professional productivity that many of their male colleagues seem easily capable of. Although these women might rationally understand that sexism disadvantages them, they still feel like failures inside if their performances do not match those of the most supported and privileged men.

These gender-based dynamics escalate even further when vulnerable career women face work setbacks that open up old narcissistic wounds. If the male partner of a distressed career woman conforms to traditional masculine relational models, he might play the knight to her damsel in distress. He might help her to figure out how to regain emotional control and "rationally" overcome her problems at work in order to maintain professional mastery. His gender role can push him away from offering quiet soothing and integrative attunement to her fragile affective state. Because the woman with a divided self has a shameful response to these unmirrored dimensions of her psychology, she is conditioned both to not expect this level of affective responsiveness and to collude with avoiding exposure.

This dynamic is well described in evolving feminist psychological theory (Dinnerstein, 1976; Chodorow, 1978; Gilligan, 1982; Jordan et al., 1991; Kaschak, 1992). Dr. Serrano frequently spoke of attuning to her husband's inner affective world in a way that would avoid overexposing him. Although she just as deeply needed the same mirroring responsiveness from him, often he could only support her by offering idealized functions through "rational" advice and guidance. At a time when she already felt like a "failure" at work, her husband's rationality left her feeling even more shameful and emotionally messy as her mirroring needs, once again, were left unmet.

CONCLUSION

Several months after Dr. Serrano's suicidal crisis, she dreamed that she and an admired male colleague were called to the bedside of a laboring pregnant woman. As her colleague aggressively tried to get this woman's baby out before she was ready to deliver, he caused her to bleed profusely. Dr. Serrano watched with shock as her colleague acted with detached professional cool in response to the crisis he had caused. As the pregnant woman was being moved for treatment, the bleeding woman became the male colleague.

In the dream there are four participants: Dr. Serrano, the admired male colleague, the pregnant woman, and the nearly born infant. These are the psychological sectors that the therapist engages when she treats a woman with a divided self in the throes of a suicidal crisis. The woman who first walks into the office, like the pregnant woman in the dream, is a woman who is bearing witness to her own distressing self-destruction. She initially presents as a highly ambitious professional (the independent-self state) who identifies with the professional masculine ideal, the admired male colleague in the dream. Hesitantly and shamefully she then allows the needy-self state, the dependent and vulnerable infant hidden inside the womb, to begin pushing its way out.

At the start of treatment the independent-self state, like the male colleague in the dream, views itself as separate from the woman carrying the needy-self sector. Feeling separate allows it to believe that it can spare itself while it traumatically separates this sector from the rest of the woman. But its separateness is only an illusion, for in the end the bleeding will kill the whole self. The male colleague and the pregnant woman share the same fate. The challenge of the treatment is to transform this divided psyche into an integrated whole.

The birth process with its pain, hard labor, and ultimate joyful delivery of a whole human being offers a metaphor for the hard-won psychological integration that these women must undergo if they are to survive. Through analysis of the repetitive and selfobject transferences, the socially rewarded but psychologically costly relational schema on which these women depend can be worked through. By understanding that their divided selves are based on a *compensatory structure* organized around authentic selfobject strivings (and not around "falsity" versus "truth"), their treatment will be more accurately and empathically attuned. While this chapter grew out of tragedy, it ends with hope as women like Dr. Serrano find their way toward healing and self-integration through an analytic psychotherapeutic relationship.

REFERENCES

Bacal, H. & Newman, K. (1990), *Theories of Object Relations.* New York: Columbia University Press.

Brightman, B. (1984), Narcissistic issues in the training experience of the psychotherapist. *Internat. J. Psychoanal. Psychother.*, 10:293–317.

Charney, D. & Russel, R. (1994), An overview of sexual harassment. *Amer. J. Psychiat.*, 151:10–17.

Chodorow, N. (1978), *The Reproduction of Mothering.* Berkeley: University of California Press.

Clayton, P. (1992), Mood disorders in women physicians. Presented at APA meeting, Washington, DC.

Council on Scientific Affairs (1987), Results and implications of the AMA-APA physician mortality project: Stage II. *JAMA*, 257:2949–2953.

Dinnerstein, D. (1976), *The Mermaid and the Minotaur.* New York: Harper & Row.

Gedo, J. (1975), Forms of idealization in the analytic transference. *J. Amer. Psychoanal. Assn.*, 23:485–505.

Gilligan, C. (1982), *In a Different Voice: Psychological Theory and Women's Development.* Cambridge, MA: Harvard University Press.

Jordan, J., Kaplan, E., Miller, J., Stiver, I. & Surrey, J. (1991), *Women's Growth in Connection.* New York: Guilford.

Kaschak, E. (1992), *Engendered Lives*. New York: Basic Books.

Kay, J. (1989), Self-psychological perspectives on suicide. In: *Progress in Self Psychology, Vol. 5*, ed. A. Goldberg. Hillsdale, NJ: The Analytic Press, pp. 169–186.

Kohut, H. (1971), *The Analysis of the Self*. New York: International Universities Press.

—— (1977), *The Restoration of the Self*. New York: International Universities Press.

—— (1984), *How Does Analysis Cure?* ed. A. Goldberg & P. Stepansky. Chicago: The University of Chicago Press.

Lee, R. & Martin, J. (1991), *Psychotherapy after Kohut*. Hillsdale, NJ: The Analytic Press.

Li, F. (1969), Suicide among chemists. *Arch. Environ. Health*, 19:518–520.

Miller, A. (1981), *The Drama of the Gifted Child*. New York: Basic Books.

Mitchell, S. (1991), Contemporary perspectives on self: Towards an integration. *Psychoanal. Dialog.*, 1:121–148.

Nadelson, C., Notman, M. & Bennett, M. (1978), Success or failure: Psychotherapeutic considerations for women in conflict. *Amer. J. Psychiat.*, 135:1092–1096.

Notman, M. & Nadelson, C. (1973), Medicine: A career conflict for women. *Amer. J. Psychiat.*, 130:1123–1126.

Pepitone-Areola-Rockwell, F. & Rockwell, D. (1981), Fifty-two medical student suicides. *Amer. J. Psychiat.*, 138:198–201.

Pitts, F., Schuller, A., Rich, C. & Pitts, A. (1979), Suicide among U.S. women physicians, 1967–1972. *Amer. J. Psychiat.*, 136:694–696.

Reiser, D. (1986), Self psychology and the problem of suicide. In: *Progress in Self Psychology, Vol. 2*, ed. A. Goldberg. New York: Guilford, pp. 227–241.

Rich, C. & Pitts, F. (1979), Suicide by male physicians during a 5-year period. *Amer. J. Psychiat.*, 136:1089–1990.

Sakinofsky, I. (1980), Suicide in doctors and wives of doctors. *Canad. Fam. Physician*, 26:837–844.

Shneidman, E. (1971), Perturbation and lethality as precursors of suicide in a gifted group. *Life Threat. Behav.*, 1:23–45.

Steppacher, R. & Mausner, J. (1974), Suicide in male and female physicians. *JAMA*, 228:323–328.

—— & —— (1973), Suicide in professionals: A study of male and female psychologists. *Amer. J. Epidemiol.*, 98:436–445.

Stolorow, R., Brandchaft, B. & Atwood, G. (1987), *Psychoanalytic Treatment: An Intersubjective Approach*. Hillsdale, NJ: The Analytic Press.

Winnicott, D. (1960), Ego distortions in terms of true and false self. In: *The Maturational Processes and the Facilitating Environment*. New York: International Universities Press, 1965, pp. 140–152.

Wolf, E. (1988), *Treating the Self*. New York: Guilford.

Chapter 12

Death of a Selfobject: Toward a Self Psychology of the Mourning Process

George Hagman

The psychoanalytic theory of mourning has changed little from Freud's original formulation (Freud, 1917) despite the extensive theoretical and clinical literature on the subject. A primary emphasis on decathexis and identification related to object loss has remained consistent regardless of school of thought and clinical method. The purpose of this chapter is to review the psychoanalytic model of mourning from a new perspective: the psychology of the self. My thesis is that mourning is essentially the transmuting internalization of the structure and function of the lost self-object. I intend to offer a reinterpretation of the stages of mourning as formulated by Bowlby (1980) and Parkes (1987) with an emphasis on the transformation of the lost selfobject's narcissistic function as the primary goal of the work of mourning.

After a brief literature review, I expand on my thesis and propose a reinterpretation of the stages of mourning along self psychological lines. This is followed by a discussion of the role of the selfobject ambience in the facilitation of the mourning process. In closing, treatment implications of a self-focused approach to mourning is reviewed.

LITERATURE REVIEW

Because the psychoanalytic theory of mourning deals primarily with the internal, psychical fate of the lost object, the impact of loss through

The author wishes to thank Peter Zimmerman, Ph.D. and Alan Roland, Ph.D. for their assistance in the writing of this article.

death on the self can only be inferred from classical theory. Freud's original notion regarding decathexis and identification implies ego change (and therefore, one would assume, self-experience), but only secondarily, as the ego alters itself in an attempt to retain the object tie. Freud's understanding of melancholia certainly assumed an altered experience of self, as hostility becomes inwardly directed; however, once again, this is in reaction to object loss. In addition, because the mourning theory predated the structural model and the terms *ego* and *self* were essentially interchangeable in Freud's thinking at that time, his mourning theory can be viewed as an early conceptualization of the bereaved self which was never fully elaborated by him.

Freud recognized the limits of his focus on object loss. As he contemplated the affective intensity of grief, Freud (1917) wrote, "Why this compromise by which the command of reality is carried out piecemeal, should be so extraordinarily painful is not easy to explain in terms of economics. It is remarkable that this painful unpleasure is taken as a matter of course by us" (p. 245). Later, in an appendix to his work on anxiety, (1927), Freud attempted to explain the pain of loss in terms of frustrated libido; although there was logic in the explanation, it failed to capture the unique agony of grief. In the end, as he himself apparently saw, Freud's model of mourning did not adequately explain the full impact of bereavement on the affective experience of the bereaved—the almost bottomless well of despair and pain that can only result from an experience of severe injury. His model may be useful in understanding the cognitive aspects of change during mourning, but it does not have the explanatory power regarding the affective impact of bereavement.

Edith Jacobson (1965), discussing the psychoanalyses of adult patients who lost parents in childhood, emphasized the narcissistic injury resulting from the loss of a love object. She wrote:

> Evidently children experience the loss of a parent . . . as a severe narcissistic injury, a castration. . . . The fact that in such children . . . the lost object becomes glorified, tends to raise that object's narcissistic value and meaning to the point of turning it into the most precious part of their own self which has been lost and must be recovered [p. 209].

Colin Parkes (1987) touched on this idea in his discussion of identity issues in adult mourning, saying, "If I have relied on another person to predict and act in ways as an extension to myself then the loss of that person can be expected to have the same effect upon my view of the world and of myself as if I had lost a part of myself" (p. 114). He was struck by the frequently violent imagery that the bereaved use in describing their painful inner experiences. Some speak of a sense of their "inside being torn out," leaving "a horrible wound," a "gap," or "unhappy void." Others experience an exquisite fragility of the self; as one widow put it, "I feel terribly fragile. If somebody gave me a good tap I'd shatter into a thousand pieces" (pp. 114–116) Parkes stated specifically that there is "empirical justification . . . that the pain of grief, like physical pain, is the experience of damage to the self" (p. 116).

Leon Grinberg (1964) spoke directly to this issue in his article on guilt and mourning. He said that object loss can be experienced as an attack on the self: "in any object loss there occurs simultaneously a loss of parts of the self, which leads to its corresponding process of mourning" (p. 368). The "cohesion" of the self is experienced as endangered, its integrity threatened. The person experiences "psychical pain" as "certain parts of the self" are experienced as menacingly lost. Psychoanalysis, Grinberg said, "gives the patient the possibility of recovering excluded parts of the self as well as the possibility of giving up those aspects which must inevitably be lost in the process of development." Through analysis, "the ego (self) will exhibit reparative tendencies towards itself, which will permit it to become stronger and better balanced" (pp. 370–371). In spite of Grinberg's emphasis on Kleinian theory, he speaks powerfully in support of a psychology of the self in mourning.

To this end, Morton and Estelle Shane (1991) recently offered an important contribution to the study of mourning in which they enhanced the psychoanalytic model with concepts derived from self psychology. In their article, they stressed that to focus solely on the experience of object loss in mourning means that "the loss of narcissistic support from that person" (p. 117) will be missed.

The Shanes pointed out how the narcissistic needs of the bereaved must be met by an empathic, responsive caregiver and milieu for the selfobject loss to be resolved. They suggested that chronic self disorders may develop when the bereaved fails to access selfobject functions in compensation for the loss. In this way, they believe, the trauma of death and selfobject failure can be mitigated so that the mourning process can proceed and be resolved successfully.

However, they did not go so far as to suggest a revised model of mourning based on their findings, and therefore, they missed the opportunity to utilize the full explanatory range and power of self psychology. Expanding on the Shanes's thesis, I offer a comprehensive reworking of the "standard" clinical model of mourning from the point of view of the psychology of the self. To this end, I attempt to show how the loss of the specific, unique, and distinct nature of the selfobject is one of the core issue in bereavement and how the rupture of the seemingly irre-

placeable selfobject bond ineluctably leads to much of the affective turmoil and dramatic, psychic change processes of mourning.

Finally, it is important to note the work of Ulman and Brothers
(1988) on posttraumatic stress disorder (PTSD). It is their belief that in
PTSD there is a "shattering and faulty restoration of central organizing
fantasies of self in relationship to others" (p. 20). Vulnerability to trauma
is "determined by the degree to which the self (in relation to selfobject)
remains organized around archaic and illusory notions of personal
grandeur or idealized merger with the omnipotent" (p. 15). Because the
self-as-fantasy constitutes the fundamental psychic reality or subjective
frame of reference (the fundamental "meaning structures" of the self),
the "shattering" of the central organizing fantasies can be devastating to
the self, resulting in the severe dissociative symptoms of PTSD.
Although bereavement does not necessarily result in this type of
"shattering" of the self, the bereaved does experience a disillusionment
and disorganization of subjective experience. Therefore, I agree with
Ulman and Brothers that what is clinically important are the vicissitudes
of unconscious and conscious fantasy organization and the impact of
selfobject loss on the structure and regulation of the affective life of the
self.

A SELF PSYCHOLOGY OF MOURNING

Each person's self-experience crystallizes over time through interaction
with others, whose activities and responses come to be experienced as
parts of the self (selfobjects). The selfobject is the internal, affectively
charged experience of the other. The quality and dynamics of function
of the selfobject in the repair, sustenance, and regulation of the self over
time is the area of study of self psychology. As the self matures, there is
a gradual decrease in the person's dependence on object interactions for
the maintenance of self structure; nevertheless, throughout life, all persons continue to require positive selfobject experiences within an intersubjective context. In the case of the death of a loved one, this selfobject
bond is ruptured, thus precipitating the mourning process.

I believe that Kohut's (1972) concept of "transmuting internalization"
can be helpful in our reconceptualization of the mourning process. In his
early model of mental self-structure, Kohut proposed that, in response to
situations of "optimal frustration," the self takes into its own structure,
through a process of breaking down and transforming, the narcissistic
functions of the selfobject. Kohut likened this process of reworking the
selfobject tie and internalizing its functions (so as to free them from
dependence on the object) to the work of mourning. Stolorow, Brandchaft, and Atwood (1987), in a recent reformulation of Kohut's concept,

asserted that the formation of self-structure occurs not in a state of frustration, but as a direct result of the process of restoration of the ruptured selfobject bond in the context of an experience of "optimal empathy" and "affective responsiveness" (see also Terman, 1988, and Bacal, 1985). In other words, Stolorow et al. stressed that the self evolves within an intersubjective context characterized by attunement and responsiveness. This has important implications for the understanding of the role of survivors in the provision of a facilitative and supportive selfobject milieu, the availability of which is a prerequisite for successful mourning.

Kohut (1972) conceptualized transmuting internalization as a developmental process in which the archaic functions of the selfobject, either in early childhood or in the context of analytic treatment, are transformed into autonomous psychic structure. However, in the case of normal mourning, the selfobject is not of an archaic nature and the bereaved possesses a sufficiently internalized and mature self-structure. Nonetheless, as Kohut stressed, even the mature self relies on others for selfobject experiences that, though not necessary for the "survival" of the self, are utilized by the person to maintain normal and fully functional levels of self-cohesion, vitality, and initiative. Therefore, the death of a loved one is experienced as a "self-crisis" that confronts the individual with a specific task, necessitating psychic work, of which only a person with adequately internalized self-structure is capable. In fact, when assessing the impact of a particular bereavement on the self of an individual, it is important to explore the extent to which the bereaved experiences the loss as a threat to his or her personal survival. Given this, we must keep in mind that the selfobject concept refers to a psychological experience that, in healthy individuals, remains available despite the physical death of the other. The normal mourning process that I discuss involves the gradual transformation of the nature of the psychological experience of the essential other (selfobject) into a form that no longer requires the other's presence. However, in cases of pathologic bereavement, the psychological experience of the essential other is dependent on his or her presence, and with that loss, the bereaved's self may be experienced as so damaged that the risk of depression, and perhaps death, is high, as is the possibility (in some cases) of psychotic decompensation. Admittedly, in spite of the continuing cohesion of the self, normal bereavement is also experienced in terms of intense psychic pain and affective turmoil. In fact, it is in the area of the selfobject's function in regulating affective experience in even the maturely developed self that the process of transmuting internalization in mourning is so crucial.

Many authors have stressed the function of affects in self-experience. Contemporary analytic theorists place affectivity, the regulation of affect, and the structuralization of affects in the center of their theories. Recent contributors from self psychology have also emphasized the primary role of the selfobject in the affective dimension of self-experience. To this end, Stolorow et al. (1987) have made an important contribution to our understanding of affect and the selfobject. They wrote that:

> selfobject functions pertain fundamentally to the integration of affect into the organization of self-experience, and that the need for selfobject ties pertains most centrally to the need for attuned responsiveness to affect states in all stages of the life cycle [p. 67].

It is through selfobject experiences that our affective life is differentiated and our experience of self articulated. Selfobjects function to synthesize affectively discrepant experiences, which is essential to an integrated sense of self. It is through the selfobject that we acquire tolerance of affect states and the use of affects as internal signals by which we manage our inner and outer lives. Selfobjects assist the person in the development and maintenance of cognitive–affective schemata which provide stability, cohesion, and vitality to the self-experience.

Stolorow et al. stressed that the healthy functioning of the self and the continuing cohesive experience of self arises from the presence, reciprocal activities, and affective attuneness of the object. Earlier, Bowlby (1980) described how the object plays a crucial role as an activating stimulus and terminating stimulus, thus playing an important part in self-regulation. The selfobject experience is also such a circular system requiring the attuned presence, actual or *potential*, of both self and object. Mourning ensues when this bond is ruptured and the intersubjective, mutually regulatory system breaks down.

As stated previously, I see mourning as the transmuting internalization of the structure and function of the selfobject (the "organizing fantasies" of the self) in response to the death of a loved one. The network of cognitive–affective schemata (self-organizing fantasies) sustained by and within the selfobject tie is traumatized, broken down, reworked, and gradually transformed in such a way as to maintain the integrity of self-experience and restore self-cohesion and vitality. Although mourning can be said to occur following any selfobject loss, it is typically the loss of those selfobjects that have been relied on to repair, sustain, and regulate aspects of the nuclear self that results in a full state of mourning. However, it is important to note that in these cases, the self has not necessarily been dependent on the selfobject in an archaic sense; therefore, the loss, though painful, does not traumatize or damage the core self-structure. Successful resolution of mourning will largely be determined by the structural integrity, cohesion, and resilience of the nuclear self as well as the availability of adequately attuned, compensatory self-objects. Pathologic mourning will typically result when the nuclear self is primarily organized around archaic selfobjects, in which case the core of the self has remained poorly structuralized and vulnerable to disruption.

Unfortunately, the nature of the focus of this chapter does not allow a complementary discussion of mourning for the lost object as an object in its own right, apart from its selfobject functions. The highlighting of the transmuting internalization of selfobject functions does not mean to imply that the experience of "object loss" is not important—far from it. However, over the years the psychoanalytic literature has dealt extensively with the problem of object loss, and my goal here is to explore an area that has been neglected. Future discussion includes issues related to what Shane and Shane (1990) called *otherness*: "The range of experiences in adult life where one serves the needs of another, where that other's emotional requirements are perceived to have priority over one's own. . . . The capacity to serve as a self-regulating other (selfobject) becomes an essential attribute of good-enough otherness" (p. 490). When one extends the concept of *otherness* to *loss*, one sees an additional side of mourning—that is, not only the loss of selfobject functions, but the loss of what life would have provided for the other. This viewpoint has particular applicability to our understanding of a mature parent's loss of a child or spouse. Without a doubt, the loss of a relationship in which one had been empathically immersed has its own special pain, its unique tasks and processes.

THE STAGES OF MOURNING

The following model has been developed from the stage models of Bowlby and Parkes, which are considered to be the "standard" models of bereavement. However, the Parkes/Bowlby model is derived primarily from ethologically based research and is therefore confined to an objective, experience-distant viewpoint. The model described here accepts the phenomenological accuracy of Parkes and Bowlby's research findings; however, it utilizes insights from self psychology to propose an alternate interpretation of their data, so as to capture, in a self-focused model of bereavement, previously unobserved aspects of the psychological process of mourning as a transmuting internalization of the selfobject.

Following the Parkes/Bowlby model, I list five "phases" of the mourning process. Although I discuss each phase separately, in reality the bereaved may move through these phases in a fluid fashion and, at times, there may be little distinction between stages. It is probably best to see this model as largely of heuristic value—more honored in the breach than in practice. Prior to the discussion of each phase of mourning, I include a quote from first-hand experiences with mourning which I believe will be helpful in the analysis to follow.

Stage 1: Rupture of the Selfobject Bond (Shock Phase)

Upon the unexpected news of his beloved daughter Jean's death, Mark Twain (Moffat, 1982) reflected:

> It is one of the mysteries of our nature that a man, all unprepared, can receive a thunderstroke like that and live. There is but one reasonable explanation of it. The intellect is stunned by the shock and but gropingly gathers the meaning of the words. The power to realize their full import is mercifully wanting. The mind has a dim sense of vast loss—that is all. It will take mind and memory months and possibly years to gather the details and thus learn and know the whole extent of the loss [p. 6].

"Reality-testing has shown that the loved object no longer exists" (Freud, 1917). The news of death is accompanied by a state of shock, disbelief, and numbness (Parkes, 1987). The recognition of the "fact" of the death may be sudden or protracted, and this will determine the length of this stage. Internal equilibrium is "frozen," and the experience of the self is dominated by apprehension, perhaps acute nonspecific anxiety, and dread. Disorganization and fragmentation of self does not yet occur during this phase. In fact, there may be a heightened sense of organization and focus within the self-experience in response to the immediacy of the trauma. Many practical issues and problems may have to be dealt with. The experience of the bond to the deceased may in fact be intensified. There is also, frequently, a defensively motivated split between the awareness of the event of the death and a belief in the survival of the deceased. As Freud (1917) noted, "opposition (*to giving up the object*) can be so intense that a turning away from reality takes place" (p. 244). Sometimes, the denial of the reality of the loss may be vigorous and stubborn. The "self-state" of this phase can best be characterized as a reflexive fortification of the self in response to an attack on its integrity. Eventually, in normal cases, the bereaved will seek to evoke the customary responsiveness of the lost selfobject, thus entering Stage 2.

Stage 2: Attempts to Restore the Tie With the Old Selfobject (Searching)

Toby Talbot (Moffat, 1982) reflected on her sorrow at her mother's death:

Grief comes in unexpected surges. As when nursing, and anything can trigger the onrush of milk. An infant in a carriage or a child crying, but also a traffic light changing, water running, a dog barking . . . Little alarms these are, transmitted to that network of nerves, muscle, hormone, tissue, and cells that constitute the physical self. Mysterious cues set off a reminder of grief. It comes crashing like a wave, sweeping me in its crest, twisting me inside out. Then recedes, leaving me broken. Oh, Mama, I don't want to eat, to walk, to get out of bed . . . Nothing matters . . . I wake from sleep in the middle of every night and say to myself, "My mother is dead" [p. 106].

The recognition of the reality and finality of death precipitates emergency attempts to retain, or recover, the selfobject bond (Parkes, 1987). Archaic affective states occur as the person struggles to restore contact with the dead. Crying, screaming, and sobbing are primitive appeals from the archaic self to the lost selfobject. "The person may revert to more archaic . . . modes of affect expression in the . . . hope of thereby evoking the needed responses from others" (Stolorow et al., 1987, p. 73). Yearnings for merger with the idealized object and fantasies of the presence of an admiring, loving object frequently accompany these affective storms. In spite of their painfulness, these affective states (in terms of self-experience) are attempts to restore the selfobject bond, at least momentarily. Gradually the experience of the selfobject's unavailability and lack of response leads to lessening attempts to regain the bond, and acceptance of the reality of loss begins to set in. The self-state may be characterized as one of intense, psychical pain (grief) in response to the recognition of self-injury. Emergency attempts to restore the self through action (crying for the deceased, pining) and fantasizing (dwelling on memories of the dead) are resorted to. The selfobject bond with the deceased is broken. The self-experience is unstable and ultimately begins to fragment.

Stage 3: Disintegration of the Self (Psychic Disorganization)

The following passage by Talbot (in Moffat, 1982) conveys the despair that may be experienced during the middle phase of mourning:

Life is a death sentence. Better not to give yourself to anything. The more you give, the more is taken from you. . . . I find myself drowning, engulfed by the disorder of the current, wanting to seize her hand to bring me to shore. Missing her so. Futilely trying to recapture the profile of elusive contours and shapes. To crystalize that deceased being. To evoke that palpable presence, the voice, inflections, and rhythms, the silences, expressions, gestures, stance, gait, the birthmarks, the quirks. But the subject . . . becomes indistinct [p. 107].

In the wake of the rupture of the selfobject bond, the self may be experienced as depleted and empty, and temporary disintegration and fragmentation of the self may occur. The object is dead, and its function in sustaining the self is lost. The person may experience depression, diffuse anxiety, sleeplessness, hypochondriasis, confusion, and loss of positive investment in life. The availability of a responsive, affectively attuned milieu of supportive compensatory selfobjects is crucial for this stage to be endured, the powerful affect states to be resolved, and the mourning process to be accomplished. The self-state of this phase results from the disintegration of fantasy structure and the disruption of self-experience. The integrity of the structures, which had previously contained and regulated the bereaved's affects, is disturbed. Periods of calm acceptance are shattered by storms of grief, panic, and rage. Despite the extremity of the self, it is important to note that, in most cases, the cohesiveness of the nuclear self is not affected. It is only in cases of pathologic bereavement that the core of the self may be damaged. In normal bereavement self-disintegration is only partial and temporary, as eventually, the person spontaneously engages in the process of self-restoration.

Stage 4: Restoration of the Self (Psychic Reorganization)

Later in her bereavement Talbot (Moffat, 1982) noted feelings of recovery and a renewed sense of self:

> Slowly I find myself being weaned from her material presence. Yet filled with her as never before. It is I now who represents us both. I am our mutual past. I am my mother and my self. She gave me love, to love myself, and to love the world. I must remember how to love. . . . Piece by piece, I reenter the world. A new phase. A new body, a new voice . . . It is like a slow recovery from sickness, this recovery of one's self. . . . My life now is only mine [p. 111].

Freud (1917) described the psychical process of this stage from the point of view of drive psychology. He said that the giving up of the object is "carried out bit by bit, at great expense of time and cathectic energy, and in the meantime the existence of the lost object is psychically prolonged. Each single one of the memories and expectations in which the libido is bound to the object is brought up and hypercathected, and detachment of libido is accomplished" (p. 245)." Later, Freud and other analysts would add identification with the lost object to this process (Abraham, 1925; Fenichel, 1945). Freud (1923) stated in *The Ego and the Id*: "It may be that . . . identification is the sole condition under which the Id can give up its objects" (p. 29). Abraham (1925) was even more explicit when he noted how the bereaved effects "a temporary introjection of the loved person. Its main purpose is . . . to preserve the person's relation to the lost object" (p. 435).

In self psychological terms, what Freud observed was the process of transmuting internalization of the selfobject into permanent self-structure which can continue to provide needed functions such as self-affirmation, mirroring, merger, twinship, and so forth, consistent with the function of the selfobject prior to the death. This is accomplished through a painful process of internal revitalization of residual selfobject functions that are gradually structuralized as an enduring, conscious image of the dead or transformed fully into the fabric of self-experience. As previously noted, Freud himself observed this process in the bereaved's compulsive recall of innumerable memories of the dead, but he stressed only the processes of identification, decathexis, and object removal. What has been missed up to this point is how memories of the deceased also evoke lost self-experience. The bereaved's memories are not simply of the deceased; they also reestablish momentarily (however partially) the narcissistic function of the lost object. To this end, these "memories" are not just static dead images from the past. They also have a dynamic, selfobject function in the maintenance and restoration of the bereaved's current self-state. Little by little, as these "lost" selfobject functions are revoked independent of the object's presence, many are "microinternalized" (Kohut, 1977), becoming part of the bereaved's self-structure. The ultimate objective of this stage is *not* the relinquishment of the self-object bond (although one of the goals of mourning is for the self to no longer depend on the presence of the deceased), but the restoration of the cohesion and vitality of the self through transformation and adaptation of the selfobject and its functions within the self-structure. Ultimately, the selfobject may eventually be integrated into the self, maintained intact as a fantasy (perhaps experienced as spiritually present) to be evoked as necessary to assist in the maintenance or repair of the self, or obtained from other relationships. It is a crucial point that this internal, psychical work cannot be fully successful unless there is adequate development of self-structure prior to the loss so that there is "maturationally preformed receptivity for specific introjects" (Kohut, 1972, p. 49) and the mourning process occurs within the context of a responsive selfobject relationship and selfobject milieu/surround. As I describe in an upcoming section, the availability of "optimally responsive" selfobjects not only plays an essential role in the facilitation of mourning, but also makes a vital contribution to the creation of new self-structure and, thus, the restoration of the self (Bacal, 1985; Stolorow et al., 1987; Terman, 1988).

Stage 5: Creative Reengagement of the Self (New Identity)

In the following passage from a short story, Thomas Mann (Moffat, 1982) wrote of the serenity and renewed pleasure in life that can follow successful bereavement:

> Is not life in and for itself a good, regardless of whether we may call its content "happiness"? Johannes Friedemann felt that it was so, and he loved life. He . . . taught himself with infinite, incredible care to take pleasure in what it had still to offer. A walk in the springtime in the parks surrounding the town; the fragrance of a flower; the song of a bird—might not one feel grateful for such things as these? . . . how tenderly he loved the mild flow of his life, charged with no great emotions, it is true, but full of a quiet and tranquil happiness which was his own creation [p. 266].

Having restructured the self after loss, and thus having regained the needed selfobject functions lost due to the ruptured selfobject bond, the person is motivated to reengage actively in the selfobject milieu and form new relationships. There is a joyful reinvestment of the restored self in new experiences and initiatives. There is an experience of greater affective stability, renewed vitality, and self-cohesion. However, the final outcome of the mourning process is not solely determined by the quality of social activity, more essential is the renewed integrity of self-experience. In most cases, the self-state has returned to its pre-loss condition; in others there may be an experience of self-diminishment, and still in others, an experience of self-enhancement and liberation (Pollack, 1989).

THE AMBIENCE OF MOURNING

Successful mourning occurs in the context of a responsive, supportive, and facilitative selfobject milieu (Shane and Shane, 1991). Without this empathic ambience and self-sustaining environment, the bereaved (having endured a traumatic self-injury) may not spontaneously engage in the process just described. There may, in fact, be an inhibition or distortion of mourning, as the person resorts to defensive measures to shore up the self in the absence of essential selfobjects. Optimally, in our society, this selfobject milieu is composed of the community, its mourning customs and rituals, and the bereaved's family. In a recent article, Joyce Slochower (1993) discussed the function of the custom of sitting shiva in Jewish culture as a facilitative milieu that provides holding and empathic responsiveness to the bereaved. This viewpoint could certainly be extended to the psychological function of mourning rituals in many cultures. However, more characteristic of modern Western society is the primary role of a relatively small network of relationships characterized by individual caregiving.

Stolorow et al. (1987) stressed this caregiver's role in creating a relationship of "affective responsiveness" to facilitate adaptation to loss and self-development. Adapting Stolorow's concepts to the condition of bereavement, it can be said that the caregiver must tolerate, absorb, and contain the bereaved's affect states, which presuppose that they do not threaten the organization of the caregiver's sense of self. They should function to "hold the situation" (Winnicott, 1960, p. 229) so that it can be integrated. The caregiver's selfobject function gradually facilitates the restoration of the capacity for self-modulation of affect and the ability to assure a comforting attitude toward oneself. Consequently, such affect will not entail irretrievable loss in the self. The expectation that restitution will follow disruption is implicitly communicated, providing support for the bereaved's sense of self-continuity and confident hope for the future (Stololow et al., 1987).

Murray Bowen (1985) gave a moving account of his work with a young widower and his three latency-age children. The young man had come to Bowen overwrought with grief and confused regarding problems arising from his wife's sudden death. An important concern was how to manage his own grief without traumatizing his children. With Bowen's support, empathy, and expert advice, the father came to be able to grieve with his children in an open yet strong and reassuring manner. He was able both to protect the children from various stressors and to facilitate their direct involvement in the mourning rituals and experience of their mother's death. Eventually, the father arranged for a viewing at the funeral parlor for himself and the children. He set up a time for them to be alone with the mother, so they could mourn her together. Bowen wrote:

> The father did a detailed account of the children's visit. . . . The children went up to the casket and felt the mother. The five-year-old son said: "If I kiss her, she could not kiss back." All three spent some time inspecting everything, even looking under the casket. The eight-year-old son got under the casket and prayed that his mother could hold him in her arms again in heaven. . . . He took a small pebble . . . and placed it in his mother's hand. The other children also got pebbles and put them in their mother's hand. Then they announced, "We can go daddy." The father was much relieved at the outcome of the visit. He said, "A thousand tons were lifted from this family today" [p. 334].

In the account just presented, the father was able to access valuable selfobject functions from Bowen, who was available as a responsive, calm, empathic presence, providing structure and self-regulatory assistance to the father. He then internalized Bowen's involvement and integrated his own grief and the needs of his children so as to facilitate a healthy mourning process for his family. In the end, he created a facilitating situation, which he then "held" for his children. Because of him, they could grieve their mother's death in the ambience of their father's strength, love, and protection. Through the father's eyes, Bowen vividly captured the positive impact of an empathic selfobject surround. The children investigated the body of their mother with curiosity and tenderness. Because of the father's involvement, they were able to "be themselves" during their final moments with their mother, as they said goodbye to her in their fashion. In terms of the children's long-term adaptation to the loss of their mother, Bowen claimed, from a brief follow-up a few years later, that he did not observe any evidence of pathological sequelae from the death. Admittedly, Bowen's later assessment was informal and perhaps superficial. However, many studies of childhood parent loss have confirmed the general truth of his observation that the chances for successful adaptation to loss are greatly improved when the child is provided with continuous, responsive, and supportive parenting from adult survivors (Krupnick, 1984).

Finally, it is important to note that, although I have emphasized the transmuting internalization of the functions of the lost selfobject, it is also true that the bereaved person, during and after the period of mourning, may utilize a number of other selfobjects that continue to be available after the death. Also, one of the outcomes just noted in the discussion of Stage 5 is a renewed ability either to seek out and use new selfobjects as replacements for the lost functions of the object or, perhaps, to meet different selfobject needs. In both instances, the responsive selfobject surround makes possible a normative and not unfortunate outcome of loss, (i.e., the replacement of the selfobject with other, perhaps somewhat different, selfobjects or group of selfobjects that serve functions similar to the lost selfobject).

TREATMENT ISSUES

From the perspective of self psychology, the goal of mourning is the restoration of the self after the rupture of a primary selfobject bond. What psychoanalysts have failed to see is the bereaved patient's struggle to transform the bond with the lost selfobject in order to secure its regulating functions within the self. Given this, the most important function of treatment is to support and protect this process by means of the analyst's empathic attunement and "holding" of the situation. The reduction of anything potentially traumatic within the analytic environment is essential. Special strategies, such as confronting the patient with the reality of death or stimulating abreaction, are invariably damaging to the empathic hold and must be avoided. Bereaved persons are exquisitely sensitive to failures in empathy and will resist and defend themselves against anyone who might, even inadvertently, interfere with the mourning process.

In the treatment of the bereaved, the focus of analysis should be on the person's struggle to repair, sustain, and regulate the self subsequent to the rupture of a crucial selfobject bond. The goal of mourning is not decathexis, but the retention of the lost selfobject functions through transformation of self-structure. The unfolding of the bereaved's selfobject needs for mirroring, merger with an idealized other, companionship, and self-efficacy in the transference provides an experience of empathic attuneness and responsiveness, thus facilitating the mourning process. In a properly managed treatment, the patient not only engages in a process of transforming the selfobject functions, but also internalizes the supportive ambience of the optimally responsive analytic relationship.

E. K. Rynearson (1987) described the treatment of a woman who suffered from a refractory, pathologic bereavement subsequent to the death of her teenage son. He pointed out how every effort to encourage the final resolution of mourning failed. In spite of years of therapy and a generally good treatment relationship, the woman remained despondent and deeply attached to the memory of her dead son. The patient would even say how she found the treatment "helpful enough," but "it will never bring my son back," she would add despairingly. Despite all efforts, the patient remained determined to continue her lonely vigil. "I began to wonder out loud," Rynearson wrote, 'how her dying son might help in reviving our therapy." He asked the patient to compose a letter from her son. He noted, "It did not feel contrived or unnatural to seek some caring and strength from an internalized 'presence' that had needed so much from us." The patient composed a series of moving and beautiful letters as if from her son, an admiring and supportive tribute to her as a mother. Rynearson concluded,

> We now look to David (the son) as a part of herself that is increasingly able to help us by becoming more alive and nurturant. David remains an obsession, but he also advises and guides as a mother would a child. I cannot say precisely what is changing in this dissociated, highly traumatized and tangled attachment, but my patient and I, and now David, are all working together [p. 497].

Rynearson's clinical approach is not a self psychological one; however, I believe that his change in treatment strategy, as just described, was consistent with the findings of self psychology, and although he may not necessarily concur, his renewed approach to his work with the patient can be usefully interpreted along self psychological lines. To this end, it may be concluded that his insight into the selfobject nature of his patient's continuing relationship with her dead son arose from his empathic emersion in his patient's state of bereavement. He became aware of the "function" of the selfobject, as he explored with the patient the positive, self-sustaining, self-repairing, and self-regulating nature of the woman's "moribund" attachment to her son. Rynearson's initial treatment goal of encouraging the patient to give up her investment in the dead threatened his patient's self-security and provoked a chronic "resistance" to the working alliance. Once he ceased to promote decathexis and began to explore the functions of the selfobject in the areas of affirmation, mirroring, and merger needs, he noted a change in the ambience of the treatment and a revitalization of the treatment relationship. Not having a self psychological viewpoint, he was not able to conceptualize his intervention and formulate his insight as an interpretation that might have been of use to his patient. Nonetheless, his intuition regarding the positive function of the bond with the son allowed him to move beyond a chronic and painful treatment impasse in the general direction of recovery.

The mourning process can be said to be successfully concluded, when the self is once again experienced as cohesive and vital, with a renewed capability and motivation for the effective use of selfobjects in the repair, sustenance, and regulation of the self. This does not mean that the lost selfobject has been abandoned—far from it. Many who have recovered from bereavement maintain powerful attachments to the dead as selfobjects, which continue to serve vital functions. In other cases, the selfobject may be fully integrated into the self, as the attachment to the dead fades from awareness. Self psychology provides us with a powerful clinical tool with which we can attune ourselves to the bereaved's struggle to maintain the integrity of self-experience in spite of the appearance of regression and suffering. It has been, perhaps, our own fear of self-injury and loss that has driven us to encourage and hasten an end to mourning, often blinding us to its self-restorative function.

REFERENCES

Abraham, K. (1925), A short history of the development of the libido. In: *Selected Papers of Karl Abraham*. New York: Brunner Mazel, pp. 418–479.
Bacal, H. (1985), Optimal responsiveness and the therapeutic process. In: *Progress in Self Psychology, Vol. 1*, ed. A. Goldberg. New York: Guilford, pp. 202–226.
Bowen, M. (1985), *Family Therapy in Clinical Practice*. Northvale, NJ: Aronson.
Bowlby, J. (1980), *Attachment and Loss, Vol. 3*. New York: Basic Books.

Freud, S. (1917), Mourning and melancholia. *Standard Edition*, 14:243–258. London: Hogarth Press, 1957.

Grinberg, L. (1964), Two kinds of guilt—Their relation with normal and pathological aspects of mourning. *Internat. J. Psycho-Anal.*, 45:366–371.

Jacobson, E. (1965), The return of the lost parent. In: *Drives, Affects, Behavior, Vol. 2*, ed. M. Shur. New York: International Universities Press, pp. 193–211.

Kohut, H. (1972), *The Analysis of the Self*. New York: International Universities Press.

———— (1977), *The Restoration of the Self*. New York: International Universities Press.

Krupnick, J. (1984), Bereavement during childhood and adolescence. In: *Bereavement: Reactions, Consequences and Care*, ed. M. Osterweis & M. Green. Washington, DC: National Academy Press, pp. 99–141.

Moffat, J. (1982), *In the Midst of Winter: Selections from the Literature of Mourning*. New York: Random House.

Parkes, C. (1987), *Bereavement: Studies of Grief in Adult Life*. Madison, CT: International Universities Press.

Pollock, G. (1989), *The Mourning-Liberation Process*. Madison, CT: International Universities Press.

Rynearson, E. K. (1987), Psychotherapy of pathologic grief and bereavement: Revisions and limitations. *The Psychiatric Clinics of North America, Grief and Bereavement. Vol. 10, No. 3*. Philadelphia: Saunders.

Shane, M. & Shane, E. (1990), The struggle for otherhood: Implications for development in adulthood of the capacity to be a good-enough object for another. In: *New Dimensions in Adult Development*, ed. R. Nemiroff & C. Colarusso. New York: Basic Books, pp. 487–499.

———— & ———— (1991), Object loss and selfobject loss: A contribution to understanding mourning and the failure to mourn. *Ann. Psychoanal.*, 13:115–131.

Slochower, J. (1993), Mourning and the holding function of *shiva*. *Contemp. Psychoanal.*, 29:352–367.

Stolorow, R., Brandchaft, B. & Atwood, G. E. (1987), *Psychoanalytic Treatment: An Intersubjective Approach*. Hillsdale, NJ: The Analytic Press.

Terman, D. (1988), Optimal frustration: Structuralization and the therapeutic process. In: *Learning from Kohut: Progress in Self Psychology, Vol. 4*, ed. A. Goldberg. Hillsdale, NJ: The Analytic Press, pp. 113–125.

Ulman, R. & Brothers, J. (1988), *The Shattered Self: A Psychoanalytic Study of Trauma*. Hillsdale, NJ: The Analytic Press.

Winnicott, D. W. (1960), *The Maturational Processes and the Facilitating Environment*. New York: International Universities Press.

Chapter 13

The Selfobject Function of Religious Experience: The Treatment of a Dying Patient

Steven H. Knoblauch

It is likely that Kohut was referring to his own experience when he wrote (1984), "One of the conditions for the maintenance of a cohesive self as one faces death is the actual or at least vividly imagined presence of empathically responsive selfobjects" (p. 19). The general applicability of Kohut's insight is here illustrated in the treatment of a dying patient. The value of a tie with the therapist facilitates a selfobject experience, which in turn provides a sense of cohesion and continuity that helps to contain, manage, and buffer emotional suffering and psychic conflict that can emerge with ensuing death.

In his most thorough description of selfobject experience, Kohut explained (1984):

> Throughout his life a person will experience himself as a cohesive harmonious firm unit in time and space, connected with his past and pointing meaningfully into a creative-productive future, only as long as, at each stage in his life, he experiences certain representatives of his human surroundings as joyfully responding to him, as available to him as sources of idealized strength and calmness, as being silently present but in essence like him, and, at any rate, able to grasp his inner life more or less accurately so that their responses are attuned to his needs and allow him to grasp their inner life when his is in need of sustenance [p. 52].

Kohut suggests a developmental line for selfobject experience and a continuing need for such experience throughout life. Since his statement was published in 1984, emphasis has been placed on the beginnings of such experience. Stern (1985), Lichtenberg (1989), and others have described infant development in terms of the emergence of self-structure through interactions with others that provide a sustaining context for the infant. How selfobject experience functions to facilitate a cohesive, continuous, and vital sense of self during other periods of life, particularly that of dying, is in need of further exploration and clarification. The description of the following case emphasizes self and selfobject experiences unique to the dying period of a patient as they emerged in treatment. Furthermore, how a selfobject experience interacts with and facilitates additionally needed selfobject experiences is examined.

The patient, Ms. L, had not experienced the kind of responsiveness in her surround that Kohut described. As a result, a significant impact of treatment emerged in the mirroring and idealizing selfobject transference dimensions. Transformations of Ms. L's self-experience were mediated such that she felt relief from her symptoms. She moved from a dreaded pattern of expecting nonresponsivity or constricting responses in her surround accompanied by a sense of "arrogant" self-control to a pattern of expecting responsiveness accompanied by feelings of "humility" and positive self-regard. In her dying days, she was able to feel good about herself and others. Central to these transformations was the understanding and interpretation of Ms. L's experiences of deity.

SELFOBJECT EXPERIENCE AND HUMAN DEVELOPMENT

One question this case study helps to address is how to conceptualize selfobject experience in developmental terms. Is the capacity for selfobject experience a linear, phase-specific development or is it shaped by specific contexts irrespective of chronology? The answer seems to be an interaction between certain sequential developmental accomplishments, particularly the capacity for representation, and the uniquely experienced contexts in which an individual is embedded as she or he develops. With this in mind, we examine the case of Ms. L and then construct an understanding of the specific developmental sequelae that help to understand her symptoms and their subsequent treatment. In framing an understanding of the case, the following observations from the self-psychological literature regarding selfobject experience are particularly relevant and helpful.

Fosshage (1992) has suggested that "within a more consistent field model self-generated and other-generated should be viewed as two poles on a continuum of selfobject experiences" (p. 223). Here Fosshage emphasizes contextual characteristics of the experience. Ms. L's experience of deity served a selfobject function that emerged in the treatment context but continued in other contexts in the absence of the therapist. What appeared to be facilitative was the acceptance and understanding of the unique meaning of her experience by her therapist.

Lichtenberg (1991) points out that selfobject experiences can be derived "from *ideation* associated with experiences that provide a powerful boost to vitalization and cohesion of the self. . . . Religion utilizes this recognition in its promise of an enduringly available protective deity" (p. 477). Lichtenberg's observation focuses on the vitalizing and cohering functions that can accrue from mental activity that substantiates the possibility of hope. Note that such ideation does not necessarily have to be derived from previous experience. It can be based in a faith emerging from a cultural context that holds out the promise of protection.

Basch (1988) describes religion as "a . . . mature, abstract, internalized source of selfobject experiences" (p. 232). Implicit in this statement is the assumption that there are also immature, concrete, external sources of selfobject experiences. I infer from this perspective an assumption of a developmental sequence to selfobject experience moving from the concrete and external to the abstract and internal. Whether this sequence can be conceptualized as linear or as a series of transformations that are context specific and reversible is not specified in the statement. Nevertheless, the idea that selfobject experience can be derived from an abstract and internal source implies the potential for such experience to emerge without the presence of another as a trigger or screen.

In short, all three theorists point to the use of experiences serving selfobject functions that 1) can occur without the use of another person, 2) are therefore self-initiated, and 3) can be sustained outside of the treatment relationship. This developmentally mature capacity utilizes experience for self-cohesion, self-sustaining, self-protecting, and vitalizing functions.

Ms. L could receive sustenance from the mirroring and idealizing selfobject dimensions of the treatment. These became the field for new relational experiences both within and outside of the treatment context that facilitated the transformation of a dreaded repetitive pattern originating in childhood to a new beginning (A. Ornstein, 1974). But, at the same time, these dimensions of selfobject experience were not able to transform the fear and loss of control generated by her current illness and anticipated death. In response to this fragmenting trauma, Ms. L utilized a developmentally mature selfobject experience precipitated by the therapist's understanding and acceptance of her sense of God. The following details illustrate the way in which this selfobject experience developed and functioned in the treatment context.

THE CASE OF MS. L

For Ms. L life was miserable and she wanted to die. She first contacted me a year before entering treatment while going through a long and harrowing divorce. During the divorce process she discovered that her cancer had recurred. Previously, Ms. L had had a mastectomy and was believed to be in remission. Now the cancer had reappeared in her bone marrow. She indicated that she might soon be needing my services but did not call back again until a year later. She was then in a panic and asked to be seen immediately.

It should be noted that at this time, the patient had a previously existing idealization of me. In that first meeting I learned of Ms. L's need for a supportive paternal figure and the disorganization and self-reproach that was triggered by the absence of such a figure. She began by indicating her hope that I would be able to help with her psychogenic dyspnea. This diagnosis had been given by an oncologist. As she talked, she exhibited distress and difficulty breathing, and described her state of panic and despair over the recent discovery that her initial prognosis had been incorrect. Previously, she was told she would live for about six more months. This period of time had expired.

Now, just before our first meeting, Ms. L was informed that the expectation for the length of time she would live with the disease had changed. The expectation was open-ended. She described her horror of having prepared to die, of having "stepped out onto the edge waiting for the angel of death to come and take [her], only to be told that there was a mistake and that no angel was coming and that, for that matter, it was not clear when the angel was coming." As she spoke, her breathing became more shallow. She began to gasp and wheeze with each breath she struggled to capture. Then, she let out a bloodcurdling scream and then again several more, which she muffled with a handkerchief cupped over her mouth. She explained that this gave her temporary relief.

As Ms. L initially struggled with her breathing and then screamed, I observed how she watched me. She seemed to be waiting for me to do something to stop her or give her a sign or command to stop. I refrained from intervening during this tense episode, sensing an important communication unfolding on a nonverbal level. After she screamed and explained, in part, why she did this, I noted the pain of the moment for both of us, her discomfort as well as mine in witnessing and accompanying her in her suffering. I suggested that as our work progressed, we might understand this "breathing problem" better.

Ms. L seemed somewhat relieved by my response and went on to describe the treatments she had undergone that were based on the "theory" that she could be healed by "physical work." Recent efforts to seek relief from her symptoms through such "body work" treatment had been unsuccessful. Born of Jewish immigrant parents, Ms. L described her mother as very resourceful and her father as distant and depressed. She did not experience her parents as being in love with each other. She had a sister three years younger who was a happy, even jolly child in contrast to her. As a child Ms. L had suffered from colic and had cried a great deal. Her mother's typical response to her crying, which continued long after the colic, was to slap a hand over Ms. L's mouth so as to muffle her crying. Ms. L's reaction as a child was to hold her breath. This was her attempt to control her crying and hold back the flow of her emotions, which were unacceptable to her mother. As she recalled these memories, I listened quietly to her. She began to feel even greater relief and her breathing improved. She speculated that this shift in her state may have been related to her memory and wondered if this were a pattern she had been repeating throughout her adult life until this very moment. She added jokingly that she knew I was the right man for her when she heard my name was "Dr. No Block."

In the next session Ms. L described a new "symptom," frequent crying spells, some of which seemed to last for hours. She stated, "I haven't permitted myself to cry for the last nine years." She associated her mother's slaps in the face to a series of slaps in the face that life had given her: her bouts with cancer, her divorce with her husband, and her difficulties raising her children. She had not given herself permission to cry in an attempt to control her experience of "life circumstances . . . out of control." As she described her attempts to control her feelings, she added, "Time is up." I noted the annoyance in her tone of voice and inquired whether these words might also refer to her experience of the treatment hour. I wondered if she felt robbed of a sense of control with me. She responded with a memory of a struggle with a former therapist who tried to get her to do some physical exercises to combat "her holding on to stress." In particular, she remembered a dream experience of "letting go" followed by three days in which she felt free of her pattern of holding in her pain. She described a kind of mystical sense of being at one with the universe. Then it stopped. She explained to me that she pushed it away: "I pushed God away. God had really touched me. I almost understood God. I've totally forgotten by now. I know nothing about God."

Ms. L's response to her therapist's impositions was to turn to God for relief. I wondered if now she was experiencing her relationship with me as restrictive and reconfiguring the organizing themes of slap in the face and withdrawal of needed support. Or was her describing the memory her way of showing me how badly she needed to find a way to reexperience the support and soothing relief that being touched by God could bring, and that she needed my help to reexperience that support and relief? I asked Ms. L about her religious beliefs and how she pushed God away. She indicated that she had never been religious and had pushed God away, "By saying let's just stop all this breathing business for now. And all this flowing. I don't know why I did this. I think it overwhelmed me. I was arrogant enough to think I could switch this on and off at my own control. The simple fact is that I have no control of anything. . . . The ship is the captain. I don't know anything about the captain. It isn't given to me to know. If I sound religious, believe me, that's just about the extent of my knowledge."

I chose not to pursue my questions about our relationship and the meaning of time restriction to her, but rather to understand her experience of God and the possible meanings of this memory. The intervention seemed to repair the rupture that the time issue had created and allow some of the meanings of her experience to unfold.

She described the struggle she had been in with her therapist for a sense of control: "I've been fighting the pleasure of "letting go" since I was a little girl, slapped hard in the face, telling herself—don't breathe out. It's too dangerous—I'm repeating that pattern now. The most effective way to hold emotions back is to hold your breath. It's horrible, but it works. That's what I did physically and emotionally; I held my breath and looked around for more trouble coming at me."

We then examined the trouble she was anticipating. She focused on the uncertainty and fear associated with her unpredictable dying process. She realized that her need to control blocked her ability to have the deific experience she once had and which she now needed in her time of despair to help her cope with feeling out of control. She experienced life as dangerous. She couldn't control what was happening to her, neither her dying nor me and my rules about treatment. She saw attempts to control as arrogant. She explained, "I need to know humility. If I don't learn humility, I'll be stripped bare. My breasts will be ripped off. I'll be poisoned. Everything I cherish will be torn away."

From this point on in treatment, Ms. L struggled to give up her control, know humility, and express to me the feelings she was experiencing. She verbally acknowledged the value of having her experience accepted by me, but she always seemed to need more in order to feel cohesive and vitalized in the face of her painful dying process. Her experience of God seemed to provide this additional organizing function for her, particularly when, as was often the case, I was unavailable to help her contain and express her feelings. In subsequent sessions, we explored her belief that holding back had contributed to her suffering, and that her "arrogance" blocked her feelings of flowing, which she characterized as the presence of God in her life. She further explained, "In all of this stuff that's happening to me now, I feel close to it again. It feels infinitely far away, as though I'll never get there again. But I'm not as far as it feels. When I cry, this all can dissolve again, and I feel hints of it. . . . Then I tighten up again . . . and hold back the crying. . . . So I'm in an unstable place, shaky on my feet, scared to death, blocked as hell."

In the next phase of treatment, Ms. L struggled to accept her feelings humbly, to flow, and thus to "know God." She began to experience relationships with others in a new way. She described a conflict with her daughter in which Ms. L was now able to express her feelings and needs, which, previously, would have eventuated in another "slap in the face" episode. In subsequent months, the content of sessions centered on conflicts in other significant relationships with her son, her ex-husband, friends, relatives, and physicians managing the treatment of her illness. Increasingly, she expressed her feelings rather than holding them back. She felt understood by others and was able to work through anger and resentments associated with past disappointments and rejections. As she reordered the meanings of past and present conflicts, she could begin to feel a sense of resolution and acceptance. She attributed these feelings to her newly found connection to God. Through this religious sense of events and relationships the repetitive pattern of holding back was transformed in that she could now articulate her affective experience.

Ms. L described her newly evolving self state as "really beautiful. And a time of intense suffering. And of almost, almost reaching whatever it is—let me say it—I'm almost reaching God. I'm purifying myself, making myself clean. Making myself worthy of whatever it is that's coming. I want to be ready for it."

In addition to reflecting her increasing sense of order and meaning in deific terms, she revealed the poignant conflict over self-worth with which she struggled, particularly in the way it pervaded her sense of inadequacy as a parent to her children and as a wife to her husband. She felt she had let them all down and felt apologetic to me about her lack of strength for our sessions or for boring me. But as she reviewed her life, her descriptions of self-experience began to shift from this sense of inadequacy toward an increasingly more positive self-concept and sense of hope.

For example, in regard to her home, Ms. L stated, "This house is becoming a sanctified place. I'm finding myself in this house. . . . I need this place in the woods to cry and yell and bathe in and be alone. I suddenly appreciate this unstable house I thought was such a burden. It's a gift to me at this time." She described a visit to her home, which reflected the degree to which she had now organized her experiences in religious terms. She explained how every moment had become meaningful to her in this way. The visit was by a man of foreign descent whose name in his language meant the same as hers—"Praise God." Their visit, though ostensibly for a quite mundane purpose, was experienced by Ms. L as spiritual and timeless. She explained to me, "All of this is what God is to me."

At this point in treatment, Ms. L now described her encounters, with others, particularly men, not in dangerous terms whereby the other would be unresponsive as with father, husband, son, and previous therapists, but as safe and sanctified with religious meaning. As an example of this, she described how she had cried in bed remembering how she had prayed for something to ease her daughter's suffering over her illness. She described her prayers being met as her daughter's husband "fell from heaven." Her use of deity as selfobject experience met her need for support in the face of death. Ironically, she could experience feelings and connection to others more in her dying than at any time previously in her life. Her immediate need was for the continuing presence of God and the affect integration facilitated by this presence.

Over time, Ms. L's physical condition deteriorated. Problems with medication and periods of extreme fatigue and difficulty concentrating undermined the frequency, duration, and focus of our sessions. During the last five months of Ms. L's life, we did not have regularly scheduled sessions. Periodically, she or I would initiate a brief phone call. She would catch me up on current events concerning her relationships with family members and the increasing deterioration of her body. Although physically exhausted, she was personally engaged up through our last contact. A few weeks before she died, she told me she could feel that death was close. The night before she died she called her son to prepare him. She had made her preparations and accepted the transition with a sense of readiness for "what comes next."

DISCUSSION

Ms. L presented with panic attacks associated with the shock of her misprognosis. She had been a patient in numerous previous psychotherapies. Her history suggests difficulties managing affects, particularly anxiety. But it is probable that she also suffered episodes of dysthymia though she did not indicate that she was so diagnosed or treated for this disorder. Her preexisting idealization of me impressed me as an important factor contributing to the rapid unfolding of transference material so early in the treatment, along with the fact that she had been through other treatments and was facing the possibility of a short time of treatment with me should she deteriorate quickly. In light of these factors, it is not surprising that the model scene (Lachmann and Lichtenberg, 1992) organizing and facilitating our understanding of the array of symptoms she was exhibiting in the first session was in fact part of the material produced in that session. It seemed that Ms. L's need for someone to listen and respond to her cries for help without slapping her in the face had been revived in the developing idealizing transference. In fact, the events of the first session may have created a new beginning (Ornstein, 1974) or mirroring selfobject experience for her.

The subsequent unfolding of meanings associated with this model scene led to a recognition that for Ms. L humility meant giving up attempts to be in control of her emotional display by holding her breath. She was able to give up that control in treatment with me because I appeared willing to listen to and accept her experiences without imposing my own meanings or behavioral requirements upon her, as she had experienced with previous therapists. So Ms. L's struggle for control could be considered as the repetitive dimension of the transference configuration having been organized by her experiences with her mother and previous therapists. In material not reported, we were also able to trace how she experienced this pattern in many other relationships such as with husband, children, and physicians treating her illness. At the same time, her experience of my responsiveness to her feelings represented a new beginning (Ornstein, 1974).

Yet, although her breathing improved and tears began to flow, the anticipation of death remained as a source of uncertainty and helplessness for Ms. L. This danger could not be removed in treatment. Thus, it became clear that the selfobject tie that unfolded as part of the treatment relationship served not just as a context for the transformation of the repetitive pattern of holding back emotions; Ms. L's need for continuity and coherence could only be met by "an enduringly available protective deity" (Lichtenberg, 1991). Because Ms. L had repudiated her religious heritage as part of her controlling pattern, she needed not just to stop holding back emotions, but also to find some way of experiencing God. She was able to access her conflict with authority in the transference as the issue of time constriction emerged. Her associations to this episode allowed us to see how she had coped with such a conflict with a previous therapist through what was initially dream ideation and later a kind of merger experience with her surround that allowed her to feel, for three brief days, freedom from her constricting pattern of holding back emotions. In the treatment with me she retrospectively characterized this as an experience of God. We can only speculate whether this was Ms.

L's personal way of reconnecting to a protective deity or a hypomanic defense against a fear of reexperiencing with me the failure in responsiveness of her father and previous therapists. Because I could not protect her from death, she needed me to help her recreate her sense of connectedness to this greater source of protection she had so briefly been able to experience once before when she had felt endangered and out of control.

There was an interesting intersubjective resonance (Stolorow and Atwood, 1992) to the relationship between the two selfobject experiences described previously. With my understanding and responsiveness, Ms. L could begin again to experience the needed presence and protection of God. With God's presence, Ms. L could work with me in the transformation of a central life problem previously organizing her experience—the holding back of emotion for fear of punishment and rejection, and the concomitant narcissistic wounding she felt in these moments. Hence, each dimension of experience for this patient contributed to the configuration of a context that made possible the other, a wonderful illustration of a dialectical relationship between two dimensions of experience constituting intrapsychic contents out of an intersubjective context. The contents were 1) the new potential for experiencing affects and relationships and 2) the experience of protection in the face of imminent demise.

This understanding can be compared to Meissner's (1984) conceptualization of belief in a religiously based moral order that "can be seen as a creative effort to reinforce and sustain the more highly organized and integrated adaptational concerns" (p. 131). Meissner also points out that "the religious concern may serve as a vital psychological force that supports the individual in his attempts at self-definition and realization" (p. 133). This understanding is consistent with the deific selfobject function that I understood Ms. L's experience to be as compared with the speculative understanding I earlier identified, of religious experience (in Freud's terms) as transference repetition. Here, the understanding would be of her religious experience as a defense against a retraumatization of constriction, punishment, or rejection by a male authority figure. This explanation is problematic in that it reduces the patient's experience to one meaning, which completely ignores the self-organizing function being accomplished, a recognition encompassed both in Meissner's perspective and my understanding of the dialectical relationship between the two selfobject experiences illustrated in this case.

SUMMARY

The treatment of a dying patient is presented as an illustration of how a selfobject tie configured on idealizing and mirroring dimensions functioned to facilitate a selfobject experience of a protective deity. The dialectical resonance of these two selfobject experiences sustained the effects of each, facilitating a transformation of the patient's repetitive pattern of holding back her emotional display for fear of punishment or rejection, and providing continuity to the experience of safety and security provided by the presence of God. This case illustrates how the patient would not have been able to experience either of these selfobject dimensions isolated from the context of the other. Furthermore, this understanding shaped the subsequent unfolding of participation in treatment by both patient and therapist.

In the treatment of dying patients impending loss of all ties and relatedness is universal. During such a period of dying the critical dimension of selfobject experience for the patient is the acceptance and understanding of her or his need to sustain the self. For Ms. L, my acceptance and understanding of how religious experience functioned to serve that need was crucial.

REFERENCES

Basch, M. (1988), *Understanding Psychotherapy*. New York: Basic Books.

Fosshage, J. (1992), The selfobject concept: A further discussion of three authors. In: *Therapeutic Views, Progress in Self Psychology, Vol. 8*, ed. A. Goldberg. Hillsdale, NJ: The Analytic Press, pp. 229–239.

Kohut, H. (1984), *How Does Analysis Cure?* ed. A. Goldberg & P. Stepansky. Chicago: University of Chicago Press.

Lachmann, F. & Lichtenberg, J. (1992), Model scenes: Implications for psychoanalytic treatment. *J. Amer. Psychoanal. Assn.*, 40:117–137.

Lichtenberg, J. (1989), *Psychoanalysis and Motivation*. Hillsdale, NJ: The Analytic Press.

——— (1991), What is a selfobject? *Psychoanal. Dial.*, 1:455–479.

Meissner, W. W. (1984), *Psychoanalysis and Religious Experience*. New Haven, CT: Yale University Press.

Ornstein, A. (1974), The dread to repeat and the new beginning: A contribution to the treatment of narcissistic personality disorders. *The Annual of Psychoanalysis*, 2:231–248.

Stern, D. (1985), *The Interpersonal World of the Infant*. New York: Basic Books.

Stolorow, R. & Atwood, G. (1992), *Contexts of Being: The Intersubjective Foundations of Psychological Life*. Hillsdale, NJ: The Analytic Press.

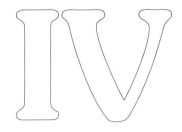

Theoretical
and Applied

The Use of Sequential Personality Testing in Analysis to Monitor the Uncovering of Childhood Memories of Abuse

Shirley C. Geller

Many adults who were abused as children have little or no conscious memory of their abuse. Frequently, such individuals enter psychotherapy for symptoms they do not initially relate to their early abusive treatment (Sands, 1991). As repression lifts and patient and therapist together begin to identify and label maltreatment and abusive events, how does the patient experience this process? How is this uncovering process revealed? This chapter seeks to provide answers to these questions.

The two patients to be discussed were and continue to be in four-day-a-week analysis with a graduate analyst who is most comfortable with a self psychology orientation. Both patients were administered the Wechsler Adult Intelligence Scale–Revised (WAIS–R) (Wechsler, 1981) and the Rorschach Comprehensive System (Exner, 1986) yearly to assess original status and change during their analysis.

ASSESSMENT DURING ANALYSIS

Although psychoanalysis has looked quite unfavorably upon any practice that interferes with the developing of the transference neurosis, and testing during analysis would be perceived as one of those practices, this graduate psychoanalyst decided to break with tradition and have her analysands assessed yearly. This was done for the following reasons. First, although analytic belief views the successful resolution of the trans-ference neurosis as a traditional measure of analytic success, current research does not bear this out. In a long term follow-up study of 17 analytic patients, Kantrowitz, Katz, and Paolitto (1987, 1990) found no correlation between the degree of resolution of the transference neurosis and four measures of psychological growth, specifically, the level and quality of object relations, the development of a self-analytic function, improved reality testing, and later growth. Second, Wallerstein (1989) found little evidence that the introduction of the interview and projective psychological tests in the assessment of 42 patients in psychoanalysis and long-term psychotherapy either delayed or impaired the treatment process. Third, the traditional concepts of resistance and defense long associated with the transference neurosis and its fullest possible resolu-tion are being questioned and redefined (Kohut, 1984; Wolf, 1988). Fourth, adherence to strict neutrality and abstinence does not pose the same problem for the self psychologist as it does for the more classical analyst. Fifth, the analytic climate is apparently becoming more liber-alized as recognized analysts are even suggesting that analysis needs to become more open to change and growth (Goldberg, 1990). Finally, the current focus on accountability and outcome measurement basic to insurance, managed health care, and national health care reform requires more specific criteria of treatment improvement. One way to provide such criteria is to utilize psychological assessment procedures on a regular (i.e., yearly) basis. In this manner, objective evidence of the efficacy of the psychoanalytic process and a show of good faith in attempting to quantify treatment outcome can be provided.

TEST AND TEST ADMINISTRATION

In this study, as stated earlier, the WAIS–R and the Comprehensive Rorschach System were employed as assessment tools. The WAIS–R is a test for measuring global and specific components of adult intellectual functioning. It consists of a series of 11 tasks requiring problem-solving and intellectual operations involving the verbal and the perceptual-manipulative spheres.

The Comprehensive Rorschach System is an objective method of assessing a person's perceptual-cognitive conceptualization using 10 inkblots. It is assumed that how a person structures and organizes an ambiguous stimulus field is directly or indirectly representative of behav-ior that can be expected in other situations requiring the same sort of structuring and organizing operations (Erdberg and Exner, 1984).

It is considered an *objective* test in that the test administration procedure, each score of the person's verbalizations of visual perceptions of
the inkblots, and the score interpretations are fixed. *This is doubly
important for its use in analysis.* The employment of the Comprehensive Rorschach System to assess change in analysis not only provides an
answer to Grunbaum's (1984) challenge for analysts to go outside the
analytic setting to validate what goes on inside of the analytic setting, but
does so by utilizing an objective process that is itself based on empirical
validation. Every verbal response the patient gives to 10 standard
inkblots is typically assigned between 8 and 15 scores (i.e., parts of the
blot the person uses to formulate his/her percept, use of achromatic or
chromatic color, use of shading, etc.). These quantified scores are further
utilized to construct ratios (e.g., achievement ratio, affect ratio, egocen-
tricity ratio), and indexes (e.g., depression index, schizophrenic index,
suicide constellation) (see Appendix A). These scores, ratios, and
indexes, which number more than 200, have been normed on hundreds
and thousands of people of various ages and diagnostic categories and
both sexes. The Comprehensive Rorschach System has empirically
related an individual's perceptual-cognitive responses to inkblots in such
a manner as to allow the generation of descriptions and explanations for
a person's thinking, feelings, and behaviors in the present, the past, and
the future. Additionally, many of the levels of personality structure that
are being measured not only have been laid down early in life, but are at
such a depth that they are minimally affected by medication, psy-
chotropic or otherwise.

The initial test administration was done at the time the patients
commenced treatment. Subsequent testing was done yearly. All the tests
were administered and scored by another psychologist[1] who was trained
and experienced in the WAIS–R and the Comprehensive Rorschach
System and institute-trained in psychoanalytic psychotherapy. The
scores for each Rorschach protocol were quantified by using an IBM
personal computer programmed with the Rorschach Interpretation
Assistance Program (Exner, 1990).

CASE ONE, MRS. A

Mrs. A, Elizabeth,[2] 41 years of age, who has completed one year of
analysis, initially entered weekly psychotherapy treatment because of her

---

[1] The author wishes to thank Kathryn E. Ward, Ph.D. for administering and scoring the WAIS–
Rs and Rorschachs.

[2] To protect the anonymity of the analysands, all names, dates, locations, occupations and
other identifying information have been changed. Whenever these identifying characteristics had
clinical significance, changes were made in such a way that the clinical picture remained intact.

11-year-old daughter. The child would go for days without speaking to either her mother or her father. Elizabeth found this difficult to understand, for she viewed her family life as comfortable and happy, and bolstered this belief by the fact that her six-year-old son showed no signs of disturbance. In essence, she perceived herself as happily married, with a contented husband, and two bright, rather special children. Relatively quickly, it was ascertained that the reason her daughter would go for days without speaking to her parents was that she felt that they were not only uninvolved with her but also made decisions for her that bore no relation to her needs and wishes. In early sessions the patient revealed that for the last four years her husband had become less emotionally available to her because of his work pressures. She in turn had become depressed, preoccupied with the emotional loss of her husband, and less available to her children. Several months after therapy was begun with the daughter, Elizabeth's husband and herself, the six-year-old son also demanded to enter treatment. The boy was refusing to attend school and having difficulty learning. Elizabeth was shocked; she saw her son as a model student. At that point all four family members were administered the Rorschach and other psychological tests. Significant disturbance was found in the whole family. Because Elizabeth was seen as playing a pivotal role in the family, analysis was suggested to her. The other three family members were referred to one of the analyst's associates.

The patient, who is an attorney and prides herself on her intellectual acuteness and immediate response to problems, felt extremely guilty about both her own depression and her insensitivity to her children, particularly in view of the detrimental effect this was having on them.

Initially, Elizabeth described her childhood, five siblings, and parents in idealized, grandiose, and special terms. Her father was portrayed by her mother as a brilliant attorney, a genius. As a result, he knew how to raise their six children and knew what was best for everyone. The children were expected to live up to his directives. The family was one that all families should emulate. Her father demanded strict obedience, insisted that feelings were a sign of weakness, and made it clear that no task was to be considered impossible. If he became upset and yelled or hit a child, it was because the child had not done what was expected.

As analytic treatment progressed, Elizabeth began remembering a terrified childhood. She remembered her parents drinking daily. She recalled being spanked painfully and frequently, often sent to her room without meals, and ridiculed for any sign of wanting anything for herself. Her father was subject to violent outbursts, at which time he would strike out. On one occasion, when she was around four, he hit her foot with a heavy tire iron. The bone in her foot is still deformed as a result. Elizabeth learned early to "read" her father's features and gestures so she could appease him before he became violent. When her techniques of appeasement did not work, she hid so that she would not be beaten. As she lay on the couch, Elizabeth recalled a childhood in which she was constantly running away and hiding from both of her parents out of fear of verbal and physical abuse.

Congruent with her childhood experiences, Elizabeth's dominant transference expectations have contained ever-present fears of criticism, hostility, and rejection from the analyst.

As Elizabeth's fantasy of having an ideal family began to deteriorate so did some of her functioning. Her migraine headaches, which she had suffered on and off since adolescence, increased in frequency and severity.

Before treatment Elizabeth had been a rather competent, aloof, and demanding career woman. She considered herself to be quite special, viewed her approach to issues as the only correct one, seldom saw herself as being at fault, and was relatively free of self-doubt.

Elizabeth's initial test scores confirmed the clinical impression (Appendix B). Her intellectual functioning was at the superior level (WAIS–R: Verbal IQ, 119; Performance IQ, 118; and Full IQ, 122). On her first Rorschach she revealed a need to distance herself from people and a certain insensitivity to the concerns of others (Texture = 0).[3] Her sense of self-importance was inflated to a point that dominated her perception of the world (Reflection = 2). And she experienced an intense inner pressure for her needs and desires to be met immediately (Animal movement = 8).

Correlation Between Uncovering Process and Test Data—Case One

Rather than adopting a "hierarchically ordered two-reality view" (Schwaber, 1983) that assumes one reality is experienced by the patient and the other is objectively "known" by the analyst, the therapist assumed a one-tier view of reality. This one-tier view, in conjunction with Gedo's (1979) belief that analytic treatment should discover the personal significance of psychic life in its specific meaning for a particular individual, led the analyst to ask the patient directly, "If you were to describe your experience during the time period you became aware that your fantasy of having had an 'ideal family' was not so but that instead you had endured a great deal of maltreatment and possible abuse, how would you describe your experience in the uncovering process?"

---

[3] Test results refer to critical but partial Rorschach elements relating to interpretations given. See Appendix B for details.

To this question Elizabeth responded: "It was a shock, a major disappointment. It left a big hole in my day-to-day life. Since my acting was based on something out of my fantasy, I didn't know how to act. Everything I did seemed pointless. My sense of depression and loneliness has increased completely. My migraine headaches increased so that some days I was too sick to get out of bed. Things came to a head in July. I had to take a week off. I couldn't work. I never missed work before. This process has also made me so much more dependent on you. I worry what I'll do next week while you're away if something comes up. That's something I would never have said a year ago. I was shocked to hear you tell me I was depressed. I never gave feelings any validity because I never was allowed to have them. Feelings that didn't fit my fantasy weren't valid so I ignored them I guess. But it's still too early to identify all of the changes."

Following a year of therapy, which included the uncovering of abusive childhood memories, Elizabeth was experiencing considerable painful emotion (SumSH > FM + m).[4] Additionally, she reported an increase in dysphoric affect (the Depression Index increased from 3 to 6). Particularly clear was her sense of recent emotional loss, feelings of great loneliness, strong need for closeness, and growing dependence on the therapist (Texture responses increased from 0 to 2). Furthermore, Elizabeth's initial active approach to life appeared to have changed to a more passive approach (Active:Passive behavior changed from 13:2 to 4:7). Moreover, she revealed a small but meaningful decline in overall intellectual functioning (WAIS–R Full IQ dropped from 122 to 115; Verbal IQ from 119 to 114, and Performance IQ from 118 to 113). Her description of not knowing "how to act" as the reality of her childhood trauma seeped into consciousness was reflected in her growing passivity and decline in intellectual functioning. Such passivity appeared to provide Elizabeth with a technique to avoid coping with the overwhelming complexity of the unconscious, negative material that was intruding upon her consciousness.

All of the preceding seem to reflect her description of her experience of the uncovering process: her description of feeling a "major disappointment," "a big hole in my day-to-day life," and an increase in her "sense of depression and loneliness."

Thus, both the Rorschach and WAIS–R seem to corroborate Elizabeth's experience of the uncovering of her abusive childhood memories.

---

[4] Weiner and Exner (1991) have reported that when the sum of a person's shading responses (C', T, Y, and V) is greater than Animal Movement plus inanimate movement responses (FM + m), it is quite likely the person is experiencing painful, negative affect.

CASE 2, MS. B

Unlike Mrs. A, whose first year of treatment has been detailed, Ms. B, 41 years of age, has begun her third year of analytic therapy. Silent idealization (Gedo, 1975, 1981) and twinship transferences have been prominent in her analysis.

Ms. B, Jennifer, entered therapy because she experienced herself becoming depressed in a manner similar to that which she had experienced 10 years ago. Ten years earlier she became seriously depressed while on a three-week vacation with her husband. It generalized into a year of agoraphobia, during which she seldom left the house. She saw a psychologist on and off over a five-year period, and the condition had gradually subsided.

During the present treatment, after almost two months of twice-a-week therapy, she began four-day-a-week analysis. Jennifer was receptive to the idea of analysis because she knew something was drastically amiss with her. She knew she would be 42 soon and was not living the type of personal productive life she had envisioned.

Jennifer suffered from school phobia as a child. And although identified as gifted, her junior high, high school, and college grades did not reflect this. She went away to college but was obliged to drop out in her third year because of failing grades.

Jennifer has always worked with animals, first for the Humane Society, and for the last 12 years as a veterinary assistant in the same animal hospital. At the time Jennifer began treatment, she rarely dared venture more than 10 miles away from her house. Her home was her refuge.

Initially, in her free association, Jennifer described a childhood in which she was almost too well taken care of. Money was freely available. Her parents were solicitous about her physical health and always rushed to treat any illness or disease. Until she left home to attend college, her mother did not ask Jennifer to do any chores or care for her personal needs.

During the first year of analysis, her separation anxiety was interpreted in terms of her being overprotected and infantilized. This in turn had limited her developing the coping mechanisms needed for achievement and interacting with the world.

During her second year of analysis, she began detailing how, when she was a child, her parents were constantly putting drops in her ears and eyes, and making her take liquid medicines. Jennifer did not feel her state of health demanded all this invasive care. Nevertheless for almost two years Jennifer continued to proclaim that although her parents may have been overprotective, they were loving and caring.

Toward the end of her second year of treatment, during one of her sessions she commented that the night before she had accidentally turned to the movie *Sybil*. She confessed that after initially viewing the film, she was never able to watch it again. This was because of the scenes in which Sybil as a child was repeatedly given enemas. She added ingenuously, "Haven't I told you my mother used to give me enemas?" She then began detailing a childhood in which she was repeatedly given enemas by her mother. She would be placed on a card table in the bathroom, usually with her father assisting. She felt she was doubly invaded: first, because she was held down while water was pumped into her and feces made to be expelled, and second, because the bathroom door, like all the rooms in the house, was to be kept open. Her younger brother could come by to watch. Jennifer's tearful screaming did not alter her parents' course of action. These routinely administered enemas began when she was around three and continued until she was eight.

At the time Jennifer entered treatment she was working as a veterinary assistant in a job that required only average intellectual skills. But Jennifer felt she was "special" and the work she was doing was somewhat beneath her. She aspired to a higher career position and was frustrated by her inability to obtain one. She felt emotionally upset a great deal of the time and was having problems not "losing it." This expression referred to the fact that she was often subject to tearful or angry outbursts.

Her test scores correlated with this clincial impression (see Appendix C). Her verbal abilities were average, surpassed by her high average perceptual-manipulative abilities (WAIS–R: Verbal IQ, 107; Performance IQ, 117; Full IQ, 113). Her sense of being "special" was confirmed on the Rorschach, where she revealed an overinflated sense of personal worth bordering on narcissistic glorification (Reflection = 1).

Jennifer's difficulty obtaining a higher-level job could be observed in her striving to accomplish more than was reasonable in light of her current functional capacities (whole responses: human-movement-responses ratios were 8:3, then 7:4). Her sense of upset was reflected in responses indicating negative emotional experiences (SumSh: FM + m ratios were initially 7:2 at the beginning of analysis and 11:8 after one year of analysis).

Her initial report of frequently "losing it" was substantiated by indications of overly intense feelings combined with unreserved expressions of affect (color form + pure color > form color +1, 3:2, and pure color = 1).

Correlation Between Uncovering Process and
Test Data—Case Two

When the therapist posed the question to Jennifer, "If you were to describe your experience during the time period you became aware that your fantasy of having had an 'ideal family' was not so but that instead you had endured a great deal of maltreatment and possible abuse, how would you describe your experience in the uncovering process?" She was informed that I was attempting to correlate her remembering of the enemas with her test data. Again, the subjective reality of the patient, not the objectively "known" reality of the analyst, was of prime importance. Therapeutic inference was suspended. To this Jennifer replied: "You do recall that I *only* remembered the enemas *after* you gave me the results of my testing, not before? The analysis has made me less anxious. It has freed me up to see things I haven't seen before. I no longer feel so bad, and I travel all over. I am not agoraphobic. It has given me insight into a lot of areas I had never considered. *But your showing me the improvement in the tests allowed me to feel secure enough to tell you about the enemas.* The test results were an affirmation that I was as intelligent as I thought I had always been, although I know I haven't used my intelligence well. The fact that I now could see all those details in the pictures (WAIS–R, Picture Completion) was proof that I really was observant. Seeing my improvement in the tests made me realize that I really had improved in two years. I was doing much better. I also began to think that maybe in another year or so I may not be coming here. I knew deep inside there was this big issue I had to discuss. I now knew I had enough tools to deal with it. So I blurted out about the enemas the day *after* you gave me the results of my testing."

As the psychologist listened to the patient's description of her experienced relationship between the test results and the uncovering process and checked the dates on her process notes, she realized that the reality described by the patient was indeed correct. Thus, in this instance, the psychological testing did not monitor the uncovering process, it appeared to have facilitated it. When Jennifer's description of the test results that allowed her to uncover her abusive childhood memories is reviewed, the freeing of her intelligence can be seen in her improved levels of intellectual functioning. On retest, following two years of therapy, Jennifer revealed a marked increase in intellectual functioning, from high average to superior (Full IQ, 113 to 125; Verbal IQ, 107 to 115; Performance IQ, 117 to 132). There was considerable improvement in her immediate auditory memory (Digit Span increased from 9 to 13) and in her ability to differentiate essential from nonessential picture detail (Picture Completion increased from 9 to 14).

An increase in productive functioning is also found on the Rorschach, in which there seems to be an increase in creative energies available to facilitate achievement (whole responses:human movement ratios changed from 8:3 to 7:4, and finally 6:5). Her experience of painful emotion is less than it has been during any time in treatment (SumSh: FM + m is 8:7 in contrast to earlier ratios of 7:2 and 11:8). And her identification with, internalization of, and empathy with people has increased (human movement responses increased from 3 to 4 and then 5). Additionally, there has been a decrease in her level of free floating anxiety (diffuse shading responses have been reduced from 2 to 1).

Because Jennifer states that she no longer feels "so bad" and now "travels all over," painful affect has apparently lessened, people are no longer such an unknown quantity, and places are not so anxiety producing.

In this chapter I have discussed some of the most obvious changes in two patients' WAIS–Rs and Rorschachs during their analytic treatment. One patient's test results appear to monitor the uncovering of childhood memories of abuse; another patient's test results seem to have facilitated the uncovering process itself, thus furthering the analytic work. Testing during treatment does not appear to have disrupted the analysis of either patient. Both continue in treatment and appear to be making significant progress.

As previously stated, although psychoanalysis has frowned upon any practice that might interfere with the unfolding transference neurosis, the empirical study of the relationship between the resolution of the transference neurosis and measurements of improvement would appear to indicate a need to reevaluate this aspect of analytic theory and technique. Additionally, having detailed cognitive and personality data on patients before and during analysis may allow the analyst to have a better understanding of the patient's personality structure than can be provided by present analytic theory alone. As a result, the analytic process may proceed at a more rapid pace.

Additionally, insurance companies are more likely to undertake and continue funding long-term treatment if they are given a clear, succinct picture of the patient's emotional disturbance, dynamics, and improvement during the treatment process.

APPENDIX A

Explanation of some Rorschach variables

Texture—T
  T = 0
  — may occur when emotional dependency needs become "neutralized."
  — relates to problems in attachment.
  — person is more guarded and distant in interpersonal contacts.
  — person is more concerned with issues of personal space than most people.
  — person is seen as selfish, uncaring, ungiving, not wanting to touch.
  — person doesn't give emotionally.

Texture
  T = 2 or greater
  — person has greater needs for closeness than others.
  — person is experiencing strong sense of loneliness.
  — person has stronger than usual needs to be dependent on others.

Reflection—r
  greater than 0
  — relates to high self-centeredness.
  — concept of narcissism.

Animal Movement—FM
  FM greater than 4
  — inner push for needs to be gratified immediately.
  — relates to unmet physiological or psychological need states.

Diffuse Shading—Y
  — related to emotional experiences that are fomented by situations of helplessness, loss of control, or concerns about the possibility of being unable to respond effectively.
  — affect associated with it can take form of anxiety, apprehension, tension, or state of uneasiness.

Achromatic Color—C'
  — relates to holding in of affect.
  — anger is most usually held in.

— associated with depression.
— can result in somatic conditions.
— is a primitive defense.

Vista—V

V greater than 0
— associated with the presence of discomfort and even pain that is being produced by a ruminative self-inspection that focuses on perceived negative features of the self.

Human Movement—M

— involves element of reasoning, imagination, and a higher form of conceptualization.
— involves concept of delay or control of impulses, during which time an active and deliberate form of ideation occurs.
— involves experiencing satisfactory human relationships so that identification with and internalization of human beings can occur.
— because people and their motivations become more understandable with identification, it involves capacity for empathy.
— an index of creativity.
— is related to capacity for fantasy, a time sense, the intellect, creativeness, delay capacity, and some aspects of interpersonal relations.

Inanimate Movement—m

— related to sensation of tension.
— reflects a sense of helplessness and loss of control over events.
— induced by situational pressures.

Color Responses

CF and C (Color Form, Pure Color) in contrast to FC (form color)
— are related to more intense, less well controlled forms of affective discharge.

Aspirational Ratio—W:M

(W) Need for achievement: (M) presence of functional capabilities such as reasoning and higher forms of conceptualization, and process of giving deliberate direction to ideational focusing that are necessary for achievement.

Depression Index (DEPI)
  — An index indicating the number of depression indexes present. The number possible is seven.

Active-to-Passive ratios
  — measure of active to passive features likely to occur in person's behavior and thought.

APPENDIX B

Wechsler Adult Intelligence Scale–Revised
(WAIS–R)

Ms. A, Elizabeth

	Beginning first year of analysis	Beginning second year of analysis
Verbal IQ	119	114
Performance IQ	118	113
Full-scale IQ	122	115

Verbal Subtests

Information	14	15
Digit Span	7	7
Vocabulary	13	14
Arithmetic	15	13
Comprehension	14	12
Similarities	13	11

Performance Subtests

Picture Completion	11	11
Picture Arrangement	10	8
Block Design	12	12
Object Assembly	14	12
Digit Symbol	12	12

Ms. A, Elizabeth

Rorschach Variables

Schizophrenic Index (SCZI)	1	0
Depression Index (DEPI)	3	6
D Score	−4	−1

	Beginning first year of analysis	Beginning second year of analysis
Adjusted D Score	−2	−1
Coping Deficit Index (CDI)	3	3
Lambda	.42	.47
EB	3:4.5	6:4.5
EA	7.5	10.5
p > a + 1	no, 2:14	yes, 7:5
Sum Shading > FM + m	no, 8:12	yes, 10:5
CF + C > FC + 1	no, 3:4	yes, 3:2
Sum 6 SpSc > 6	no, 2	no, 2
Intellect > 5	no, 3	no, 5
3r + (2)/R	.48	.50
Pure H < 2	no, 3	no, 3
H < [(H) + Hd + (Hd)]	no, 3:2	no, 3:3
Zd	+0.5	−2.0
X+%	.56	.68
F+%	.38	.75
X−%	.11	.00
Affect ratio	.50	.57
R	27	22
P	3	4
Hypervigilance Index (HVI)	no	no
Obsessive Style Index (OBS)	no	no
M	3	6
M−	1	0
FM	8	4
C'	5	4
T	0	2
m	4	1
V	0	2
Y	3	2
Pure C	0	2
FD	1	2
r	0	0
W:M	12:3	8:6
a:p	13:2	4:7
Ma:Mp	3:0	3:3
AG	1	1
COP	1	2
S	4	1

APPENDIX C

Ms. B, Jennifer

WAIS–R

	Beginning second year of analysis[5]	Beginning third year of analysis
Verbal IQ	107	115
Performance IQ	117	132
Full-scale IQ	113	125
Verbal Subtests		
Information	14	13
Digit Span	9	13
Vocabulary	12	12
Arithmetic	8	9
Comprehension	12	14
Similarities	12	12
Performance Subtests		
Picture Completion	9	14
Picture Arrangement	9	9
Block Design	14	14
Object Assembly	14	18
Digit Symbol	12	12

---

[5] The author's decision to use the WAIS–R to assess change in analysis was made during the patient's second year in treatment.

Ms. B, Jennifer

Rorschach Variables

	Beginning first year of analysis	Beginning second year of analysis	Beginning third year of analysis
Schizophrenic Index (SCZI)	1	2	1
Depression Index (DEPI)	5	4	5
D Score	0	−3	−3
Adjusted D Score	0	−3	−3
Coping Deficit Index (CDI)	2	2	5
Lambda	.50	.13	.75
EB	3:4.0	4:6.0	5:1.5
EA	7.0	10.0	6.5
p > +1	no, 0:6	no, 4:9	yes, 7:6
Sum Shading > FM + m	yes, 7:2	yes, 11:8	yes, 8:7
CF + C > FC + 1	yes, 3:2	no, 3:7	no, 0:4
Sum 6 Sp Sc > 6	no, 0	no, 3	no, 1
Intellect > 5	no, 0	no, 1	no, 1
3r + (2) / R	.57	.33	.49
Pure H < 2	no, 4	no, 5	no, 5
H < [(H) + Hd + (Hd)]	no, 4:2	no, 5:3	no, 5:3
Zd	−1.5	+3.5	0.0
X+%	.43	.33	.49
F+%	.57	.33	.53
X−%	.24	.30	.20
Affect ratio	1.10	.69	.67
R	21	27	35
P	6	3	7
Hypervigilance Index (HVI)	no	no	no
Obsessive Style Index (OBS)	no	no	no
M	3	4	5
M−	0	1	0
FM	2	7	7
C'	3	4	3
T	2	4	4
m	0	1	0
V	0	2	0
Y	2	1	1
Pure C	1	0	0
FD	0	1	0

	Beginning first year of analysis	Beginning second year of analysis	Beginning third year of analysis
r	1	0	0
W:M	8:3	7:4	6:5
a:p	5:0	8:4	5:7
Ma:Mp	3:0	3:1	2:3
AG	0	0	1
COP	1	2	0
S	2	6	4

TABLE 1. SOME AREAS ASSESSED BY THE
COMPREHENSIVE RORSCHACH SYSTEM

The degree that the individual:
1. perceives the world and people accurately and conventionally.
2. focuses on him/herself. Correlates with the concepts of narcissism, grandiosity, and entitlement.
3. is capable of reasoning and creativity and has the capacity for delay. Correlates with the concept of ego processes and empathy.
4. has uncontrollable thoughts (unconscious) bombarding him/her that relate to unmet physiological or psychological need states. Correlates with the concept of id processes.
5. has the normal need for physical closeness. Relates to Bowlby's explanation of attachment and to the diagnostic categories of paranoid and sociopath.
6. expresses affect in a highly controlled, somewhat controlled, or uncontrolled manner.
7. is able to resist being swept away by his/her needs, conflicts, and emotions.
8. is feeling overwhelmed by forces he/she is not able to respond to effectively. Correlates with the concept of free-floating anxiety.
9. is experiencing depression, plus the specific forms of thought that cause it.
10. is experiencing disturbances in logical thinking, plus the specific forms of thought disturbance that occur.
11. is experiencing physical tension.
12. is having difficulty coping with daily living.
13. is feeling overwhelmed by thoughts and feelings he/she cannot control. Relates to the concept of unconscious forces dominating the personality structure.
14. has the capacity for productive, in contrast to unproductive, introspection.
15. is hypervigilant, uses intellectualization as a defense, or engages in obsessive thought.
16. adequately processes information.
17. is infantile and dependent in contrast to being intellectualized, aloof, and self sufficient.
18. is open to affective experience.
19. is likely to attempt suicide.

Additional Areas of Assessment:
20. What is the quality of the person's interpersonal life (e.g., collaborative, adversarial, empty, passive versus active)?
21. What are the person's predominant affects and defenses?
22. What is the quality of the person's self and object representations (view of self and view of others)?

REFERENCES

Erdberg, P. & Exner, J. E., Jr. (1984), Rorschach assessment. In: *Handbook of Psychological Assessment*, ed. G. Goldstein & M. Hersen. New York: Pergamon, pp. 332–347.

Exner, J. E., Jr. (1986), *The Rorschach: A Comprehensive System. Vol. 1.* 2nd ed. New York: Wiley.

—— Cohen, J. B. & Mcguire, H. (1990), *Rorschach Interpretation / Assistance Program (version 2).* Asheville, NC: Rorschach Workshops.

Gedo, J. (1975), Forms of idealization in the analytic transference. *J. Amer. Psychoanal. Assn.*, 23: 485–505.

—— (1979), *Beyond Interpretation.* New York: International Universities Press.

—— (1981), *Advances in Clinical Psychoanalysis.* New York: International Universities Press.

Goldberg, A. (1990), *The Prison House of Psychoanalysis.* Hillsdale, NJ: The Analytic Press.

Grunbaum, A. (1984), *The Foundations of Psychoanalysis.* Berkeley: University of California Press.

Kantrowitz, J. L., Katz, A. L., Paolitto, F., (1990), Follow-up of psychoanalysis five to ten years after termination: I. Stability of change. *J. Amer. Psychoanal. Assn.*, 38:471–496.

—— —— —— Sashin, J. & Solomon, L. (1987), Changes in the level and quality of object relations in psychoanalysis: Follow-up of a longitudinal, prospective study. *J. Amer. Psychoanal. Assn.*, 35:23–47.

Kohut, H. I. (1984), *How Does Analysis Cure?* ed. A. Goldberg &, P. Stepansky. Chicago: University of Chicago Press.

Sands, S. H. (1991), Dissociative disorders: The nature of the self and the transference. Paper presented at the 14th Annual Conference on the Psychology of the Self, Chicago, Illinois, October.

Schwaber, E. (1983), Psychoanalytic listening and psychic reality. *Internat. Rev. Psycho-Anal.*, 10:379–392.

Wallerstein, R. S. (1989), Follow-up in psychoanalysis: Clinical and research values. *J. Amer. Psychoanal. Assn.*, 37:921–941.

Wechsler, D. (1981), *WAIS–R Manual: Wechsler Adult Intelligence Scale–Revised.* San Antonio, TX: Psychological Corporation.

Weiner, I. B. & Exner, J. E., Jr. (1991), Rorschach changes in long-term and short-term psychotherapy. *J. Personality Assess.*, 56:453–465.

Wolf, E. S. (1988), *Treating the Self.* New York: Guilford.

Chapter 15

On the Capacity to Be Creative: A Psychoanalytic Exploration of Writer's Block

Richard H. Tuch

Developing an ability to be creative is believed by some to be a reasonable gauge of the success of psychoanalytic treatment. Winnicott (1971) wrote that "it is only in being creative that the individual discovers the self"; creativity generates an originality that reflects the individual's true self whereas imitation, the repetition of what others have created or what is commonly accepted, reflects the individual's false self.

Creativity is not easy to measure. Accordingly, analysands whose life endeavors hinge on the capacity to be creative provide a unique opportunity to study what enables people to be creative. The case that follows is that of a man who became depressed after the play he'd written became a commercial success. After recovering from this depression he continued to write, but was never satisfied with the poems and short stories he'd turn out. He wished to be able to write something that drew deeply from within himself. Eight years lapsed between his initial writing success and the beginning of his analysis. During that interval he lived a fairly aimless life.

In the first year of his analysis the patient began to write a novel. He completed the novel several months before terminating his analysis. How the patient developed the ability to access his inner life in order to be able to write is the subject of this chapter.

WRITER'S BLOCK

Surprisingly little has been written about writer's block. Bergler (1950), who takes credit for introducing the term, felt that, as a group, creative writers harbored a wish to be orally frustrated by their preoedipal mothers. Such oral masochistic wishes, Bergler reasoned, could be defended against through the act of creative writing because writing eliminated the frustrating mother by establishing the writer as both giving mother and recipient child. ("I give myself, out of myself, beautiful words and ideas.") This comes close to Bion's statement (McDougall, 1991) about how "good writers make such a demolition of the breast." According to this theory, if the writing defense falters and the oral masochistic wishes become conscious, then the primary motive to write ceases and writing block ensues.

Whereas Bergler saw writing as a defense, not writing (writer's block) can also serve as a defense. Ceasing to be able to write may defend against the emergence of unacceptable impulses that might otherwise become conscious were writing to proceed. When writing represents one's anal productions, an obstinate constipation (writer's block) may develop in order to defend against one's anal aggressive wishes to smear. When writing becomes erotized and takes on a phallic meaning ("making a liquid flow out of a tube onto a piece of white paper"—Freud, 1920), it may then become inhibited owing to objections of the superego. When writing represents an "aim-inhibited, socially acceptable way to fulfill the elements of one's grandiose/exhibitionistic strivings" (Kohut, 1971), conflicts may arise owing to fears that one's wishes to be mirrored will once again be painfully frustrated.

Writer's block may also represent a classical case of what Freud (1916) referred to as "those who are wrecked by success," whereby the superego equates successful writing with an oedipal victory and as a result forbids it from occurring.

Writing creates a world over which the writer has total control in regard to the nature of relationships and the outcome of conflicts. Through his writings the writer creates an alternative world as a way of dealing with life's potential frustrations and disappointments. Accordingly, writing functions much like childhood play, which helps children master the inevitable unpleasantries that result from having to depend emotionally on others. Writers who fear succumbing to the seductive lure of such a fantasy world (who fear "regressing in the service of the ego"—Kris, 1952) abandon writing to avoid such a fate.

Writing blocks may also develop as a way of abandoning activities believed to jeopardize one's object relations. McDougall (1989, 1991) writes about a woman named Benedicte who suffered from writer's block. When Benedicte was 15 years old, her mother discovered and destroyed writings she had spent hours working on, writings that were Benedicte's way of maintaining a link with the father she had lost when she was younger. Benedicte developed writer's block to hide this secret link to her father, a link that threatened her relationship with a mother who needed to be the patient's "one and only." Having writer's block became Benedicte's way of maintaining the fragile relationship she had with her sole surviving parent. In a similar vein, when writing is equated with one's aggressive impulses, writer's block may develop as a defense against the potentially destructive effect that one's words ("symbolically concretized into weapons") can have on one's objects (McDougall, 1991).

Writing can also be motivated by the need to articulate a coherent, faithful definition of oneself. This process relates both to Mahler's (1975) concept of individuation and Stolorow and Atwood's (1992) concept of self-delineation. For many, the task of defining oneself approaches completion by the time one reaches adulthood. However, if conditions fail to promote this process, or otherwise interfere with it, the need to define oneself may persist into adulthood. This occurs, for instance, when parental needs interfere with the child's attempts to individuate, or develop a well-delineated sense of self. Such was the case with McDougall's Benedicte: "To create is to claim one's right to a separate existence and an individual identity—and the patient accordingly saw writing as disloyal to her mother." When distinguishing oneself from one's objects through one's writings is believed to be intolerable or destructive to one's objects, writer's block may ensue as a way of safeguarding these relationships.

If originality is evidence of one's having developed a coherent, faithful definition of oneself, then plagiarism and writer's block must reflect an inability to reveal one's true self. Drawing upon Winnicott's work, Hutter (1982) describes plagiarism as the act of "hiding behind someone else's words or experiences to the point of claiming them as one's own." He presents the case of a patient with writer's block who was "forever substituting what she felt to be someone else's more authentic experience for her own fragmented or negative sense of self."

Through writing, writers may lessen their sense of emotional isolation. By drawing readers into their private world, writers actualize a wished-for shared experience. The acceptance of their work can act to reassure them that their needs and feelings are neither unfathomable nor unacceptable. Basch (1985) writes about how "affect attunement leads to a shared world, without affect attunement one's activities are solitary, private, and idiosyncratic. If, for whatever reason . . . affect attunement is not present or is ineffective during those early years, the lack of shared experience may well create a sense of isolation and a belief that one's affective needs generally are somehow unacceptable and shameful." A writing block may develop when writers feel they can not risk the chance of repeating the childhood trauma of offering up their inner feelings only to yet again be misunderstood or condemned.

Being motivated to write is the necessary but insufficient requisite for writing. Besides being motivated, one must also have developed particular psychological capacities and processes that facilitate the writing process. For instance, to write successfully, writers must be able to sufficiently disguise the autobiographical aspects of their writings (Freud, 1908). If they are unable to do so, their writings may prove so idiosyncratic as to make them inaccessible to most readers. Readers will then be unable to "find themselves" in the story. Writers must also be able to modify their unrealistic grandiose expectations as to just how much fame, impact, or adulation they can expect their work to yield. In addition, writers' grandiose beliefs that "no one can understand me because I am so unique and superior as to be unfathomable to others" can interfere with their attempts to put pen to paper in an attempt to make an understandable and acceptable piece of art. Difficulties in any of these areas can result in writers' inability to produce creatively.

Being able to write creatively also requires the integration of one's identifications and the neutralization of sabotaging internal objects. Kohut (1977) spoke of Mr. M, whose interest in writing developed out of an identification with his "word-loving, language-wise father." The patient's interest in writing waned, however, when his father withdrew from him, resulting in the patient's developing writer's block. McDougall (1991) states that "creative work in any field requires the integration of the universal bisexual wishes of childhood and the failure to identify with the potential fertility of both parents due to impediments in this integration is a frequent cause of serious intellectual and creative inhibition." It is also necessary to work through the internalization of destructive objects in order to feel sufficiently free to write creatively. For instance, McDougall (1991) writes about how Benedicte "fell prey to an internalized mother . . . who sabotaged the daughter's creative productions."

What follows is a single case report of a man who underwent a three-year analysis. With the help of that analysis he was able to overcome his difficulties writing creatively. Two points must be made before the case is presented. First, though the term *writer's block* is usually understood to refer to creative blocks that develop in the course of a work in progress, for the purpose of this chapter the term will be expanded to include *any* instance of creative inhibition, including those that exist before a planned work has been started. By broadening the usually accepted definition to include instances where individuals intend to write but haven't yet been able to, it is hoped that a more satisfying psycho-analytic exploration of inhibited creativity will result. Second, this chapter is about what one patient and his analyst came to understand about that particular patient's difficulties writing. Whether these dynamics apply to other such cases remains to be seen. This case study should not be read as a general statement about writer's block per se.

CASE REPORT

When the patient, Mr. L, first came to see me, he was in his late 20s. He was suffering from a severe depression that had paradoxically developed after a farce he had written had been successfully produced. Mr. L's depression responded to the antidepressant medication I prescribed for him. He came to see me intermittently over the eight years that led up to his being analyzed. Typically, he would return to treatment whenever he'd experience a physical ailment or insomnia, both of which caused him to feel as if he were "falling apart." Once back he would resume the explorative work we had intermittently undertaken. Even though he gravitated toward working psychoanalytically, he expressed doubts and suspicions about psychoanalysis. He would limit sessions to one a week and would repeatedly and inexplicably break off treatment after a period of weeks or months. Even though he stayed in treatment for progressively longer periods of time each time he resumed treatment, he nonetheless remained suspicious of the process throughout.

After years of living an undirected life, Mr. L returned to graduate school and felt he was "finally getting somewhere." The anxieties he experienced facing his qualifying exams motivated his final return to treatment before beginning analysis. Once back, Mr. L spoke of how he had grown weary of his recurrent depressions. He had begun to view the bitterness he felt over his childhood as a sign that he had not outgrown childhood as others his age had. He also expressed concerns that he had not been able to develop a relationship with a woman. Feeling the need to address these issues "once and for all," Mr. L agreed to begin psychoanalysis. Additional symptoms that brought Mr. L to analysis included (1) obsessive fears about his "true nature," (2) a persistent sense of alienation, and (3) intense anger that he feared was sufficiently strong to potentially lead to his becoming a mass murderer.

Converting Mr. L's psychotherapy into a psychoanalysis was facilitated by the fact that we had always worked in a psychoanalytic mode. I had conducted the psychotherapy in such a way as to promote the transference, even though an understanding of the transference wasn't achieved until the analysis began. I saw Mr. L four times weekly throughout the course of the analysis.

Mr. L grew up in the Midwest and was the middle of three children. He described his father as someone who had strong opinions and always had to be right. He had felt close to his father when he was quite young. The two had shared an interest in science fiction movies. But as time went on his father withdrew from him and grew critical of his continuing interest in movies. His father considered these interests "escapist and masturbatory." Mr. L's father warned him that if he continued to pursue these interests he would ultimately be seen by the world as alien and unfathomable. The father proposed that the way out of being condemned to a life of aloneness was to abandon his errant ways and accept the father's "guidance" as to how he should live his life.

Mr. L described his mother as someone who neither cared for nor was interested in him. Anything he got from her he felt she gave begrudgingly. She would tell him "he wasn't worth shit" and that he was a "good for nothing." At times, the patient would become enraged at his mother. He would say cruel things to her when he felt she had been particularly neglectful of him. This was followed by his feeling deep shame and remorse, taking his behavior as proof that he was "truly a monster."

Shortly after beginning the analysis, Mr. L became intensely interested in E, a woman whom he had met at school. Though he had always been interested in women, he rarely dated and was never able to form a long-term, intimate relationship with a woman. He feared that he was a repressed homosexual.

Mr. L began to feel he needed E more than she would ever need him. He could not imagine what he had to offer her. He imagined her as his savior and dreamed of her helping him out of his own personal prison of feeling alone and unfathomable. But he worried that he could become entirely too dependent on her and feared that his neediness would drive her away. He did, in fact, become exquisitely sensitive to nuances in E's behavior. Any chance encounter with E was yet another opportunity to see whether she was truly glad to see him. An overly matter-of-fact reaction on E's part would send the patient into despair.

As the analysis progressed, Mr. L became aware of just how prone he was to feeling let down by others. The anger he would feel when disappointed by others was so intense that it made him feel as if he was capable of murder. In fact, there were times early in the analysis when the patient became so enraged by my intermittent misunderstandings of him that I had fantasies of his bringing a gun to the subsequent session and killing me. The patient feared that either his neediness or his anger would ultimately destroy any relationship he had come to depend on.

Mr. L had come to believe that no one would be capable of understanding him or accepting him for who he was. He feared that E would be unable to fathom how he could have gone as long as he had without being with a woman. He felt ashamed of his wishes and needs. He wanted to date E, but felt she would not allow him his idiosyncrasies or his insecurities, and instead would expect him to be more self-assured and less needy than he in fact was. Mr. L longed for love and acceptance from E, but felt he would never be able to prove himself worthy of her.

Mr. L's relationship with E seemed to serve two functions. First, it seemed to be a way of splitting the transference, of needing from two what he felt would be too scary to need from just one. Being aware of how enraged he could become when he felt disappointed or misunderstood by me, the patient developed a parallel relationship to ours that he remained emotionally involved in throughout the course of analysis. His love for E, however, remained unrequited. Dreams indicated that the other purpose of the relationship with E was to help the patient, as he got closer to me, reassure himself that he wasn't a homosexual, something he had feared most of his life.

Whereas Mr. L's relationship with E served as a vehicle to reexperience the longings for love and acceptance he had yearned for from his mother, Mr. L's relationship with me more closely paralleled that which he'd experienced with his father: "You want to control and make me into what you want me to be. You feel you are always right and insist I fit into your vision of me." This sense of my requiring him to capitulate to my vision of who he is and what he should become added to the patient's fears of homosexuality. He watched carefully for instances when my interpretations seemed to be more about me than about him. When he felt that this was the case he would become enraged with me and would forcefully resist what he interpreted as my efforts to make him into my image. He insisted that I see the legitimacy of his anger and feared I would dismiss it as unprovoked and unfathomable (i.e., that I would think he was "getting upset about nothing"). Paradoxically, he himself wished that his anger *was* about nothing, and he invited me to say just that to help him give it up. The intensity of his anger scared him, just as he felt it would scare anyone whom he tried to get close to. He feared, however, that once he was without his anger, he would be open prey to my attempts to mold him.

Mr. L realized he needed help from another to be freed from his "mental prison" of feeling alien and unfathomable, but he feared that were he to accept help from another, he would then be required to be totally obedient to that person's vision of him. This conflict constituted one of the patient's basic dilemmas at the outset of analysis. He resolved the conflict by withdrawing angrily (particularly when I disappointed him) and turning his sense of being different and alien into a sense of being superior. He turned his belief that others would never understand him into a point of pride. He felt a kinship with the Japanese author Mishima, who proudly held on to his sense of special-ness—of being unlike others. "You will never understand me/be able to understand me" expressed both a bittersweet sense of triumphant supe-riority and a painful sense of hopeless despair and alienation. The patient used this sense of superiority as a way of compensating for his sense of not fitting in and being unlovable. Once this defense became something to be proud of, a formidable resistance to the analysis had been established.

Mr. L's vision of himself as unfathomable was reinforced by his own inabilities to understand "what the big deal was" about his childhood. He himself lacked the capacity to empathize with the pains of his own childhood. He would dismiss his complaints as nothing more than self-pity and would attack my attempts to empathize with his experiences as an invitation to self-indulgence. He felt that my attempts to help him understand and reexperience this time of his life would only lead to a heightening of his anger and resentment. He could not imagine a sce-nario in which his being more in touch with his pain would lead to a bet-ter understanding of what he'd experienced, and why. He feared that I would nurture his anger and heighten it to the point of his becoming a murderer, or alternatively, that his anger would prove unwarranted, leading to its dismissal, which would then leave him defenseless and invalidated.

A pattern soon developed in which the patient would feel misunder-stood by me or injured by my interpretations. We discovered, over time, that these experiences of feeling misunderstood by me had occurred before and had been responsible for his having broken off treatment in the past. These experiences recurred for most of the first year of analy-sis, the patient hearing my interpretations as attempts to get him to accept my views of him as more correct than his own. If I were ever to have an idea he hadn't yet come up with, he experienced it in this light. When I would ask the patient to explore an assumption or perspective that he held, he felt I was judging it as "wrong," incorrect, and without merit. I interpreted that the patient felt I was acting like his father, who always had to be right and who was still waiting for the patient to recog-nize how wrong he'd been all along.

Mr. L responded by talking about his literary agent, who claimed that his own analysis had resulted in his becoming a Republican. The patient felt that I too might turn him into someone who was "part of the machine." He wondered if someone who owned the kind of luxury car I did could ever understand someone who never wanted one. Wouldn't I, he wondered, interpret his not wanting such a car as nothing more than a denial of his envy? Wouldn't I find it hard to accept any differences between him and me as valid? Gradually the patient became less defensive in response to my attempts to explore the meaning of his feelings. I too changed, becoming considerably more sensitive to the ways in which I would phrase things and becoming cognizant of how I could be dismissive of the patient's experience.

Mr. L felt that, in essence, his father had said to him, "Either accept my view and be accepted into the fold, or, if you persist in this masturbatory escapism that you call your life, no one will understand you or accept you and you will live life as an isolated alien." The patient's response to this was, "So be it!" He went off to New York and lived on the fringes, even to the point of shooting heroin. He turned his father's prophecy into something to be proud of. He was different—but better on account of it!

Several months after beginning the analysis, the patient felt he wanted to try getting off the antidepressant medication he had been on for some time. Mr. L had been doing much better since beginning the analysis, so his decision seemed reasonable. He discontinued the medication, only to become severely depressed in a matter of weeks. He considered going back on the medication, but I wondered whether a different medication might be indicated. Even though I was quite capable of making such a pharmacologic decision, my concern that discussing medication with the patient might contaminate the transference led me to recommend that he go to a colleague for a psychopharmacologic consultation. Though he did not entirely understand my reasoning, Mr. L nonetheless complied with my wishes.

The following week the patient protested angrily that my request that he go elsewhere for medication represented "orthodoxy" on my part. He felt I was imposing my own issues and needs onto his analysis. In response to these "charges," Mr. L expected me to become defensive and dismiss his interpretation as groundless transference distortions. Insofar as he understood my recommendations as having more to do with my own needs than with his own the patient had been right. I had recommended the consultation out of concern that this control case be "properly conducted."

The interpretations I made to the patient regarding this situation reflected three points: (1) I acknowledged that I had indeed imposed my own needs onto his analysis, (2) I demonstrated an appreciation of how my actions had affected him, and (3) I accepted his reactions as reasonable given what he'd experienced in the past. These interventions tended to soften the patient's defenses, which permitted him to accept the idea that the intensity of his affective response had been overdetermined and accordingly needed to be understood as having to do with more than just the situation at hand. For instance, the patient had interpreted my unwillingness to handle his medications as meaning that I only wanted to deal with a part of him. As he put it, I was willing to feed him but did not want to have to deal with his soiled diapers. Our work together resulted in the discovery that he was reexperiencing with me something of what he had originally experienced with his mother.

Repeated experiences of this nature between the patient and myself during the course of his analysis led to a more thorough understanding of the empathic failure Mr. L had experienced as a child and the effects these failures had had on him. In this way, the analysis became a vehicle for reexperiencing the pain of feeling misunderstood, dismissed, and of having others' needs continually put ahead of his own.

Shortly after beginning the analysis, Mr. L set out on a task he had never been able to approach, namely, that of writing a serious novel. Initially he was unable to share the contents of the novel with me, figuring I would tamper with the work by trying to analyze it. Working through his concerns that I was primarily interested in imposing my ideas on him put the patient in touch with one of his basic quandries: "Can another truly understand and accordingly help me without my having to utterly capitulate to them?"

His associations suggested that he feared that analysis was equivalent to being "buggered" by his father, the ultimate influence and submission. He talked about fearing that the novel he was writing might lead to his feeling as if he were an imitator, because, "you can only be so original." He knew that all writings were derivative and he was aware of how his own writing had been influenced. I suggested he feared that I could influence him to such an extent as to turn him into what I wanted him to be, which would then cause him to feel like an imitator. I wondered whether he was frightened by the part of him that wanted to feel close to me. Might not this wish for closeness cause him to feel easily influenced by me, I wondered. Might not his feeling influenced by me make him feel like a woman, or like someone who had been turned into a homosexual by being buggered? The patient responded by reiterating his feelings that to need someone is to be weak and therefore unmasculine.

I suggested that when the patient is angry, he feels strong and special, but in the end this leaves him feeling isolated and alone. Mr. L said he felt that the only alternative would be to become vulnerable and influenceable. He then remembered a novel about a paralyzed man who had to find some way of letting people know he was still alive inside. He was touched by the story and became tearful as he retold it. He felt the story had to do with his own childhood when he had felt paralyzed and unable to communicate with others. He spoke of how he had begun to confide in people, something he thought he would never be able to do.

He expressed an awareness that he had grown to rely on me and feel close to me, and feared a time when he would no longer be able to be with me.

The completion of his novel became pivotal in Mr. L's development. We realized that what he primarily sought from his readers was a sense that they considered the work "understandable." He wished that his book would prove, once and for all, that the world didn't regard him as alien. However, he feared that the book could prove so idiosyncratic that no one would be able to relate to it and his father's prophecy would be realized. Wouldn't others, he worried, view his novel as little more than an attempt to be understood? Wouldn't his need to be understood be so transparent as to interfere with the novel's success? He feared that the readers would have contempt for him as a "spoiled child" who was complaining about nothing. "After all, my siblings turned out reasonably well, so what's my problem?" reasoned Mr. L. "I hadn't seen myself as having had a valid reason for why I am the way I am. I hadn't been able to write because my life made no sense to me and I'd assumed it would make no sense to others."

Mr. L had begun the novel in his first year of analysis and terminated his analysis coincident with feedback he received from those he had asked to critique his work. The feedback turned out to be generally quite positive. What stood out to most readers, however, was that while the father figure character had been well developed, the narrator (who corresponded to the patient himself) hadn't been given enough background to permit the reader to understand what made him "tick." Breathing life into this character became the final task of the patient's analysis—to be able to draw upon his own experience in order to make the character understandable.

Mr. L questioned whether he could get his readers to feel the narrator's pain and see how his behavior was understandable given what he had been through. He felt that Mishima's point was that he had never been understood and now no longer wanted to be. Mishima abandoned all hope of being understood and ultimately suicided. Mr. L felt that he was still willing to risk trying to be understood even though he knew he was likely to lose his sense of specialness and superiority in the process.

At one time, Mr. L had shared an interest in science fiction movies with his father. Subsequently, his father withdrew and berated him for his continued interest in films. It was as if the father took the patient to the movies and left him there. Now Mr. L wanted to engage me and engage his readers as a way of reestablishing the shared experience he had once had with his father. I myself began to experience an urge to act as a collaborator in the writing of the novel, and I suspect this countertransference reaction was in response to the patient's wishes to draw me into a shared experience that he had always longed for.

As Mr. L struggled to develop the narrator, he was increasingly able to draw upon his own life to fill in the narrator's character. His capacity to do so represented one of the most significant changes he'd experienced in the course of his analysis. He had come to question what he'd internalized from his father, namely, the idea that his affective life was something no one else would be able to relate to. I suspect this change occurred as a result of the patient's having allowed himself to bring this side of himself out in the analysis.

Mr. L never asked me to read his novel. I didn't have to. What he had sought from his readers he had already gotten in the course of our work together. He had risked revealing his true self and was pleased to discover that not everyone experienced him as his father had.

After succeeding at developing the narrator, Mr. L felt it was time for him to cut back and ultimately end the analysis. He feared I would punish him if he carried out this plan. He worried that if he left the analysis I would be waiting for him to fail in order to tell him, "I told you so," when he needed to return. Rather than becoming enraged and acting these feelings out, as he would have done in the past, the patient was now conversant about these issues and fears. He was able to quickly bring them up for discussion, with much less affect than he had expressed in the past, and he was just as able to get beyond these concerns. These changes in the patient's behavior led me to consider his idea about termination timely and appropriate.

At the end of the analysis, Mr. L said, "For ten or twelve years, I didn't know where my next idea would come from. Now I know I have stories within." He said, "Now, when I have a bad night, I have a book to remind me that I don't have to lose myself entirely. I have a book now that I can pick up—it's a partner."

In the final days of analysis, Mr. L quoted a *New Yorker* magazine article in which a writer described the outcome of his own analysis. That writer saw his psychoanalysis as resulting in the relinquishment of certain personal beliefs and, as a result, in his "being accepted into the club of good old boys." My patient expressed gratitude that this had not been true of his own analysis, as he feared it might. He felt that he had been allowed to find himself and be himself, for which he expressed gratitude.

DISCUSSION

The predominant transference exhibited during Mr. L's analysis was that of a mirroring transference that manifested itself in the patient's exquisite sensitivities to misunderstandings and slights. He initially felt that I needed him to accept and conform to my views and that this need precluded me from being able to see things from his perspective. His father's inability to set his own needs aside long enough to be able to empathize with his son left the patient distrustful of anyone who held out hope that things might be different this time. Times that I would fail the patient by virtue of my intermittent inability to be attuned to him reinforced this distrust of others and accordingly reinforced his withdrawal into a state of superior isolation ("haughty grandiosity"). This superiority ("I'm so unique and special as to be unfathomable to others") acted defensively as a kind of consolation ("compensatory structure") that wasn't easily relinquished.

Mr. L had turned his shame over feeling different into triumph—something to be proud of. Working through these empathic failures played a major role in helping the patient relinquish his sense of superiority (his primitive grandiose-exhibitionistic trends) so that he could both write and accept his need for emotional sustenance from others. No single interaction between the patient and myself was demonstrably curative of his writer's block. Instead, change occurred gradually as a result of transmuting internalizations. Over time the patient became less sensitive to empathic failures and was less inclined to withdraw into states of haughty grandiosity.

Gradually, the patient allowed himself to experience and reveal the longings for understanding and acceptance that lay beneath his grandiose veneer. He had found my reactions to him to be different than what he had expected, given how his parents had been. Even though I was intermittently misattuned to him, my understanding of how my misinterpretations affected him softened his defenses. He came to accept his longings for understanding and acceptance and ceased feeling that such longings would inevitably lead to his having to become what others needed him to be. As a result, Mr. L began to understand and empathize with what he had experienced as a child. For the first time, his childhood feelings made sense to him. This development of self-empathy was followed by his developing faith that his novel would prove understandable to others.

The idea that I might be capable of understanding him was experienced by Mr. L as something he both longed for and feared. It was feared because it challenged the patient's sense of specialness and accordingly threatened the support he derived from his sense of superiority. The patient feared losing his sense of superiority without having something to put in its place. Paradoxically, being empathic with an aspect of another's experience may prove unempathic to that person's more pressing need to hold to a sense of not being understood by others.

Hoping to be liked and understood became unacceptable to Mr. L for many reasons. He feared that the intensity of his needs for validation and understanding would drive away those he needed just as it would destroy the quality of his novel. He feared that if he allowed himself to experience neediness, he would then feel frustrated, become enraged, and attack those he needed things from. This would result in his feeling guilty and depressed. He would feel as if he had driven away the very ones he needed.

Mr. L also feared becoming vulnerable to the influence of those he sought validation and understanding from. He feared that were he to feel accepted, it would come at too high a price, requiring, as it had with his father, that he utterly capitulate to the views of others. He would then have to admit that there was nothing legitimate about the path he had taken in life, that in the end it proved "just to have been a phase."

Mr. L felt his father would use the patient's success to support his father's contentions that he *had* been a reasonably good parent, "for how else could you have turned out all right?" In this context, the patient's success meant his own position about what had gone wrong between him and his father was without merit and therefore dismissable. The idea of having the better part of his life dismissed in this way acted as a resistance to the patient's wishes to succeed (thus producing yet another dynamic for a "success neurosis"). Mr. L maintained the position of failure to rob his father of the material upon which his father could base such a triumph. This is reminiscent of McDougall's (1991) patient who felt that "if writing meant speaking in her mother's language and emptying 'contents' to which her mother would lay claim, then Benedicte would rather not write at all!" Mr. L's failure served as living proof that his father had been wrong. It served as an indictment of the father's parenting style. But in order to feel vindicated, the patient had to remain unproductive and unsuccessful, thus supporting his father's contention that the patient would never "make it" unless he gave up his idiosyncratic, masturbatory ways. As Bob Dylan said, "There's no success like failure, and failure is no success at all."

The impulse of wishing one's father dead is usually interpreted as deriving from one's Oedipus complex. An additional interpretation arises when one considers instances in which the parental selfobject needs preclude the child's being able to develop a cohesive sense of self. Under such circumstances, a child may feel "it's either he or I" and may equate his or her individuation with the murder of the parent. I strongly suspect that that was the case with Mr. L. His father would physically portray himself as injured whenever spoken up to by his son, as if to say, "You're killing me!" Such communications are likely to reinforce the idea that being oneself is detrimental to one's objects.

It appears as if Mr. L's main writer's block developed around a conflicted wished for shared experience, one that could lead the patient to feel that his affective life was understandable and acceptable to others. This wish was in conflict with transferential fears that his novel would be met with blank stares. He worried that people would wonder "what the hell he was talking about." If this were to be the case, his father would be proved right, and he would feel defeated and injured once again. Accordingly, the function of the writing paralleled the function of the analysis—to be able to share his innermost experience and feel understood by others in the process. Accomplishing this feat in the analysis helped undo his sense of feeling alien, isolated, and alone. His father's "spell" had been broken.

Through the course of the analysis the patient developed insight into what he had been unconsciously using the writing to accomplish, namely, to compensate for or undo what he had internalized of his father's attitudes toward him. One might say the patient had too much riding on the novel's success (in regard to how it would be received) for him to be able to write unencumbered. Once this was understood and that burden was lifted from the creative process, the patient proceeded to complete his novel and his analysis.

REFERENCES

Basch, M. (1985), Interpretation: Towards a developmental model. In: *Progress in Self Psychology, Vol. 1*, ed. A. Goldberg. Hillsdale, NJ: The Analytic Press, pp. 33–42.

Bergler, E. (1950), *The Writer and Psychoanalysis*. New York: Doubleday.

Freud, S. (1908), Creative writers and day-dreaming. *Standard Edition*, 9:142–153. London: Hogarth Press, 1957.

—— (1916), Some character-types met within psycho-analytic work: Those wrecked by success. *Standard Edition*, 14:316–331. London: Hogarth Press, 1957.

—— (1920), Inhibitions, symptoms and anxiety. *Standard Edition*, 20:77–156. London: Hogarth Press, 1957.

Hutter, A. (1982), Poetry in psychoanalysis: Hopkins, Rossetti, Winnicott. *Internat. Rev. Psycho-Anal.*, 9:303–316.

Kohut, H. (1971), *The Analysis of the Self*. New York: International Universities Press.

—— (1977), *The Restoration of the Self*. New York: International Universities Press.

Kris, E. (1952), *Psychoanalytic Explorations in Art*. New York: International Universities Press.

Mahler, M., Pine, F. & Bergman, A. (1975), *The Psychological Birth of the Human Infant*. New York: Basic Books.

McDougall, J. (1989), The dead father: Early psychic trauma and its relationship in sexual functioning and creative activity. *Internat. J. Psycho-Anal.*, 70:205–219.

—— (1991), Sexual identity, trauma, and creativity. *Psychoanal. Inq.*, 11:559–581.

Stolorow, R. & Atwood, G. (1992), *Contexts of Being*. Hillsdale, NJ: The Analytic Press.

Winnicott, D. W. (1971), *Playing and Reality*. New York: Basic Books.

Chapter 16

The Guilt of Tragic Man

Janet T. Droga
Peter J. Kaufmann

Heinz Kohut (1977) characterized the classical view of man as motivated by the satisfaction of his drives, dominated by the pleasure principle, and bound up in inner conflict. He called him Guilty Man. In contrast, he portrayed the self psychological view of man as motivated by a need to fulfill and express his nuclear program and complete the development of his aims and ideals. Ultimately, in Kohut's view, man's failures dwarf his successes and he falls into "guiltless despair" (p. 238) over never having realized the basic pattern of his nuclear self. This despair is a result of having been tragically deprived of the requisite responsiveness that would have enabled him to achieve his aims. Therefore, Kohut named him Tragic Man. It is our thesis, however, that Tragic Man may also feel guilty. Our purpose in this chapter is to examine the concept of guilt and its place within self psychology.

In the spirit of George Klein (1976) in his groundbreaking paper, *Freud's Two Theories of Sexuality*, we perform a "theorectomy" (Stolorow, 1976) on the concept of guilt in the treatment of patients with self disorders by stripping away its metapsychological garb and proposing a *clinical* theory of guilt. Klein asserted that metapsychology positions subjective experience within an impersonal, mechanistic, biologically based system involving forces, energies, and structures. Clinical

A version of this chapter was presented at the American Psychological Association's Division of Psychoanalysis (39) Annual Spring Meeting, April 15, 1993, in New York City and at the Sixteenth Annual Conference on the Psychology of the Self, October 30, 1993, in Toronto.

We are very grateful to Frank Lachmann, Ph.D., James Fosshage, Ph.D., and Ruth Gruenthal, C.S.W. for their helpful comments and editorial suggestions.

theory, on the other hand, is concerned with personal meanings and motivations. It arises from and remains within the individual's unique subjective universe (Stolorow, 1976). This position falls well within the paradigm shift that is currently occurring in psychoanalysis—a shift from a positivistic to a relativistic science, from an objective to a subjective observational stance, from an intrapsychic to a field theory (see Fosshage, 1992, for an excellent discussion of this paradigm shift), a shift that Kohut was instrumental in advancing.

Infancy research provides the underpinnings for the shift in paradigm away from the fixation–regression model and offers support for a continuous construction model of development and psychopathology (Zeanah et al., 1989), findings that support our position of remaining open to the specific contextual meanings of our patients' experience of guilt. Zeanah et al. (1989), in exploring the implications of developmental research for psychodynamic theory and practice, put forth a good argument for "individualizing" psychotherapy with adults. They reason that conflictual themes are no longer seen as being rooted in specific phases of development; rather, they are embedded within a relational context and are drawn out of the reconstructed "moments" (Stern, 1985) that arise from the patient's narrative. They conclude that "preconceived formulations concerning ontogenetic origins of psychopathology are no longer valid" (p. 665).

Guilt has traditionally been viewed as arising out of the oedipal situation (Freud, 1923). It develops as a consequence of conflicts between sexual and aggressive instinctual wishes and the injunctions of the superego. Kohut (1984) viewed guilt as inextricably bound up in and derived from Freud's drive-based structural conflict model. In his development of self psychology theory, he needed to delineate and remove his new formulations from this classical point of view to highlight his discovery of the selfobject dimension of experience. In doing so, we contend, Kohut did not give his full attention to the issue of guilt and thereby underemphasized its presence in the empirical domain. In addition, when he did address guilt, Kohut at times placed his own experience-distant theoretical spin onto the expression of guilt by positing that it is secondary and reactive to a failing selfobject milieu. In viewing the consequences of selfobject failure, Kohut emphasized how normal development was arrested, leaving a deficit of normal psychic structure. He deemphasized the schemas, organizing principles, representational configurations, or relational configurations (Fosshage, 1994b; Stolorow, Brandchaft, and Atwood, 1987; Lachmann and Beebe, 1992; Mitchell, 1988) that were formed in response to the kind of selfobject milieu in which the individual developed. These schemas or configurations could include the individual's tendency to experience guilt in particular situations.

At a national conference on the Psychology of the Self (Beverly Hills, October 1992), one of the main panels was entitled "Reassessing Shame and Guilt." However, the one paper presented was devoted entirely to an exploration of shame (Morrison, 1994), in which the presenter stated, as an aside, that classical theory had already adequately dealt with guilt. It was left to one of the discussants (Fosshage, 1994a) to include guilt in his remarks, thus illustrating our contention that self psychology theory does not adequately address or explore the patient's experience of guilt in the clinical situation.

FREUD'S VIEW OF GUILT

Freud's formulation of guilt reflects the following general assumptions:

1. Individuals are motivated to satisfy sexual and aggressive drive derivatives.
2. Psychopathology reflects underlying structural conflicts among the psychic agencies of the mind (the ego, superego, and id).
3. The Oedipus complex is central in the formation of the superego and the pathogenic conflicts that afflict neurotic individuals.
4. The individual fears his or her conscience as he or she once feared the parent, becoming particularly prone to feeling guilty if he or she experiences the murderous–competitive or incestuous derivatives of the now forbidden Oedipus complex.
5. In feeling guilty, the individual feels "bad" or "wrong" as he or she once did when criticized by his parents and fears retaliation for misdeeds.
6. Neurotic individuals may be vulnerable to experiencing guilt over oedipal "victory," when a particular event or act signifies a triumph over the rival parent in the oedipal triangle.

Friedman (1985) criticizes Freud's concept of guilt in that it is restricted to fear of the superego or fear of internalized parental authority. By doing so, Freud left out what we commonly understood as guilt, the sense of distress that arises when one feels one has injured or failed to help others with whom one is concerned. Friedman argues that Freud's restricted conception reflected his assumption that children are motivated by self-interest and fear and that children invariably perceive their parents as powerful providers who will either dispense or withhold needed love and protection. In making these assumptions, Freud left out the possibility that individuals may be motivated by basic concern for others and that an individual's feeling of injuring others may be more likely to arise when he or she is dealing with weak, vulnerable, or damaged parents.

KOHUT'S VIEW OF GUILT

Kohut (1971), in working with patients who exhibited narcissistic disorders, claimed that "narcissistic personalities are in general not predominantly swayed by guilt feelings (they are not inclined to react unduly to the pressure exerted by their idealized superego). Their predominant tendency is to be overwhelmed by shame" (p. 232).

Kohut's only explanation for guilt is embedded in the classical model. Although implying that guilt may be minimally present, he also indicated at times that he did not expect to find evidence of guilt in these patients. The absence of guilt was based on the postulation that narcissistic patients were essentially arrested at an early developmental level in which the superego as a structure of the psychic apparatus did not as yet exist.

Clinically, Kohut (1977) recognized the presence of guilt in patients in whom structural conflicts are primary. Although theoretically advocating a basic shift in emphasis away from the "psychological surface (the content of the rage, the patient's guilt about his destructive aims)" (p. 124) to the underlying narcissistic injuries that secondarily evoked these affects, he acknowledged that, at times, "for tactical reasons, the dynamics of the rage–guilt cycle will often temporarily occupy a prominent position on the analytic stage" (pp. 124–125). In those patients exhibiting persistent negative therapeutic reactions despite a thorough analysis of structural conflicts, he suggested that "the analyst should consider not only the effect of unconscious guilt feelings (a negative therapeutic reaction), but also, and *foremost*, the presence of a persistent structural defect—often within the realm of an unrecognized disturbance of the self" (pp. 46–47, italics added).

Kohut placed the phenomenon of guilt within a structural conflict model and assumed unconscious guilt to be associated with a negative therapeutic reaction. He implied that guilt should be considered but, at least in those patients with intractable symptomatology or pathological guilt, he relegated its importance to a secondary position vis-à-vis the exploration of a possible defect in the structures of the self. Kohut also assumed a deficit in structure instead of considering the structure that individuals do develop in response to selfobject failure.

Kohut (1982, 1984), in our view, later moved away from the dichotomy of Guilty Man and Tragic Man. He shifted to viewing all pathology as involving a range of self disorders in response to selfobject failure across development. He subsumed oedipal phase disorders within the larger rubric of self disorders. In this sense, it could be interpreted that Guilty Man became one kind of Tragic Man (likewise, see Fosshage, 1994a).

OTHER VIEWS OF GUILT WITHIN SELF PSYCHOLOGY

Other writers within self psychology (Stolorow, et al., 1987; Bacal and Newman, 1990) have also noted Kohut's inadequate treatment of the phenomenon of guilt. Bacal and Newman likewise point to the close tie of guilt with "forbidden drives" as the reason for its lack of relevance to self psychologists and call for a closer scrutiny of this concept. They cite Thomson, who regards guilt as a prevalent self experience arising out of conflict between the self's needs and those attitudes and values of the parents that are antithetical to those needs. Bacal and Newman continue with a personal communication of Markson who states that guilt is "often associated with the feeling that the subject's attempt to have its selfobject needs met are injurious to the selfobject. From this perspective, guilt is the outcome of conflict between the pursuit of selfobject needs and the sense of the suffering of the selfobject" (p. 241).

In addition to noting that the pathogenic role of guilt, along with the concepts of superego and superego conflict, is traditionally formulated in terms of drive theory, Stolorow et al. (1987), highlight and underscore what they see as the core conflict in the development of many patients. As children, many of the patients were required to fulfill selfobject needs of their parents to maintain vitally needed ties to them. Therefore, any attempt on the part of the child to articulate, delineate, or otherwise give voice to his or her own differentiated strivings leaves the child forever vulnerable to painful states of guilt, self-loathing and "a perception of himself or herself as omnipotently destructive" (p. 91), a state Stolorow et al. (1987) referred to as "self-demarcation guilt" (p. 95).

Lichtenberg, Lachmann, and Fosshage (1992) regard guilt as an affective response that emerges developmentally at 18 months as the child becomes sensitive to the distress of others. Originally, guilt reflects the attachment motivational system and functions to inhibit the child's aversive antagonism, which could jeopardize his or her attachments. It integrates the child's altruistic feeling for others with his or her concern for preserving needed ties. As the child develops, guilt may be triggered by motives that reflect any of the motivational systems depending on how parents have responded to the child's pursuit of these motives.

Like Stolorow et al. (1987), these writers observe that children can become guilty about pursuing exploratory–assertive activities when parents perceive these pursuits as antagonistic and rebellious. The parents may not only prohibit this behavior, but also label the child as malicious or bad for manifesting it. Subsequently, the child will confuse assertion with antagonism and regard the carrying out of his or her own agenda as evil.

Goldberg (1988) also emphasizes that guilt arises out of self–selfobject relationships. He views the formation of guilt as a way to sustain a threatened or ruptured selfobject bond. When the child's behavior evokes anger from the parent and threatens a disruption of the selfobject tie, the child reacts with anger at the potential loss and turns the anger inward. The resulting guilt serves to restore the bond with the parent.

Fosshage (1994a) relates guilt to shame. He concludes that "guilt is on the same continuum as shame—that is one feels badly about oneself—and guilt addresses those shame-ridden experiences that have the additional element of having hurt the other person" (p. 41). Fosshage supports our thesis that "guilt . . . is referring to a type of self experience and does not require . . . the invocation of the superego concept as part of a metapsychological mental apparatus theory" (p. 41). He encourages the reconceptualizing of Guilty Man and Tragic Man "not as complementary, but Guilty Man as one form of Tragic Man" (p. 43).

GUILT

Before turning our attention to clinical material, we briefly put forth our view of guilt. The definition of guilt we use does not derive from any one metapsychological position within psychoanalysis but captures the experience of guilt that our patients have described. Here we are taking a phenomenological approach to guilt that we would like the reader to adopt when considering the clinical material that follows. The subsequent discussion explicates the kinds of guilt emerging from the patients' material and is related to some types of guilt already described in the literature.

We concur with the conception of guilt as the feeling of distress that arises when one feels that one has injured others with whom one is concerned (Friedman, 1985; Fosshage, 1994a). We believe that this emphasis best captures the remorseful feeling that people commonly identify when they describe experiences of guilt.

Friedman (1985) defines guilt as "the appraisal, conscious or unconscious, of one's plans, thoughts or actions as damaging, through commission or omission, to someone for whom one feels responsible" (p. 529). He elaborates that the experience of guilt has affective, cognitive, and motivational components. Affectively, the feeling of guilt combines a sense of empathic distress, or feeling what the distressed person is feeling, with depressive anxiety (Klein, 1948), feeling badly about having harmed the loved other. Cognitively, the content of guilt involves the belief that one's plans, thoughts, feelings, or acts have harmed a person for whom one feels responsible. Friedman stresses that this belief may derive from inaccurate or irrational interpretations of events in order to emphasize the clinical possibility of helping someone by correcting their distortions. We amend Friedman's emphasis by asserting that an individual's subjective elaborations of events are based on lived experience in which significant others (parents) and/or the individual viewed the individual's activities as destructive. We also stress that parental appraisals of the effects of a child's actions and thoughts have a significant impact on how the child comes to evaluate his or her own behavior and what he or she sees as being injurious. Friedman, drawing on the work of Martin Hoffman, indicates that an individual's sense of responsibility for others results both from a biologically based altruistic concern for others and from the effects of growing up in a nuclear family, which tends to generate a significant feeling of responsibility. Friedman's positing of a biologically based developmental line (see also Kriegman and Slavin, 1990) raises interesting issues about human motivation that go beyond the scope of this chapter. It is our view that the individual's sense of responsibility for others will depend greatly on the familial context in which he or she develops.

Individuals are motivated to avoid or reduce the experience of guilt and preserve the sense that one is not damaging to others, often because guilt is painful and self-diminishing. To prevent oneself from feeling guilty, a person may avoid an intended, guilt-provoking action. After having had a guilt-provoking thought or feeling or having committed a guilt-provoking act, a person may make reparation to the damaged other through thought or action with the hope of undoing the damage and decreasing the sense of guilt. After becoming guilty, a person may also defend intrapsychically against being aware of this feeling to protect himself or herself and maintain the sense that he or she has not damaged the other.

THE GUILT OF TRAGIC MAN

In considering the guilt of Tragic Man, our focus is on the experiences of guilt manifested by a particular type of patient whom we have encountered in our clinical practice. Stolorow et al. (1987) characterize these patients as growing up with idealized yet vulnerable parents who expected their children to meet their needs. When the children failed to satisfy parental expectations, they evoked parental disapproval and shame which caused the children to feel guilty and ashamed. Accepting their parent's evaluation of their behavior, the guilty children perceived that their actions had in fact injured the blaming parent. Because of their own neediness, these parents required a state of oneness with their children which led them to experience even their children's normative acts of self-expression and self-delineation as damaging (Stolorow et al., 1987, p. 91). Thus, these children learned to feel guilty about self-assertion.

These patients have become "shackled" to parental bonds dictating that they strive to satisfy parental requirements and deny self-demarcating strivings that clash with parental expectations (Stolorow et al., 1987). At moments when they feel they have failed to meet parental expectation because of inevitable limitation or the wish to pursue independence, these patients feel guilty toward the enraged parent.

By presenting this type, we do not mean to imply that these patients represent the only group or the main group of patients with self disorders for whom guilt is a significant experience in pathogenesis. In the spirit of George Klein, we argue for understanding the particulars of each patient and for appreciating the extent to which guilt may be a significant factor in his or her psychopathology as well as the varied meanings that guilt may have for this person. We emphasize that the experience of guilt during development and treatment may be a more important factor in determining psychopathology than self psychologically oriented theories have previously stressed.

CASE ILLUSTRATIONS

Ann, a 38-year-old divorced economist, presented for treatment complaining of difficulty in both completing her research and developing a satisfying relationship with a man. She described experiencing significant vacillations in self-esteem and being prone to feeling ashamed, especially if she perceived that she had fallen short of achieving her ambitions.

As she began the analysis, Ann felt unsure about what to discuss. She thought that the analyst should set the agenda. After the analyst conveyed interest in what Ann wanted to consider, Ann expressed embarrassment about making her thoughts and feelings the focus of attention. Was she important enough? She also worried that she was indulging herself by talking so much about her concerns. She assumed that the analyst must mind that Ann was being so selfish. While the analyst might not express displeasure now, Ann was sure that the analyst would become fed up with Ann's self-centeredness sooner or later and would rebuke Ann for it.

When the analyst and Ann explored why Ann felt embarrassed and worried about becoming the focus of attention in treatment, they discovered that Ann expected the analyst to react like her mother. Ann had experienced her mother as being depressed throughout childhood; dissatisfied with her role as a homemaker, which prevented her from pursuing her career aspirations; and discontented with her marriage to her unresponsive husband. Ann always felt that her mother wanted to be the focus of attention. She also perceived that her mother fundamentally expected her to share and remedy her mother's depressed state. In Ann's view, her mother would brighten in her mood and would approve of Ann as long as her daughter followed this agenda. That meant offering comforting and reassuring words whenever her mother was particularly despondent, displaying her academic achievements for her mother's self-congratulation, and obeying her mother's opinionated teachings.

When Ann focused on her concerns instead of adhering to her mother's agenda, she typically experienced her mother's wrath. Ann recalled how enraged her mother would become with her at these moments, criticizing Ann for her selfishness and self-centeredness and lamenting how she was causing her mother additional aggravation. Ann observed that these attacks were more vehement if her mother perceived that Ann was exhibiting traits like her father, was showing more interest in her father than in her mother, or was receiving more attention from her father than he showed toward his wife. In response to these tirades, Ann felt ashamed of her failings in her mother's eyes and felt guilty about having done something bad that had upset her depressed mother further.

Ann realized that these experiences with her mother had led her to expect the analyst to become blaming if Ann accepted the opportunity to make her agenda the focus of treatment. As these sources of her initial embarrassment and worry were clarified, she felt more comfortable formulating and focusing on her concerns in session. A mirror transference gradually emerged in which Ann relied on the analyst's interest to bolster her self-esteem as she defined her ambitions and her means of trying to attain them. She became more sensitive to fluctuations in her experience of the analyst's attentiveness to her. She underwent a lowering of self-esteem and a loss of self-confidence when she felt that the analyst was disinterested or preoccupied; she felt an increase in her self-regard and belief in herself when she perceived that the analyst was "there for me." Attuned to what she saw as the analyst's agendas for her, Ann also wondered if she could defy these implicit dictates and still retain the analyst's support and interest. She tested out the unconditional nature of the analyst's interest by pursuing career plans on her own that took her away from therapy for periods of time. She was greatly relieved when the analyst accepted her absences without enraged criticism and maintained an expression of concern for Ann. By experiencing the analyst's alignment with her self-delineation, Ann was better able to assert herself in battles with her domineering colleagues and lovers who reminded her of her mother. She then completed several research papers that reflected her unique perspective in a subject area that she associated with her father.

Ann was invited to participate in a discussion panel based on her research. She felt that she had held her own in the presentations and debate while her proud mother watched her from the audience. Yet, in the session following this triumphant performance, Ann became aware of feeling very guilty toward her mother. Why?

In the process of exploring her feelings of guilt, it emerged that Ann felt guilty about surpassing her mother, knocking her mother out of the way, and becoming the dominant one in their academic competition. Here, Ann had publicly presented and defended a major research work whereas her mother had never even been able to write such a piece. Ann also felt bad because she had been publicly acknowledged for her independent viewpoint, whereas her mother remained unrecognized. Ann could bask in the limelight of center stage; her mother remained isolated and alone. Why hadn't she ever enabled her mother to go public? Further inquiry revealed that as Ann became the dominant one in her relationship with her mother, she wouldn't need her mother anymore in the way she had needed her during her childhood. She could then differentiate herself from her mother, become responsible for herself, and leave her mother behind. Ann felt that this self-assertion would be like killing off the domineering mother of her childhood.

Ann represented someone who manifested a self disorder as evidenced by the emergence of a mirroring selfobject transference, fluctuations in her self-esteem and proneness to feeling ashamed. Her experience also included feelings of guilt. Her mother's failure to "mirror" her perspective had left Ann feeling that she was essentially unimportant. Her mother's lack of interest in Ann's independent pursuits and her mother's failure to provide "a gleam in the eye" for Ann's efforts at self-delineation contributed to Ann's uncertainty about her ambitions and her ability to realize them. Her mother's critical attacks when Ann acted autonomously also led Ann to feel anxious and guilty about taking independent action. As we clearly see from what emerged after the panel presentation, Ann was plagued by guilt after succeeding in such action: guilt about surpassing her mother, differentiating from her mother, and having more than her mother.

Although guilt over competitive success is frequently referred to as oedipal guilt, we do not understand this guilt as resulting simply from a biologically determined oedipal complex, but rather as one emergent within a relational context. What could be seen as Ann's oedipally based guilt, which was inevitably derived from Ann's incestuous and competitive wishes, emerged because Ann's mother would attack more whenever Ann became engaged with her father in any way. This is an example of the lack of attuned parental responsiveness to Ann's normative competitive and affectionate strivings during the oedipal phase (Kohut, 1977, 1982, 1984).

Max, a 35-year-old scientist, presented for treatment complaining of experiencing a pervasive sense of being unreal and of experiencing periodic states of acute anxiety that had afflicted him over the several months since he had decided to pursue an emotional commitment with his new girlfriend. He thought that his symptoms might be related to the loss of both of his parents who had died some years before but whose deaths he had never mourned.

During the initial sessions, Max complained that his symptomatic state was persisting because he could not rely on the analyst for relief. He was afraid to expose his "feelings and foibles" to the analyst for fear that the analyst would be angry at him and would feel burdened by him.

When the analyst inquired into the bases for these fears, Max revealed that he was afraid that the analyst would react to him like his alcoholic mother had previously responded. His mother had a long history of depression and anxiety and had resorted to alcohol and occasional use of minor tranquilizers to medicate her symptoms. When she was drunk or hung over, she was neglectful of Max. She also could become verbally abusive toward him. At times, she would deride Max for what she saw as his social and athletic shortcomings. Max remembered that she would become especially angry when he expressed his need for her attention or when he became upset over her rebuff of his needs. He recalled how he became more distant from his feelings when she raged at him or criticized him. At those times, he would feel that his experience wasn't happening, that his experience was "unreal."

When his mother was intoxicated, she would sometimes cry to Max about her suffering, literally shedding tears on his shoulder. Max would not know how to relieve her, yet he felt that she was appealing to him to make her feel better. Her appeal for help made him feel more guilty about expressing his needs to her, as this self-assertion seemed to burden her further and add to her evident suffering.

When his mother sobered up, she typically apologized to Max for her mistreatment of him and for her emotional out pouring. She also encouraged Max to develop the emotional self-control that she lacked. Max then felt that his mother "didn't really mean" her drunken misbehavior. He also felt that he should be more self-denying and protective toward her in order to make her happy.

As a result of this inquiry, it was understood that Max expected the analyst to react like his inebriated mother. This understanding enabled Max to relax his self-protectiveness somewhat and to begin the process of mourning his parents' deaths. Crying over the loss of his parents relieved Max's "unreal" state. A selfobject tie with the analyst emerged that had idealizing and twinship aspects. Max experienced the analyst as being someone who was very much like him and who helped Max tolerate and integrate the pain of his grief (Stolorow et al., 1987).

As Max mourned his parents' deaths, he gained greater access to a wider range of feelings and to meaningful memories. He felt more "real" as a result. He also was able to reduce his fear of retraumatization sufficiently so that he could become emotionally involved with a woman. Significantly though, Max still was unable to feel "real" on a consistent basis and to fully enjoy his new life with his girlfriend. Further inquiry revealed that improvement would mean that he was abandoning and thus hurting his "handicapped" mother.

In a sequence of sessions, Max's guilt toward his mother was identified, explored, and linked to the restriction of his ability to resolve his symptoms and change. In the first session, Max reported that he had just returned from a successful vacation with his girlfriend during which he had enjoyed himself and had felt predominantly "real." Since returning from his trip though, he had been vacillating between feeling more "real" and feeling more "unreal," especially at transition points in his day when he reflected on himself. What became evoked at these "alone" moments was explored and tied to possible memories of his father's death or his mother's drunken unavailability. Yet none of these formulations resonated with what Max was feeling. He left the session wanting to find some understanding that would enable him to stay feeling "real."

At the beginning of the next session, Max reported that he had a dream that he felt was related to his unstable state. He explained,

> In the dream, I am with a handicapped woman. She only has one arm. I love her though and I am trying to help her do everything. Despite her condition, she is able to do more for herself. At one point, I look at her and she even seems able to swim on her own. I want to leave her for an attractive woman I see who has two arms, seems more intact. But I can't leave her. I feel that I will hurt her if I go, so I stay with her.

Reflecting on the dream, Max associated the one-armed woman with his mother, thinking that his mother had always seemed unarmed to deal with the emotional problems that beset her. Loving her, he had felt obliged to be her helper, even if it meant putting his own feelings and needs aside. He realized how much he had diminished his importance, minimizing the significance of his interests in order not to upset her further and make himself feel guilty. Though she seemed capable of caring for herself, swimming on her own after his father's death, he could never leave her, maybe in part because of how that leaving might have hurt her. The analyst then interpreted that it was difficult for him to hold onto the feeling from his vacation and the accompanying sense of being "real" because that would mean that he was leaving his handicapped mother and hurting her. Max laughed in response, remembering a rare time when he and his mother had gone to the beach together after his father's death. He had taken a walk away from her along the water and had stayed away for over an hour, socializing with acquaintances whom he had met along the way. When he had returned, she had been in tears, lamenting that she thought he had drowned. Max remembered how guilty he had felt in response to her being upset. He wondered whether he still associated enjoying his own life with a hurtful abandonment of his mother, which was especially guilt-provoking because he had never succeeded in making her "whole."

Max represents another example of someone with a self disorder who was restricted by a sense of guilt. He presented with difficulty in the maintainance of self-esteem and a sense of reality, suggestive of a self disorder. These symptoms were ameliorated in the context of a selfobject transference with idealizing and twinship components that emerged during the treatment. His mother's drunken mistreatment of him and her failure to validate and alleviate the painful affect that she evoked led Max to develop dissociative tendencies to protect himself from fragmentation and self-loss. He then utilized these tendencies to protect himself from mourning his parents' deaths which compromised his sense of reality. His mother's punitive response to his expression of need, coupled with her suffering, led Max to feel guilty about the pursuit of his own needs. In the sessions just reviewed, Max's feeling "unreal" reflected his effort to undo the guilt he felt about pursuing his own enjoyment with his girlfriend and thereby abandoning his mother. By feeling "unreal," he "disarmed" himself and returned to stay with his handicapped mother.

Both Ann and Max manifest what writers have termed *separation guilt* (Modell, 1971, 1984; Weiss and Sampson, 1986) and *survivor guilt* (Modell, 1971, 1984: Niederland, 1981). In the following, we elaborate on the views of several writers who have described separation and survivor guilt and illustrate how Ann and Max manifest these phenomena.

Our intention here is not to suggest that these two types of guilt exhaust the types of guilt that Tragic Man may experience, but instead to indicate that individuals who manifest self disorders may experience a variety of types of guilt depending on their developmental histories. Ann, for example, felt guilty about gratifying her competitive feelings toward her mother, a variety of guilt traditionally termed as *oedipal guilt* in the literature. The types of guilt also may include variations not previously noted. For example, we have encountered patients who could be characterized as experiencing *existence guilt*, as their very conceptions and births were experienced by a parent as having had an injurious impact.

SEPARATION GUILT

In the chapter "On Having the Right to a Life" from *Psychoanalysis in a New Context*, Modell (1984) defines *separation guilt* as guilt over separating from members of one's nuclear family. In Modell's view, individuals who experience separation guilt feel that they have no right to a life, which really means a right to a separate existence. Those who experience separation guilt not only feel disloyal for abandoning family members, but feel "that their differentiation from those who remain in the nuclear family will cause the death of the latter individuals" (p. 68). Modell observes that this sense of causing the death of family members derives from the unconscious fantasy that separating from family members and having something for oneself will deprive those family members of vital substance. In his clinical experience, Modell observes that patients who manifest separation guilt tend to negate and undo all pleasure that they could experience with self-respect in an effort to punish themselves for the assertion of individuality implicit in having the pleasure. This negation undoes their separation from family members.

Weiss and Sampson (1986) maintain that separation guilt can be the crucial factor in preventing individuals from changing restrictive ties to their childhood attachments. Sampson (1976) writes:

> A crucial factor in a patient's continuing attachment to infantile objects and to infantile gratifications is unconscious guilt about wanting to turn away from early objects, to exercise self-control and to run his own life. Thus therapy is not a process in which a patient gradually and reluctantly renounces infantile satisfactions. Rather, in the course of therapy a patient gradually comes to feel reassured that he may relinquish infantile object ties and pleasures without harming the analyst and without being overwhelmed by guilt towards earlier objects [p. 261].

Clinically, Weiss and Sampson (1986) note the many ways that patients' self-destructiveness may reflect efforts to comply with a parent or identify with him or her to prevent harmful separation or to make repair for a separation that has occurred.

Applying this concept to Ann and Max, we can see that Ann experienced her good performance on the discussion panel as a guilt-provoking assertion of separation from her mother, whereas Max perceived his enjoyment on vacation with his girlfriend as a guilt-evoking step toward leaving his mother. Ann felt that her performance meant that she could be responsible for herself and could leave her mother behind, experienced as killing off the domineering mother of her childhood. Max associated his vacation enjoyment with a hurtful abandonment of his disarmed mother.

SURVIVOR GUILT

As Friedman (1985) notes, the concept of survivor guilt was introduced into the psychiatric literature by Niederland (1981) who used it to describe the guilt experienced by Holocaust survivors. Niederland observed that Holocaust survivors experienced symptoms like depression, anxiety, and psychosomatic conditions after pursuing and succeeding at their new lives. Niederland attributed these symptoms to the outcome of the survivors' identification with loved ones who had perished. These patients felt and seemed dead. Niederland maintained that these identifications were motivated by survivor guilt, an "ever present feeling of guilt for having survived the very calamity to which their loved ones succumbed" (p. 235).

Modell (1984) expands the concept to encompass more subtle forms of survival that elicit guilt because the survivor feels that he or she has more than less fortunate members. Modell maintains that this type of guilt grows out of individuals' comparing themselves to other family members and feeling that "to have something good means that somebody else would be deprived" (p. 75). He hypothesizes that everyone has "an unconscious bookkeeping system that accounts for the available 'good' within a given nuclear family so that the current fate of other family members will determine how much good one possesses" (p. 76). Thus, if an individual feels that he or she has done better or has been more fortunate than other family members, then the individual will be prone to feeling guilty about having gotten more than his or her fair share and having taken this portion from others in the process.

Considering Ann and Max, we also can see that they display this kind of guilt. Ann felt guilty about basking in the public limelight while her mother remained unacknowledged. Max felt guilty about enjoying his vacation while his mother had been emotionally handicapped and unhappy. Both patients then felt guilty about having more than their mothers. In addition, Max felt guilty about enjoying himself and feeling happy after his father died. Epitomizing survivor guilt, Max wondered how he could live and enjoy himself when his father was dead.

GUILT INTERMINGLED

In distinguishing different types of guilt, we also note that varieties of guilt can be intermingled in a patient's experience so that the experience may reflect, for example, separation and survivor guilt or separation and oedipal guilt. In his article "The Waning of the Oedipus Complex," Loewald (1979) even implied that murder through asserting independence is an inevitable aspect of everyone's oedipal resolution. He wrote:

> In an important sense, by evolving our autonomy, and by engaging in non-incestuous object relations, we are killing our parents. We are usurping their power, their competence, their responsibility for us, and we are abnegating, rejecting them as libidinal objects. In short, we destroy them in regard to some of their qualities hitherto most vital to us [p. 758]. It is no exaggeration to say that the assumption of responsibility for one's own life and its conduct is in psychic reality tantamount to the murder of the parents [p. 757].

We would amend Loewald's universal assertion by questioning which familial contexts particularly lead individuals to experience oedipal resolution as a type of parricide through self-delineation. Still, following Loewald, we stress that types of guilt may be intermingled in the patient's experience. It can be helpful to patients, then, if we can help them grasp the multiple meanings that the experience of guilt has for them so that they can more fully understand themselves. Through this process, we can enable them to feel more free to self-differentiate, compete, and have more for themselves.

CONCLUSION

In this chapter, we argued that the dichotomy that Kohut drew between Tragic Man and Guilty Man should be reconsidered. Patients who manifest self disorders experience guilt, which contributes to shackling them to the pathogenic past. Kohut underemphasized the guilt of Tragic Man because he associated the concept with Freud's theory, which he sought to replace. In addition, he both stressed the selfobject experiences from which individuals benefit and emphasized the deficits that individuals manifest when they are deprived of these experiences. Consequently, he did not adequately address the repetitive relational patterns that individuals develop in response to previous selfobject failures (Stolorow et al., 1987; Lachmann and Beebe, 1992). These patterns may include tendencies to experience guilt when strivings to self-delineate, compete, and have more are felt to be damaging to other family members. By appreciating the repetitive relational patterns, guilt could be allotted a more rightful place in the understanding of pathogenesis and treatment. While we emphasized separation and survivor guilt in this chapter, we are not suggesting that these types exhaust the varieties of guilt that patients may experience.

The fact that guilt, or for that matter any other feeling, should be fully explored in the treatment situation is implicit in the stance of sustained empathic inquiry within an intersubjective field. However, because of Kohut's limited discussion of guilt, the need to explore guilt remains merely implicit in our theories of therapeutic action and technique within self psychology. Furthermore, we risk the danger of overlooking its importance in the patient's experience in our efforts to reach the postulated "deeper" problem of an injured self unresponded to by the caretaking surround. Because guilt is so closely associated with classical formulations, this eventuality is very probable. Consequently, it is important to explicitly state that guilt must be fully explored whenever and however it arises in the analytic arena, both in its meanings within the patient's life history and in how it operates in the present to further organize the patient's experience of self, other, and self with other.

REFERENCES

Bacal, H. A. & Newman, K. M. (1990), *Theories of Object Relations*. New York: Columbia University Press.

Fosshage, J. (1992), Self psychology: The self and its vicissitudes within a relational matrix. In: *Relational Perspectives in Psychoanalysis*, ed. N. Skolnick & S. Warshaw. Hillsdale, NJ: The Analytic Press, pp. 21–42.

—— (1994a), Commentary on Andrew Morrison's "The breadth and boundaries of a self-psychological immersion in shame." *Psychoanal. Dial.*, 4:37–44.

—— (1994b), Toward reconceptualizing transference: Theoretical and clinical considerations. *Internat. J. Psycho-Anal.*, 75:265–280.

Freud, S. (1923), *The Ego and the Id. Standard Edition*, 19:12–59. London: Hogarth Press, 1961.

Friedman, M. (1985), Toward a reconceptualization of guilt. *Contemp. Psychoanal.*, 21:501–547.

Goldberg, A. (1988), *A Fresh Look at Psychoanalysis*. Hillsdale, NJ: The Analytic Press.

Klein, G. (1976), Freud's two theories of sexuality. In: *Psychology Versus Metapsychology*, ed. M. M. Gill & P. S. Holzman. *Psychological Issues*, Monogr. 36. New York: International Universities Press, pp. 14–70.

Klein, M. (1948), On the theory of anxiety and guilt. In: *Envy and Gratitude and Other Works: 1946–1963*. New York: Delacorte Press, 1975, pp. 25–42.

Kohut, H. (1971), *The Analysis of the Self*. New York: International Universities Press.

—— (1977), *The Restoration of the Self*. New York: International Universities Press.

—— (1982), Introspection, empathy, and the semicircle of mental health. *Internat. J. Psycho-Anal.*, 63:395–407.

—— (1984), *How Does Analysis Cure?* ed. A. Goldberg & P. Stepansky. Chicago: University of Chicago Press.

Kriegman, D. & Slavin, M. (1990), On the resistance to self psychology: Clues from evolutionary biology. In: *The Realities of Transference: Progress in Self Psychology, Vol. 6*, ed. A. Goldberg. Hillsdale, NJ: The Analytic Press, pp. 217–250.

Lachmann, F. & Beebe, B. (1992), Representational and selfobject transferences: A developmental perspective. In: *New Therapeutic Visions: Progress in Self Psychology, Vol. 8*, ed. A. Goldberg. Hillsdale, NJ: The Analytic Press, pp. 3–15.

Lichtenberg, J., Lachmann, F. & Fosshage, J. (1992), *Self and Motivational Systems*. Hillsdale, NJ: The Analytic Press.

Loewald, H. (1979), The waning of the Oedipus complex. *J. Amer. Psychoanal. Assn.*, 27:751–775.

Mitchell, S. (1988), *Relational Concepts in Psychoanalysis*. Cambridge, MA: Harvard University Press.

Modell, A. (1971), The origins of certain forms of pre-oedipal guilt and the implications for a psychoanalytic theory of affects. *Internat. J. Psycho-Anal.*, 52:337–346.

—— (1984), *Psychoanalysis in a New Context*. New York: International Universities Press.

Morrison, A. (1994), The breadth and boundaries of a self-psychological immersion in shame: A one-and-a-half person perspective. *Psychoanal. Dial.*, 4:19–35.

Niederland, W. G. (1981), The survivor syndrome: Further observations and dimensions. *J. Amer. Psychoanal. Assn.*, 29:413–426.

Sampson, H. (1976), A critique of certain traditional concepts in the psychoanalytic theory of therapy. *Bull. Menn. Clin.*, 40:255–263.

Stern, D. (1985), *The Interpersonal World of the Infant*. New York: Basic Books.

Stolorow, R. D. (1976), Radical surgery for psychoanalysis. *Contemp. Psychol.*, 21:777–778.

—— Brandchaft, B. & Atwood, G. E. (1987), *Psychoanalytic Treatment: An Intersubjective Approach*. Hillsdale, NJ: The Analytic Press.

Weiss, J. & Sampson, H. (1986), *The Psychoanalytic Process*. New York: Guilford.

Zeanah, C., Anders, T., Seifer, R. & Stern, D. (1989), Implications of research on infant development for psychodynamic theory and practice. *J. Amer. Acad. Child/Adolescent Psychiat.*, 26:657–668.

Chapter 17

Looking at Patient Responses: Judging Empathic Attunement

Sanford Shapiro

Self psychology and the concept of empathic inquiry—of staying connected with a patient's experience—have changed the way I hear clinical material. But sometimes—when, for example, a patient needs to complain, and have an adversarial selfobject response—what I think is empathic turns out to be unempathic (Wolf, 1988). This type of patient feels misunderstood and complains. Yet when I try harder to be understanding, the patient becomes anxious. If, however, I lose patience, the patient suddenly feels better. Being empathic, I come to realize, is letting the patient complain and fight. Over time, I have learned intuitively when to try harder to be understanding and when to just be patient and survive the patient's complaints.

Teaching students, however, has been more difficult. Students want to know how to judge when to try harder and when to stay patiently in what I like to call a survival mode. Some ideas from outside of self psychology have helped me in teaching students how to make this assessment.

Ten years ago, colleagues in San Francisco introduced me to the ideas and empirical research of Weiss and Sampson and their control mastery theory (Weiss, Sampson, and the Mount Zion Psychotherapy Research Group, 1986). Since that time—in a mutual collaboration—I have taught my colleagues about self psychology while immersing myself

An earlier version of this chapter was presented at the 16th Annual Conference on the Psychology of the Self, Toronto, Canada, October 30, 1993.

in the study of their research. Control mastery theory is slowly finding its way into the psychoanalytic literature (Silverman, 1989; Eagle, 1993). Little, however, has been written about it in the self psychology literature.

Although not all of control mastery theory is compatible with self psychology, two concepts—looking at patient responses and unconscious guilt—are useful to self psychologists. I have now integrated these ideas into my work and teaching. The goal of this chapter is to introduce and make understandable to self psychologists the ideas and empirical research of the San Francisco Psychotherapy Research Group.[1] I will review control mastery theory in general and focus in detail on the research concerning patient responses and unconscious guilt.

PATIENT RESPONSES

A patient's response to an interpretation does not refer just to the patient's words, but also to the patient's affect and state of integration. A patient may agree with my interpretation but in a compliant fashion—there is no sense of aliveness. That signals me that I am off track and not in empathic attunement. Or a patient who was previously feeling disorganized and chaotic now boldly disagrees with me or strongly objects to my interpretations in a clear, well-organized manner. Although I take the complaints seriously, I also feel reassured that I am on track, that this patient has now achieved a new level of integration and is expressing the aversive motivational system (Lichtenberg, 1989).

The Psychoanalytic Process: Theory, Clinical Observation and Empirical Research (Weiss & Sampson, 1986) is the culmination of 14 years of empirical research on the psychoanalytic process. Two terms introduced, "pathogenic beliefs" and "patient's tests," cause much confusion to self psychologists. I will review how these terms are defined and show how they can be helpful to self psychologists.

Weiss, after carefully studying detailed process notes, developed a theory that patients come to analysis unconsciously knowing what they need to get better. He theorized that a patient's difficulties result from unconscious "pathogenic beliefs" of danger—a danger that arises if certain developmental goals are pursued. These grim beliefs are irrational and are based on early relational experiences. An example of a pathogenic belief is the following thought: *If I become more independent and self-sufficient, I will be hurting my mother.* When, in the course of a new relationship, these beliefs are disconfirmed, the patient

---

[1] This group, under the direction of Weiss and Sampson, was previously called the Mount Zion Psychotherapy Research Group.

becomes free to develop new strategies for achieving developmental goals.

Weiss believes that each patient has an unconscious plan to get better, a plan that subjects the analyst to tests. These tests, when passed by the analyst, will disconfirm the pathogenic beliefs. In Weiss's theory, when a pathogenic belief is disconfirmed, the patient improves. When the analyst fails a test, a pathogenic belief is confirmed, and the patient gets worse.

An example is a patient who, for the first six months of her analysis, was scrupulously punctual. Then she started coming late—often ten or twenty minutes late—apologizing profusely each time. Thinking this was a resistance, I wondered if the chronic lateness was an expression of underlying anger toward me. She felt hurt and criticized by these interpretations. Gradually she became depressed and discouraged, our treatment alliance was disrupted, and an impasse developed. Then, with the help of self psychology, I became able to understand that she was trying to develop a sense of her own individuality, to give up being the compliant, good little girl. With these interpretations her mood improved, her sense of confidence returned, and the treatment alliance was reestablished.

I realized that she came late because she was busy taking care of other business. She was, for the first time, doing things for herself—not just for everyone else (including me). Her pathogenic belief was that doing something for herself was selfish and hurt others. She believed that she did not have a right to do something just for herself. Her test was to take care of herself and see if that hurt me.

When I interpreted the lateness as anger directed at me, I failed the test and confirmed her belief that taking care of herself hurt me. When I understood that she was feeling the freedom to decide how to run her life, whether to stay at her office and finish her work or come to her appointment, I passed the test and her pathogenic belief was disconfirmed.

EVALUATING RESPONSES

Weiss and coworkers demonstrate with their research that direct observation of a patient's immediate response can determine whether the analyst's intervention is "pro-plan" or "anti-plan." When the analyst's behavior or intervention disconfirms the pathogenic belief (is pro-plan) the patient's immediate response is bolder, stronger, and more insightful. When the analyst confirms the pathogenic belief (is anti-plan) the patient's immediate response is more diffuse, anxious, and resistant.

When, for example, a patient complains about a lack of progress in therapy, careful attention can determine if there is progress or if this is a setback. If the patient is more anxious and fragmented in his or her complaints, the analyst is "anti-plan" (has lost empathic connection and has failed the patient's test.) If the patient, however, was previously feeling chaotic and disorganized and now complains in a bolder, stronger, more integrated fashion, then the analyst is "pro-plan" (is providing a vital selfobject function and is passing the patient's test). Thinking *this is just a test* can help the analyst stay calm (Weiss, 1993).

Weiss's theory was subjected to empirical research. A completed analysis had been audio recorded, and the recordings, plus process notes of some hours, were made available to the research group. The treating analyst, in a different part of the country, knew nothing about Weiss or his theory, and he had recorded the analysis for his personal research. Working from a classical model, he considered the terminated analysis a success.

One group of research workers, reading transcripts of the opening hours, formulated the patient's "plan." Plan formulations have four parts: the patient's GOALS are inferred; OBSTRUCTIONS, or pathogenic beliefs, are inferred; TESTS that the therapist will be subjected to are predicted; and INSIGHTS that will help the patient are predicted (Curtis et al., 1988).[2]

After formulating the patient's plan, the researchers then looked at samples of the analyst's interventions excerpted from transcripts of the recordings. Without knowing the patient's responses, the workers rated each intervention on a Likert scale from "pro-plan" to "anti-plan."

A second group of research workers, knowing nothing about the plan formulated or the analyst's interventions, looked only at transcripts of the patient's responses, rating them on a Likert scale from "bold, strong and insightful" to "diffuse, anxious and resistant." There was a statistically significant correlation between interventions rated as "pro-plan" with patient responses that were rated as bold, strong, insightful responses; and "anti-plan" interventions correlated with diffuse, anxious, resistant responses.

PATIENT'S TESTS

Weiss believes that patients unconsciously test their therapists to determine if conditions are safe. When therapists pass such tests, uncon-

---

[2] Control mastery therapists infer a patient's plan in the first few hours and use this formulation to guide their interpretations. I prefer a "wait and see" mode of investigation. Patients have good reasons for their behavior, and by monitoring their responses to my interventions, their plan will become clear in time.

scious mental contents can emerge spontaneously into conscious awareness (Gassner, Sampson et al., 1982). "The patient tests the therapist
from the beginning to the end of treatment. He is vitally interested in
finding out how the therapist will react to his plans. Will the therapist
oppose his goals, or will he be sympathetic to them and encourage him
to pursue them? The therapist's ability to recognize the patient's tests
and pass them is central to therapy. The success or failure of a therapy
may depend on this" (Weiss, 1993, p. 92).

Weiss describes two types of tests: transferring tests and passive-into-
active tests. In a transferring test, the patient will anticipate a traumatic
response from the analyst similar to one received from earlier caregivers.
This test is easily passed by sensitive analysts who, for example,
respond in a validating or acknowledging way when the patient is
expecting to be criticized or discounted. Taking a patient seriously may
disconfirm a pathogenic belief that the patient's complaints will injure
the analyst. It may also meet developmental needs in the selfobject
dimension of the transference (Stolorow and Lachmann, 1980).

Passive-into-active tests involve a patient, in an identification with a
traumatizing parent, subjecting the analyst to abuses similar to those
experienced in childhood. For instance, a patient subjected to criticism
and humiliation in growing up will, in an attempt at *control* and *mastery*, subtly provoke and belittle the analyst, while carefully monitoring
the analyst's responses. If the analyst acts hurt or becomes defensive,
the patient's belief will be confirmed—that the patient is supposed to
organize around meeting the analyst's needs, even at his or her
expense—and the patient will continue to feel vulnerable and
responsible. If, however, the analyst survives the attack, can take care of
himself or herself and not blame the patient, then the pathogenic belief
will be disconfirmed. Seeing the analyst as strong—not vulnerable—the
patient will then identify with the analyst's strength in the process of
mastering the underlying feeling of vulnerability.[3] Passive into active tests
are more stressful for therapists than are transferring tests: "When the
patient transfers, he endows the therapist with the authority of a parent,
so the therapist tends to feel relatively safe. However, when he turns
passive into active, the patient assumes the role of the traumatizing
parent, and the therapist may feel considerable strain" (Weiss, 1993, p.
105).

---

[3] Weiss believes that analysts may do the right thing for the wrong reasons. After reviewing the
analyst's process notes in the case of Mrs. C, Weiss believes that the patient made progress despite
the fact that the analyst's interpretations were totally out of tune with what the patient was working
on. Something about the analyst's personality and manner passed some important tests (Weiss,
personal communication, 1987).

Weiss believes that pathogenic beliefs may be directly modified through experience and insight. Because pathogenic beliefs are frightening and debilitating, patients are unconsciously highly motivated to change them and highly active in their efforts to seek out experiences that will disprove them (Bush, 1994).

UNCONSCIOUS GUILT

In discussing pathogenic beliefs, Weiss elaborates on the concept of guilt. He gives unconscious guilt more central importance than does self psychology, and he links it to unconscious pathogenic beliefs: "Irrational unconscious guilt stems from distorted unconscious beliefs about having done something bad in the fundamental sense of doing something hurtful or being disloyal to another person toward whom one feels a special sense of attachment or responsibility, such as a parent, sibling, or child. . . . [This model of guilt] emphasizes the primacy of the individual's fear of hurting others as the deepest unconscious layer of the experience of guilt" (Bush, 1989, p. 98).

Weiss describes two types of guilt: separation guilt and survivor guilt. Based on early traumatic experiences—not on unconscious drives—children can develop beliefs that separation or self-individuation will hurt a parent (separation guilt), or that whatever they get for themselves will be at someone else's expense (survivor guilt). Self psychologists have contributed much to our understanding of separation fears, that is, the extent to which children will go to protect themselves against a loss of vital connections with caregivers (Kohut, 1984; Stolorow, Brandchaft, and Atwood, 1987). Weiss adds another dimension with his belief that children also have conflicts because of love and feelings of loyalty toward caregivers.

I believe the two conflicts, fear of loss and fear of being bad or disloyal, have a figure–ground relationship to each other. Sometimes the fear of loss will be more in the foreground; sometimes it is the fear of being disloyal. An example is a patient struggling to express her criticism of me. I interpreted that she was afraid of losing me if she expressed her complaints. "I'm not afraid of losing you!" She said, "I know you will hang in there with me, but I don't want you to see me as *bad*." She then told me that complaints to her mother resulted in her mother accusing her of being "evil." Her mother saw the "devil" inside her. At another time in the analysis, she was reluctant to tell me her critical feelings for fear that I would be hurt and would withdraw from her. This time she wasn't worried I would think she was bad—she feared losing the connection with me.

CASE ILLUSTRATION

The following case illustrates how concepts from control mastery theory and self psychology helped me deal with a challenging clinical problem. Separation guilt was a major factor blocking this patient in her self-individuation development. And a lack of affect integration handicapped her ability to appreciate inner emotional needs and feelings (Shapiro, 1991). She needed me to provide affect-attuning selfobject functions, and she needed to subject me, unconsciously, to tests to help resolve separation guilt.

Angel, a 19-year-old college student, worried me. An attractive, willowy girl, she first consulted me after being found asleep in the back seat of her car in a closed garage with the motor running. Fate intervened when a roommate accidentally stumbled upon her. Angel did not feel depressed. She felt something was wrong with her, that she just did not belong in this world. "Something is wrong with my thinking," she said. "I need help."

The analysis lasted five months.[4] Although we made good contact in our first session, the connection vanished over the weekend. We met five times a week, and each of our meetings left me feeling frustrated and anxious. She would talk about anything that I suggested. I wanted to know about her, but I couldn't find the key to her mind. My anxiety increased as I knew that she could commit suicide at any time and without warning.

She was protecting herself because she felt vulnerable and was afraid to trust me. After two weeks of feeling disconnected, I shared my feelings of frustration with her, and she relaxed. I then inquired whether disconnection from family and friends left her feeling sad, lonely, and in pain. Her reaction to my saying things like "sad" or "lonely" or "pain" was immediately to think: *It's not good to feel that way; You don't want to feel that way.* These feelings, which had been disavowed, could now be appreciated and integrated into the organization of her self-experience. She realized that she had been in a rut, and she now thought that it would be a long road out of her prison. She told me about being paralyzed with self-consciousness, often holding her breath around other people.

I now found myself subjected to a series of tests as she began to assert her individuality. For example, she was floundering when she came in and complained that I did not help her to get started. "You could at least say hello when I come in," she said, and then she apolo-

---

[4] Intensive work with young people with developmental arrests often can achieve much progress in a short time.

gized for being rude. I interpreted this statement as her fear that she was hurting me when she asserted herself. Her response was bold and insightful. She said that taking care of herself was being mean, and that made her feel guilty.

She looked for my permission to take off her shoes, to sit with her feet tucked under and to bring a drink to the session. I interpreted her feeling of pressure to figure out what I expected so that she could comply. Her response was to realize the pressures she felt from family and friends to do things "right" and her feeling of shame if she did not comply. She feared that she would hurt her mother if she took care of herself, and she now realized that she automatically—and unconsciously—felt that it was her duty to take care of others, even at her expense. Something must be wrong with her, she had reasoned, because she could never do enough—people were always needing more from her. She had finally decided that she just did not belong in this world.

As I systematically interpreted her separation guilt in the transference—her feeling that being more independent would hurt me—she became bolder and stronger. She became less compliant, reached out more to her friends, and, to her surprise, people responded positively. Saying no to one of her friends was a new experience. "It was like getting a piece of gunk off of me!" she said. She subjected me to further tests by now barraging me with personal questions like where do I live, how old am I, and do I have children. Appreciating her newfound courage in reaching out, I answered each question without hesitation. She became anxious after telling me that she did not like one of my paintings. She feared that expressing her own ideas and opinions would hurt me if they did not agree with my way of thinking.

Becoming more insightful, she now realized how isolated she was from friends. Everyone expected her to listen to their problems, but no one reached out to her. "People look to me to be a den mother," she said. "At my last birthday party I could have been dead or not there—it wouldn't have mattered." When she shamefully described feeling irritated in another situation, I pointed out that she sounded apologetic. She then recalled how, in growing up, complaining was not nice and was not allowed. She had gotten the message that complaints, or any expressions of painful feelings, would hurt other people. After the first month of therapy, when her friends now asked what happened to her, she could talk about her suicide attempt. Becoming more aware of her feelings, she now felt more in control and less afraid. Hope had returned.

Life now excited her, and after three months of therapy, she wanted to reduce the sessions to three times a week. She explained that our appointments were a "touchstone" for her, a place where she could organize and focus. Now she wanted time to think about things before coming in. Staying connected with me was no longer a problem; she could pick up where she left off, even after the weekend break. I experienced this as a test to see if I needed her to fulfill my therapeutic ambitions. I understood that she wanted to see what she could do on her own, without talking to me first, an idea I thought worth trying. With her increasing self-confidence, she developed new relationships and had new experiences of mutuality, intimacy, and aliveness. She then began canceling and missing appointments.

I understood the missed appointments as tests to see if I trusted her to run her own life, or if I needed her to meet my narcissistic needs, like her mother. At one point, however, after not seeing or hearing from her for a week, I became anxious, I began to doubt my assessment, and I called her. I wakened her and she was angry. She said, "I am not feeling well. Do you want me to come in?" I said that I had not meant to intrude, that I had wondered if there had been some misunderstanding. She said that there was no misunderstanding, but she again failed to appear for the next appointment. Later that day she called and left a message apologizing for being rude by not calling me.

At the next appointment, she asked anxiously if I still wanted her as a patient. I said that I had called because I felt anxious; I had not meant to pressure her. When I heard that she was not well, I realized that she was taking care of herself and was not off somewhere trying to commit suicide. I didn't think she would commit suicide, I added, but I didn't know her that well yet. "You can't always be sure," she said sympathetically. She said that she felt guilty for wasting my time. I said that she was responsible to pay for the time, but the time was hers to use in whatever way she felt was best. She brightened and said, "Yes, I did feel this was one place where I would not have to worry." I said that our goal was for her to be able to take care of herself without having to worry about taking care of me and everybody else first. When her initial anxiety changed into a confident brightness, I felt reassured that I had passed her test and reestablished an empathic connection.

In the following weeks, she came to the appointments intermittently, only sometimes calling to cancel. Her insightfulness and assertiveness, however, continued to blossom, and she continued to have meaningful new experiences. I was impressed that her relationship with her mother now improved, and they developed a strong connection. She did well during my vacation, and she told me that she wanted to cut the sessions down to twice a week. She explained, "There is a danger zone, a time when something is not right with your thinking, and there is a reality zone, a time of discovery and of learning new things." She was no longer in danger, she was continuing to learn new things, and she felt certain that her progress would continue. She asked what I thought. I said that I did not know what was best, but I would encourage her to follow her hunches and see what happened. If things continued to improve, that would be a good sign. If problems arose, we could reevaluate the decision. She thought about her earlier high school experiences, and she wondered what she might have done had she been feeling this good then.

The next session she came on time, albeit reluctantly, and felt puzzled. Coming to the sessions no longer felt the same. She asked me why I thought she did not want to come. I asked if anything had come up in our last session that distressed her. When she said no, I said that perhaps the original reason for coming (i.e., that something was not right with her thinking) no longer applied. Perhaps it was time to reassess our goals and review our options.

She asked me about options, and I said that one option was to take a break, to have a period of time on her own and then meet with me and review her experience. Another option would be to change our focus and explore underlying issues. Thinking that this was a resistance, I said that I would encourage her to continue the therapy and explore underlying issues, especially if she hoped to have a family someday and wanted her children to have better experiences. She said that made sense, but she did not want to have children, and, quite boldly, she said she did not want to look at underlying issues. She wanted to take a break. She worried that if she stopped, she could not come back. When I explored the idea of her continuing, she became more diffuse and anxious. When I explored the idea of taking a break, she became bolder and more confident. Taking my cue from her responses, we agreed to stop and meet in six weeks for a reevaluation.

At the six-week follow-up she came on time and reported continued progress. She said, apologetically, that she did not miss the sessions. I interpreted her fear that feeling independent and self-sufficient would be hurting me. She immediately brightened and reported that she had finally confronted her roommate with her dissatisfactions, and their relationship had improved. She also reported that she felt strong enough to finally quit her heavy cigarette smoking. Her parents, too, had changed, and they were now reconsidering their values—they were learning from her.

She recalled that she stopped laughing in junior high school when she started learning to "be a lady." She had worried that people thought she was weird, and she felt that there was something about her that put people off, something unpleasant or unattractive. Now she felt happy, laughed a lot, and no longer worried as much about other people's reactions. She was pleased that she no longer felt something was wrong with her, and she wanted to terminate the therapy. Four months later I received a Christmas card with a note: "Everything has been great lately. It's exciting to look forward to the new year. Thank you very much for your help. You helped me begin to make enormous changes in my life. I feel better than I've *ever* felt."

DISCUSSION

Angel had become organized around taking care of others. Self-initiative became inhibited to the point where she lost her ability to feel alive and real. She assumed that her growing sense of paralysis was her fault. She was a failure, a burden to others, and it was her duty to purge the world of her shameful presence.

Self-disclosure of my feeling frustrated passed a test showing her that I would work with her and not leave her to fend for herself. The pathogenic belief that she did not have a right to have help, that she had to do everything on her own, was disconfirmed. She then felt safe enough to test me further by asserting her individuality while carefully monitoring my responses. Transferring tests involved her anticipating my withdrawing from her, like her mother, if she didn't comply with my expectations. A passive-into-active test was her withdrawing from me, as her mother did from her, and looking to see if I would become anxious as she did. The time when I did become anxious and called her, I failed the test. She came in to the next session anxious and compliant, anticipating that I no longer wanted her as a patient. The failed test was not a technical error. It was an inadvertent disruption characteristic of any therapy, and I viewed it as an opportunity for further investigation.

Overcoming her pathogenic beliefs allowed an arrested developmental process to resume its natural course. I anticipate that further growth will take place spontaneously. Further therapy may or may not be necessary in the future but, in any event, the danger is over.

CONCLUSION

I believe that experienced therapists from differing theoretical perspectives intuitively infer their patients' plans, and they unconsciously past tests that disconfirm their patients' pathogenic beliefs. I believe that such therapists also unconsciously provide selfobject functions for their patients that help overcome developmental blocks.

When treatment goes well, one can trust one's theoretical beliefs. When treatment bogs down, however (i.e., when impasses develop), then one can be helped by looking at contributions from other theoretical points of view. In classical theory, treatment impasses are viewed as "negative therapeutic reactions," or manifestations of forces arising solely from within the patient. In both self psychology and control mastery theories, impasses are seen as the result of something gone awry in the intersubjective field: either the analyst is not seeing something from the patient's perspective, or the analyst is failing a test. The analyst needs to become immersed further in the patient's subjective world (Atwood and Stolorow, 1984) or needs to infer better the patient's plan.

Self psychology has contributed much to the literature on patients' struggles with fears of loss and rejection, and their need to maintain vital ties. Sometimes, however, the fear of hurting the loved object is more significant than the fear of losing the loved object. Addressing the concepts of separation guilt and survivor guilt is a helpful contribution of control mastery theory.

Fundamental to self psychology is an appreciation of the selfobject function of affect attunement in the development of affect integration (Socarides and Stolorow, 1984/85). One aspect of affect integration is the ability to identify, and put into words, internal feeling states. The development of speech helps to process painful feelings. A block in the development of affect integration leaves an individual vulnerable to being overwhelmed by tension and secondary feelings of chaos, fragmentation, or paralysis.

In the case of Angel, after bridging our early disconnection by disclosing my frustration, I discussed her experience with her. I asked about such feelings as isolation, loneliness, sadness, pain, frustration, and irritation. It scared her to talk about such feelings. They were dangerous—they threatened vital relationships. As a result, self-validation, spontaneity, and self-initiative became inhibited, and Angel lost her ability to feel alive and real. People always needed something, and Angel found herself laboring to fill their bottomless pits. She in turn felt covered with "gunk" and paralyzed. Her mounting frustration meant that something was wrong with her, and she concluded that she did not belong here. I understood her suicide attempt as a desperate attempt to take care of herself, to reverse a relentless feeling of enslavement. I said that she was like the citizens of New Hampshire, whose state slogan is "Live Free or Die!"

My providing the selfobject functions of identifying and validating her affect states helped her to consolidate her sense of self and improve her self-esteem. She stopped performing and started being. I also provided the selfobject function of being used as a test object. Repeatedly she subjected me to tests to see whether I expected her to organize around my needs, or whether I would understand and validate the authenticity of her needs.

Observing her immediate responses to my interventions helped me stay on track. With some patients, my attempt to be "understanding" when they want to reduce sessions or terminate leads to anxiety. They feel rejected and unwanted by me. With Angel, however, my understanding her wish to stop resulted in her increased boldness and insightfulness.[5]

There are many ways to understand a therapy. This case shows how the self psychology concept of selfobject functioning and the control mastery concept of passing tests to disconfirm pathogenic beliefs complemented each other and helped me keep my bearings while working with this challenging patient.

REFERENCES

Atwood, G. & Stolorow, R. (1984), *Structures of Subjectivity: Explorations in Psychoanalytic Phenomenology.* Hillsdale, NJ: The Analytic Press.

Bush, M. (1989). The role of unconscious guilt in psychopathology and psychotherapy. *Bull. Menn. Clin.,* 53:97–107.

—— (1994), Control mastery theory and intersubjectivity theory. Presented at the Conference on the Intersubjective Perspective: Control Mastery and Self Psychology, November 13, 1994, San Francisco, California.

Curtis, J. T., Silberschatz, G., Sampson, H., Weiss, J. & Rosenberg, S. E. (1988), Developing reliable psychodynamic case formulations: An illustration of the plan diagnosis method. *Psychotherapy,* 27:513–521.

Eagle, M. (1993), Enactments, transference, and symptomatic cure—A case history. *Psychoanal. Dial.,* 3:93–110.

Gassner, S., Sampson, H., Weiss, J. & Brumer, S. (1982). The emergence of warded-off contents. *Psychoanal. Contemp. Thought,* 5:55–75.

Goldberg, A. & Marcus, D. (1985). Natural termination: Some comments on ending analysis without setting a date. *Psychoanal. Quart.,* 54:46–65.

Kohut, H. (1984). *How Does Analysis Cure?* ed. A. Goldberg & P. Stepansky. Chicago: University of Chicago Press.

Lichtenberg, J. (1989). *Psychoanalysis and Motivation.* Hillsdale, NJ: The Analytic Press.

Malin, N. (1990). Returning to psychotherapy with the same therapist: A self-psychological perspective. *Clin. Soc. Work J.,* 18:115–129.

Shapiro, S. (1991), Affect integration in psychoanalysis: A clinical approach to self-destructive behavior. *Bull. Menn. Clin.,* 55:363–374.

---

[5] The abrupt termination raises the question of a "flight into health." But suddenly stopping treatment can also meet developmental needs. Patients may need to have the experience of seeing what they can do for themselves and still feel the therapist's support. These patients may return for more therapy, with either the same therapist or a different one, and work on other issues. This is a natural developmental experience and is not a shortcoming of the original therapy (Malin, 1990; Goldberg, 1985). To interpret the stopping only as "running away" or "acting out" prevents these patients from feeling pleased with their accomplishment.

Silverman, L. H. (1989). Commentary on a new view of unconscious guilt. *Bull. Menn. Clin.,* 53:135–142.

Socarides, D. D. & Stolorow, R. (1984/85). Affects and selfobjects. *The Annual of Psychoanalysis,* 12/13:105–119. Madison, CT: International Universities Press.

Stolorow, R., Brandchaft, B. & Atwood, G. (1987), *Psychoanalytic Treatment: An Intersubjective Approach.* Hillsdale, NJ: The Analytic Press.

——& Lachmann, F. (1980), *Psychoanalysis of Developmental Arrests.* New York: International Universities Press.

Weiss, J. (1993), *How Psychotherapy Works.* New York: Guilford.

—— Sampson, H. & the Mount Zion Psychotherapy Research Group (1986), *The Psychoanalytic Process.* New York: Guilford.

Wolf, E. (1988), *Treating the Self.* New York: Guilford.

Chapter 18

Psychohistory, Cultural Evolution, and the Historical Significance of Self Psychology

Hans Kilian

The purpose of this chapter is to show the psychohistorical relativity of psychoanalytic knowledge and the consequences of its nonperception and denial in clinical theory and practice.

Psychoanalysis reaches the proud age of 100 this decade. Since Freud published his *Studies on Hysteria* in 1895, his baby has become an old lady. Her lifespan is approaching a second turn of the century. This gives me some good reasons to look with you at the problems of psychohistorical change in the last hundred years and at their consequences for psychoanalytic theory and practice. One hundred years of psychoanalysis were of course 100 years in the history of childhood and in the history of upbringing too. We saw 100 years of cultural change in the relationships both between the genders (or sexes) and the subsequent generations. We must realize that this change caused in part by psychoanalysis, also rebounded to have an effect on psychoanalysis itself. What's more, 100 years of psychoanalysis were accompanied by 100 years of change in mental and psychosomatic illness. Above all, however, we had 100 years of economic and social history which more fundamentally transformed the life of the individual, the family, the coexistence of nations, and mankind as a whole than millenia before.

Heinz Kohut Memorial Lecture, 1993.

I shall have no time to go into detail about all these developmental lines of the cultural and psychohistorical change we have been witnessing during this century. But I hope I can give you a useful theoretical key that will open the door for a synoptic understanding of both the history of psychoanalysis and its psychohistorical reality context. In this connection, I shall try to point out the specific relevance of self psychology at the present time.

But let me first introduce the centennial old lady as a whole in her present state. At first glance, psychoanalysis is in the best of health. In spite of her age the lady is basically viable and seems to be capable of further development. At least she isn't complaining about any aches and pains. But as everybody knows, appearances are sometimes deceptive. In fact, the old lady is suffering from an increasing confusion of terms and conflicting theories that stem from different periods and stages of her development. The older psychoanalysis grows, the more difficulties psychoanalysts of different groups and schools have in communicating and understanding what they are saying to each other. Another consequence is that a growing number of patients don't feel understood because they are often seen in the light of older theories that don't describe their real problems.

What are the deeper causes of the old lady's confusion? Is it curable? What should be done to resolve the problem? To answer these questions, we first need a diagnosis. A historian of science or an epistemologist would simply say she is stricken with a severe model crisis. That would be right, but that's not all. That's only a diagnosis of symptoms that doesn't help her cure her troubles. Let's go one step further. You are self psychologists. So you know that founders of scientific schools of thought and their theories are very often selfobjects whose adherents cannot go beyond them, much less dismiss them from their minds without being traumatized. Therefore, you could also say that the centennial lady is stricken with an uncured selfobject disorder. I agree to that, but that's not all either. That's only a statement about her subjectivity, which doesn't help her gain more scientific cohesion and objectivity. It's true that the old lady also suffers from bad sight (a defect of vision), which diminishes and distorts her perception of reality. She is affected by historical agnosia and agnosticism. That means she isn't able to see to which extent human reality changes in the course of social history. I guess it's because she has been used to perceiving her patients and their problems just through the glasses of an invariant metapsychology. You might say she needs glasses with interchangeable lenses to correct the historic time shift between her own subjective perception and her patients' quite different reality. Though her bad sight is chronic, it's not organic. It's only functional. In principle, it would be possible to correct it by learning historical vision. That's not much more difficult than it is for children to learn how to see and draw in spatial perspective. Historical vision is not a vision in spatial perspective but an imaging of changing structures of subject and reality in spatiotemporal perspective. You can also say it's a perception of psychohistorical processes of self and other in the context of changing reality.

The old lady's poor sight is in reality a lasting consequence of the historical fact that her father and untouchable selfobject, Sigmund Freud, could never give up his utopian hope that psychoanalysis was destined to become a natural science of the unconscious mind. Around the turn of the last century he actually tried to become a university professor with a theory of the sexual causes of hysteria he hoped to be compatible with natural sciences. I wonder whether he ignored or underestimated therefore the psychohistorical dimension and specificity of mental disorders. In fact, he excluded himself and several generations of his devoted disciples from any chance of envisaging and managing the problem of the psychohistorical change of mental illness in an adequate way. You could also say that the time wasn't ripe for that. Be that as it may: it seems to me the venerable lady cannot get rid of her confusion without giving up her childhood dream that she was meant to be a princess of highly regarded science. To overcome her model crisis, she should first of all establish her true scientific identity. As her childhood dream to become a princess of natural science wasn't realistic, it made her fall behind the times instead of helping her keep pace with them. Indeed, she is lagging behind. I have forgotten to mention it. That's because you see her lagging only when she gets up from her armchair, beside or behind the couch. It's a heavy blow for her, because she had dreamed of moving ahead of the times with her father's chosen few from the ancient Viennese circle. What could be done to help her part with her outdated models of thought and make a fresh start with more realistic ideas? You could say she needs a piece of advice she can most likely and most easily find by turning to self psychology.

Let me add to this another suggestion. A hundred years after Freud's *Studies on Hysteria* I would like to recommend to her a vocational training: "Studies on Historia"! She needs some careful study in psychohistory and social history, too, which are only possible now, at the approach of another century. It is only now that we possess a sufficient overview of the history of psychoanalysis and its changing background of reality. It was Heinz Kohut who cleared the way for a new psychohistorical approach to psychoanalysis. He discovered the historical dimension of the self. With his theory of the self and selfobject relations he crossed the Rubicon that separates the territory of the classical natural sciences from the territory of the evolutionary and historical sciences. As long as the ego is considered by psychoanalysis as a homeostatic system of functional regulation, its location is on the classic natural scientists' side of the Rubicon. Therefore, you cannot speak of a history of the ego. But you can speak of the history of the self.

One hundred years of history of psychoanalysis are at the same time 100 years of the history of a culturally developing self and culturally changing relations of self and other. The history of the paradigmatic changes in psychoanalysis took its course from the "Ancient Times" of Freud's topographical model to the "Middle Ages" of structural theory and its derivatives and finally, from the latter, to the current times of Kohut's self psychology. The essence of the argument is that these three phases of the history of psychoanalytic theory and practice correspond to three phases and stages of social history and cultural evolution in the 19th and 20th centuries. Here are their basic features.

The 19th and 20th centuries have been a period of accelerated cultural development during which three phases of the economic and social history of mankind follow, intertwine, and overlap. They are 1) the preindustrial agricultural society, which was fused with the patriarchal rule-and-role culture of feudalism; 2) the economy of free competition and its large concentration in the big cities of industrial society; and 3) the decentralized growth of postindustrial society and the so-called tertiary sector of service and service trade professions.

These three phases correspond to three stages of the sense of reality and of the development of human relations (relating to the other as an object, as a selfobject, and as a whole subject as is possible with reciprocal empathy). What's more, the three phases correspond to three phases of historical change of mental illness and, most important for us, three phases of the history of the self.

First, there is the phase of the tradition-directed role-self of the patriarchal rule culture. Without having a theory of the self, David Riesman introduced the term *tradition-directed* social character around 40 years ago. It's understandable that Freudian psychoanalysts at that time didn't know what to do with his theory, which seemed to be unrelated to their field.

Second, there is the phase of the "inner-directed" ego-self of the urban society with free market competition. The "inner-directed" ego-self has been most typical of the middle classes of this society.

Finally, there is the phase of the postpatriarchal self, which is emerging step by step in the framework of an expanding postindustrial society. As concerns the third phase, the most important for self psychology, I choose a different issue than David Riesman used. In my view, his well-known concept of an "other-directed" social character covers only a part of the problems and developmental stages of a newly emerging postpatriarchal self. Since he wrote his book *The Lonely Crowd* in 1950, there has been a collective crisis in the development of an other-directed self, which gave birth, among other things, to Kohut's work and self psychology. I will try to show that the emergence of self psychology indicates a level of psychohistorical development, in which Riesman's other-directed social character begins to develop further into an autonomous postpatriarchal self. I will explain this later in more detail.

But there is another point of contact with well-known American thought that is relevant and even indispensable for psychoanalysis. It is important to recognize that the accelerated technological and economic changes in many areas occur more quickly than the change in human relations, thought, and self. Put simply, human development falls behind technological development. This doesn't apply just in the sense that human beings (as a consequence of such a developmental retardation) don't fulfill the requirements of adaptation to the current state of things in reality. It means also that those lagging psychohistorically behind become unavoidably deceptive selfobjects for their fellow beings and descendants, because they are unable to counteract the dehumanization of the changing human life-world. In other words, they are not capable of contributing to its continuously renewed humanization, which, in the course of current history, must be achieved again by every generation. That phenomenon applies also to psychoanalysis itself. What is called a "cultural lag," that is, the lagging behind of human abilities to resolve current problems in a realistic and creative way, has only been partly described by the American sociologist William F. Ogburn. He did not include the areas covering psychic structures (the structures of self, thought, and human relations) in his very fruitful theory. I am trying, by means of an extension of the visual field to mental structures, to fill the gap.

That leads me back to psychoanalysis and its history. I will examine in greater detail its three paradigmatic stages and their reality context. Freud developed his topographical model at a time of transition that led from a declining patriarchal culture of feudalistic origin to an expanding economic system of rising free competition. In Central Europe there was a long-term overlapping of two historical cultures and two conflicting value systems. Feudalistic loyalty to absolute patriarchal lords and free competition or rivalry as practiced in an "open society" are incompatible principles of different social systems. The contradiction of the two conflicting value systems remained unnoticed or denied by most of Freud's contemporaries. Therefore these conflicts became contents of what Freud called "the unconscious." Freud's ambience was characterized by a continuing melting down process of Central European corporate systems, by a weaker cohesion of patriarchal families and a growing crisis of authority. Where did this crisis come from?

According to its medieval self-image the traditional patriarchal rule culture had to be understood as a social system of reciprocal loyalty of lords and their subordinates or dependents. Obedience and submission to the lords were supposed to be rewarded with protection and support. The 19th century saw the decay of this social system and the collapse of its justifications. Meanwhile, the course of social history was quite different in the Protestant and Anglican sea-trading countries, which were leading by several centuries of free competition and the development of an "inner-directed" ego-self. However, in Central Europe there was a feudal-like cast or class society that prevented social ascent from a lower to a higher level. That was the difference between America and most of continental Europe.

When Freud treated his first patients, such as Dora, the capacity of more and more holders of authority positions to supply protection was diminishing. Inversely, their needs and demands for further continuing loyalty and unconditional obedience were progressively growing at the same time. That's what economists call "scissors of demand and supply." But we must bear in mind that this gap, or these scissors, didn't concern material goods but human relations. A preestablished balance of human relations got collectively lost, and this loss of balance remained unnoticed by most people alive then. That was the social climate and the psychohistorical reality context of Freud's discovery of the Oedipus complex. Freud believed that he had discovered a basic problem of human life, which had its sources in the innate instinctual drives of prehistoric primal hordes and in conflicts between the paternal headmen of the hordes and their descendants. Under the influence of Darwin's biological theory of evolution he conceived a purely psychobiological view of the disorders he was confronted with. He didn't consider causal conditions like an imbalance of human relations and a historical crisis of authority, which provoke a collective activation or eruption of the hidden volcano of human instincts.

Let us take a quick look at the psychohistorical aspects of Freud's psychoanalytic technique, which was derived from his first topographical model. Freud applied the technique of direct interpretations of presumably repressed drive wishes. Seen with the eyes of today's analysts, his technique was quite an authoritarian one. Doctors used to have a heart-to-heart talk with patients at that time. They used to explain what should be thought of things or what had to be done. Within such an ambience there was no need for psychoanalysts to make detours with a long-winded defense analysis or waste time with continuous, patient efforts to achieve empathic understanding. That's typical of a subject-to-object relationship between doctors and patients. The analysis was successful when the patient was able to replace his or her former identification with the patriarchal superego or "father-imago" by another identification with a protecting paternal selfobject. In contrast with his or her former superego and "father-imago" the new selfobject was mostly an analyst who at that time usually no longer believed in God. Like Freud, he was in most cases an atheist who believed in reason and in ideals or ideas derived from the philosophy of the Enlightenment. That's to say from a philosophical movement of the Age of Reason whose adherents agreed to emphasize the ability of individuals and society to change for the better by means of reason and insight—on condition that they aren't prevented from this by suppression and ignorance. Freud added to this the condition that they aren't prevented from insight by repression or denial. In fact, repression is the inner form of suppression. The effect of repression is indeed a suppression of a part of the self. By discovering the effects of repression and denial Freud contributed to a timely progress of the Enlightenment, suited even to the reality context of present-day "open society." That was one of his outstanding and lasting merits. However, the theory and technique of Freud's topographical model were still characterized by "patricentric thinking," which prevailed in Central Europe before World War I. Freud revised his topographical model in the 1920s.

The following Middle Ages of psychoanalysis, with the unquestioned predominance of structural theory and egopsychology, lasted through the dark decades of the middle of the century. It was the epoch of the middle-class crisis of the industrial society, which was also the era of the disruption crisis of traditional culture. That was a time of latent collective anxiety, increasing withdrawal from reality, and compulsory reaction formation against Enlightenment-born ideas of human emancipation. It was a collective reaction formation against centrifugal tendencies and forces whose purpose was to prevent, by means of violence, a further decay of patriarchal culture. It culminated in a wave of collective antisemitism that lead to Nazism, World War II, and the Holocaust.

The common denominator of what I call the Middle Ages in psychoanalysis was the dominance of defense analysis. Both the method of defense analysis and the structural theory were developed by Freud at the time of class warfare in European industrial society, which had become disunited and polarized and had lost its traditions and cultural integration. It was not just by accident that Freud developed his theory of structural conflicts of id, ego, and superego at the same time that industrial society was consumed by growing structural conflicts and economic crises. Both in psychoanalysis and in the social reality the issue was defense against the dangers of conflict and the disintegration of a poorly cohesive system. In society these were the classes and interest groups. On the subjective level they were the conflicting parts of an ego-restricted mind and self that had lost the former integrative superstructures of the traditional culture. Hysteria was no longer the most frequent psychic disorder of this period. The leading role went to character neuroses and psychosomatic symptoms in which problems of latent depression and chronically stimulated fear and aggression played an important part. Especially in Central Europe the disorders were mainly neurotic conflicts suffered by the impoverished middle classes: they shared the interests of the poor and the ideals of the rich, ruling, and educated classes. Because they could not satisfy their own needs by active participation in the clashes of class and interest groups of their time, they were susceptible to developing neurotic symptoms.

In the technique of defense analysis there was a shift from the antagonistic approach to more or less technocentric and functionalistic thinking. Functionalistic thinking reduces problems of social and human life as if they were only a matter of homeostatic regulation and balance of closed systems. This type of thinking excludes from consideration both history and system transcendent development of self and other in a changing world and grew out of the loss of utopian hopes to heal psychic sufferings by means of making the unconscious conscious, as Freud tried to do at the beginning. During the second third of the 20th century most analysts became pessimistic and no longer believed in the basic goodness of human nature. Like Freud, they believed in the evil of an innate instinct of destruction, which had to be restrained by a technique of consistent taming. Therefore, they did not believe in reason and empathic understanding, but in technical rules, particularly the technical priority of analyzing aggressive impulses. The restricted code of technocentric thinking and the dominance of defense analysis were by themselves a defense, which in this way counteracted a persistent disintegration anxiety and fear of catastrophe. Technocentric and functionalistic thinking is in fact quite reductionistic. Though it defends against a threatening disintegration anxiety, it is only at the price of reducing and restricting both creativity and autonomy.

By the 1960s, technocentric thinking had become an unrecognized source of transference and countertransference difficulties, because the social-historical reality context had changed again. These difficulties cropped up because functionalisticly thinking analysts could not recognize the self-selfobject needs of a newly emerging postpatriarchal self. They couldn't understand why their familiar technique and mode of thinking became suddenly ineffective or were psychohistorically incongruous with the novel narcissistic disorders they were confronted with. The problems of most young patients were no longer those of a fearful middle class. They suffered from the labor of an evolving but not yet firmly established postpatriarchal culture of postindustrial society, which is based mainly on the so-called tertiary sector of service and service trade professions.

What are the problems of people who carry on these new professions? Instead of producing material goods, service professionals, like advertising experts and counselors, perform and sell services brought about by brainwork. Put simply, most of them are brainworkers who sell what they produce by thinking. As a consequence, many of them get used to thinking about only what they are able to sell and what meets the demands of a market for salable and buyable brainwork. In doing so they are liable to disregard human thoughts, feelings, and values that contrast with the values of the market. So they deny a part of their own true selves. As a consequence many of them develop a self dependent on the acceptance of others, especially important others and selfobjects. That's the problem of the "other-directed" self. Individuals with such a self often have difficulties taking a firm stand of their own and becoming themselves reliable selfobjects for their fellow beings, whose feelings and selfobject needs they used to disregard. Their descendants of the next generation are increasingly susceptible to self-disorders and selfobject disturbances. These problems are seriously aggravated when the self also loses its rootedness in the past, its perspectives of social success, and its hopes and ideas of a better future. Being reduced to live only in the present means living a life whose contents are nothing but permanently available selfobjects or compensations.

Since the 1960s and early 1970s there has been a vigorous tendency toward the restoration of human values and the human self in the framework of a further developing postpatriarchal culture. It became obvious that the tertiary sector of the postindustrial service professions is not only a field that gives rise to new problems of human adaptation, it also offers chances of human development and social emancipation that were out of reach for earlier generations. The service culture is growing into a social system of human rights, self-regulation, information processing, negotiation, and relationships based on reciprocity, cooperation, and partnership. In contrast with the traditional patriarchal culture of the past, stability of the individual self and social stability are no longer primarily mediated and ensured through internalization of authority. The structural framework of postpatriarchal culture favors the ability to empathize, or more precisely, to facilitate the unfolding of others by what I call "catalytic empathy."

Kohut was the trailblazer of a fundamental paradigmatic change that opened the third phase of the history of psychoanalysis. I will call his approach a "postpatriarchal psychoanalysis," because it meets the needs of a further developing and ripening postpatriarchal self. Its theory and practice are no longer confined to models and techniques of homeostatic drive and defense regulations within a closed mental system. They correspond to what Waddington and other contemporary evolutionists conceived of as "self-transcendent" processing structures in "open human systems in transition." At the same time this advance opens the door for setting up a holistic perception and interpretation of subject and reality. Kohut's most important contribution consists in developing empathy as a scientific method of dealing with the self of another. I define the heuristic value and historical significance of Kohut's theory as the "scientific discovery of the other." His work is not only a timely progress of clinical theory and practice, but also a valuable contribution to the restoration of human values and the sense of human self on the collective level of present day cultural evolution.

Individuals of today who have a postpatriarchal character structure are, like Freud's patients of that era, caught in a cultural warp. Therefore they are exposed to what we call now selfobject disturbances. This is so because the selfobject matrix of contemporary everyday life is not yet sufficiently prepared to provide children, young people growing up, and couples in relational crises with a cultural mirroring and validation of their newly emerging cultural identity and self-awareness. Quite the contrary, the selfobject matrix of contemporary everyday life is a transitional one, which is partly shaped by inertial and defensive resistances against this emerging postpatriarchal self-awareness.

Until this point I have given an overview of the three sociohistorical fields that characterize the history of psychoanalysis. Now I shall proceed to draw my conclusion: A psychoanalyst at the end of the 20th century is well advised to realize that physical contemporaries are not always necessarily psychohistorical contemporaries. To be a good psychoanalyst, one would have to recognize that symptoms appearing to have similar attributes and structures do not always necessarily have the same origin, nor are they related to the same developmental stage of psychohistorical evolution. That is not only a theoretical problem, but a very serious practical one in present-day psychoanalysis. There are psychohistorical time shifts and time lags between psychic sufferings and psychoanalytic notions or ways of technique, which lead to endless psychoanalytic processes as a consequence. They remain mired as if they were stuck in dead-end streets. One cannot deal correctly with such a psychohistorical time lag, except by exploring the problem in every single case instead of evading it.

Analysts have to synchronize their tools and theories with the real problems of their patients and not inversely by synchronizing patients with the ill-fitting tools and inflexible rules of a fool of a prehistoric psychoanalyst whose name was Procrustes. Psychoanalysts should learn and be able to use what I call "psychohistorical empathy." That means including also a good grasp of cultural evolution and social reality in empathic understanding. This enhances and makes empathy possible even with a different psychohistorical kind of individual self. Only the two together provide us with the theoretical competence and practical ability to deal in a reliable way with psychohistorical relativity and the asynchronism that may exist between us and our patients. The specific relevance of self psychology for contemporary problems lies in the fact that it opens the door to overcoming the growing time lag and cultural lag of traditional psychoanalysis. Neither the patricentric theory of the Oedipus complex nor the reductionistic approach of ego psychology are suitable instruments for the analysis of the selfobject problems of the postpatriarchal self. According to the degree to which self psychology is specifically prepared to unfold such abilities and competences, it will be the key, the most suitable way, or even the "royal road" to attending a further development of an autonomous and self-transcendent self (i.e., a self that meets the requirements of our time).

The present time is actually the scene of the psychohistorical birth of an autonomous postpatriarchal self. This new self is passing through a process of psychohistorical separation and individuation that dissolves the bounds of preautonomous patriarchal identifications. In self-psychological terms this means that the historical birth of an autonomous postpatriarchal self is a process of detachment from a development-thwarting selfobject matrix of a psychohistorically older culture. A psychoanalytic theory relevant to the emerging postpatriarchal culture presupposes a holistic theory of self and other. If self psychology did not already exist, that is, if Heinz Kohut had not invented it a little more than 30 years ago, it would and should have been invented in any case, because the structural change of psychohistorical life conditions and contemporary cultural evolution make self psychology a psychohistorical necessity.

REFERENCES

Freud, S. (1895), Studies on hysteria. *Standard Edition*, 2:7–305. London: Hogarth Press, 1955.

Ogburn, W. (1964), *On Culture and Social Change. Selected Papers*, ed. O. D. Duncan. Chicago: University of Chicago Press.

Riesman, D. (1950), *The Lonely Crowd*. New Haven, CT: Yale University Press.

Waddington, C. H. (1975), *The Evolution of an Evolutionist*. Ithaca, NY: Cornell University Press.

Author Index

Subject Index